'The effect of Connolly's oratory was remarkable. If it did not arouse the wild and whirling enthusiasm evoked by the outburst of a demagogue, it created enthusiasm of a different kind. It compelled assent as well as respect; it carried conviction and it aroused enthusiasm of the more lasting kind, a quiet, enduring enthusiasm which forced the hearer to act on Connolly's side rather than cheer his words.' Cathal O'Shannon

'A thoroughly worthwhile exercise. . . . The Irish-Scottish-American soul of Connolly bursts through the pages' *Irish Independent*

Samuel Levenson, born in Worcester, Massachusetts, has been a teacher, a public relations expert, and an editor as well as a writer. He is a member of the Labour History Society of Ireland and of the American Committee on Irish Studies.

JAMES CONNOLLY
Belfast, 1913

JAMES CONNOLLY
A biography

Ω——————————————————————

SAMUEL LEVENSON

QUARTET BOOKS LONDON, MELBOURNE, NEW YORK

Published by Quartet Books Limited 1977
A member of the Namara Group
27 Goodge Street, London W1P 1FD

First published by Martin Brian & O'Keeffe Limited, London, 1973

Copyright © 1973 by Samuel Levenson

ISBN 0 7043 3108 X

Printed in Great Britain by litho at The Anchor Press Ltd
and bound by Wm Brendon & Son Ltd
both of Tiptree, Essex

For Leah

Contents

Acknowledgements

I am grateful to Nora Connolly O'Brien and Roderic Connolly for relating to me memories of their father; to D. Stuart of Edinburgh and the late Owen Sheehy Skeffington for providing additional information; to the staff of the National Library of Ireland for supplying copies of the extensive Connolly material collected by William O'Brien; and to Michael Mullen, general secretary of the Irish Transport and General Workers' Union, for furnishing data, brochures and photographs.

For advice and other forms of assistance I am happy to thank Charles McCarthy, Basil Clancy, and the Rev. Prof. F. X. Martin, O.S.A., all of Dublin; C. Desmond Greaves of London; Granville Hicks of Grafton, New York; Father Thomas Halton of Washington, D. C.; Edward J. Chapin of Sterling, Virginia; Yale White of Worcester, Massachusetts; and Timothy O'Keeffe of London.

Most of all I am grateful to my wife Leah, whose enthusiasm, patience, critical eye, and skill as an editorial secretary are only a few of the elements she contributed to the making of this biography.

Samuel Levenson

Worcester, Massachusetts
January 1973

Introduction

AMONG the most remarkable periods of Irish history was the first part of this century, the years, say, from 1900 to 1920. During this time the Abbey Theatre was established, a great labour conflict took place in 1913–14, and on Easter Monday 1916 a desperate band of Irish patriots captured the centre of Dublin and held out against British power for six days. By promptly executing the leaders of this Easter Rising, the British ensured that there would eventually be an independent Irish Republic.

Great writers flourished during this era: William Butler Yeats, John M. Synge, Sean O'Casey, and, overseas, James Joyce and George Bernard Shaw. There were also lesser talents: George Moore, Lady Gregory, Padraic Pearse, Joseph Plunkett, Thomas MacDonagh and James Stephens. There were nation-builders Arthur Griffith, Douglas Hyde, Sir Horace Plunkett, Standish O'Grady, a youthful Eamon de Valera, and the Belfast industrialist William James Pirrie. Patriots included Sir Roger Casement, Maud Gonne, and Countess Markievicz (born Constance Gore-Booth). George Russell (AE) could fit into a dozen categories. Other colourful characters came from all religious groups and economic levels: Jim Larkin, the labour firebrand; John O'Leary, the Fenian; Francis and Hanna Sheehy-Skeffington; Tom Kettle; Oliver St John Gogarty, the original of Joyce's Buck Mulligan; and Sarah Purser, Dublin portraitist and acid-tongued hostess.

Of this remarkable generation, the 'most remarkable political thinker' was James Connolly. This is the opinion of Owen Dudley Edwards, of the University of Edinburgh, and author of the most recent book about Connolly (see bibliography). Mr Edwards calls him 'the most profound mind and the greatest theoretician among the founders of the modern Irish state'.

There is no question in the mind of Edwards and other writers that Connolly was an Irishman. Since his parents came from Ireland, and he 'died for Ireland', I shall not dispute the opinion. But it is worth noting that the Irish are notably generous in such matters. Connolly was born and raised in Scotland. Aside from the period he spent in Ireland as a British soldier in his youth, he lived there only from 1896 to 1903, and from 1910 to the time of his execution in 1916. For most of his life he was a Marxist and an atheist. Connolly must therefore be classed with such unlikely Gaels as Jonathan Swift, Oscar Wilde, G. B. Shaw and Maud Gonne, rather than with Joseph Mary Plunkett.

The Connolly encomia are numerous, and increase on each anniversary of the Easter Rising. Here are a few samples from AE, Liam O'Flaherty, and others. 'A sombre concentrated man of great ability, all his faculties under complete control, ready for use, a fine speaker, very impressive by his mere mastery over his matter . . . By his death Ireland lost the only labour leader it had with brains and high character.'

'The only Irish philosopher of consequence that we have had in Ireland since the days of Bishop Berkeley.'

'James Connolly had his heart in both the national and economic camp, but he was a great-hearted man, and could afford to extend his affections where others could only dissipate them.' 'The most vital democratic mind in the Ireland of his day.' 'A man of genius and character.' 'A born leader of men, a most extraordinary man.' 'With the possible exception of Robert Emmet, there is not in the whole gallery of Irish revolution a more commanding figure or interesting personality than that of James Connolly.'

Representative of many tributes from the left is one from Dr David Thornley, of the Irish Labour Party. He considers Connolly 'the only Marxist leader of any importance, apart from Lenin, to apply with complete logic Marxist teaching on the proper tactics for the proletariat in the context of imperialist war'. (It is interesting but irrelevant at the moment to note that Dr Thornley goes on to suggest that the 1916 Rising was 'in a sense one of the first of this century's "Popular Fronts"', and perhaps 'the only one in which it was the Marxists who got taken for a ride'.)

The difference between these opinions of Connolly and those held during his lifetime is vast. Except for a few disciples, he was feared and abhorred by all classes and groups of society. A glimpse of the contemporary attitude appears in the journals of the inveterate Dublin playgoer Joseph Holloway. On 1 August 1910, he was conversing with Mrs Dudley Digges in the vestibule of the Abbey Theatre when 'a stout-built block of a fellow in a bowler hat came in, and Mrs Digges recognised him as . . . a socialist, anarchist, and she did not know what, whom she met in America. He had just come over to preach his gospel in Ireland a few days ago. She went over to speak to him and then brought him over to introduce him to me . . . There was a good deal of the Irish-American about him, and he looked a determined bit of goods.'

James Connolly, then forty-two years old, was just beginning his second attempt to rid Ireland of capitalism and British rule. This biography attempts to explain how and why he became such a 'determined bit of goods', and to describe what happened to him thereafter. Connolly attracted my attention not because he ended up as a famed Irish patriot, but because he is a splendid example of a type which interests me—the professional revolutionary, syndicalist, anarchist, the legendary 'outside agitator' who haunts the dreams of the middle-class.

Connolly, no legend, was returning to Ireland after seven years in the United States spent in various jobs from life insurance agent to machinist. But his prime occupation had been to propagandize for the Socialist Labor Party of Daniel De Leon; the Industrial Workers of the World in the days of Big Bill Haywood and Joe Hill; and the Socialist Party of America in the days of Eugene Debs and Morris Hillquit.

During the next six years he made a lasting impact on Ireland. First and foremost, he commanded the insurgents during the Easter Rising of 1916, and was executed as a result, together with Padraic Pearse, Sir Roger Casement and others. During those years he published two important brochures he had written in the United States, took a hand in founding the Irish Labour Party, assisted Jim Larkin in the notable Dublin labour struggle of 1913–14, and helped build what is today the largest trade union in all Ireland.

But the suspicion and distrust, especially on the part of the middle- and upper-classes remained undiminished. It is exquisitely revealed in a letter written by one Louie Bennett to a friend in America. I shall transcribe here a large part of it (the full text is contained in R. M. Fox's biography of Miss Bennett) because it conveys in such detail the popular reaction, and because the writer was such an intelligent and well-meaning person. The daughter of a Protestant family of auctioneers and valuers, she became a suffragette and pacifist in her middle years, and then a sympathizer with labour, having been shocked by the struggle of 1913 into recognition of the conditions under which Dublin workers toiled and lived. Eventually she became the devoted and militant secretary of the Irish Women Workers' Union.

When Miss Bennett met Connolly in 1916 a few weeks before the Easter Rising, he was 'acting general secretary' of the Irish Transport and General Workers' Union. He was 'acting' because Jim Larkin, the firebrand who had founded the union, was still expected to return some day from the United States. In essence the Connolly that Louie met was not far removed from the thin, ill-fed young man she might have seen fifteen or twenty years earlier preaching revolution on a mist-shrouded street corner in Dublin; or the stocky, badly-dressed editor selling copies of his paper, the *Harp*, to people attending radical meetings at Cooper Union in New York City.

Though this was Louie's first meeting with Connolly, she already knew quite a lot about him. She had heard him talk before working-class audiences and 'often wondered how he held them, as I imagine he must be talking far above their heads. For me it was an intellectual effort to follow him'.

She knew also that 'he was one of the best suffrage speakers I have ever heard and a thorough feminist in every respect; he taught the Transport Union of Dublin to support and respect the women workers' struggle for industrial and political rights'. She described him as

physically, intellectually and in character powerful to an exceptional degree. Medium height, heavy build, bulldog type of body and head—broad brow; broad, heavy, strong-jawed face, dark hair, sallow, light-blue eyes, crafty in expression. I have always had an immense admiration for the man, but the expression of his eyes has always disappointed me and inspired misgiving.

The expression of his 'strong northern face' was 'dour and hard. He always struck me as utterly lacking in geniality . . . a man capable of deadly and merciless hatred. His very smile was cynical and joyless . . . The iron had eaten into his soul and he is through and through embittered'.

She was pleased that he had none of the 'personal magnetism' attributed to Jim Larkin, since she had been disgusted by Larkin's 'wild ravings'. As a speaker Connolly

never carried his audience to the wild enthusiasm Larkin did, though he was immensely popular with the people. As an orator he appealed to the mind, not the emotions . . . During Larkin's reign, he quietly played second fiddle, did all the donkey work. But we all knew him as a power, and when Larkin left, Dublin (and many others) hoped that a wiser cycle of the Labour movement in Ireland had begun. For Connolly did not blaze against every section of Dublin social life. He recognized that forces were working down as well as up towards a solution of Labour problems, and he seemed ready to meet those who were timidly approaching social problems from the outside. I think that if he had devoted himself to the Labour movement he might eventually have revolutionised Dublin conditions.

Instead, Miss Bennett thought, the passions of World War I obscured the clarity of his intellect. He became infected with war fever. 'He thought he saw in the war a chance of grasping freedom for Ireland, and from that moment Labour took second place in his thoughts . . . I think hatred of England is the dominating passion of Connolly's life. And he has deluded himself into the belief that industrial conditions cannot be improved in Ireland until she is free from England. He said so to me and I heard him say it publicly.'

Miss Bennett was visiting Liberty Hall, headquarters building of the Transport Workers' Union, to see Helena Molony, secretary of the women's branch of the union. The hope was that Louie would help to reorganize it but she was reluctant to have anything to do with a labour organization that was so filled with a passion for national freedom. Connolly came in and joined their discussion. Miss Bennett found him 'particularly dour and antagonistic . . . not prepared to make any terms with me. He insisted over and over again in answer to my arguments that I did not really want to help the women . . . At last I said plainly that I was a pacifist first and before everything, and I wouldn't give up that principle for trade unionism'.

Louie decided, on leaving, that Connolly 'was an autocrat at Liberty Hall and that he meant to dominate the women's department there just as he did every other department'.

She concluded by telling her friend that

In many ways he was a power for good. Like Larkin, he insisted upon temperance. But he maintained better order in Liberty Hall than Larkin had done. He reorganized the whole place and had it painted and cleaned up and all the offices set in good working order.

It is not surprising that, no matter where he lived—in Scotland, England, Ireland or the United States—Connolly met with this reaction. He was an advocate of class struggle, an avowed Marxian socialist, with ideas about colonial revolutions, women's liberation, industrial unionism, and the tyranny of religious organizations that still have significance in many parts of the world today. He was one of the first to recognize that, by combining the forces of nationalism and socialism, both would be strengthened. He was strongly in favour of women's rights, to the extent of permitting women to become full members of his Citizen Army.

Within the socialist parties to which he belonged, he alienated many comrades because he fought the tendency to make socialism synonymous with atheism or free thought. He considered it only common sense not to alienate the workers more than was necessary. On the other hand, he vigorously rebutted clerical charges that socialism had anything to do with theology, and took delight in pointing out the frequent occasions on which the Roman Catholic Church, allegedly the great benefactor of the Irish people, had aided and abetted British rule over them.

Connolly placed special stress on the need for organizing workers into industrial unions, believing that their strength would be the only guarantee that, when the workers voted socialism into effect, the vote would be heeded.

Connolly used both the printed and oral word to foment revolution. He wrote brochures, articles, leaflets, words to 'proletarian' songs, and even two plays. He spoke on hundreds of street corners, in scores of draughty auditoriums, in dozens of towns and cities.

He was constantly under surveillance by the police and government authorities. The object of scorn by the press, and the butt of all respectable people, he lived and moved in a miasma of hatred. Anarchist and atheist were the most common insults hurled at him, but there was sufficient variety to keep things interesting. Once, as a young man in Dublin, he ran for public office. The opposition candidate, by Connolly's own account, was able to convince Catholics that Connolly was a bigoted Protestant, Protestants that he was a Catholic rebel, Jews that he was an anti-semite, anti-semites that he was Jewish, manual labourers that he was a journalist on the make, clerks and professionals that he was an ignorant labourer. Connolly's birthplace was variously given as Belfast, Derry, England, Scotland and Italy, depending on what area would best antagonize the voter.

James Connolly is now considered a founding father of the Republic of Ireland, and the patron saint of Irish trade unionism. But uneasiness lingers in a nation which is fundamentally cautious, conservative, agrarian, and pious. It cannot wholly accept a man who lived so fundamentally at odds with its basic institutions and precepts. A possible indication of this lasting distrust is that no adequate biography of Connolly appeared until forty-five years after he was executed—and even then the publisher was a British, Marxist firm. Published in 1961, *The Life and Times of James Connolly* is a splendid detailed account, the product of ten years of research and writing by a man whom I have had the pleasure of meeting several times, C. Desmond Greaves. The book is so good that the question arises as to whether another is needed.

My reasons for replying in the affirmative are as follows:

One. There is room for a biography which highlights Connolly as a person and as an individual rather than as a figure in a history of the Irish working class. The Greaves book is filled with much economic and political data which are extremely useful in placing him in the context of his period and in displaying his accomplishments as a socialist agitator and labour organizer; but Connolly the man emerges more clearly when much of this material is excised. For many readers a shorter biography is preferable in any case.

Two. While I share fully Mr Greaves's admiration for Connolly's integrity and courage, I think it is time to point out that certain flaws existed in his thinking and in the thinking of his colleagues. They failed utterly to anticipate the problems that would confront a socialist government once it gained power. Hence, they offered no practical guidelines for meeting these problems. In the contemporary world, states that are governed by communist parties have failed to discover a procedure for the peaceful and democratic accession of new leaders; for stimulating free and honest debate on major issues; for organizing 'democratic centralism'; for encouraging the uninhibited expression of artistic talent. The emergence of even one Stalin makes a mockery of the utopia that Connolly envisioned. Those nations where socialist parties are in control are socialist in name only; they have failed notably to nationalize the means of production and they seem to have an unfailing tendency to lapse into opportunism.

Nor do I believe in the 'correctness' of all of Connolly's actions. I doubt the wisdom, for instance, of the Easter Rising. I am inclined to agree with most socialist thinkers of the time that it was only a *putsch.*

17

What else can one call an endeavour so lacking in popular support, so hopeless of success?

Three—and most important. In 1968, at the age of eighty-seven, William O'Brien died, leaving to the National Library of Ireland an enormous and invaluable collection of material about James Connolly. For the first time a researcher could use this treasure trove. Its existence had long been known but the collection had been jealously guarded by Mr O'Brien. On rare occasions he would hand to some researcher who happened to gain his favour a copy of a single letter or memorandum. One of the surprises of this collection, which consists of personal letters, song books, pamphlets, bills, union agreements, and every other kind of material is a lengthy correspondence (almost one hundred letters, many fifteen pages long) between Connolly in America and J. Carstairs Matheson, a school-teacher who edited a socialist paper in Scotland.

O'Brien was an extraordinary man—as able in his own way as Connolly and Larkin were in theirs, and just as important to the Irish labour movement. An account of the man, written by Arthur Mitchell, is found in the Autumn–Winter 1971 issue of *Studies*, published in Dublin. Sean O'Casey saw O'Brien as a man animated by 'a frozen sense of self-importance; and the clever, sharp, shrewd mind at white heat behind the cold pale mask was ever boring a silent way through all opposition to the regulation and control of the Irish labour movement'. (*Inishfallen, Fare Thee Well*.) The value of his thirty-year control of the Irish Transport and General Workers' Union is still a matter for discussion. Some maintain that he built up the union's membership and treasury by sacrificing its true influence and radicalism; others argue that the union inevitably reflects the nature of a country that, despite the outbursts of violence that surface from time to time, is basically conservative and slow-moving.

By occupation O'Brien was a tailor. He was thirteen years younger than Connolly. When he became active in union affairs, one of his early achievements was, as the following pages will show, to engineer Connolly's return to Ireland in 1910. A bachelor, a non-drinker, and a non-smoker, he was burdened by a clubfoot and a chilly temperament, but he was a superb union administrator and strategist. His conflict with Jim Larkin when Larkin attempted to regain control of the union upon returning from the United States must surely be ranked as one of the longest and bitterest wars in the annals of trade unionism.

The world has changed enormously since Connolly's day. What would he have made of television, nuclear weapons, a Communist

China and Russia, men walking on the moon, and Richard Nixon? He would have been puzzled by these changes but would soon have discovered that today, as in his day, some people were still fomenting and implementing revolutions.

Futile as revolutions may be as an instrument of basic change, the mere threat of armed rebellion has often speeded the introduction of constitutional reforms. John O'Leary consistently held that little could be accomplished without the presence of men assembled on the hillside, 'either in hope or desperation'. Sean O'Faolain asserts that, in the long and painful history of Ireland, the seeker of progress through constitutional means never once won a reform 'without the Rebel as the real force behind him'.

It can also be argued that so long as governing institutions insist on restricting or banning peaceful movements for reform, revolutions and 'revolutionists' (Connolly's term) will appear periodically, whether for good or ill, to the end of time.

Such speculation was completely foreign to Connolly's nature, and he would have nothing to do with it.

I

JAMES CONNOLLY was born in 1868 in one of the teeming stone warrens of an Irish ghetto in Edinburgh called the Cowgate. Almost all the circumstances of his birth and upbringing were long enshrouded in obscurity or error, partly because the annals of the poor are meagre, partly because Connolly wanted it that way.

For years it was believed that he was born in County Monaghan in 1870. Even today some people—Connolly's son Roderic is one of them—are reluctant to accept the fact of Connolly's Scottish birth. Roderic, now approaching seventy, points out that the family farm in the Vale of Anlore, Ballybay, County Monaghan, was in possession of the family as late as 1913. At this time Connolly was faced with the choice of settling on this farm, at the urging of his wife, or of going to Dublin to assist Jim Larkin in waging the great labour conflict of that year.

In an unsigned biographical note to *Labour in Ireland*, a collection of Connolly's writings, the writer, probably Desmond Ryan, evades the issue by stating that Connolly was born 'of Co. Monaghan parents and was reared in Scotland'. William O'Brien, Connolly's closest friend and colleague, accepts his Scottish birth and the Edinburgh Corporation records seem conclusive. They show that on 20 October 1856 a man named John Connolly and Mary McGinn, twenty-three-year-old members of the Irish community in Edinburgh, were married there at 17 Brown Square; that their first son John was born there on 31 January 1862; that a second son Thomas was born on 27 April 1866; and that the third son, James, was born at 107 Cowgate, on 5 June 1868.

James Connolly's reluctance in later life to reveal the place where he was born is easy to understand. This undersized, ill-schooled, poverty-stricken man was constantly engaged in an unequal battle to free Ireland from the rule of capitalism and of Britain. His only instrument was the influence he could muster among the Irish masses. Obviously, birth in Scotland was not an asset. (Neither was service in the British Army, another fact he kept well hidden.) But he could not escape his heritage. Among the Irish in both the southern and northern parts of Ireland and in the United States, he was always stamped as some kind of alien. He talked with an accent strange to most of them—not a burr, not a brogue, but the kind of dialect that prevailed in the Irish ghetto of his youth. It was easy enough for Connolly to keep his secret for he was temperamentally averse to talking or writing about himself. He abhorred 'the cult of personality' (the term was unknown, of course, in his day) when applied to anyone, including Jim Larkin and himself.

John Connolly, his father, was born in Ireland, worked originally as a farm labourer, and probably had some knowledge of Gaelic. The girl he married was a domestic servant, and her family did come from County Monaghan. When the two families came to Scotland is unknown. Two years after John married, he entered the service of the Corporation of Edinburgh as a rubbish collector. His job was to remove dirt and dung at night when the streets were free from traffic, and at times to cart ashes on a Saturday. The work was arduous and ill-paid, leading to a strike in 1861 which won for the carters a raise to fifteen shillings a week.

The eldest son, also named John, spent a few years in blind-alley occupations, following the custom of unskilled workers, then joined the First Battalion, Royal Scots Regiment, under the name of John Reid at the age of fifteen. He was dispatched to India in 1877. When he returned, he became interested in socialism, and preceded James into the movement.

Thomas, the second son, was more fortunate. After learning the trade of compositor's assistant, perhaps on the Edinburgh *Evening News*, he emigrated, and nothing more is known about him.

James followed his brothers in attending school at St Patrick's, a few hundred yards from his birthplace, and then worked in the same printing office as his brother Thomas for a year or so. He was perhaps eleven years old when he started. From this period comes Connolly's reminiscences of reading by the light of embers, whose charred sticks served him as pencils. From this possibly came a squint which he carried through life—although it has also been attributed to his talking in the open air and sunlight during much of his life.

He was plagued by other physical handicaps—a stammer which he mastered only with great difficulty; and a slight bowlegged condition which may have been due to a trace of rickets (malnutrition). And he never grew over five feet six, although his frame was sturdy enough.

As a printer's devil, Connolly washed inky rollers, fetched beer or tea for the adult workers, filled cans of oil or ink, and acted as an errand boy and the butt, no doubt, of many jokes. When the factory inspector made his infrequent visits, James was hastily summoned from his multifarious duties and planted on a high stool behind a case of type. But the manœuvre was discovered and he had to be dismissed.

It is verifiable that Connolly was working in a bakery at the age of twelve. As with Maxim Gorki, then undergoing the same experience, this place became a place of mingled torment and romance. He started work before six in the morning and toiled until late at night. Often as he staggered to his job in the murky light of early morning, he would pray fervently that the shop would by some miracle be burnt down when he got there. When he returned home to sleep, bone-tired, he would have nightmares in which flour bags and loaves of hot bread played a devil's dance in his head. After a year of this dreary experience, his health broke down. He then obtained work in a mosaic tiling establishment—presumably Messrs Hawley's in Frederick Street. It was also a depot for supplying marble and chimney pieces from manufacturers in England. The establishment seems to have had a certain air of elegance, for in one of its advertisements it stated that it would teach 'mosaic' to 'ladies'. The firm presumably lost interest in employing James Connolly when he became fourteen because it could hire younger boys.

So at the age of fourteen, Connolly faced a dilemma common to children of the working class. He solved it in the same fashion his brother had—by joining the Second Battalion of the Royal Scots Regiment, falsifying his age and his name since he could not produce a correct birth certificate. However nationalist an Irish lad might be, he was committing no act of apostasy by enlisting; he was following the custom of the day. The choice was between taking the Queen's shilling or starving. So many Irish preferred the latter course that the Fenians could say, without exaggeration, that often entire battalions of British troops were enrolled as members of their rebel ranks.

(The fact that Connolly joined the Royal Scots, not the King's Liverpool Regiment as given in the Greaves' biography, was discovered by David Stuart, of Edinburgh, who is interested in Connolly. Mr Stuart wrote to me that he got his original lead from the daughter of James's older brother, John, and then checked the records at the Royal

Scots Museum at Glencorse and Edinburgh Castle. He was also able to correct the date of James Connolly's marriage by consulting the records of the Roman Catholic Church in Perth.)

Connolly first set eyes on Ireland when he was a British recruit. His regiment was stationed at Cork, in the south. One night he spent on Spike Island, in Cork Harbour, guarding Myles Joyce, who was soon to be executed for his part in a massacre of landowners. The trial made a great furore at the time, with many people believing that Joyce's inability to speak English was the only reason he was convicted. The event gave Connolly much cause for thought, and so did the nationalist publications which fell into his hands during his stay in Ireland.

When the Regiment was transferred to the Dublin area, Connolly became acquainted with the city and confessed later, 'I love Dublin.' One reason was that here he met his future wife, Lillie Reynolds. On an evening outing he tried to hail a tram at Merrion Square to go to Dublin's seaport, Kingstown (now called Dun Laoghaire), a few miles away. Ignoring his wave, the driver left him standing beside another would-be passenger—'a young woman of his own age, fair, small and refined in an unassuming way'. They entered into conversation, their friendship quickly ripened, and by the end of 1888 they had decided upon marriage. Connolly was twenty, his fiancée a year older and a few inches taller.

Lillie came of a non-Catholic County Wicklow family. Her father had died when she was young, and her mother had to struggle to bring up four children in a little house in the Dublin suburb of Rathmines. As early as she could, Lillie entered domestic service with the Wilsons, a family of substantial means, whom she met probably because both families were members of a social group connected with the local Church of Ireland.

In 1889, about four months before Connolly's seven-year enlistment period was up, the Regiment was ordered to the depot in Aldershot, England, prior to going overseas. Connolly could not endure the thought of leaving his fiancée and took strong action. He deserted the army and fled to Perth, north-west of Edinburgh, where he had a distant relative. Lillie went there to meet him and get married, but when she arrived she found he had left and gone to Dundee, a larger and more industrialized city, where another relative lived.

At this remote date it is difficult to know what Connolly was thinking about. Perhaps he felt he had to go into hiding for fear of arrest; he may have been ashamed of his penniless condition; he may have had 'bridegroom fever'; he may have heard that work was to be found in Dundee; or he may have wanted to join in an interesting free-speech fight which was being conducted by the socialists there (of which more later). If the last were true, Lillie was receiving for the first time an intimation of what her life with Connolly would be like; he would be a loyal devoted husband, but the cause would always come first.

Six love letters from Connolly to Lillie have been preserved from this period. They are not as helpful as they might be since some are undated; other Connolly letters are missing, and so are all of Lillie's replies.

In a letter dated 7 April 1889, Connolly thanked Lillie for her generous contribution to the 'distressed fund' and explained that it was 'want of cash and the necessary habilaments' which prevented him from meeting her. But he hoped to do so before she left Perth. Meanwhile, he had obtained temporary work in Dundee, adding, 'I could get plenty of work in England, but you know England might be unhealthy for me—you understand.'

In an outcropping of youthful pride, he made a point of his hesitation in writing. 'For the first time in my life I feel extremely diffident about writing a letter. Usually I feel a sneaking self-confidence in the possession of what I know to be a pretty firm grasp of the English language from one in my position.'

In the event, it appears that Her Majesty never made an attempt to track down the deserter. Because of the transfer to Aldershot, the records of the battalion became confused and when the next muster was held, it was thought that Connolly had served out his term. Connolly never knew this, and could not understand why he was never apprehended.

In another letter to Lillie, Connolly expressed surprise that she had not received his last and explained once more that he had received her letter and obtained work. He had also received the socks she had knitted for him. His landlady had commented that 'the lass who sent you those didn't make a fool of you'.

To Lillie's complaint that she 'could not warm to the Perth people', he replied that Scotsmen were pious, hypocritical sharks, but pure gold when good. The remainder of the letter is of interest as containing Connolly's first written words on social questions. He told Lillie that Dundee contained more Irish people per head of population than any other place in Britain, and that they came from every county in

25

Ireland. Women worked while husbands were unemployed. According to the census there were eleven women working for every two men.

The last two letters were written from Edinburgh where Connolly had found a job. They dealt with arrangements for the marriage in Perth, a somewhat difficult matter since Lillie was now in London and the banns were to be published in Edinburgh.

'Now for another distasteful job,' Connolly continued. 'You know before a Catholic can marry a Protestant he must obtain what is called a dispensation from the Archbishop. I have applied for this dispensation, and I am informed it can only be granted on condition you promise never to interfere with my observance of my religion (funny idea, isn't it) and that any children born of the union should have to be baptised in the Catholic church. Now, I know you wont like this, especially as the priest will call on you to ask you. But Lillie, if your brother attended chapel for nearly a year for the sake of his sweetheart, surely you will not grudge speaking for a quarter of an hour to a priest, especially as the fulfillment of these promises rests with ourselves in the future, though I'd like you to keep them. Your brother, you know, had to make the same promises, though perhaps he did not let his family know.'

It was typical of the man, in his second letter from Edinburgh, to juxtapose the following ideas: 'How I am wearying to get beside you, and hear your nonsense once more. It is such a long time since we met, but I trust this time we will meet to part no more. Wont it be pleasant. By the way if we get married next week I shall be unable to go to Dundee as promised as my fellow-workmen in the job are preparing to strike on the end of this month for a reduction in the hours of labour. As my brother and I are ringleaders in the matter it is necessary we should be on the ground. If we are not we should be looked upon as blacklegs, which the Lord forbid.'

Unable to read these portents of her future life, Lillie Reynolds was married to James Connolly at St John's Church, Perth, on 20 April 1890 (not St James's Church on 13 April, as Greaves has it). The young couple proudly took possession of a home of their own at 22 West Port, almost on the corner of the Grassmarket, one of the parts of Edinburgh most densely populated by the Irish.

Connolly's job in his native city was similar to that of his father and brother but 'not as good'. By 1889 his father John had served thirty-one years as a permanent employee of the city council's 'Cleansing Department', but in that year he had suffered an accident which left him almost totally incapacitated. He was given light work as caretaker of the 'Public Convenience' in the Haymarket section, but the council was careful to reduce his wage of almost £1 a week to one-third of that amount. John Connolly, the eldest son, had temporary status in the Cleansing Department, from which he could no doubt graduate to a more privileged position. Banking on that prospect, in 1890 he married the daughter of another sanitation department driver. James was employed by a firm which received contracts from the Cleansing Department only during emergencies, and hence his employment was more erratic. However, he was a good worker, a non-drinker, non-smoker and 'steady', unlike his more flamboyant brother, and thus received work fairly regularly.

James's mother died of 'acute bronchitis' about this time, and thereafter his father, who seems to have been a gentle, kindly and intelligent man, spent his time conversing with others who were retired or unemployed, and attending socialist meetings. Unskilled himself in the ways of the urban jungle, he could do nothing to give his children a start in life, as the saying goes, but when they decided that only radical reform could solve society's problems he had the good sense to refrain from trying to alter their convictions.

During his remaining six years in Edinburgh, Connolly became increasingly interested and active in left-wing politics. It is time to consider those external and internal factors which led him into this area.

II

WHAT were the factors that made Connolly a radical and revolutionary?

One of them, obviously, was his upbringing in the squalid, teeming 'little Ireland' areas of Edinburgh—Cowgate, Grassmarket and Salt-market. Bitter poverty, unemployment and underemployment were characteristics of these areas. The income of the average family was one or two pounds a week. Living conditions were squalid; 13,000 families occupied single rooms. Cholera and typhus were rampant. One in five babies failed to reach its fifth birthday.

It was a world remarkably similar to the big-city slums of today. Drunkenness, brutality, taking of drugs (at this time laudanum), 'crime in the streets', oppression of a minority by the majority, and police corruption flourished. In the all-white, all-Irish ghettoes of Edinburgh, it was unsafe for respectably dressed people to walk in the streets. Outside their own areas, the Irish were fair game for any Scotsmen or English they encountered. (A full account is contained in James E. Handley's splendid study, *The Irish in Scotland*.)

One of the conditions which particularly irked Connolly was the custom of paying the weekly wages in a pub. He referred to it more than once with the greatest bitterness, and early became an abstainer.

The wonder is not that Connolly became a revolutionary but why so many others failed to do so. There were plenty of persons and organizations pointing the way towards a remedy. Both nationalist and socialist organizations were in existence. Connolly was thirteen when H. M. Hyndman founded the parent organization of the Social-Democratic Federation, which eventually became the British Socialist Party. Connolly was sixteen when William Morris broke away from the Federation to found the Socialist League. During his youth Connolly was reading their literature, as well as the *Penny Readings*, patriotic miscellanies issued from 1884 onwards by the Sullivans, editors of *The Nation*.

In addition there was in Edinburgh, unlike Belfast, Glasgow or Dublin, a tradition of dissent and of sympathy towards Irish nationalist aspirations. It may be attributed to vestiges of Scottish national organizations which survived the union of 1707, the presence of political refugees from the Continent, and a strong literary, intellectual and academic ambience.

Tradition has it that Connolly received his first teachings in nationalism from an uncle who, under the name of MacBride, had been an active member of the Irish Republican Brotherhood. A more certain cause for Connolly's anti-British wrath was his service in the British Army at a most impressionable age. The evening he spent in Cork Harbour as guard over Myles Joyce had scarred him. Connolly spent the whole night brooding over the impending execution.

His bitterness towards the British Army was a lasting thing. Many years later, Connolly, returning home, found his son Roderic, then twelve, engaged in conversation with a recruiting sergeant dressed in full regimentals. The sergeant was trying to induce Roderic to become a drummer boy. Connolly led his son into the house, harshly told him never to accept the King's shilling, and then went outside again to tell the sergeant what he thought of the British Army and its non-commissioned officers. Roderic had never seen his father in such a towering rage.

During the battalion's stay in Dublin beginning in 1885, Connolly probably attended some open air meetings conducted by socialists. The prime evidence for this is that a few years later he felt free to advise Keir Hardie how to present the socialist case in that city. During his year in Dundee (1889), the local socialists were conducting a great free speech campaign. Two branches of the Social-Democratic Federation had been holding frequent open-air meetings in Barrack Park and High Streets. Late in March 1889, the magistrates issued proclamations forbidding public meetings in these areas. The Social-Democratic Federation took up the challenge, and a gathering estimated by the local press as 20,000 strong heard vigorous protests voiced in Albert Square.

The speakers then led the crowd to High Street, where they were promptly arrested. On the following Sunday, 1 April, several meetings were held, to which speakers came from Glasgow and Edinburgh. One of them was John Leslie of the Social-Democratic Federation and first secretary of the newly established Scottish Socialist Federation. It was at this time in Dundee that Connolly became acquainted with Leslie, and was welcomed by him into the socialist movement. Which socialist organization he joined is a detail. Both in Dundee and in Edinburgh, during the eighties and nineties, there were numerous socialist groups; while their leaders were often opposed to each other, many of the rank and file held joint membership.

There were many reasons why Connolly was attracted to the socialist movement. For one thing, the socialists, of whatever breed, supported the trade unions whenever they were active—including the many strikes that took place in Dundee during his stay there. For another, the socialists alone of all British groups supported Irish national demands. They urged complete separation of Ireland from Britain, an agrarian revolution, and tariffs to protect Irish industrial development. *Justice*, the organ of the Social-Democratic Federation, supported the movement for Home Rule, saying: 'Only in Dublin can the Irish people control their laws. Let the two agitations go side by side.'

III

CONNOLLY spent the years from 1889 to 1896 in Edinburgh. They were both wonderful and dreadful years. They were wonderful because during this period he became aware of what he could do as a writer, speaker, organizer, and thinker, guided by the 'magic searchlight' of Marxism. He found mentors and colleagues in the study of Marxism. The principal one was John Leslie, who became the Edinburgh secretary of Keir Hardie's Independent Labour Party when it was formed in 1894. Son of a Scottish father and an Irish mother, Leslie was a fluent and witty speaker, an omnivorous reader, and capable of writing poetry as well as prose. His only political work, *The Present Position of the Irish Question*, laid the basis for much of Connolly's thinking.

Another mentor was Leo Meillet, who had been mayor of a commune in Paris. In 1889 he told Edinburgh's first meeting to commemorate the commune that 'without the shedding of blood there is no social salvation'. And there were others: Andreas Scheu, formerly an Austrian journalist and a militant atheist; Robert Banner and John Lincoln MacMahon, members of the Scottish Land League; and the Rev. W. Glasse, who subsequently translated the *Internationale* and helped to establish a University Socialist Society. There was also Connolly's brother, John, who had become interested in several socialist groups, and was now secretary of the Scottish Socialist Federation. James no doubt looked up to his older brother as one usually does, and it was probably John who brought him into Leslie's circle. These years in Edinburgh were wonderful also because here Connolly's first children were born: Mona, a year after his marriage; Nora, a few years later; and Aideen, his third daughter, in March 1896, shortly before the Connollys left Edinburgh.

But they were also dreadful years because of the constant poverty which beset him and the hard struggle that he and the other socialists had to get their ideas accepted. Even the trade unionists were hostile; when the Scottish Socialist Federation organized a demonstration on behalf of the eight-hour day in May 1890, the Trades Council, the local association of trade unions, refused to participate.

The routine of socialist activity into which Connolly was drawn consisted of three weekly meetings; the most important of which was the public meeting held each Sunday in the East Meadows in the summer, and in various halls during the winter. The mid-week meeting generally consisted of a lecture by one of the members, often John Leslie. The Friday 'business meeting' of the Scottish Socialist Federation was often replaced by 'reading and discussion', especially when the organization began in 1892 to meet at Connolly's flat at 6 Lothian Street. It was a pleasant, salubrious area, surrounded by bookshops and colleges; Lillie, though not interested in politics, enjoyed company and gladly offered tea to all comers.

In a world where the majority of the people had only the haziest notion of what socialism was, and were apathetic or hostile towards it, it was necessary for those who believed in it to learn as much as they could. Socialist literature was in its infancy. Marx's *Capital* and the *Communist Manifesto* were available, but above the heads of some of the members. Bellamy's *Looking Backward* helped, and so did the writings of William Morris. Even refutations of socialism were gobbled up because of the possibility of gleaning from them additional information about the labour theory of value, dialectical materialism, and other aspects of Marxism.

But slowly things began moving. In 1892, the Trades Council agreed to participate in a demonstration for the eight-hour day upon the invitation of John Leslie, Independent Labour Party secretary, and James's brother John, secretary of the Scottish Socialist Federation. The procession marched through the streets to Queen's Park where a resolution demanding the eight-hour day was passed.

John Connolly, one of the speakers at the demonstration, was thereafter dismissed from his position with the city. The Edinburgh Trades Council, believing that he had been fired because of his participation in the demonstration, protested to the Cleaning and Lighting Committee of the Town Council. After first refusing to consider the communication, the Committee held a hearing, found that John Connolly's complaint was not substantiated, and recommended that the Town Council take no action. The Town Council accepted this decision. In August the Trades Council decided that the investigation had been unsatisfactory but 'owing to the difficulties surrounding the case was unable to recommend any further action being taken. The difficulties were summarized in another sentence: 'the men best able to give direct proof were liable to the same treatment Connolly received'.

While John sought other work, James took over his tasks as secretary of the Scottish Socialist Federation. An immediate result was a marked change in the branch reports appearing in *Justice*. Whereas John's reports had been flamboyant and ornate, the passionate logic of James's mind appeared in his very first report. It was his earliest printed words. From the start he took his job seriously. He wanted his reports to be letter perfect, and he pored over them, consulting Lillie in matters of grammar, spelling, and punctuation. In his first report, he stated that the Scottish Socialist Federation had decided to send a delegate to the International Conference at Zürich with a free hand in all matters but one: he must vote against the admission of the Anarchists. The SSF was bitter against the Anarchists because it felt that they had broken up the Socialist League and were forcing it to function as an organization increasingly drawn towards the Social-Democratic Federation.

Connolly also announced the possible formation of a speakers' class and invited suggestions as to the best manner in which such a class should be conducted. Apparently this subject was on his mind, since he was acting as chairman for John Leslie. As a neophyte, he carried the platform and was learning the art of oratory by standing on it before an often empty street.

In the 12 August 1893 issue of *Justice*, Connolly announced the intention of the Scottish Socialist Federation to establish a branch in Leith, the seaport of Edinburgh. And here is a sample of his earliest prose:

The population of Edinburgh is largely composed of snobs, flunkeys, mashers, lawyers, students, middle-class pensioners and dividend-hunters. Even the working-class portion of the population seemed to have imbibed the snobbish would-be-respectable spirit of their 'betters' and look with aversion upon every movement running counter to conventional ideas. But it has won, hands down, and is now becoming respectable. More, it is now recognised as an important factor in the public life of the community, a disturbing element which must be taken into account in all the calculations of the political caucuses.

Leith on the other hand is pre-eminently an industrial centre. The overwhelming majority of its population belong to the disinherited class, and having its due proportion of sweaters, slave-drivers, rack-renting slum landlords, shipping-federation agents, and parasites of every description, might therefore have been reasonably expected to develop socialistic sentiments much more readily than the modern Athens.

In his next report, Connolly castigated an official of the Glasgow Trades Council for remaining a member of a co-operative society even though he knew it paid less than trade-union rates; and he poured scorn on an association of bottle manufacturers for refusing to deal with strikers because foreigners were among their number. 'It was all very well', he wrote, 'to employ a foreigner at starvation wages and so cut down the wages of the native—but to treat with the foreigner ... Why it was preposterous!'

On 5 June 1894, James Connolly became twenty-six years old. He was rapidly moving into the very centre of the socialist movement in Edinburgh. His new rooms at 21 South College became a hive of socialist activity. More and more the work of the Scottish Socialist Federation and the Central Branch of the rapidly growing Independent Labour Party came to revolve about him. He began to develop as a speaker. On the first occasion he spoke, Lillie stood beside the platform waiting for him to begin. But when the fateful moment came, her heart failed her and she fled.

That may have been the occasion on Saturday, 13 May 1894, when Keir Hardie was advertised to speak at East Meadows, to support the candidacy for Parliament of Councillor Beevers of Halifax. Some hundreds waited in the rain for him, and there was an ominous silence when Connolly mounted the platform to apologize for his absence. He had been notified of the time and place, Connolly explained, but had failed to arrive. Then came a characteristic Connolly touch. Connolly promised that an apology would appear in the *Labour Leader* for this breach of faith. And the paper did in fact go to the length of publishing the complaint, although no explanation was given.

During the same month Connolly spoke at Falkirk, near Glasgow, at the 'second outdoor meeting of the newly formed branch of the Scottish Socialistic Federation'. He had 'a large audience notwithstanding the heavy showers', the local paper reported. 'The meeting resulted in a good collection, a large sale of literature, and several names being added to the membership role.' The man who sent

34

Connolly this clipping added: 'You are the first Socialistic speaker that has interested a Falkirk audience. You are father of the work. Look well after your child.'

As secretary of the Central Edinburgh Branch of the Scottish Labour Party, Connolly was thrilled at the opportunity of entering into correspondence with several important people of the time, notably James Keir Hardie and Robert Bontine Cunninghame-Graham. A few letters from this period have survived. On 28 May 1894, Connolly wrote to Hardie asking that the party release Mr Beevers from any obligation to run for Parliament from the Central Edinburgh area since a candidate from nearer home had been found. He urged the Independent Labour Party not to allow the impression to get around that it had played any role in selecting him. In other words, the multitudes held the ILP in even greater disfavour than the SSF. Expecting the workers to accept the ILP choice without demur would 'simply arouse every prejudice against us and deprive us of the opportunity of dilating on the cliqueism of the Liberal caucus'. The new candidate was William Small of Blantyre.

On 3 July 1894, Connolly wrote to Hardie:

As an Irishman who has always taken a keen interest in the advanced movements in Ireland, I was well aware that neither the Parnellites nor the McCarthyites were friendly to the Labour movement. Both of them are essentially middle-class parties interested in the progress of Ireland from a middle-class point of view. Their advanced attitude upon the land question is simply an accident arising out of the exigencies of the political situation, and would be dropped to-morrow if they did not realise the necessity of linking the Home Rule agitation to some cause more clearly allied to their daily wants than a mere embodiment of national sentiment of the people.

He then suggested a plan for forcing the hand of Redmond and his clique. Since there was the nucleus of a strong Labour movement in Ireland, a well-billed meeting held in Dublin, with Hardie presenting a rebellious, anti-monarchical, outspoken speech on the fleecings of landlord and capitalist, and the hypocrisy of both political parties (Liberal and Conservative) would 'knock the bottom out of the Irish opposition to our movement'.

By September 1894, Connolly had apparently become disillusioned with the choice of Small and asked Cunninghame-Graham to run in his place. Born in London forty-two years before, Cunninghame-Graham had been educated at Harrow, had written popular books concerning his travels in Latin America, had taken part in the dock strike of 1887, and had helped found the Scottish Socialist Party. While admitting that Small was a fool, Cunninghame-Graham pointed out that he himself lacked funds to participate in such a campaign; that he was 'the worst candidate in the world, as I hate elections, and soon get tired of meetings', and that Small's 'domestic difficulties' were not valid grounds for dropping the man. In another letter dated 5 October, Cunninghame-Graham laid down certain conditions before he would contest the seat—namely, an invitation not only from the Scottish Socialist Society but from the Independent Labour Party and, if possible, the Trades Council, and a petition bearing at least 1,000 signatures. These conditions were apparently impossible to meet, and the matter was dropped. However, Cunninghame-Graham did serve later as a member of Parliament from Scotland. He died in 1936, at the age of eighty-four.

Meanwhile, an economic depression which had started in 1893 showed no signs of lifting. A miners' strike was impending, and the working class was in an increasingly militant mood. Connolly's work in Leith began to bear fruit in the establishment there of a large branch of the Independent Labour Party, which acknowledged its indebtedness to the propaganda of the Scottish Socialist Federation.

In Edinburgh the SSF formed a women's branch which met at 21 South College Street. A 'rambling' club and a cycling club were also established, both of which combined recreation with socialist propaganda. A man named Dickenson began to publish an *Edinburgh and Leith Labour Chronicle* in October 1894, which gave full publicity to all SSF and ILP activities. On its front page Connolly read the words of Camille Desmoulins, which he quoted often during the next thirty years: 'The great appear great because we are on our knees. Let us rise'.

The Scottish Socialist Federation now decided to run a candidate for the Town Council from the St Giles Ward. The two obvious candidates were John Leslie and James Connolly. Both had lived in the parish for many years and Connolly had been born there. Both were Irish and Catholic. Leslie was better known, but Connolly was on the way up. He had made rapid strides as a public speaker, surpassing first his brother John and then Leslie himself. The issue was probably decided by Connolly's possession of a house and a minimum of economic stability which, for all his intellectual gifts, Leslie lacked. Connolly was adopted as Socialist candidate on 22 October 1894, a week before nominations had to be filed. Two hundred people heard him state his programme. His principal plank was housing. He demanded the end of one-roomed houses in St Giles. New houses should be built at rents based only on building costs and upkeep. Unoccupied property should be taxed. High-salaried city officials should receive no pensions, but other employees should have a retirement plan. He was against the Fountain Bridge improvement scheme, for the water scheme, and for the amalgamation of Edinburgh parishes.

The Liberals were the favoured party among Irish voters at this time, principally because their leader Gladstone had courageously introduced an Irish Home Rule Bill in 1886 and again in 1892. In the interval, Gladstone smashed Parnell's political life, following the disclosure of Parnell's romance with a married woman; but this episode had not materially decreased Liberal popularity among the Irish voters, since almost all the Catholic priesthood had joined to bring down the haughty, frail 'uncrowned king of Ireland'.

The Liberals, whose official candidate was named Mitchell, were properly contemptuous of the Socialists, describing them as 'a few noisy fanatics'. Another Liberal candidate named Gardiner had been refused the official nomination but ran anyway, requesting support 'as a Catholic and an Irishman'. He loftily described Connolly as a 'young man of no business ability advocating ideas repugnant to all right-thinking men'.

Connolly conducted a vigorous campaign both at indoor and out-door meetings and in print. Five hundred attended the first indoor meeting after his nomination. Pavements were chalked white with his name by enthusiastic supporters. He held an open-air meeting for the municipal truck drivers at Kingstables Road, where the chairman was too tongue-tied to speak and presided silently while Connolly addressed his fellow-employees from a cart.

During the election campaign and for some time afterwards, Connolly contributed a monthly article to the *Labour Chronicle* under the pseudonym of 'R. Ascal' in which he discussed local and national issues with insight and wit. He made it clear, there and elsewhere, that he was appealing principally to 'the mob, the lower classes, the great unwashed, the residuum, and other such great names' that organs of the upper classes 'are so fond of applying to the masses'.

He attacked the Liberals and Conservatives as 'two sections of one party—the party of property'. He urged the St Giles Irish to learn how foolish it is to denounce tyranny in Ireland and then to vote for tyrants and instruments of tyranny at their own door. Perhaps they will see that the landlord who grinds his peasants on a Connemara estate, and the landlord who rack-rents them in a Cowgate slum, are brethren in fact and deed. Perhaps they will realise that the Irish worker who starves in an Irish cabin and the Scots worker who is poisoned in an Edinburgh garret are brothers with one hope and destiny. Perhaps they will see that the same Liberal Government which supplies police to Irish landlords to aid them in the work of exterminating their Irish peasantry, also imports police into Scotland to aid Scots mine owners in their work of starving the Scottish miners.

But though Connolly's meetings were large and enthusiastic, he had difficulties from which his opponents were free. The Scottish Socialist Federation was denied the use of church halls, and many of its supporters were not on the voters' roll. The publication of a new electoral list was the signal for every debt-collecting agent to make a bee-line for the slums. Hence, those who were poorest preferred to sacrifice their rights as citizens for the sake of retaining a room and a bed. This circumstance told heavily against Labour candidates, since their supporters often chose to be voteless 'lodgers' with no ascertainable address.

Some of the bitterest invective delivered against Connolly came from the Irish National League, made up almost entirely of Roman Catholics, which supported the Conservatives. The leaders of the League, termed by Connolly a 'crew of hucksters', urged Connolly's defeat in the interests of 'faith and country'. While Liberals used the fact that he was a Catholic against him, the League called him an atheist in disguise. Church-goers were planted at the polls to spot and report Irish and Catholics who voted for Connolly. In the election, the official Liberal candidate Mitchell came first, with more than a thousand votes. The Conservative candidate got half that number. Connolly received 263 votes and the unofficial Liberal candidate Gardiner received 54.

In his analysis of the votes, Connolly wrote, rather proudly: 'The official Liberals were able to obtain a majority of only four to one over a party the most revolutionary and the most recent in public life, with no electioneering organization, and with a candidate known to earn his bread by following an occupation most necessary in our city life, but nevertheless universally despised by the public opinion of aristocratic Edinburgh.'

In a more philosophical vein, he pointed out that 'The election of a Socialist to any public body is only valuable in so far as it is the return of a disturber of the political peace.' It did not even mean the immediate realization of whatever palliatives were set before the electors. Such palliatives 'are in themselves a mere secondary consideration of little weight, indeed, apart from the spirit in which they will be interpreted'. In other words, he considered reforms as subordinate to the larger aims of socialism. But the struggle for reforms was an essential part of achieving socialism, and with this in view he announced a further electoral effort would be undertaken next year.

November 1894 opened what proved to be one of the worst winters in Scottish history. It marked the beginning—or rather the intensification—of a wintry period for Connolly as well. The City Cleansing Department met the crisis simply by working its regular men overtime—without using private contractors. Connolly, now completely unemployed, attempted to make himself independent and pursue unhindered his main interest, Socialism. In February 1895 he found a small shop at 73 Buccleuch Street, where he set up as a cobbler. Unfortunately, his skill was not equal to the venture. A schoolgirl who sympathized with the socialist cause (Anna Munro, who later became a prominent suffragette) collected all her family's footwear and took it to Connolly's shop for repair. Not a pair could be worn again. The shop suffered from other obstacles. During this winter of 1894–95, few people were willing to travel the distance, in the biting winds over piled-up snow, from the Cowgate to Buccleuch Street.

The business also suffered from the fact that Connolly was more interested in politics than in profits. He announced the availability at his shop of tickets for socialist meetings long before he thought of mentioning that he mended boots. When he did think of advertising, however, he used it with wit and originality. The Labour movement at the time seemed full of cobblers. It was the victimized man's retreat; most people possessed the implements of the trade, or they could be cheaply acquired. In the *Labour Chronicle*, which advertised several such shops, Connolly's advertisement stood out. It read:

Socialists support one another. Connolly, 73, Buccleuch St. repairs the worn-out understandings of the brethren at standard rates. Ladies boots 1/6d., gents 2/6d.

During the winter, preparations were made for the so-called Poor Law elections which, for the first time, would put the operation and control of welfare under democratic administration. The Scottish Socialist Federation once more ran Connolly for St Giles's Ward, but this time the weather discouraged enthusiasm, and his opponent was none less than Monsignor Grady of St Patrick's Rectory, who 'knew the St. Giles poor and wanted to help them'. He asked the electors not to support him merely because he was a priest; he was a taxpayer as well. In the elections held in April 1895, Monsignor Grady got 523 votes, another candidate polled 480, and Connolly could muster only 169, almost a hundred fewer than the previous time. However, one of Connolly's statements from this campaign is worth remembering: he stigmatized 'the folly of handing over the care of the poor to those who have made them poor'.

The severity of the winter and widespread unemployment made the Trades Council a little less reluctant to join forces with the radicals. On 23 February 1895, it joined with the Independent Labour Party and the Women Workers Federation in holding a demonstration and in sending a deputation to the Town Council to demand work. After the demonstration, a concert was given for the purpose of raising relief funds. But the Trades Council refused to proceed with a May Day demonstration; hence, it was conducted jointly by the Independent Labour Party and the Scottish Socialist Federation. In addition to the usual resolution calling for an eight-hour day, there was another which termed war 'a barbarous mode of settling international disputes' and urged 'that in the future the question of peace or war shall only be decided by the direct vote of the whole people'.

All this was exciting to Connolly—much more exciting than running a doomed cobbler shop, though equally unprofitable. With the sardonic remark that he was going out to buy a mirror to watch himself starve to death, Connolly left his store, locked the door behind him, and took charge of another shop at 65 Nicholson Street. This was the new headquarters of the Scottish Socialist Federation, of which Connolly had again become secretary in May 1895.

At this time a distressing incident occurred which undoubtedly helped to sour Connolly on Edinburgh and all its works. Keir Hardie, founder in 1894 of the fast-growing Independent Labour Party, had been impressed by Connolly's abilities on various trips to Edinburgh and Leith, and would have wished the Scottish Socialist Federation to join the Independent Labour Party. When a bye-election took place in one of the local districts, he sent a copy of the ILP manifesto to Connolly and asked him to have it printed and distributed. Hardie suggested that the document be signed by the local committee of the ILP rather than his own. Since Connolly was a member of the Socialist Election Committee for Parliamentary Purposes, a loose combination of all these socialist and labour groups, he thought that he was competent to send the order to the printer, and announced to the Committee that he had done so. But to his surprise he found that he had invited a storm. The Committee refused to co-operate in any way and wrote to Keir Hardie sharply reproving him for communicating with Connolly.

Greaves interprets the fracas as an indication that 'Connolly was becoming more than a local leader now, and was experiencing the jealousy of lesser men for the first time'. Envy of the speed with which the upstart Independent Labour Party was taking root, and the lack of clear organizational demarcations also played a part. There is other evidence that Connolly was acquiring some competence and reputation as an agitator. In 1895 a socialist lecturer named Connell, about to leave England on a tour of Scotland, was told that there were two Irishmen in Edinburgh that he must meet: John Leslie and James Connolly. The visitor found Connolly a very self-contained man, who seemed to care little whether people agreed with him or not. He spoke with great deliberation, choosing his words carefully. Connolly told his visitor that once socialism had taken root in Ireland it would grow more rapidly there than in any other country. Connell, in sum, thought Connolly much too quiet and thoughtful ever to become any kind of militant leader. The passion and intensity, even rudeness, that Connolly showed at times were apparently abated in the presence of this older and more famous lecturer.

In mid-June 1895, aged twenty-seven, Connolly began to seek full-time work as a political propagandist or organizer outside of Edinburgh. His friend Currie, who edited the Scottish Socialist Federation notes in *Justice*, wrote on his behalf that, after fighting two elections, Connolly could find no employment in his native town; that he was a fluent speaker, with a good strong voice which seemed to have been specially created for outdoor propaganda; that he had a thorough knowledge of his subject; and that his untiring zeal and perseverance had made him 'a martyr whose martyrdom would have been saved if certain men had been honourable enough to fulfil an obligation entered into, or at least give some reason for nonfulfilment. Connolly has more than sufficient time on his hands and if any branch of the S.D.F. or I.L.P. is wishful to have an efficient and capable lecturer or organizer, letters addressed to James Connolly, 65, Nicholson Street, will always find one.'

In his desperation, Connolly was equally willing to remain in Edinburgh if he could get lecture engagements from time to time. A month after Currie's boost in *Justice*, an advertisement appeared in the *Labour Leader* to the effect that Connolly was open to book dates for lectures. Terms would be provided by Dan Irving, Social-Democratic Federation Club, St James Hall, Burnley. There seems to be no record that Connolly received any engagements of this sort.

Willy-nilly, Connolly devoted his main efforts during the next six months to building up the Scottish Socialist Federation (converted after September 1895 into the Edinburgh Branch of the Social-Democratic Federation). His work involved arranging and promoting, together with the Independent Labour Party, a series of lectures held that autumn at the Operetta House, which held 1500 people. In this way Connolly saw, heard, and became at least superficially acquainted with some of the notables of the time—Eleanor Marx, Edward Aveling, Ben Tillett, Tom Mann, and H. M. Hyndman. At the Hyndman meeting the audience voted a pledge (proposed by Connolly and seconded by Leo Meillet) to support Socialism, but what made the evening outstanding was that, for the first time in Edinburgh history, the Trades Council was officially represented at a socialist gathering. That some day a Labour Party pledged to socialism would take office in England was undreamed-of.

Connolly's situation was becoming desperate. While the Social-Democratic Federation was becoming increasingly successful, he was ploughing back every gain into increasing the scale of its propaganda, while he himself approached destitution. He went so far as to apply to the Chilean Government (through its office in Paris) for assistance in emigrating to that country. Leslie persuaded him to delay his departure only by promising to write a special appeal in *Justice*. It went as follows:

Here is a man among men . . . I am not much given to flattery, as those who know me are aware, yet I may say that very few men have I met deserving of greater love and respect than James Connolly. I know something of Socialist propaganda and have done a little in that way myself, and I also know the movement in Edinburgh to its centre, and I say that no man has done more for the movement than Connolly, if they have done as much. Certainly nobody has dared one half what he has dared in the assertion of his principles. Of his ability I need only say, as one who has had some opportunity of judging, he is the most able propagandist in every sense of the word that Scotland has turned out. And because of it, and for his intrepidity, he is today on the verge of destitution and out of work. And we all know what this means for the unskilled workman, as Connolly is. Now this should not be—most emphatically should not be . . . Connolly's case is scarcely an encouragement for others to go and do likewise. Leaving the Edinburgh Socialists to digest the matter, is there no comrade in Glasgow, Dundee, or anywhere else who could secure a situation for one of the best and most self-sacrificing men in the movement? Connolly is, I have said, an unskilled labourer, a life-long abstainer, sound in wind and limb (Christ in Heaven! how often have I nearly burst a blood vessel as these questions were asked of myself!). Married, with a young family, and as his necessities are therefore very great, so he may be had cheap.

There was indeed a response to this desperate appeal—and, happily, from Dublin, the scene of some army years and of his courtship. The Dublin Socialist Club invited him to become its paid organizer. The expenses of the migration to Dublin were met by a subscription raised by John Leslie and others. Connolly and his family left early in May 1896. He took with him his precious library of books on socialism and Irish history, pads of writing paper, and a sheaf of cuttings concerning the 1889 London dock strike that he had once collected. He was almost twenty-eight years old—and these possessions represented all his savings, unless one counted a mind and tongue honed to agitation and revolution.

His brother John agreed to accommodate the Edinburgh comrades at his home and, for a time, wrote the notes in *Justice*. Leslie went off to Falkirk; other pioneers of socialism also drifted off. The old 'speaker's corner' in Edinburgh crossed the railway tracks into a new area. But Edinburgh and Scotland had left their mark on Connolly. There he had found his *métier*, trade, profession—call it what you will. It was not a respected or well-paid occupation, but it was one that suited him.

So he was off to Dublin as a professional revolutionary. It cannot be seriously said that Dublin was ready for him—not even the tiny band of radicals who comprised the Dublin Socialist Club.

IV

CONNOLLY's first task in Dublin was to round up persons who, at some time or other, had been members of one or more of the forlorn socialist organizations that had existed since the 1840's, convert them to his hard-line, class warfare type of socialism, and build on this base a viable radical party.

The first meeting of the Irish Socialist Republican Party took place in the snug of a pub on Thomas Street on 29 May 1896. Of the eight founding members, five sipped lemonade only. A man named Dorman proposed that Connolly be appointed organizer at a salary of £1 per week. The resolution was seconded by J. T. Lyng, and was passed unanimously.

Until Connolly's arrival, Dorman was the man who delivered the socialist message each week on the Custom House steps. He was a kindly, lovable, pleasant man, a retired naval officer whose socialism was largely humanitarian. The Lyngs were typical Dubliners, young, talkative, bursting with energy, but without political experience. Others were soon added: another Lyng brother; three O'Briens (Thomas and Daniel were in their twenties, and William in his teens); and J. Carolan. Jack Mulray, an apprentice tailor, though not a member, sympathized with the group and was in daily contact with Connolly, who passed his shop every day as he climbed the stairs to his office in 67 Abbey Street. (Mulray made a pair of trousers for Connolly which did not take into account Connolly's bowlegs; the result was cause for laughter for many years.) Except for Dorman, they were a young group, who wore their hair long, and their numbers were small. A newspaper commented that the Irish Republican Socialist Party had more syllables than numbers, consisting mainly of 'a Scotto-Hibernian', meaning Connolly of course, 'and a long boy', referring to Tom Lyng, who was six feet tall. Their small numbers, youthfulness, and touches of Bohemianism were not characteristics

44

likely to attract support from the trade unionists whose backing they sought.

On the organizational level, Connolly informed all members that the financial secretary, T. J. Lyng, would visit them once a week to collect dues (no longer called subscriptions), and that the club rooms would be open every night. His next step was to begin a series of open-air meetings. The first one was held on 7 June 1896. It was announced in the local papers as follows:

Irish Socialist Republic. Great Public meeting in favour of the above will be held at Custom House on Sunday next 5 p.m. Mr. Jas. Connolly, late of Edinburgh, and others will address the meeting. Mr. Alexander Blane, ex-M.P. will preside.

Blane was a prominent Parnellite who lost his seat after the break-up of the Irish Nationalist Party.

Meetings at the Custom House were held each week thereafter. By the end of June, two more stands were occupied: one at Phoenix Park on Sundays at 6 p.m., and one at St James's Fountain each Tuesday at 8 p.m. The Fountain meetings were discontinued after one was broken up by the throwing of cabbage stalks and loud cries of 'You're not an Irishman.' The Custom House meetings continued until October when bad weather and Dorman's departure for the south closed the season.

At these last meetings, the Party could proudly distribute its manifesto, published in September 1896. It called for the establishment of an Irish Socialist Republic based upon public ownership of the land and of all instruments of production, distribution and exchange. It called for agriculture to be administered as a public function under boards of management elected by the agricultural population and responsible to them and the nation at large. Industry was to be conducted under the same principles.

To stem 'the tide of migration by providing employment at home', and to mitigate 'the evils of our present social system', the Party announced certain immediate objectives:

1. Nationalization of railways and canals.

2. The replacement of private banks by State ones, with popularly elected boards of directors that would issue loans at cost.

3. The establishment in rural areas of centres where the latest agricultural machinery would be lent to farmers at a rent covering cost and management alone.

4. A graduated income tax on all incomes over £300 in order to pay pensions to the aged, infirm, widows, and orphans.

5. Establishment of a minimum wage and a 48-hour week.

6. 'Free maintenance for all children.'

7. Gradual extension of the principle of public ownership to all the necessaries of life.

8. Public control and management of the national schools by popularly elected school committees.

9. Free education up to the highest university grades.

10. Universal suffrage.

In its final paragraphs, the manifesto declared that the subjection of one nation to another, as of Ireland to the British Crown, was a barrier to the free political and economic development of the subject nation, and could serve only the interests of the exploiting classes of both nations. It ended with the notice: 'Branches wanted everywhere. Enquiries invited.' The entrance fee—presumably for single members— was six pence, and the minimum weekly subscription was given at one (old) penny.

Both in language and ideas, the statement showed the direct influence of the inaugural manifesto of the Social-Democratic Federation of 1883, *Socialism Made Plain*, but differed in one major aspect. At a time when the socialists of oppressed nations were frequently taken to task for their 'nationalism', the Irish manifesto called the struggle for national independence an inseparable part of the struggle for socialism. It foreshadowed the present era when national independence, for better or worse, has become an end often more greatly desired than socialism.

Because of a strike in the building trades, Connolly's pound a week was not forthcoming, and life was very hard until September. Connolly then found work as a labourer on the construction of a new drainage system. His daughter Nora has written touchingly of how the last family treasures were sold or pawned in order to enable him to buy the clothing he needed before he could start work.

The infant Irish Socialist Republican Party dared to suggest to the Dublin Trades Union Council that it set up a committee to oppose at the polls a Member of Parliament who had vigorously denounced the building trades strike. The Council agreed to throw its full weight against him, but it refused to accept the further suggestion that a joint committee be established to do so. The Trades Union Council also continued to join with the Liberal nationalists to hear the annual Barrington lectures, 'bacchanals of mental confusion that outraged even the Fabians'. Connolly took up the ideological gauntlet with a series of lectures at Foresters Hall, and in December 1896 addressed the Fabians on 'Why We Are Revolutionists', arguing for the formation of a new working-class party.

During these years, among middle-class intellectuals and artists, the first stirrings of interest in reviving the ancient Gaelic tongue and ancient pre-Christian mythology were taking place. It was not a nationalist movement, had no roots among rural or urban proletarians, and was opposed by the Church. Connolly, like most others, certainly did not consider it, in the words of Padraic Pearse, as 'the most revolutionary influence that has ever come into Irish history'. Instead, he was re-examining Irish history along his own lines. On 31 July 1896, he heard a republican give a lecture on 'The Social Side of the Irish Question'. The speaker, Fred Ryan, argued that the ideas of James Fintan Lalor provided the solution for Ireland's difficulties. Lalor believed that the rural proletariat were 'the true owners of the soil, and advocated expropriation of the landlord class and the nationalization of the land. He urged the peasants, as the first step towards this goal, to refuse to pay rent. At the same time he boldly demanded the complete independence of Ireland from the British Crown.' In 1848 Lalor started a journal in Dublin called the *Irish Felon*. In it he asked, 'Who will draw the first blood for Ireland? Who will win a wreath that shall be green forever?' The magazine was promptly suppressed and Lalor was put in prison. The following year he died of tuberculosis.

Even in these early days, Connolly was quick to distinguish among Irish revolutionists those who shared his deeply rooted class solidarity. He set to work producing Lalor's writings as a pamphlet, with an introduction by himself. He sent a copy to the *Shan Van Vocht*, a periodical founded in Belfast by Alice Milligan, a Protestant Republican. The paper was the voice of the Young Ireland societies; behind it was the shadowy influence of the Irish Republican Brotherhood, the surviving Fenian organization. *Shan Van Vocht* reviewed the pamphlet —Connolly's first—favourably.

Connolly now proceeded, in three lengthy articles published during October 1896 in the *Labour Leader*, to lay down his basic thoughts regarding the past, present, and future of Ireland.

He began by arguing that:

The Irish question has in fact a much deeper source than a mere difference of opinion on forms of Government. Its real origin and inner meaning lay in the circumstance that the two nations held fundamentally different ideas on the vital question of property held in land.

The difference was that primitive communism, the first stage of all civilized societies, survived longer and blossomed more copiously in Ireland than in other countries in Europe. The English government was 'astute enough to perceive that the political or national subjection of Ireland was entirely valueless to the conquerors while the politically subjected nations remained in possession of economic freedom'. For this reason, it declared the public clan lands to be the private property of the chief, to hold in fief for the Crown. Primitive communism was thus replaced by a form of feudalism.

The Irish people, ran Connolly's argument, refused to accept the change until after the break-up in 1649 of the Kilkenny confederation, when the clans were dispersed. The demand for the restoration of the common ownership of land then fell into abeyance in the face of the need to recover political freedom. The Irish middle class stepped into the breach and secured its own economic position by ruthless exploitation within the framework of British institutions while preserving its political influence by lip-service to Irish nationality. Home rule was merely a device to place this class at the head of a local Parliament that would have no real political power but would simply act as a device for better exploiting the Irish people. Its dream of an industrialized Ireland successfully competing against the older capitalist countries was impossible in a world afflicted with over-production and periodic slumps. The Irish could succeed only by becoming the 'lowest blacklegs in Europe'.

The alternative conception of small-peasant ownership Connolly thought even more utopian. New methods of agricultural production were being introduced throughout the world. Modern machinery, which alone made possible production at a competitive price, demanded great capital outlay. 'The days of small farmers, like small capitalists, are gone,' he declared. Since, in any case, the present 'owners' of the land had little historical title to it, and since it was 'manifestly impossible to reinstate the Irish people on the lands from which they have been driven', the only solution was land nationalization. The community as a whole would receive collectively what had been stolen from their forebears individually.

In the last of his three articles, Connolly described the final result of the monopolization of land and industry by the landlords and capitalists in classic socialist terms. The workers today, he said, are 'deprived of everything by which they can maintain life', and must 'seek their livelihood by the sale of their capacity for work, their labour power'. They must sell it or starve. The remedy was a revolutionary change in the structure of society—the establishment of an independent socialist Ireland, not an industrial Home Rule hell created under the specious project of 'developing our resources'.

1897

With the beginning of the new year, several committees developed throughout Ireland for the purpose of commemorating the rising of 1798, an ill-starred attempt by the brilliant and dashing Protestant, Wolfe Tone, to plant the principles of the French Revolution on Irish soil.

In an article entitled 'Nationalism and Socialism', published in *Shan Van Vocht* with an editorial disclaimer, Connolly told these committees that, if modern nationalism was to be something more than a mere morbid idealizing of the past, it must demonstrate to the Irish people that it 'is also capable of formulating a distinct and definite answer to the problems of the present', and offer 'a political and economic creed capable of adjustment to the wants of the future'.

As elements of such a creed, 'all earnest nationalists' should declare their aim to be a republic: 'not a capitalist monarchy with an elected head' as in France, nor a plutocracy like the United States, but a republic that would be a 'beacon-light to the oppressed of every land'. He brushed aside the objection that such a stand would alienate middle-class and aristocratic support, saying that if the only way to conciliate these groups was by promising them that the victorious masses would not interfere with their privileges, it was better not to conciliate them at all. The masses in any case would refuse their support on such a basis. Indeed, any freedom so achieved would prove illusory and spurious, Connolly explained in a passage which still rings with prophecy:

If you remove the English army tomorrow and hoist the green flag over Dublin Castle, unless you set about the organisation of the socialist republic, your efforts would be in vain. England would still rule you. She would rule you through her capitalists, through her

49

landlords, through her financiers, through the whole array of commercial and industrial institutions she has planted in this country and watered with the tears of our mothers and the blood of our martyrs. England would still rule you to your ruin, even while your lips offered hypocritical homage at the shrine of that Freedom whose cause you betrayed.

Alice Milligan, the editor of *Shan Van Vocht*, was so impressed that she urged her young brother Ernest, then an eighteen-year-old law student, to look up Connolly while on a visit to Dublin from Belfast. Ernest found him living in a one-room tenement on Charlemont Street with his young family which had been augmented by another daughter, Ina (called Agna in Nora Connolly's reminiscences). Milligan described Connolly as of medium height, thickset, and 'though terribly earnest in conversation', endowed with a rich sense of humour. The young man, a member of the Gaelic League (the Irish language society) and a liberal nationalist of sorts, was at once disturbed and fascinated by Connolly's Marxism. 'Politics are based on the stomach,' Connolly told him, 'and economic causes have moulded history.' At a meeting in Foster Place, Ernest Milligan met members of Connolly's party and was given to read George's *Progress and Poverty*, Blatchford's *Merrie England*, Bellamy's *Looking Backward*, Ruskin's *Unto This Last*, and Charles Booth's *Labours of the People*.

Upon his return, Milligan established a branch of the Irish Socialist Republican Party in Belfast known as the Belfast Socialist Society. As usual, what response there was came from the youth, but even they had some difficulty in assimilating Connolly's republican Marxism.

In Cork another spark was lit, as proved by an article in the *Shan Van Vocht* of 12 March 1897 written by a young man named Con O'Lyhane. An honours graduate of a technical school, he wrote in support of Connolly's refusal to participate in mere worship of the past and urged the '98 Commemoration Committees to rededicate the nation to the aims of Tone's United Irishmen. Meanwhile, Connolly's party was holding indoor educational meetings in Dublin, conducted in the same style as the Edinburgh Socialist Democratic Federation. All members gave lectures. Tom O'Brien spoke on the Land League and Daniel O'Brien on Wolfe Tone. Guest speakers were Alexander Blane and Alice Milligan. In the spring of 1897, outdoor meetings were resumed. Meanwhile, Connolly's *Labour Leader* and *Shan Van Vocht* articles were collected and published as a pamphlet under the title of *Erin's Hope, the*

End and the Means. It was a proud moment for the self-educated, indigent agitator.

In May 1897 the Commemoration movement held a large demonstration in Phoenix Park, with the Dublin Trades Council represented but not the heretical Irish Socialist Republican Party. To get around such bans, Connolly founded the 'Rank and File '98 Club', with T. J. O'Brien as secretary. It was a 'front organization' typical of those which later generations of radicals were to join. The new club's one pound subscription to the Dublin executive committee for the centenary was readily accepted. The aim of the club was to disseminate a knowledge of what it considered to be the true aims of the United Irishmen. Jack Mulray, the tailor, was one of its first members.

Meanwhile, a great number of organizations of quite a different stamp were preparing to celebrate the sixtieth anniversary of the ascension of Queen Victoria to the throne. Diamond Jubilee Day was 22 June. The Independent Socialist Republican Party decided to celebrate the day in its own way with a meeting in Foster Place on the 21st. The principal speaker was to be Maud Gonne, but the celebration, under the slogan, 'Down with the Monarchy; long live the Republic', expanded far beyond that.

Maude Gonne, six foot tall and 'the most beautiful woman in Europe', was the daughter of a Colonel in the 17th Lancers. When Maud was four, her mother died, and the girl was brought up by an assortment of nannies and aunts. In her early youth, she became enamoured of land reform and other nationalist causes. In Dublin she attended the Contemporary Club, where she met the veteran Fenian John O'Leary, whom William Butler Yeats regarded as the embodiment of 'Romantic Ireland'. It was then but a step to the Celtic Literary Society, where she met Alice Milligan's circle. At the National Library she became acquainted with Connolly, who studied there during his long periods of unemployment. She did not accept his Marxist doctrines but appreciated what they had in common—a devotion to the poor people of Ireland, a willingness for action, and great physical courage.

In 1897 she was thirty-one years old, two years older than Connolly. She did not get married until she was thirty-seven. Her marriage to John MacBride was a failure, lasting only a few years. The pursuit of her by the poet W. B. Yeats before her marriage, and after she was separated from her husband, comprises one of the most astonishing and hilarious of love affairs in literary history. All this was well known in Dublin literary and patriotic circles. Not so well known is the fact that, before her ill-starred marriage, she lived for many years in Paris with a French journalist to whom she bore two illegitimate children.

Readily joining with Connolly in preparing the anti-Jubilee demonstrations, she obtained a window in Parnell (then Rutland) Square from which lantern slides could be thrown on a large screen. To dim the festive lights which could compete with the slides, it was arranged with city workers that electrical faults would occur at the appropriate time. Daniel O'Brien made a large black coffin on which were inscribed the words 'British Empire'. To lead the procession which was to accompany it through the streets Connolly obtained the services of a workers' band whose instruments would represent small loss if the police destroyed them. Maud Gonne then set to work turning out black flags embroidered with the facts on famines and evictions which had marked Victoria's reign, the fruits of Connolly's research.

The convention of the '98 Commemoration Committee was in session on Jubilee Day, as an act of contempt for the Crown, when the band appeared. The chairman promptly suspended the sitting so as to allow the delegates to join the procession. Such was the simple nature of political protest at the time. At the head of the procession was a rickety handcart draped in the semblance of a hearse and bearing the coffin. It was pushed by a member of the Irish Socialist Republican Party. Maud Gonne and Yeats were in the procession, distributing their black flags, as it moved solemnly down Dame Street to the sound of a funeral march.

By the time the procession reached O'Connell Bridge, police from Dublin Castle, the seat of British rule, were clubbing heads to disperse the spectators. Connolly soon saw that the procession could not cross the bridge. In a flash of inspiration he ordered the coffin to be thrown into the Liffey River, crying out, 'Here goes the coffin of the British Empire. To hell with the British Empire.' Connolly was promptly arrested and spent the night in prison. Maud Gonne sent him his breakfast, paid his fine when he appeared in court, and he was released.

But his arrest did not halt the day's demonstration. As planned, the city was in a black-out when night fell, but a large crowd gathered around Maud Gonne's magic lantern in Parnell Square. Even though the events at O'Connell Bridge had attracted some of the younger men, many women, children, and old people remained to watch. These were baton-charged by the police, and one old woman was killed. The indignant crowd surged down to Sackville Street (now O'Connell Street) and smashed all windows with portraits of the Queen and other

Jubilee decorations. It was Connolly's first demonstration and, though it was not impressive, it won headlines in foreign newspapers, and satisfactorily showed that not all Ireland worshipped Queen Victoria. A few black flags flew in Limerick, and one was flown from the municipal flagstaff of Cork, after Con O'Lyhane and his friends stormed the fire station and tore down the Union Jack.

Two months later the Duke and Duchess of York visited Dublin, and again great efforts were made to encourage a demonstration of loyalty, especially by 'pensioners, constabulary, police and civil servants'. The ISRP announced a special meeting in Foster Place on the evening Their Highnesses were scheduled to arrive, but only to commemorate the landing of the French fleet at Killala during the '98 Rising. All '98 Committees were invited to give their support. When the speakers reached Foster Place, they found it occupied by police who ordered them to disperse. Under protest, they walked to the rooms of the Irish Socialist Republican Party in Abbey Street where a sizeable crowd was addressed by members Stewart, Lyng and McDonnell. This meeting was eventually broken up, and forty Royal Irish Constabulary stood guard outside the premises until early the following morning.

Connolly then announced that the suppressed meeting would take place on the following Sunday at Foster Place. Two special banners were prepared for the occasion. One was a red flag showing a royal crown transfixed on a pike, with the legend 'Finis Tyranniae'. The other was green, with a sunburst and the words, 'Truth, freedom and justice in Ireland.' On Sunday, when the flags were unfurled, a battle royal took place. A series of baton charges forced the demonstrators out of Foster Place. Connolly marched his followers to Abbey Street, where the police repeated the performance. A third attempt to hold a meeting, this time at the Custom House, was even more brutally smashed. No arrests were made, but some socialists were injured.

Maud Gonne wrote Connolly a letter following one of these demonstrations (which one is unknown since the letter is undated) saying:

Bravo! all my congratulations to you! You were right and I was wrong about this evening. You may have the satisfaction of knowing that you saved Dublin from the humiliation of an English jubilee without a public meeting of protestation. You were the only man who had the courage to organise a public meeting and to carry it through in spite of all discouragement—even from friends!

Though the meetings were legal, no 'reputable' newspaper voiced any outcry against their harassment. In a country under British rule, where legality is so prized and police brutality so condemned, this fact speaks volumes regarding the socialist movement's lack of influence and power, and for the dislike in which it was held, by the masses of English and Irish alike.

* * *

It is important to realize that Connolly was never an anarchist. Even in the days when he was most under IWW and Syndicalist influence, he felt that politics and political parties could play an important role in achieving revolutionary ends. It was the parties in existence that he could not tolerate; the party he wanted did not exist.

All this he made clear in two articles he wrote at that time. In *Irlande Libre*, a periodical published in Paris by Maud Gonne, he repeated what he had said before: that the Irish struggle had occupied itself with political emancipation to the neglect of the property question, and that the Irish Socialist Republican Party was hostile to the 'purely bourgeois parties which at present direct Irish politics'. He ended by alleging that not only the Irish but the British masses had been without 'political existence' for the past 700 years, and by urging the French workers to support a programme that would emancipate Ireland from Britain, and Irish socialists from dependence on capitalist parties.

In the *Shan Van Vocht*, he pointed out that Irish workers received much lower wages than British ones. Three-quarters of them earned less than 15s. a week. This he attributed partly to the overcrowded state of the labour market in Ireland, but also to the workers' acceptance of the political leadership of their economic oppressors. He urged the election of a socialist majority in Parliament that would serve as a weapon against those members of the privileged orders who sought to preserve British rule. It would amount to a declaration of moral insurrection which might prove the precursor of a military insurrection. Socialists should participate in Parliament because, at the least, they could do everything existing parliamentarians could do, and in addition they could call 'attention to the evils inherent in that social system of which the British Empire is but the highest political expression'. The alternative, Connolly maintained, was to leave the parliamentary factions unchallenged to form a permanent barrier between the Irish people and the outside world.

In a following editorial, Alice Milligan professed full sympathy with Connolly's views on labour and social questions but she remained adamant in her objection to political action, to 'an Irish republican party at Westminster'. She stood with John Mitchel in refusing to take any oath of allegiance. But she was willing to let the matter be debated. A number of letters followed, to which Connolly replied in October 1897. He quoted from various Home Rule parliamentarians who deemed 'separation from England was undesirable and impossible', and insisted an alternative political policy must be urged in both England and Ireland.

Most of the readers of the *Shan Van Vocht* apparently remained unconvinced. Rejecting the notion that 'Irish Republicans should become politicians', Alice Milligan said that those advocating this course 'are taking the broad road that leads to destruction', and warned that 'such a party would inevitably be in alliance with the English Labour Party'.

In the meantime, Connolly left Charlemont Street and went to live in another one-room tenement at 54 Pimlico. The landlady was a Protestant who ignored her tenants and their frequent shabby visitors except on certain ceremonial occasions. Every time a child was born, she presented the parents with a chicken and a pint of whiskey. But there was one time when Lillie feared that trouble was brewing. Because of Connolly's growing fame as a speaker, he was stopped on the way home and asked to speak to the tenants of some buildings in the Coombe area. They had received notice to leave after refusing to pay a rent increase. When Connolly told Lillie that he had agreed, she looked at her tiny room full of squawling children and asked, 'Was that wise?' But on 22 October 1897, he addressed the indignation meeting held in Gray Square.

It was during this period that the Home Rule elements, who had hitherto held aloof from the '98 Commemoration Committees as republican and unconstitutional, decided that they were becoming too popular to ignore. They proceeded therefore to hold a commemorative meeting on 4 October, with Dillon, Harrington, O'Brien, and Joseph Devlin as speakers. This action created a sharp division in the Commemoration movement. Some wished to welcome the Home Rulers as newly converted fellow-Irishmen, others to reject them as constitutionalists and monarchists manœuvring for popularity. It was difficult to withstand the petty flatteries, the opportunity to appear on a platform with noted leaders, the fear of appearing disputatious at a time of national rededication. Yeats, a Protestant who was not a republican, urged Connolly and Maud Gonne to participate. Connolly replied by addressing a meeting of his party's '98 Club, in the Drapers Hall.

For a short period it looked as if the Irish Socialist Republican Party counterattack would work. Attendance at meetings (ISRP at 7 p.m., followed by the '98 Club meeting at 9.30 p.m.) grew, stimulated in part by the introduction of the singing of patriotic and revolutionary songs, a practice always dear to the Irish. At a special meeting of the '98 Club on 21 December, with Connolly presiding, a resolution was proposed and passed unanimously which urged the Commemoration Executive Committee to exclude members of the parliamentary party from an official or controlling influence in the commemoration proceedings.

1898

But the Home Rulers were not to be stopped. In January 1898, following a split in the Executive Committee of the Commemoration Clubs, a Centennial Association was formed which effectively took over the clubs. The ISRP's '98 Club thereupon disaffiliated. It still met on Sunday evenings but its members gradually became assimilated into the ISRP. At the end of March 1898, the new association held a meeting with its platform decorated with Joseph Devlin; William Martin Murphy, Dublin's biggest capitalist and an avowed royalist; and representatives of the clergy. In April the dissidents capitulated, and the association absorbed the Centenary Committee. From this point onwards, the development of a single and triumphant Home Rule Party in Parliament became a certainty. Even among Irish left-wingers the trend towards acceptance of something less than independence became stronger.

Connolly fought back as best he could. In the January 1898 issue of the *Labour Leader*, he answered a critic who reported that 'many English Socialists' considered the ISRP agitation for Irish independence 'a mere chauvinism' that served only to 'perpetuate national rivalries and race hatreds'.

In reply, Connolly envisaged a period when 'under a socialist system every nation will be the supreme arbiter of its own destinies, national and international; will be forced into no alliance against its will, but will have its independence guaranteed and its freedom respected by the enlightened self-interest of the social democracy of the world'.

The statement that the party's ideals 'cannot be realised except by the paths of violent revolution is not so much an argument against our propaganda as an indictment of the invincible ignorance and unconquerable national egotism of the British electorate . . .

'Seeing that the Home Ruler disavows all desire for separation, our English comrades are prone to draw favourable comparisons between him and the Socialist Republican.' The fact is, Connolly went on, that the Home Ruler's sole aim 'is to reproduce in Ireland all the political and social manifestations which accompany capitalist supremacy in Great Britain'.

This was Connolly's first passage of arms with the doctrine which seeks to justify imperialism on the grounds that it unites nations. Subject countries must not revolt; their emancipation must be left to the social revolution in Britain. After the British workers have obtained power, they will grant the others freedom, within the Empire of course. It was a doctrine that Connolly was to fight for the rest of his life.

It is the nature of the revolutionary that he lives as much in the world he envisages as in the real world. Even as the Home Rulers were consolidating their power, Connolly was boasting in the *Labour Leader* that the Irish Socialist Republican Party had sprung from 'obscurity to public recognition, and even approval', and that its struggle for republican principle had found entrance 'into the most remote parts of the country'. Abroad, its influence had been so far acknowledged that 60,000 leaflets had been issued by Daniel De Leon's Socialist Labor Party of America, embodying an appeal to Irish Americans to support the SLP in the municipal elections.

Connolly followed up this contact by urging Irishmen abroad to take up associate membership in the ISRP at a shilling a year. The first to avail himself of this opportunity was Edward Aveling, son-in-law of Karl Marx. From America came a response which was later to draw Connolly across the Atlantic.

Meanwhile, he had been conferring with Maud Gonne regarding a famine in counties Mayo and Kerry. Potato blight was rampant, while floods made the bogs inaccessible and added a fuel famine to the potato famine. Together, Connolly and Gonne drafted a manifesto, which drew liberally on quotations from the Fathers of the Church. The manifesto was entitled *The Rights of Life and the Rights of Property*. A cogent paragraph ran as follows:

In 1847, our people died by thousands of starvation, though every ship leaving an Irish port was laden with food in abundance. The

Irish people might have seized that food, cattle, corn and all manner of provisions before it reached the seaports, have prevented famine and saved their country from ruin, but did not do so, believing such action to be sinful, and dreading to peril their souls to save their bodies. In this belief we know now they were entirely mistaken. The very highest authorities on the doctrine of the church agree that no *human* law can stand between starving people and their right to food, including their right to take that food whenever they find it, openly or secretly, with or without the owner's permission.

After giving Connolly £25 to print the manifesto, Maud Gonne left for Mayo, arranging to have the copies shipped to her before he himself left for Kerry. (The story of her activities in Belmullet, Foxford, and Ballina are told in her memoirs, *The Servant of the Queen*.) Connolly departed Dublin in mid-March 1898, with an assignment to report the famine for Daniel De Leon's *Weekly People*, organ of the American Socialist Labor Party. He returned to Dublin in mid-April, and delivered two lectures at Foster Place, on 24 April and 1 May 1898. In the audience was a young Kerryman named J. J. Kelly, who afterwards became famous under the name of 'Sceilig'. He joined with Connolly in condemning the heartlessness of the Government, but was so upset by the socialist doctrines he heard that he began to heckle. Connolly recognized him as a genuine republican and Gaelic enthusiast, and invited his interrupter to the platform, where unity against imperialism was once again restored.

Connolly's articles on the famine appeared in June 1898. There was nothing doctrinaire about his explanation of the causes of the famine. He did not attribute it to the existence of an alien government nor to landlordism except to a minor degree. It was caused by the failure of the system of small farming, and the restricted mental horizon of the peasants; they could have prevented the blight if they had been prepared to co-operate. Under these circumstances, state action was required, Connolly wrote. The Home Rule Party was not averse to it, but it was anathema to their Liberal allies. Hence the post-Parnellian factions staged their demonstration and left it at that. He concluded with the wry observation that the British Members of Parliament had paid for their own seats and sat quietly in them; the Irish members, however, were paid by their supporters, hence felt it necessary to create good harmless scenes on occasion and had become adept at it.

From April to August 1898, when the centenary fell due, the commemorative movement continued its course. Maud Gonne co-operated sadly with the new body. Yeats followed her example with lagging interest. Connolly had many an argument with her, much to Yeats's displeasure, for Yeats had no head for politics. When 15 August came, Maud Gonne was so disgusted at the tame but grandiose speeches that she refused to take part in the proceedings.

During the same spring and early summer, Connolly constantly reminded the reformists of the Centennial Committee that they were commemorating a revolutionary. In the outdoor propaganda, he lectured them thoroughly on 'Socialism and the '98 Celebrations'. He pursued the same subject at a meeting held at the grave of Wolfe Tone in Bodenstown. But the Irish socialists had no lack of other subjects. They gave the Dublin workers their views on the tramway system, the rise in the cost of bread, old-age pensions, the Spanish–American war, and the Italian insurrection. To the apostles of sobriety, the socialists gave a lecture on 'Socialism and the Temperance Movement'. Trade unionists were offered a sermon on 'Trade Unionism and Socialism'.

During this period Connolly resolved that the Irish Socialist Republican Party must have its own publication. Only in this way, he felt, could he reach more people with these socialist commentaries. Only in this way could he 'expose' the failure of the Home Rulers to make an issue of the famine and of the Commemoration movement. There was so much he had to say about 'the coming social revolution', 'disarmament and Socialism', and 'the coming European war'. From beginning to end he had this conviction in the importance and efficacy of periodicals as instruments of change. This *Workers' Republic* was only the first of many periodicals he was to edit. But there was more to it than that. He had learned by bitter experience that a dozen badly paid radicals could hardly support a full-time organizer. He must have hoped that the magazine would flourish, and provide enough revenue to make up the difference. It was not many months later that he discovered the error in this calculation too. But at the moment he was hopeful.

In July 1898 Connolly left for Scotland to seek financial support for the paper. At Glasgow he obtained a loan of £50 from Keir Hardie. At Edinburgh, his next port of call, he received some subscriptions and was 'assured of a great many who will take the paper regularly and also get it into the newsagents'.

Connolly found a small printer to undertake the job. P. T. Daly, later secretary of the Dublin Trades Council, set much of the type. An advertisement in *Justice* described the new Irish weekly, selling at a penny a copy, in the following words:

> A literary champion of Irish Democracy, advocates an Irish Republic, the abolition of landlordism, wage-slavery, the co-operative organisation of industry under Irish representative governing bodies. Every Friday, 1st issue August 12th. Ask your newsagent.

The paper was offered to the world at a meeting held in Dublin on Sunday, 14 August 1898, when Connolly spoke on 'Wolfe Tone and the Irish Social Revolution'. The inaugural number accused the new sponsors of the centenary of distorting the meaning of 'United Irish' to mean a 'union of class and creed', and scoffed at the idea of a revolutionary party that took no account of social injustice. What, it asked was the 'feasibility of uniting in one movement underpaid labourers, and over-paid masters?'.

Connolly wrote that Tone's 'social ideas were such that he would have been a rebel even had he been an Englishman. His principles could only be realised in a socialist republic.' He summed up the matter by adding, 'Apostles of freedom are ever idolised when dead but crucified when living.' Connolly was writing his own epitaph.

In the same issue, Connolly castigated religious sectarianism, using as his launching pad the enthusiasm of Irish Catholics in America for the Spanish–American War. He said that, while the Home Rulers were preaching Faith and the Fatherland, linking national demands with a single religious belief, Catholic Irishmen were fighting Catholic Spaniards, and Protestant workers were on strike in Belfast against Protestant employers. What the *Workers' Republic* wanted was 'To unite the workers and to bury in one common grave the religious hatreds, the provincial jealousies, and the mutual distrusts upon which oppression has so long depended for security'.

Lanky Tom Lyng was busy from dawn to dusk selling the new paper to the crowds that had come into Dublin for the commemoration celebrations. In succeeding issues the weekly, though it had only eight pages, dealt with both current events and general socialist principles, the latter congealed, so to speak, from speeches in Foster Place. Connolly elaborated on such matters as the capitalist origin of modern war, which he attributed to the struggle for markets, on the inevitable instability of a peasant proprietary, and on the need for political action by trade unionists.

In the 1 October issue, Connolly made his first attempt to grapple with the question of the Irish language, whose revival was being pushed by the newly founded Gaelic League. His first judgement was sceptical: 'You cannot teach starving men Gaelic.' He saw in the replacement of the Irish language by English simply an illustration of Marx's dictum that 'capitalism creates a world after its own image'. A few years later he attributed the spread of English to the Irish mercantile class during the industrial revolution. Not until he was in America, ten years later, did he give his mature opinion: the suppression of one tongue by another was an illustration of imperialism, and the defence of a people's mother tongue was an integral part of the defence of the soil. After his return to Ireland, he set about learning Irish himself.

Connolly had in mind establishing a national Irish weekly comparable to *Justice* or the *Leader*, and during the first weeks prospects seemed bright. The open-air meetings of the Irish Socialist Republican Party ensured a regular sale, and in Belfast young Milligan found a wholesaler who would distribute the paper to news stands. But the Belfast socialists mistrusted the new paper's nationalist flavour, and failed to rally around it when a Catholic bishop condemned it and the wholesaler was forced to discontinue distributing it. For a time Milligan distributed it himself at key positions in Belfast, but opportunities both there and in Dublin gradually declined, and at the end of October 1898 the weekly discontinued publication. It had run for fewer than a dozen issues.

Towards the end of the year, the system of electing local representatives had been completely overhauled, under provisions of the Irish Local Government Act. It was one of a series of Conservative Party measures designed to 'kill Home Rule with kindness'. The Irish Socialist Republican Party put forth E. W. Stewart as its candidate for the North Dock Ward. In the January elections he was defeated, partly because the party, lacking financial resources, had to confine its election propaganda to open-air meetings at Spenser Dock. The *Evening Telegraph* refused to accept advertisements for these meetings on the ground that Stewart's leading opponent was being maligned.

V

1899

AFTER the elections, Connolly visited Cork, where he spoke to what the *Cork Constitution* called a 'fairly large' audience on his favourite subject, 'Labour and the Irish Revolution'. His main point was that the class which ground the Irish workers down economically could never lead them to national victory. 'We should have done with this middle-class leadership', which meant 'middle-class patriotism', and 'middle-class compromise', he told his listeners. The task of the Irish workers was 'to give to patriotism a purer and a nobler significance, and by organising, to shatter forever the system which condemned the people to misery'.

Back in Dublin, Marxist education resumed. Connolly spoke on the 'technical terms of scientific socialism'. Bradshawe discussed the class struggle and 'Are We Utopians?'. T. J. O'Brien lectured on the differences between the old and new socialism, as represented by Robert Owen and Karl Marx, respectively.

But Connolly himself was in dire financial straits. On 11 March 1899, he wrote to Daniel O'Brien that he had succeeded in getting a job performing heavy manual labour for the City of Dublin

but found myself unable for it. At least I worked Thursday, was not able to go out on Friday, tried again on Saturday (today) but was not allowed to start.

So I have now reached the end of my financial tether, and having been on short commons so long, am unable to perform such work when I get it. My reason for writing to you is to tell you that as the Organiser (?) business is a failure—7/- per week—and as I don't like to be drawing money from a few comrades—some of whom can ill afford it, perhaps, I am wishful, as a last resort before shaking the dust of Ireland from my feet, to try again my luck at the pedlar's pack. The reason I abandoned that line before was that I had never a sufficient stock to start with, and as a consequence two days good selling left me stranded until I scraped together sufficient for another start.

He then asked O'Brien for a loan of two pounds to purchase a stock for a peddlar's pack.

It lowers me in my own opinion to ask this, but it would tear my heart-strings out to leave Ireland now after all my toil and privation—and unless I succeed in this instance the welfare, nay the mere necessity of feeding my family will leave me no alternative.

This letter provides the only evidence we have that Connolly had once tried his hand at peddling, and that, less than three years after landing in Ireland, he was already considering the possibility of leaving it.

Instead of pursuing either alternative, Connolly turned again to magazine publication—this time with costs cut to the bone. He would eliminate the commercial printer and set the type himself. He procured a small hand press, a case or two of type, and the necessary accessories. He was the editor, contributor, composing-room staff, and, except when he could get help, machine-room staff as well. Each new issue would appear only when its predecessor had sold out. The first issue of the revived *Workers' Republic* was dated Friday, 12 May 1899. The logotype was designed and cut from linoleum by Carolan who, being unemployed, helped Connolly with the printing.

Leaflets and pamphlets were produced on the same press in the same size. The paper appeared most regularly when Connolly was unemployed. A pound or two was scraped together from every possible source to keep them both going. Connolly was not far from the truth when he described the first series as 'so weekly that it almost died', and the second appeared 'whenever it was strong enough to get out'.

During the summer of 1899, it became apparent that Great Britain was intent on establishing its 'rights' in South Africa, although war with the South African Republic (Transvaal) and the Orange Free State was not declared until 12 October. From the first Connolly recognized the war as purely imperialistic and threw all his forces into the struggle. They were not very formidable, consisting of the paper, a few pamphlets, and a party that numbered fewer than one hundred members and was so weak that it held no regular delegate conventions. The party's connections with the broad trade-union movement were slight. Those of its members who were trade unionists lived a double life—they were trade unionists on week days, socialists on Sundays. When there was no regular socialist activity, Sunday was doubly a day of rest. Nevertheless, the party had branches in Dublin and Cork, with groups of supporters in Belfast, Limerick, Dundalk, Waterford and Portadown; and most of the party members were strong in their faith. Most of the members were young, and some were undeniably talented.

At ISRP meetings held from June onward, both at Phoenix Park and Foster Place, Connolly strove to bring the significance of the Transvaal crisis home to the workers. At the first meeting, Maud Gonne sent a message of support and urged that protest meetings be held all over Ireland. The authorities had not yet adapted themselves to the new position and the police did not interfere when a resolution was moved condemning Britain's 'criminal aggression' and urging the Irish in the Transvaal to take up arms against Her Majesty's Forces. It was probably the first protest against the coming Boer War that was made anywhere in the British Isles . . . for whatever it was worth.

In the *Workers' Republic*, Connolly said the purpose of the war was to enable 'an unscrupulous gang of capitalists to get into their hands the immense riches of the diamond fields'. 'Such a war,' he said, 'will undoubtedly take rank as one of the most iniquitous wars of the century.' It corroborated 'the truth of the socialist maxim that the modern state is but a committee of rich men administering affairs in the interest of the upper class . . . There is no pretence that the war will benefit the English people'.

He pointed out that the reason British troops could be transferred from Ireland to the Transvaal was because the Government could rely on the Home Rule Party and the Royal Irish Constabulary to keep the country quiet.

But if the working class of Ireland were only united, and understood their power sufficiently well, and had shaken off their backs the Home Rule–Unionist twin brethren, keeping us apart that their class may rob us, they would see in this complication a chance for making a long step forward towards better conditions of life and, seeing it, act upon it in a manner that would ensure the absence from the Transvaal of a considerable portion of the British Army.

He was indicating here that England's difficulty ought to be Ireland's opportunity. If a revolutionary situation appeared, Ireland should take advantage of it, peacefully if possible, forcibly if necessary.

In July 1899 Connolly made his stand on violence perfectly clear. There was no sense in debating whether 'constitutionalism' or 'insurrectionism' was the better way. Neither was likely to be successful unless and until there was perfect agreement 'on the end to be attained'. The '98 Commemoration had been started by physical force men who stood for national independence as exemplified by Wolfe Tone but, because they were unclear as to the kind of society they wanted, they had ended by electing within twelve months persons to their governing committee who were notorious for their royalist proclivities. Physical force, which was a means, had been made the test of advanced nationalism instead of the social system, which was the end. Connolly concluded:

> Socialists believe that the question of force is of very minor importance; the really important question is of the principles upon which is based the movement that may or may not need the use of force to realise its object.

Irish sentiment against the Boer War gradually rose. Maud Gonne founded a women's nationalist organization which conducted propaganda against war and enlistment. Some students at Trinity College, Dublin's Protestant university, organized a pro-Boer Society and held stormy meetings. Trade unions began to take an interest. The *United Irishman*, edited by Arthur Griffith, a young journalist recently returned from South Africa, threw its weight on the side of the Boers.

After 1916 Griffith's Sinn Fein slogan eventually became the term under which all anti-British and pro-independence movements were lumped. But at this time he was poor, unknown, sincere, pursuing an unphilosophic and ill-defined goal of Irish nationality. The Irish Republican Brotherhood helped to finance his paper, but Griffith was no republican. What he advocated was a dual monarchy similar to that of Austria–Hungary. Far from being anti-imperialist, he desired an Anglo-Irish Empire in which Britain and Ireland would jointly exploit the lesser breeds. He expressly denied the equality of the African and Asian peoples. He was not above referring to 'Anglo-Jews' and 'Niggers', and drew no distinction between capitalist and worker. To Connolly, Sinn Fein represented the small-trading class which, jealous of the big cross-Channel mercantile interests, wanted to share the spoils, not abolish them.

At times Griffith and his party could grow rebellious and even anti-clerical, but they accepted no part of Connolly's progressive ideas. Griffith 'listened to Connolly's open-air meetings with a glum face'. He sought no strengthening of the working class; he feared that the concessions it might wring from big business, which could afford them, might ruin the small employer. Griffith gave little publicity in his paper to Connolly's activities, but Connolly was thankful for what he received. The legend that there was a long and intimate connection between the two men is unfounded.

Several protest meetings were sponsored by a loosely knit 'Irish Transvaal Committee' during the autumn. The most famous one took place just before Christmas, when Joseph Chamberlain, British colonial secretary and leader of the Liberal-Unionists in the House of Commons, was scheduled to receive an honorary degree from Trinity College. It was announced that Michael Davitt, William Redmond, and Councillors Nannetti and Cox would speak in protest at Beresford Place. At the last moment, police posters appeared banning the rally. The only dignitaries—if that is the word—who assembled at Abbey Street for the trip to Beresford Place were Connolly, Maud Gonne, and the veteran Fenian John O'Leary. Joining them later in the cart was Member of Parliament Pat O'Brien, who explained that he was substituting for Michael Davitt.

Though there was room behind, Connolly climbed beside the driver. When the group turned the corner of Abbey Street, the officer in charge of a police cordon ordered them back. The driver hesitated, and the police at once pulled him from his seat. With a skill based on his experience as a driver of dust carts, Connolly seized the reins and drove through the police barricade, scattering both police and populace as the swaying wagon drove through.

At Beresford Place a huge crowd was assembled. 'We haven't much time,' said Connolly. O'Leary called for silence and Maud Gonne read the protest resolution. Hardly had the applause died down when the mounted police arrived. They dispersed the crowd and, seizing the reins, led the cart into the Store Street police barracks. The superintendent in charge held puzzled consultations with his subordinates. 'We can't keep them here,' he said. There was nothing in his instructions that told him what to do with a captured O'Leary, Connolly, Maud Gonne, a Home Rule M.P.—and a cart. He finally approached

Connolly, still in the driver's seat, and said severely, 'You can't stay here.'

'We don't want to,' Connolly said, with accuracy.

The gates were opened, and the party was turned out to freedom—but it was made clear that any attempt to return to Beresford Place would mean a repeated arrest. Such being the case, Connolly drove along Abbey Street, across O'Connell Bridge, and to Foster Place, where the meeting was resumed. A new crowd assembled, and Maud Gonne announced that the resolution passed in Beresford Place would again be read. As Connolly disputed the matter with protesting foot police, O'Brien, M.P., called for three cheers for the Boers, after which the mounted police arrived and charged the populace. Accustomed to horses, the crowd simply gave way, and re-formed behind them. But gradually the cart was separated from the audience and there was little more to be done than to arrange for an indoor meeting which took place the same night. During the excitement, another group of police raided the premises of the Irish Socialist Republican Party and smashed the press that printed the *Workers' Republic*. The weekly had suffered another death.

1900

During 1900 the classical Establishment methods for combating revolution—reform and repression, the carrot and the stick—were working well. Fortunately for Connolly, he was so busy fighting back that he did not have time to estimate his chances of success.

Following passage of an act reforming methods of electing local Irish officials, several Labour candidates were elected to office in January 1899. By September 1899, Connolly was criticizing these representatives for using 'the name of Labour as a cover for the intrigues of a clique', for breaking solemn pledges, and for the lack of inspiration and leadership. Nevertheless, in January 1900, the Irish Socialist Republican Party itself plunged into a municipal campaign, contesting North Dock Ward with Tom Lyng as the candidate. The campaign to discourage Irishmen from enlisting in the British Army to fight the Boer War was in full swing, and Connolly had difficulty in dissuading his followers from inserting a plank in the platform denying the right of employment to ex-soldiers. 'I'll resign if you put that in,' he said with hard practicality.

All labour candidates, including Lyng, suffered resounding defeats.

Connolly attributed them to the 'arrogance and weakness' shown by labour representatives elected the previous year, but it is doubtful whether anything could have beaten back the tides of chauvinism and opportunism that were sweeping the country. The appeal of Home Rule to mild republicans was strengthened when the Irish factions in Parliament merged at the end of January 1900 into a single group known as the United Irish League. Headed by John Redmond, it attracted many nationalists who felt that this was the broad highway to Irish freedom.

Stronger republicans—Keir Hardie and his Independent Labour Party—were losing sympathy with Connolly's group after hearing reports that Connolly was leading mobs through the streets 'brandishing the Boer Flag and shouting for an Irish Republic and for the defeat of Britain in the Transvaal'. Bruce Glasier, a reporter who was touring Ireland on behalf of the Fabians, wrote in Blatchford's *Clarion* of March 1900, 'How I envied him his self-indulgence and irresponsibility. How straight and broad, but ah! how exhilarating seemed the path along which he was careening with the policemen at his heels.'

Adding the Fabians to his long list of opponents, Connolly retorted:

Ireland has not until last year received much attention from the Fabian gentry. The Irish worker had not the municipal franchise, therefore Fabian gas and water schemes would have been lost on him. But as soon as he obtained the franchise and manifested the desire to use it in a true class spirit, the cry went up for the Fabian missionaries. In order to prevent the Irish working class from breaking off entirely from the bourgeois parties and from developing a revolutionary tendency, the Fabians sent their lecturer to Ireland, to induce the Irish working class to confine themselves to the work of municipalising, and to fritter away their energies and break their hearts on the petty squabbles of local administration, to the entire neglect of the essential work of capturing the political power necessary for social reconstruction.

Most socialists, including Blatchford, and most socialist organizations supported the English Government in the Boer War, but a few individuals—J. Ramsay MacDonald, Pete Curran, Mrs Pankhurst—resigned in protest from the Fabian Society. The number of Irishmen volunteering for the British Army gradually fell off, despite unemployment and strong recruiting efforts. Some republican papers kept up such an outspoken attack on living conditions in the army that Connolly, for once outmatched in militancy, confided in Mulray that he feared they might bring direct official attention to him.

To combat this rising sentiment against the war, the Government decided to send Queen Victoria to Ireland, and the establishment made great preparations to receive her. Special ships brought thousands of shipworkers from Belfast to line the route for her arrival; children were given a holiday, and a great 'treat' for them was announced by the Lord Lieutenant who ruled Ireland for the Queen. Workers at the great Guinness brewery were given a holiday and an extra shilling in their pay envelopes, and a huge stand was erected for them to cheer from.

Connolly responded by issuing a manifesto which called monarchy 'a survival of the tyranny imposed by the hand of greed and treachery in the darkest and most ignorant days of our history'. He argued that the only birthright necessary to qualify for public office should be the birthright 'of our common humanity'; he denied all allegiance to the institution of royalty; and he asserted that 'the mind accustomed to political kings can easily be reconciled to social kings—capitalist kings of the workshop, the mill, the railway, the ship and the docks'.

Maud Gonne arranged a 'counter-treat' for the children, which was attended by many thousands and seriously affected the success of the Lord Lieutenant's event. The Transvaal Committee arranged a torch-light demonstration, outside its office at 32 Abbey Street, which the police charged with batons. Dispersing the mob, they picked out three editors—Connolly, Griffith, and O'Leary Curtis of the *Weekly Independent*—and knocked them to the ground. A second procession starting from Capel Street was ambushed at Green Street by 200 policemen who paid little attention to the age or sex of the demonstrators. When members of the Irish Socialist Republican Party returned to Abbey Street to get their bicycles, the usual method of transportation in those days, a third charge was made. During the entire month of March that the Queen spent in Ireland, there was continuous turmoil. At the height of the tumult, Connolly was called away to Edinburgh. His father had suffered a cerebral haemorrhage on 3 April and died seventeen days later. Connolly registered the death, remained for the funeral, and then hurried back to Dublin.

With the British Army suffering repeated defeats, and unemployment growing, the Government launched an attack on civil liberties. In mid-April 1900 it seized the entire issue of Griffith's *United Irishman*

69

because it contained an article, 'The Famine Queen', written by Maud Gonne. To take up the slack, on 11 May 1900, the *Workers' Republic* resumed publication. It met with protest from a surprising quarter; from printers who accused Connolly of depriving them of employment by producing it with voluntary labour. He replied brusquely that by the same token he robbed the barbers by shaving himself.

The revived weekly was distributed at a series of open-air meetings held at Foster Place, where ISRP speakers demanded freedom of the press and the curbing of police brutality. But these few voices received little attention and were finally stilled when a total ban was placed on public meetings in Dublin, following the 'khaki election', which returned the Conservatives to power on a wave of jingoism. But force and repression were not the only effective tools. It was possible to pacify many workers by offering them higher wages and better working conditions, concessions made painless to the Establishment by the expansion of imperialism which tapped fantastic new sources of wealth in distant countries. Since some of this wealth trickled down to them, these workers did not probe too closely into the manner in which it was obtained.

In 1900 an international socialist congress was held in Paris. Representatives of the Irish Socialist Republican Party were Stewart and Lyng; Connolly was probably unable to attend because he was out of funds. The congress had varying effects on the Irish. It was the first such congress ever to recognize the right of Ireland to national freedom. Even Arthur Griffith was moved to cheer. On the other hand, after the German socialist Rosa Luxemburg delivered a brilliant speech attacking the 'nationalist heresy', embodied in the attempt to reconstitute Poland, few of the socialists present considered the Irish position as truly revolutionary.

The main debate revolved around the right of the socialist deputy Millerand to become part of the French Government. After many hours of bitter argument, a compromise resolution was introduced. It avoided the question of whether Millerand was right or wrong in entering a reactionary capitalist government, but criticized him for not obtaining the sanction of his party first. Ireland voted against the resolution, thus taking the more extreme position.

Connolly fervently supported this stand. In a letter published in the 25 May 1901 issue of *Justice*, he called the presence of Millerand in the French cabinet 'an injury to Socialism all over the world' and 'an international scandal'. He argued that the revolutionary proletariat should 'accept no government position which it cannot conquer through its own strength at the ballot box'; and he pointed out that, since Millerand's entrance into the cabinet, no fewer than twelve strikes had been broken by the use of the military. His conclusion was that: 'What good Millerand may have done is claimed for the credit of the bourgeois republican government; what evil the cabinet has done reflects back on the reputation of the Socialist party. Heads they win, tails we lose.' As may be observed, Connolly was developing a trenchant blunt style which left no room for misunderstanding.

In October 1900 the *Workers' Republic* was revived for the fourth time, and was distributed on news stands. But unemployment was still rife in Dublin, and Connolly's wages from the Irish Socialist Republican Party were being paid with decreasing regularity. For Christmas he brought home two shillings. The family had no Christmas dinner and no presents. Lillie was again pregnant. Her only son, Roderic, was born 11 February 1901.

Undaunted by these harsh personal circumstances, Connolly continued to preach pure socialism in the pages of the *Workers' Republic*. Some of these essays were reprinted in 1901 in a pamphlet called *The New Evangel*. In one article he took note of the trend towards government ownership of railways and municipal enterprises. While recognizing it as a sign that the 'overweening belief in the all-sufficiency of private enterprise' was being discarded, he nevertheless argued that to call this trend socialistic was in the highest degree misleading. If state ownership and control were socialism, then the army, the navy, the police, the judges, the jailers, the informers, and the hangmen would all be socialist functionaries. Socialism requires

ownership by the state of all the land and materials for labour, combined with the co-operative control by the workers of such land and materials . . . To the cry of the middle class reformers, 'Make this or that the property of the government,' we reply, 'Yes, in proportion as the workers are ready to make the government their property.'

In another essay, Connolly explained why his party sought the downfall of the Liberal and Home Rule parties with a zest that 'even the most bigoted conservative could never hope to excel'. It was because of the futility of their attempt to 'blend the principles of progress and reaction', leading only to the 'shedding of their members at both ends'. Socialists sought to demolish the reform parties in order to hasten the day when the political battlefield might be left clear for the only parties possessing a logical reason for existence.

This challenge was issued at a time when the Independent Labour Party was busy conciliating the Liberal and Home Rule parties. Hardie's *Labour Leader* was becoming ever more fulsome in its praise of Redmond's followers. By May 1901 Hardie was extolling Redmond's partner, John Dillon, and in September he toured Killarney with a Member of Parliament who, 'although not a member of the Land and Labour League . . . is yet full of a passionate desire to serve the poor'. This was not enough for Connolly. He continued to hold Hardie in personal regard, but their political association ceased.

VI

WITH CONDITIONS the way they were in Ireland, Connolly became
eager to make a lecture tour of England. His purpose, as always in this
and future tours, was, first, to raise funds by adding members to his
party and subscriptions to his magazine; and, second, to spread the
gospel of 'true' socialism as opposed to reform socialism.

Justice again published the announcement of his availability, and
the Social-Democratic Federation leader in Lancashire, Dan Irving,
arranged the itinerary. It had been hoped to make one continuous
tour, but not enough English branches requested Connolly's services
to make this possible. For them and the executive committee of the
Federation as well, the Irish stand on the Millerand question had been
too strong. The Scottish branches, on the other hand, were
unconcerned.

The Scottish part of Connolly's tour began in Glasgow, where he
addressed a May Day meeting on Glasgow Green under the auspices
of the Social-Democratic Federation. He concluded a week of propaganda with a meeting in Jail Square. After returning to Dublin for a
brief interval, he resumed his tour at Falkirk at the beginning of June.
One of his audience here wrote:

> He possesses an attribute comparatively rare among socialist lec-
> turers, that of being at the same time simple and perfectly intelligible
> to the ordinary man, and also perfectly accurate and rigid in his
> adherence to scientific verity.

This is not a bad description of a Connolly lecture, assuming, of
course, that one is willing to attribute a degree of scientific verity to
Marxism.

Despite bad weather and some opposition from—strangely enough—temperance groups, Connolly held several meetings in Aberdeen, then Leith, and finally Salford in Lancashire.

Dan Irving had arranged that the Social-Democratic Federation of South Salford and the Independent Labour Party of West Salford should share the expenses of the week's campaign. Both organizations were in the doldrums, with empty meeting rooms and no activity. Connolly spoke at street corners every night of the week, concluding with a rally which brought in some new members. 'Comrade Connolly's visit put new life into the branch,' wrote one participant, and a return visit was arranged for September.

While in Salford, Connolly received word from Murtagh Lyng that the tram-car workers in Dublin desired to form a union and had requested the help of someone from the Irish Socialist Republican Party. Connolly wrote back that the logical person to assist them was Tom Lyng, not himself. 'Tom is on the ground, is known to a number of these men, has conversed with them on the matter; urged them to form their Union, and there would consequently be nothing strange in him organizing it . . . I know Tom will say that he is not so capable of doing this work as I am, but I fancy I am as good a judge in this matter as he is, and I believe he could manage the job with infinite credit to himself and us.'

At first sight it appears that Connolly's action in passing over an opportunity for what would presumably be a paying job as organizer does great credit to his magnanimity. But Connolly then goes on to say that he was booked up for speaking engagements to the end of September or beginning of October; and to take on this organizing job would require him to break these engagements, thereby leaving behind him 'a very resentful feeling . . . a feeling from which the party as well as I would suffer.' This story fails to hold water. The amount of resentment would have been infinitesimal. The simple truth is that he was finding himself as a speaker, an agitator, and a writer, and preferred—probably *needed*, in a deep psychological fashion—to develop his talents along those lines rather than settle down to a regular job organizing the tram-car workers. One thinks, not for the first time, 'Poor Lillie.'

The same letter concludes, typically enough, with a request for additional membership cards and literature, and a condemnation: 'I hear Tom Lyng and Arnall are the only ones really taking part in the open air propaganda. It is a damned disgrace.'

This kind of nagging criticism was one of the elements that eventually helped to cause the disintegration of the Party. Murtagh Lyng, newly elected secretary of the Party, plaintively responded on 3 August 1901:

> I think your own experience here, and the knowledge you have had of the difficulties under which things are carried on here might have led you to infer that if all your orders and wishes, etc. have not been attended to with the promptitude you desired, there has been some reason *more* or *less satisfactory* for the seeming neglect. I quite recognise that working for us as you are, you have every right to expect that we should by our efforts here show that we appreciate your interest in us, still you must be prepared to make allowances in view of difficulties here. As a matter of tactics I think the tone of some of your remarks have been much too *vitriolic*—tending to produce the opposite effect on some of us to what you desired.

Unperturbed, Connolly wrote to Murtagh on 26 August to pass on a complaint from a man in Pendleton that his order for literature had not been filled. He asked what had caused the delay in publishing the latest issue of the *Workers' Republic*; and concluded fretfully: 'I would be obliged if some one would drop me a letter to let me know how things are going, and what about the pamphlet for next issue, and are the Americans subscribing still?'

Lyng answered by describing a recent successful meeting, 'with a great crowd', 'with any amount of questions' and with two new members joining. Connolly unbent sufficiently to express his pleasure that

> you are doing so well with meetings and getting so many new members. There were so many evil prophets in Dublin saying that the movement would go slump if I left Dublin that your progress since I left has been doubly gratifying to me—proving that the I.S.R.P. was well able to stand on its own feet, and that its growth depended upon correct principles and not upon one's personality. If all those who can work for Socialism in Ireland would work I might content myself in exile, and never would be missed, which would be a greater tribute to my work of the past five years than if my presence was indispensable.

Murtagh Lyng's letter to Connolly dated 2 October 1901 makes the first reference to the drinking club idea, the rock upon which the Party eventually was shattered. Murtagh said the matter was being discussed of dispensing liquor at the club rooms, but the first results were poor—the two brewing companies approached were indifferent. The letter concluded typically enough: 'No move has been made re indoor lectures or elections yet, probably there will be after next Tuesday when new officials will be appointed, and may galvanize the show into a bit of life. At present I am feeling a bit tired and not devoting much time to things here.' Murtagh was here expressing the feelings of many later socialists: 'Socialism takes too many evenings.'

On his return to Salford, Connolly found his best prospects among the Irish who worked in the Pendleton mines. They had established a branch of the Irish Socialist Republican Party in the interval, and now it was holding its first meeting. The chairman made it clear that the branch had been started in order to challenge Home Rule policies within England. In his address Connolly dealt with the differences between the 'fakirs' (reformists) and the 'clear-cuts' (revolutionaries). These terms, both imported from the United States, had received wide circulation at a recent Social-Democratic Federation held in Birmingham, where the Scottish branches had split, some falling under control of one group, others under another.

Then Connolly laid down the challenge; the fakirs could follow Redmond, the clear-cuts must follow the Irish Socialist Republican Party. The Home Rule parties, said Connolly,

> were always the open enemies or the treacherous friends of the working class, but the revolutionary parties have always been in favour of full political and social freedom . . . I hope that every Irish worker will join, and be as zealous in co-operating with the militant revolutionary class at home in working for the full emancipation of their class and country, as the Irish of Great Britain have been in helping the middle-class movement of Home Rule.

At the same time Connolly made it clear that the new ISRP branch in Salford must not compete with either the Independent Labour Party or the Social-Democratic Federation. It could accomplish this by confining its membership exclusively to those of Irish birth or descent.

During the meeting, at which many members were enrolled, Connolly gave a glowing account of the ISRP in Ireland, mentioning its strong branches in Dublin and Cork. One of his listeners, who later became a Labour MP, thought that 'Connolly was one of the most convincing speakers I ever heard in my life, a man with a great passion for the cause of the labouring classes, and probably a greater passion for the cause of Ireland.'

After a visit to Reading where he held large meetings but gained no recruits, he joined Len Cotton in Oxford, where the struggle was consistently difficult owing to the high spirits of the students and the conservatism of the local authorities. Following precedent, trouble began at Connolly's first meeting, when a combination of aristocratic students and plebeian scoffers gathered round the platform and began to sing and shout. They threw stones at Connolly and threatened to tear down the red flag, forcing Connolly to abandon the meeting after an hour.

As Connolly and Cotton marched down Cornmarket Street, the crowd attempted to seize the platform from Cotton, and the pole, which was seven feet tall and thick as a broom handle, from Connolly. With amazement, Cotton watched Connolly break the pole across his knees as if it were a match and wield it with ease among the nearest hoodlums, four of whom he laid out. The police then intervened. The socialists were separated and in the mêlée Cotton lost sight of Connolly. He appeared at dusk, having spent all this time searching for his hat, which had been knocked off in the fracas. Further meetings were held, but were so stormy that it was impossible to take collections. This meant that Connolly did not receive his expenses, and the Oxford branch issued a public appeal for donations.

In London he held meetings at Finsbury Park and Highbury Corner under the sponsorship of the North London Socialist Club, a branch of the Social-Democratic Federation. Connolly was at his wittiest. Noting the worsening economic prospects of the traditional Irish immigrants who for years had gone to the Eastern Counties for harvest work, Connolly said: 'They used to be waylaid by farmers wanting to give them a job,' but since the introduction of agricultural machinery, 'they now were waylaid by the farmer's dog, wanting to give them a bite.'

He considered the willingness of some capitalists to sponsor reforms as natural enough: 'If the workers ask for the capitalist baker's shop, he will throw the loaves at them to keep them out.' When a listener asked why he called his socialist party republican, he responded, 'I cannot imagine a socialist party being in favour of a monarchy.'

From London, Connolly wrote Murtagh Lyng on 14 October 1901:

The meetings here are awful. McEntee assures me that the smallest meeting we ever had in Foster Place would be considered a 'demonstration' here. Certainly my meetings have been the smallest I have had in England. They said that my meetings were big meetings, but a large proportion of the crowd were Irish and Scotch comrades from other branches in London, who come up to see me personally. So I must still adhere to the opinion I gave Hazell when he asked me my opinion of London. I told him the only hope for it was a 'big fire'.

With sly humour, he told about a comrade recently back from Dublin

who was enthralling the members by telling them how our fellows were working up to 12 o'clock at night printing the W.R., and every night in the week. He spoke about the police raids, and I gave them to understand in an off-handed sort of way that police raids were part of our routine business, and that if we had not one at least once a month we felt as if there was a gap in our life.

During his absence Connolly had been elected to the Dublin Trades Council by the United Labourers Union. The Labourers now went further by supporting his nomination as Labour candidate for the Town Council from the Wood Quay Ward. His nomination was approved on 13 November. Two other members of the Irish Socialist Republican Party ran for office at the same time: MacLoughlin for Councilman, and Stewart for Alderman, both in the North City Ward. 'If I don't die fighting for Ireland,' said Connolly, 'I'll leave people behind who will.'

As usual, Connolly's campaign consisted for the most part of open-air meetings, his favourite location being in New Street. The support of the Trades Council did not do much to make Connolly respectable; he received the usual amount of vilification. Sermons were preached in which he was termed an anti-Christ, and Catholics were forbidden to vote for him under pain of excommunication. It was charged that his children attended Catholic school only to camouflage his atheistic beliefs. The polling booths were deliberately located (says Greaves) in a schoolroom attached to a Catholic church so that the voters would be reminded of their duty by a priest as they entered.

Under these circumstances, it was not surprising that Connolly lost by a vote of 431 to 1,424. Stewart and MacLoughlin also lost by decisive majorities.

1902

The pattern for Connolly's life as an itinerant socialist agitator became firmly fixed in 1902. His letters written in the spring and summer of that year come from Falkirk, Leith, Glasgow, and Kirkcaldy in Scotland; and from Salford, Accrington, Nelson, Ashton-under-Lyne, Bolton, Pendleton, and Hyde, in England. The last four months of 1902 he spent touring the United States on behalf of the Socialist Labor Party.

But during the early part of the year, and between trips, Connolly managed to get much work done in Ireland as well. He and his fellow party members, Stewart and MacLoughlin, made their voices heard in the deliberations of the Trades Union Council. With the assistance of P. T. Daly, who represented the printers, they induced the Council to approve various proposals for assisting occupants of the dreadful tenement houses that made Dublin notorious, and to press these proposals upon the city authorities. These proposals called for assessing unoccupied houses; for the establishment of tribunals to fix fair rents; for continued occupation by tenants pending decisions by the tribunals; and compulsory registration of all tenement houses. Connolly's request that the city carry out its building work by hiring workers directly instead of through contractors was also approved by the Trades Council. So effective was the work of the ISRP members that Stewart and MacLoughlin were elected to the Council's executive committee and in September 1902 Stewart was elected president of the Council. Stewart was a great conversationalist, skilled in satirizing the foibles and weaknesses of others, but less ready to accept ridicule of himself. Greaves says that he 'could cherish implacable hatreds on the most slender grounds'. We shall hear more of Stewart later on.

In January 1902 the publication of the *Workers' Republic* was suspended, and an appeal was issued for donations to replace the hand press with a more efficient and rapid machine. Apparently, such a machine was found, and the weekly reappeared in March. It contained

79

an article in which Connolly referred bitterly to the opposition the Home Rulers had given his candidacy, while they were now supporting the candidate of the Social-Democratic Federation in Dewsbury.

On the same printing machine, the Irish Socialist Republican Party published an appeal to English Socialists, urging them not to support the Home Rule Party. Such support, it was argued, might bring them a few Irish votes, but it held back the day when Irish socialists would stand beside them in the common struggle. Connolly was constantly infuriated by this tendency of socialists, liberals, and reformers of every variety to consider the demand for Irish freedom as completely crackpot. However, this particular appeal met with some favour among militant leftists, and was published in the German magazine *Vorwärts*, the French publication *Le Petit Sou*, the *Weekly People* of the American Socialist Labor Party, and *Justice*, organ of the Social-Democratic Federation.

During the spring of 1902 Connolly toured Scotland, making speeches, conferring with comrades, discussing the possibility of combining the *Workers' Republic* with a proposed new Scottish weekly, and writing hasty instructions to Thomas J. Lyng, successor to Murtagh as secretary of the Irish Socialist Republican Party in Dublin.

Those letters which have survived tell us where Connolly was on different days, and what he was thinking about. From Leith on 4 April, he wrote to Lyng naming places where bundles of the pamphlet *Erin's Hope* should be sent; wondered about the possibility of urging subscribers to the *Workers' Republic* to form reading circles; and concluded: 'Any further word from America?'

The last item referred to discussion then taking place about the possibility that Connolly might tour America on behalf of the Socialist Labor Party, USA. The SLP had republished *Erin's Hope* in February, and soon after had invited Connolly to visit the US. Connolly's own trade union, the United Labourers of Ireland, was eager for him to go and was prepared to offer some financial assistance. The union wished to obtain first-hand information about the conditions of workers in America, the land which provided so much help to the Home Rule movement. This desire, it is needless to say, was hardly spontaneous; it had been instilled and carefully nurtured by Connolly himself.

During the next few months other details were worked out with Henry Kuhn, national secretary of the SLP: the Irish comrades should pay the expenses out, the American party the passage back; the

Irish visitor would not be allowed to request collections and donations for this party but would have the same opportunity to sell subscription blanks to the *Workers' Republic* as representatives of *The People* had. Connolly later alleged that only after these details had been settled was the question discussed as to what Irishman would go, and that it was Kuhn who suggested Connolly. Technically, Connolly may have been correct in this statement—but only technically.

On 5 April, at Falkirk, Connolly met a young Scotsman named J. Carstairs Matheson and discussed with him the possibilities for strengthening De Leon and SLP sentiment within the Social-Democratic Federation. Ever since the publication of De Leon's *What Means This Strike?*, published in February 1898, these SLP sympathizers—called Impossibilists by the opposition—had been impatient with Hyndman's chauvinism, his identification of finance-capital with Jewry, and his tendency to compromise. Connolly and Matheson discussed in particular ways of circumventing Harry Quelch, editor of *Justice*, the publication supported by the Social-Democratic Federation. Together the two men worked out the idea of publishing a new monthly to act as organ of the dissenting Scottish federations of the Social-Democratic Federation. Called *The Socialist*, it would be published in Dublin on the press owned by the Irish Socialist Republican Party. The same editorial matter would be published in both the *Workers' Republic* and *The Socialist* whenever it seemed appropriate. Thus both financial and editorial problems would be simplified, it was thought.

On 21 April, Connolly wrote from Glasgow that no copies of the *Workers' Republic* had been received so far, and enclosed five shillings to pay off part of a personal debt to Lyng. 'I wish I was in a position to make it more and pay it oftener,' he added, in the authentic tones of a man as proud as he was poor.

At the end of the month Connolly addressed the May Day meeting sponsored by the Social-Democratic Federation in Edinburgh. The Independent Labour Party and the Edinburgh Trades Council had been eager to participate but the SDF members had refused their request. The SDF in Scotland, under De Leon influence, disapproved of trade unions that had no political goals, and even denied the possibility of socialists boring from within to transform such organizations. The only proper goal was to establish a new trade-union movement stamped with socialist aims from the start. As a staunch SLP supporter, Connolly agreed, but added a few pragmatic touches. To extreme socialists, he urged the necessity of fighting for social changes (in Aberdeen he urged that trams be permitted to run on Sundays). To moderate socialists, he preached the necessity for class warfare and revolution. To all his listeners, he called for Irish national freedom.

After spending a week in Aberdeen, Connolly visited Falkirk, where a vigorous down-with-monarchy manifesto was issued to mark the coronation of Edward VII. On his way back to Dublin, Connolly spent a week in Salford, where pro-De Leon sentiments were strong among all groups.

At Salford, Connolly devoted one of his talks to the effects on society of a new economic institution, the trust. In a few years it would be publicized in the US by Ida M. Tarbell, Upton Sinclair, Lincoln Steffens and other muckrakers. Connolly drew much of his text from J. A. Hobson's *Evolution of Modern Capitalism*, the first book published in England (in 1896) to analyse 'the imperialist phase of capitalism'. Connolly argued that the existence of trusts 'proved that industry could be carried on without competition at all'. It was futile for the working classes to think of hindering the development of trusts, since their growth was due to laws inherent in society itself. The working classes, he maintained, should instead organize to capture the political power of the state and then transfer to it all productive property.

During the last week of May 1902, Connolly was back in Scotland, writing Lyng on the 26th that he would accept no further speaking engagements in Scotland and England beyond 31 August, since the US trip was confirmed. He gave Lyng directions on how to increase the number of party branches in short order so that he, Connolly, would not be embarrassed by American questioners on the strength of the ISRP. He reported that 'The Scotch paper idea was in great danger of falling through owing to various causes—your state of indecision about the paper coming out being one of them—but recent events have enabled me to revive it and it is now under discussion again.'

On 29 May Connolly wrote to Lyng expressing his disappointment at the Cork members:

. . . their oracular statement of the impossibility of carrying on the propaganda, not only in Cork, but in Ireland as a whole is calculated to make one sick. I think it would be a good idea for you to write to them and tell them what you knew of the conditions under which the propaganda was carried on by us in Dublin before it was possible to 'arrange with Connolly'. If they have any shame at all it ought to make them blush.

Connolly then discussed ways of financing his American trip. He suggested that

> we press the S.L.P. to allow of a collection for our funds to be taken up at the close of each meeting I address, this collection not to be mentioned in placards or other advertisements, or in any other way until it is announced by the Chairman. I do not see how they could object to that. Then you should decidedly print a good few collecting sheets, so that if I meet with any enthusiastic *Irish* sympathisers I can give them one each to collect for our own funds.

In a letter from Kirkcaldy (the birthplace of Adam Smith), dated 2 June, Connolly was worried 'that the delay in getting out the W.R. will result in losing all our orders from English branches, or at least a great part of them'. He hoped that Lyng was getting 'some favourable replies to advts about meetings and branches. You would smile if you could only hear the way I dodge around the question I am always being asked relative to *how many Branches* we have in Ireland. I want a few branches even if they are only on paper.' Had Louie Bennett read this letter, she would have been confirmed in her opinion of his 'crafty' eyes.

A week later, he wrote to William O'Brien from Edinburgh to the following effect:

> Thank you and McLoughlin for your services to me in the matter of clothes. I quite understand your difficulty on the night of my leaving Dublin; you will also understand my embarrassment. The whole circumstances of the suit, tho' I may say, made them the dearest I have ever worn, although I have paid no cash. That a suit begun in November should not be completed until April and that I had to approach the parties concerned so often and vainly until I felt like a beggar—all this combined to so humiliate me and outrage my self-respect that it at one time nearly, indeed actually, made me resolve never to go back to Dublin again. But having once put my hand to the plow I cannot turn back, and as a matter of fact the movement in Ireland, and Ireland itself, is so twined up in my very existence that I could not abandon it even if I would.

Back in Dublin, Connolly found that printing of the first issue of *The Socialist* was 'in a much more backward state' than he had expected. He got the paper out in mid-July but dated it August, thus giving the members in Scotland ample time to dispose of the issue and making it certain that the next issue would be on time. Three more issues were printed in this fashion before Connolly left for his American tour. They were attended with all kinds of difficulties—the late receipt of copy; the belief of George Yates, the most prolific contributor, that he could edit proof without regard to cost; and the difficulties involved in buying paper and paying wages for a congenitally-impoverished organization, the ISRP.

All these matters Connolly discussed in letters written at this time to Matheson, editor of *The Socialist*. These letters began a lengthy correspondence between the two men. Of the 81 letters which have survived, 44 were written by Connolly, most of them during the period 1903 and 1910 when he was living in the US. Some of these letters are 10 and 15 pages long.

In his letters Connolly describes events taking place in the socialist stream. He practically never mentions the major political parties, candidates, or issues. The letters discuss the Socialist Labor Party, why it deserved to fail, why it was booted out of the Industrial Workers of the World, and why an honest socialist could join the Socialist Party and still maintain his integrity. Connolly devoted so many pages to berating the machinations and duplicity of Daniel De Leon that Matheson more than once—and quite correctly—accused him of being obsessed by the subject.

There is very little in these letters about Connolly's personal emotions or reflections, or how he managed to feed his family. From them we could easily get only the picture of a fanatical agitator who allowed his family to live in a hovel and eat the most meagre of fare while he fought the class struggle.

It is true that Connolly had little interest in making a living; his goal was to liberate the working class. He lived by a battle plan. Nevertheless, there are obvious offsetting factors to this picture: for one, the absence of all the letters he wrote to his wife and children, presumably filled with intimate details on family life and budgets, and personal reactions to the places and people he met on his travels; two, the presence of stories about a warm-hearted, tender father given by all of his children, without exception.

Even longer letters were written by Matheson. For his part, he described events taking place in the socialist life of Scotland to a Connolly avid for news about his old causes and comrades. Matheson evidently held Connolly in great respect as a sort of proletarian hero. As early as 1905 he was attempting to find a way by means of which Connolly would return to the British Isles. One gets the impression from these letters that Matheson would have wanted to establish a warmer, more personal relationship with Connolly, who was some eight years his senior, but none developed.

Matheson was a devoted socialist, a man of intelligence and integrity. I am tempted to quote at length from his thirty-seven long letters, if only to remind people that it was people like him, in the millions, who achieved whatever social gains and economic benefits we now enjoy. It would be easy to give a full pen-portrait of the man—by chance he provides it himself in one of his letters—but I shall try to abbreviate the description.

In 1910 an anonymous letter appeared accusing the editor of *Forward*, organ of the Independent Labour Party, of sacrificing his convictions in order to seek a seat in Parliament. The editor, claiming that he knew the identity of the writer, described his characteristics in searing words. Matheson feared that the description could only point to him, and in great agitation sought Connolly's advice on how to defend himself.

He confessed that he had indeed attended Edinburgh University, but did not claim to be a 'superior person', nor a Nietzschean. At the university

I did not hide my opinions. I didn't know very well how to express them, one doesn't often possess this gift at 21, but I did my best . . .

I am not a speaker. I have tried and you have heard me try and know that I have no gift that way. My efforts excite 'the grief of friends and the derision of foes'. You will remember the disjointed fragments of a speech I gave at the social held in Glasgow before your departure. I do not think it is 'hiding one's opinions' to reserve his propagandist efforts for channels which are best suited to his capacities . . . As for 'risk', I have never been in a position in which I was called upon to risk anything, beyond the ordinary risks of a socialist. I know that about 3 years ago I applied for a situation in Kilmarnock Academy, which I was anxious to get. I was placed upon the list. Another man was chosen, fresh from the University, who had never taught in his life before. Some days afterwards a member of the Board remarked casually to one of the staff of the school that I 'seemed to be a great socialist'. I don't say that decided the appointment, but there it is. I have never claimed that I had run great risks, but I have never avoided any risk that I was called upon to undergo and I have never evaded any risks by denying or hiding my socialism.

Connolly sometimes made a parade of his belief that only proletarians could be trusted to advance the cause of the worker. He did not live up to this creed in his actions, as indicated by his willingness to trust not only Matheson but others high on the social scale. It is interesting to know that, at various times, such people existed and were willing to meet him on a plane of equality.

During the months prior to his departure for the US, Connolly continued to shuttle back and forth between Scotland, northern England and Ireland. He wrote from Falkirk on 23 June 1902, suggesting to Tom Lyng a way of expediting the shipment from Belfast to Dublin of a new (second-hand) printing press. On 12 July he wrote irritably from Salford: 'I think it is absolutely disgraceful that you have not sent me an acknowledgement of the receipt of that 12/6d I sent on Monday. Further I think I am *entitled* to hear how the machine is working.' Two days later he wrote Lyng from Accrington that the copies of the *Workers' Republic* that had been ready in Dublin before he left had not yet arrived and that 'this neglect to send them here is inexcusable'. Apparently he had been sent a proof of the first copy of *The Socialist*; he thought it looked 'all right, but it is a pity you put Matheson's signature at the bottom of *every* article; there was no need to sign the shorter ones. I hope the comrades will make every effort to get out this first edition.' He mentioned that he had received from the US a circular publicizing his tour of that country, and said: 'The statement that they have hired Cooper Union, which as you know is the biggest hall in New York, causes a cold chill of nervousness to creep down my spinal column.'

On 21 July, he wrote from Nelson (in Lancashire) telling Lyng to use the front-page article of *The Socialist* in the next issue of the *Workers' Republic*, and enclosed copy for both magazines. In an undated letter from the same place he enclosed a drawing of a *Workers' Republic* subscription card to be pre-printed and sold at American meetings. The last sentence of this letter, cryptic but significant in view of later events, read: 'I do hope you are doing something to master that disgraceful conduct in the Club-room on Sundays.'

After visiting Ashton-under-Lyne, Connolly wrote from Bolton on 26 July that he was worried about the lack of progress being made in raising funds for his trip; '... when you take into account the circumstances that I will require something to keep me alive while I am in Dublin preparatory to going to the States, and that my wife will also require something while I am on my voyage the problem assumes big dimensions.' He suggested that the ISRP try to obtain a letter from the Dublin Trades Council endorsing his trip as helpful in obtaining information concerning US conditions of labour, the status of trade unionism, and the like. Connolly thought the endorsement would be useful to him in America and might open the way for a few lectures to trade union groups when he returned.

From Hyde, in southern England, Connolly wrote on 8 August that he had seen his portrait in the Socialist Labor Party organ, the *Weekly People*, as part of the build-up for his trip; after seeing such an awful travesty of his features, he was convinced that the American trip was destined for failure. Continuing in this humorous vein, he added: 'The fiend who wrote that preposterous biography and created a new birthplace and a new year of birth for me, will, I hope, suffer in this life all the tortures of the damned ... The yahoo!' It was this biography that established the legend that Connolly had been born in 1870 in County Monaghan, Ireland, instead of Edinburgh in 1868. The author was Murtagh Lyng, writing under a pseudonym.

Connolly spent the entire following week in Salford, the bustling textile and commercial city located across the Irwell River from Manchester. Salford's population was then about 100,000. It was among the Irish workers of this city that Connolly felt most comfortable. During the week he lectured on such topics as trade unionism, the revolutionary mission of the working class, and the relationship between labour and republicanism.

The Salford comrades gave Connolly a great send-off on 16 August, at the clubrooms of the Social-Democratic Federation. In response to the toast to his health, Connolly told his listeners not to attach such great hope and importance to the awakening of the middle class. He thought that the working people, with all their limitations and faults, were showing a disposition to accomplish their own emancipation and would eventually do so. He was always sorry to see working men lacking in faith in their own class for, generally speaking, they were better able to grasp broad issues than men of the middle and upper classes. The average middle-class man, though superficially well educated, was quite unable to grasp any problem outside his own narrow environment. It was the working class that had in the main built up and still sustained the socialist organizations. There was no justification for relying on the middle class as the ultimate instrument for emancipating people from present conditions.

Connolly returned to Dublin for a few days and, on 30 August, sailed from Londonderry to the land of Daniel De Leon.

VII

Of all groups seeking to create a revolution in the US in 1902, the Socialist Labor Party seemed to be the most likely to succeed. It had a relatively large membership, and regularly ran candidates for local and national offices; it had a history dating back to 1874; it had in Daniel De Leon a leader of unsurpassed brilliance; it had an affiliated trade union, established on industrial, not craft, lines, known as the Socialist Trade and Labor Alliance; it produced propaganda by the ton (a daily newspaper, weekly, and monthly in English, and weeklies in German, Swedish, Yiddish, run off on high-speed presses); above all, it seemed to have a clear understanding of the strategy required to effect a revolution, the strategy laid down by Karl Marx.

True, there was an upstart rival—the Socialist Party just formed by a merger of the Social Democratic Party of Eugene Debs and Victor Berger with the group of dissidents from the Socialist Labor Party led by Morris Hillquit. In a few years another new group would drain off still more strength from the De Leon organization—the Industrial Workers of the World.

But at the moment Connolly had reason to be dazzled by the strength and size of the Socialist Labor Party. He was soon to learn that most of that strength was concentrated in New York; that most members were foreign-speaking immigrants; and that the branches in the hinterlands were small, beleaguered, and impoverished. But to Connolly it seemed an impressive organization, particularly when compared with his own organization—that handful of youthful dissidents who had the temerity to call themselves the Irish Socialist Republican Party.

The reception the SLP had prepared to kick off Connolly's tour was certainly one to impress a man who had recently been an Edinburgh rubbish collector, a failed cobbler, and an incompetent ditch digger— a man, furthermore, held in contempt by almost the entire population of Dublin. For weeks in advance the SLP papers had been republishing material from the *Workers' Republic*, even insignificant matter like 'Home Thrusts', which were signed by 'Spailpin', and resembled the miscellanies of 'R. Ascal'. Of the inaugural meeting held at Cooper Union, in New York City, the *Weekly People* reported: 'The opening of the doors ... was like the breaking of a dam and the release of a torrent. At 7.30 o'clock all the approaches to the hall were jammed with the waiting crowd.'

A resolution of welcome and an introductory speech by Daniel De Leon preceded Connolly's talk. The resolution said that Connolly was visiting the US to enlist the interest of Irish Americans in the socialist movement and to destroy the influence upon them of the Home Rulers and bourgeoisie, 'to the economic detriment of the Irish working men in this country, therefore be it resolved: That we ... cordially welcome him to "our" shores and give his mission our emphatic endorsement.'

After beginning his talk by saying, correctly enough, that he had never talked before such a large audience, Connolly delivered an elementary exposition of the class struggle, especially as it concerned Ireland. He represented, he said, only the Irish working people; he could not represent the entire Irish population because of the irreconcilable conflict of interests between this group and the capitalist group. The rest of his talk was similar hard-core socialist doctrine—tenets that gave little room for reform or for non-political trade unionism.

If we can believe the account given in the SLP paper, Connolly's address was followed by 'tumultuous applause'. The audience cheered at the top of their voices, rising in their seats and throwing their hats in the air. The demonstration lasted several minutes. Pressmen crowded round Connolly. What historic Irish family did he belong to? What kings was he descended from? 'I have no ancestors,' he told them. His people were poor like himself.

There was good reason for the Socialist Labor Party to embrace Connolly. The Party's labour arm, the Socialist Trade and Labor Alliance, was losing out to the American Federation of Labor, and it was hoped that Connolly could swing some of the Irish working men back. De Leon also hoped that Connolly, upon his return, would act as the disseminator in Europe of SLP ideas and propaganda.

This man, Daniel De Leon, was an authentic genius, with talents not much inferior to those of Lenin. His roots were Latin American, and probably Jewish (Sephardic). He was born 14 December 1852, and was thus sixteen years older than Connolly. His birthplace was the

Dutch colony of Curaçao, the island forty miles off the coast of Venezuela. After the death of his father, a surgeon in the Dutch Army, De Leon was sent away at the age of fourteen for schooling, first in Germany and then in the Netherlands. At the age of twenty, De Leon came to New York where he taught Latin, Greek and mathematics at a school in Westchester County. He entered Columbia Law School in 1876 and graduated two years later with honours in constitutional and international law. For a time he probably practised law in Texas (a period left in intentional obscurity by De Leon because the radical labour movement at the time was hostile to lawyers), but in 1883 he became a lecturer in international law at Columbia. A New York street-car strike in 1886 evoked sympathies which rapidly led him, by way of Henry George and Edward Bellamy, to the Socialist Labor Party. As a result he was eased out of his lectureship at Columbia.

The party De Leon joined in October 1890 was a loose and quarrelsome association of socialist propaganda groups with a membership of fewer than 1,500, most of them Germans. Only two members of the National Executive Committee spoke English. The party had been unable to ride the successive waves of radicalism which shaped themselves into the Knights of Labor and the Henry George, Bellamy, and Populist movements of the eighties and nineties.

De Leon rose quickly to leadership in the SLP. In 1892 he became the editor of its newly founded English language organ, the *People*, and held this post until his death in 1914. He was repeatedly an SLP candidate for state offices in New York, made national lecture tours for the party, initiated in 1896 the Socialist Trade and Labor Alliance as a rival to the Knights of Labor and the American Federation of Labor, and in 1905 helped to found the Industrial Workers of the World. At the same time he translated many socialist classics by Marx, Engels, Kautsky and Bebel, a drama by Ferdinand Lassalle, and nineteen of Eugene Sue's proletarian historical novels.

For twenty-four years De Leon worked to make the Socialist Labor Party the spokesman for the American working class. To this effort he brought enormous resources of scholarship and admirable native endowments of intellect and nerve. He gave himself to the cause with a passion which surpassed even that of Eugene Debs.

He lived an abstemious life, finding pleasure in sailing a small boat on Long Island Sound, basking on a Connecticut beach, and tending a vegetable garden. He was married twice; first to a Venezuelan woman whose son Solon, born 1883, was still alive in 1967; and second, to a woman from Kansas, four of whose children reached maturity.

Brilliant in thought, and admirable in so many ways, De Leon had one fatal flaw: he was his own greatest admirer. He could not conceive that anyone could understand and solve a political, economic, or organizational problem as well as he could. His egotism drove him into disputes with hundreds of able persons who became dissident and disillusioned; Connolly was only one of them.

But at the moment all was harmony. The Cooper Union meeting seemed likely to serve well its purposes of introducing Connolly to US workers and to inaugurate the SLP election campaigns of 1902. Connolly's part in the latter was to tour the country and convince the Irish that voting for socialism was not contrary to their national or religious heritage—a large task. Most of the Irish he never managed to reach; they were too busy fitting into the American world of work and politics. Those who still maintained a casual interest in Irish freedom felt that Home Rule was good enough. Connolly spent countless and fruitless hours trying to convince this latter group that a clean break with both England and capitalism was the only proper route for Ireland.

It was a rigorous tour, with few meetings attaining the height of enthusiasm apparent at Cooper Union. Some of the meetings were held in the open air. But Connolly talked to good audiences at Yonkers, Tarrytown, Peekskill, Paterson, and the audiences increased as he neared Boston. Word of his heresies had apparently reached that city, and when he spoke in Faneuil Hall a number of Irish moderates tried to stampede the meeting by walking out in the middle of his speech. Connolly cried after them, 'The truth has hurt them, and like all such they run away from it.' He obtained more subscriptions for the *Workers' Republic* from that than from any other meeting, his second best being at Duluth, Minnesota. At Lawrence, Massachusetts, a similar Home Rule protest was staged.

After a month in the east, Connolly slowly drifted west. On his way he covered various towns in New York State, spending several days in the vicinity of Troy, where he had cousins (every Irishman has cousins in the United States), and reached Buffalo by 16 October. Almost every night he slept in a new town; no evening was without its lecture. From St Paul and Minneapolis he went to Salt Lake City. A week later he was in California where he spent nearly two weeks. On 18 November he spoke at Pioneer Hall in San Francisco. At San Jose, he made a remark which sheds a great deal of illumination on the reasons why he never made a frontal attack on the Catholic Church, as so many of his comrades were wont to do. In answer to a question, he made clear his belief that, if socialism ever became victorious, the Church would make its peace with that doctrine in the same way that it had learned to live with so many other doctrines that had once been repugnant to it. His exact words were: 'This institution will exercise the precaution of not placing all its eggs in one basket, for fear they may be broken.'

From Los Angeles, Connolly went to Colorado where the meetings were quite unsuccessful, owing to a lack of preliminary work. But he managed to fill the Court House at Grand Junction, despite competition from 'Captain Jinks of the Horse Marines' at the opera house. He 'made many witty remarks in his economic speech', which was devoted to proving that capitalism was independent of religion by comparing economic development under governments which were Catholic, Protestant, and 'Freethinker' (namely, France). After a short visit to Canada, Connolly gave several speeches in Detroit. He spent Christmas week in Troy. His farewell meeting was held at the Manhattan Lyceum Annex in New York, where he was given another ovation and 'tremendous cheers, ending with a rousing "tiger" '.

It had been a long and arduous trip, with many one-night stands, endless train rides, and uncomfortable, makeshift lodgings in homes often overcrowded and almost always poorly prepared for visitors, however well-intentioned the hosts. But he was irked more by the shiftlessness of his comrades back in Ireland. From St Paul, Minnesota, he wrote to Daniel O'Brien on 3 November:

I have just received a letter from Tom Lyng in which, among other things, he makes the remark that you in Dublin 'expect to get the W. R. out in a few days'. This letter is dated 16th October, and I want to know the meaning of that delay. Here am I, knocking life out of myself travelling from 200 to 600 miles every day at least, and talking every night, canvassing hard for subscriptions and in order to get them telling everybody that the paper will appear more regularly in the future than in the past, and you people at home have not the common manliness to try and stand by my word by getting out the paper as promised. You may think it all a joke, but I think that you all ought to be damned well ashamed of yourselves. Is it so hard a job for you to get together enough matter to fill a paper once a month—such a terrible strain on your nerves! I am ashamed, heartily ashamed of the whole gang of you. If some of you do not think the cause of the Socialist Republic worth working for, why in Heaven's name do you not get out of the Party? We would be better starting again with half a dozen men as before than be cumbered by the presence of a crowd who are only Socialists because it gives them the reputation for originality. I was always opposed to the idea of expelling men unless for breach of principle, but I am inclined now to believe that such leniency was criminal and that it would do us good were we to expel some more men for making promises to the Party and not keeping them in time to be of service.

Two other preoccupations recur in many missives from the US: his fear that the Irish comrades were not preparing vigorously enough for the elections scheduled for 15 January 1903; and worries about the drinking club. On 23 September: 'I hope you have settled that club nuisance. Now that you have the Coercion Act, it behoves you to exercise every care possible to keep clear of all disreputable connections. I am fretting over that thing, in case you get any trouble with it.' On 3 October: 'I am getting anxious as I have not heard from you relative to that club—it is the bane of my life now—that fear that you will get into trouble over it.' On 16 October: 'I am glad to hear that the club is more decent, but I think we would be well rid of it.' Tom Lyng replied finally: 'The Club is now restricted to ISRP members and friends properly introduced by them.' Lyng added that the new arrangement meant a decrease in revenue. On 3 November: 'Glad to hear the club is restricted to members.'

For the most part, Connolly did not like America. He disliked its climate, its customs, and its people. Of its weather, he wrote: 'It is fearfully hot here for me, but the Americans say it is exceptionally cool. It is obvious to me that hell will be a greater punishment to us than to the Americans.'

He sent back to Ireland a copy of an injunction issued by a court against a weavers' strike, with the comment: 'The injunction should be a fine object lesson to Irish workers of the liberty enjoyed under the stars and stripes by the working man fighting for better conditions.' He questioned the very idea that the Irish working man was improving his lot by emigrating to the US. In an article published towards the end of his tour in *Detroit Today*, he wrote:

The increasing emigration from Ireland inspired my journey. The population of Ireland is only 4,000,000 and, as there is an annual emigration of 40,000, it is becoming quite a serious question as to how long the Irish nation will exist at this rate of deportation. Naturally we desire to find out whether those people who emigrate are really permanently benefited by the change; or rather whether they could not achieve as great a change for the better in their economic conditions by making a more determined stand at home. We believe—that is, the Irish Socialist Republican Party—that the conditions in America are not so rosy as they are painted by Irish middle-class politicians, and that if Irishmen were to remain at home and fight for socialism there, they would in the near future attain to better conditions of life than is possible by merely throwing themselves on the labour market of the United States.

Undoubtedly the standard of comfort here is much higher than at home, and to that extent the fortunate worker who gets employment is for a time improving himself. But the intensification of labour is greater here than at home, machinery is developing more rapidly, and in my opinion the worker is an old man in this country when he is still regarded as being in the prime of life at home. In other words, the emigrant sacrifices his future for his present for the sake of a few extra dollars.

In his final New York address, Connolly confessed his surprise and shock at 'the absolute disregard for law' that prevailed in the US. Ignoring a basic tenet of socialism, that the law was nothing more than a way of legalizing expropriation and oppression, Connolly said: 'Breaking law is regarded as a common occurrence, and instead of meeting with disapproval it is considered smart . . . This is an individualistic country and in no country is individualism so systematically pursued, both as a theory and as a policy.'

Connolly attributed this individualism to immigrants who came to seek their fortune regardless of the interests of the community, and to the lack of a traditional ruling class that to some extent acted as a restraint upon the capitalists. He found the same spirit of individualistic lawlessness prevalent in the trade unions. They were not curbed by old traditions, and looked on betrayal by their leaders as a piece of smartness rather than a matter calling for disapproval. Indeed, he believed that on the whole the US was behind England in its conception of the class struggle.

Nor did he exempt the Socialist Labor Party from his strictures. In the *People* he wrote, humorously only in part:

Allow me to say that in one respect the S.L.P. is thoroughly American. It has its full share of the American national disease, swelled head. When I am asked what I think of America I say, 'I don't think much of it,' and watch the wonderment on the face. I am not grumbling about this egotistical feeling. It is of course highly natural towards any other nationality except the Irish; to us it is only ridiculous. In course of time we will no doubt succeed in making you realise the fact.

In airing these opinions, Connolly probably did not realize how typical they were of those of other European visitors. Neither did he realize that he was stepping on Daniel De Leon's toes. For one of De Leon's profoundest convictions (he inserted it as a comment in Connolly's valedictory speech when it was printed in the *People*) was that 'The United States is the country on which the emancipation of the workers of Europe depends'. De Leon may have been similarly unappreciative of an off-hand comment that Connolly made in his Salt Lake City talk (also printed in the *People*): 'De Leon struck me as a somewhat chirpy old gentleman with an inordinately developed bump of family affection.' Connolly meant, of course, to be humorous but he was hitting on a delicate point. De Leon, only fifty at the time, affected the manner of a venerable sage, and could hardly have been pleased at this description.

Two minor disputes he had with SLP sections did not increase his affection for America. When the Troy, NY, members endeavoured to bludgeon him into giving three speeches in a row, although it had been warned that he would not do it, he 'went on strike at Troy, and did not speak for three days. This was the first rest I had had for 31 days, and I was determined to have it.' When he did consent to speak, a member named Passano made an offensive remark, which Connolly refused to countenance. He complained to the National Executive Committee, which obtained apologies from both the Troy Section and Passano.

The second rhubarb concerned an item in the *Workers' Republic*, which some Minneapolis members claimed was an endorsement of the Social Democrats. When they asked Connolly to repudiate the item, he hotly replied that 'the *Workers' Republic* was published for Ireland and not for America, and if the comrades in Minneapolis thought we were going to publish the paper to suit American politics they were vastly mistaken'. The Minneapolis comrades then refused to push the magazine subscriptions, and as a result 'out of one of the finest meetings

I have addressed I got only three subscriptions'. The letter describing this altercation was sent from St Paul, Minnesota, on 3 November. It contained a postscript: 'Last night I received a letter from Troy, New York, apologising for their conduct, and this morning I received a deputation from Minneapolis apologising for theirs. So all is friendship again.'

There were, of course, large gains from his trip. He had dispatched to Ireland more than sufficient funds (he was sure) to keep the *Workers' Republic* afloat for many months to come. He had been warmed by his reception as spokesman for the working class of his country; his vision had been enlarged; his self-confidence had been increased. But, for the reasons indicated, he was glad the trip was finished, and neither desired nor expected to return. Connolly was thirty-four, but still an innocent with regard to the traps that life sets for man. In nine months, he was again on a boat headed for the US.

VIII

THE CIRCUMSTANCES which led to Connolly's unexpected return form a dolorous account. First came his defeat in another municipal campaign. He ran again from the Wood Quay Ward, and again with the support of only a single union, the United Labourers. He had only two brief weeks in which to campaign. His election manifesto made no mention of freedom or Home Rule for Ireland, or of any immediate reforms. It called solely for 'a system of society in which the land and all houses, railways, factories, canals, workshops, and everything necessary for work shall be owned and operated as common property'. The only method suggested for achieving this goal was for the working class to establish a political power of its own.

An interesting part of his election address was his description of how he was defeated the previous time, how

> the paid canvassers of the capitalist candidate . . . gave a different account of Mr. Connolly to every section of the electors. How they said to the Catholics that he was an Orangeman, to the Protestants that he was a Fenian, to the Jews that he was an anti-semite, to others that he was a Jew, to the labourers that he was a journalist on the make, and to the tradesmen and professional classes that he was an ignorant labourer; that he was born in Belfast, Derry, England, Scotland and Italy, according to the person the canvasser was talking to.

Connolly received 243 votes, about half his previous vote. This result did nothing to increase the confidence of the ISRP members in their 'organizer'. Few of them considered that the vote might have been greater had they campaigned harder. Many of the members were unemployed and used the party headquarters as a sort of club house, while Connolly toiled over the pages of *Labour in Irish History* in a corner.

But the internal discord had other roots. As mentioned earlier, a licensed bar was in operation in the headquarters, and, when Connolly left for America, a committee was elected to manage the bar and the headquarters, look after the printing machinery, etc. On his return, Connolly found the funds he had collected so painfully in dozens of American cities to pay for subscriptions to the *Workers' Republic*—the funds he had carefully remitted with almost every letter sent home— had been spent in making good losses incurred by bad management of the bar. When Connolly moved to depose the committee because it had not kept proper accounts, ill-feeling arose. It increased when membership figures and the accounts failed to tally. The explosion took place at a meeting held on 18 February when Connolly proposed payment of a bill in order to avoid foreclosure of the printing press. The motion was rejected. Stunned, Connolly protested that the printing machine had to be kept running, and that the Party was under a contractual obligation to its new American subscribers to keep publishing. He received little support, whereupon he tendered his resignation.

He told his wife when he returned home, 'I resigned as a protest in hopes of proving they were pursuing a suicidal policy.'

'They wouldn't accept?' Lillie asked incredulously.

'Wouldn't they? They did.'

During the next few weeks the conflict was compounded by the decision of *The Socialist* no longer to use the ISRP press, by an argument concerning payment of the rent for the clubrooms, by resignations and threats of resignation by various members. Not one to do things by halves, Connolly himself applied for membership in a branch of the Social-Democratic Federation but, before the branch could take action, he swallowed his pride and rejoined the ISRP. It was all in vain, however. Both he and the other members knew that the situation had deteriorated beyond repair.

A partial account of these events is revealed in letters written by Connolly at the time. On 9 March 1903, he wrote to Matheson:

The curious thing is that the whole fight is being fought out 'round the corner', so to speak, from the real issue. The only thing that is discussed is the financial situation, and the other point is only noticeable by the fact that all the moderates are aligned against us and all those who have no use for moderation are for us. Of course, my position on the finance is sound in itself, and I am in dread that as a consequence of their carelessness with the money they will not be able to fill out the American subscriptions, which you will realise would leave me in a most undesirable light in the eyes of our American comrades, if I continued in the party and made no public and vehement protest. What aggravated the situation was your action in withdrawing *without warning* the printing of the 'Socialist'. Counting on your 4 pounds per month they had spent money which they otherwise might have had foresight enough to husband. Since I withdrew they have had a great searching of hearts and much mutual recrimination; many members who were not present at the meetings when the fights were on have turned up since and threatened their resignations also, and the general opinion seems to be that the element who have charge can not run it; that they might do well enough for an ordinary branch of a 'big' organisation, but can not handle the peculiar position *we* have to work in.

However that may be I am resolved to let them try. They need not complain of my desertion, they have now, thanks to my efforts principally, as they themselves admit, got machine, presses, type, a whole printing establishment in fact, and a good reputation politically. Socialism in Dublin stands now in a position such as seven years ago its most ardent advocates did not hope to see it in, and it ought to be able to walk alone. I think that if my side comes uppermost the Kangaroo element will resign, and if they do I may rejoin but it will only be at most a minimal connection in order to keep them together until the angry passions are quiet. I leave Dublin in any case at the first opportunity. Of course if those present in possession hold their own I will *have to git*, as it would only be a short time until they kangarooed openly.

Connolly concluded by telling Matheson that he had requested the Scottish District Council of the Social-Democratic Federation to sponsor him in a series of lectures as it had done the previous year, but had received no reply. Even if he received the appointment, he would need

to fill up the interval between now and the opening of the SDC campaign; if I could do that . . . I would have time to arrange about a domicile for my family. As to work I would 'prefer', well, Chancellor of the Exchequer would do. But I have been a proofreader, a tilelayer (ten years ago); a while you wait shoemaker, a mason's labourer and a carter. It is so long since I did hard manual labour that I feel queer at the thought of it. So you can best assist me if you can devise a plan whereby I can keep the wolf from the door, and yet be doing something, until that SDC business comes off.

On 21 March Connolly wrote to William O'Brien, the twenty-three-year-old tailor who was financial secretary of the ISRP, as follows:

I desire to inform you that in reference to the unfortunate dispute arising out of your unfortunate motion about the rent, and my ill-judged action upon it, that I feel your loss to the movement so keenly that after due deliberation upon it I have resolved to make you an offer.

It appears that in resigning you and your friends (of course I except Stewart) were actuated by the belief that I am an obstacle to the progress of the party, that I am a danger to Socialism in Dublin. Now I do not know upon what facts such reasoning is based, but that is beside the point. I believe that you, being a much younger man, and having fewer ties to embarrass you than I have, are a help and a hope of the Socialist movement here, and also that you could be depended upon to run the movement upon the same lines as in the past—the only lines that can be permanently successful. Therefore, I make you this offer: I am willing if you will agree, to retire from all participation in the party, to resign my membership and go out in order that you may come in. As I have proven that the men who were slandering me could not even attempt to defend their charges before my face, I can now leave the party without fear that men are left in it who would defame me.

To sum up if you consider my presence in the party an insuperable obstacle to your resuming your membership, say so, and I am willing to go out. It shall never be said of me that I kept back the movement anywhere.

Three days later he wrote to Matheson: 'At present we have conquered the hidden Kangy tendency; it was an awful débâcle. Stewart and four members resigned. Stewart's expulsion was moved but he escaped by one vote. But their looseness with the cash has almost killed us.' As for Matheson's mention of a possible job opportunity in Falkirk, Connolly said his decision would have to wait until he could look around while lecturing in Scotland, and 'see how the land lies. The trifling circumstance of having a family to lug around makes it undesirable for me to settle precipitately upon any plan or place. Not that I can wait with equanimity for I have not been so poverty stricken for six years. I have only drawn 20/- wages since I returned from America.'

On 8 April 1903, Connolly wrote to Matheson:

I am wearying for my Scotch tour to commence. It is the center-piece of my plans for the whole year as I intend (D. V.) to go to America in the Autumn and bring my family out after me. This is the outcome of our little Kang episode. We squelched the reptiles, but they dissimulated so well that, as you saw, my kindly intention to drag their scalps around as a trophy in the public gaze was frustrated and I have no doubt they will be allowed to crawl back. They may not Kang again, but in any case I consider that the party here has no longer that exclusive demand on my life which led me in the past to sacrifice my children's welfare for years in order to build it up. I only wish I had known it in America before I came home, as when there I received tempting offers to stay, and it is not likely that having rejected them once I will receive them again.

Connolly had been back in Ireland only three months when he made this fateful decision.

His feelings about the break-up of the Party were not always so philosophical. In August he wrote to O'Brien:

As you say the conditions under which I existed in Ireland were very hard to my family and myself, but hard as they were they were not hard enough to drive me from the country. No, the glory and pride of that feat was reserved for my quondam comrades, whose willingness to believe ill of me, and to wreck my work, seems to have grown in proportion to the extent I was successful in serving them.

When members used me as an intermediary with comrades beyond the sea, and then dishonoured their obligations to those comrades, when my vehement protest against such action was represented by one member as the result of anger at not getting a good job, when another member asked the business meeting to refuse me membership because I wanted to live upon the Party and had kept it back in the past by doing so, when a traitor, whose treason is only limited by his opportunities, twisted my every word out of all meaning it could bear and had his interpretation accepted for the sake of doing me an injury, and when a section of the party withdrew in alliance with a man who had openly declared he would 'wreck the party in six months', Ireland was scarcely habitable for me.

These things have changed the whole course of my life, but my conscience is clear, as my judgment was correct; let those who are responsible for those acts be assured that no amount of belated praise can gild the pill, or sweeten the bitterness of my exile.

My career has been unique in many things. In this last it is so also. Men have been driven out of Ireland by the British Government, and by the landlords, but I am the first driven forth by the 'Socialists'?

The ISRP by now was so weak that it could hold no more meetings, outdoors or indoors. Much of the blame for its collapse must certainly be attributed to Connolly's own personality. He was unable to understand the feelings of those who did not share his own convictions. He was even more impatient with those who shared his feelings but did not act twenty-four hours a day upon them. He could not understand people who failed to realize that continued and regular issuance of the *Workers' Republic* was vitally necessary to speed the day of liberation; and that subscriptions to this magazine were a holy contract, to be lived up to against all obstacles. More than that, Connolly could not tolerate the Irish (perhaps human) fondness for blurring issues, for postponing unpleasant decisions, for engaging in humorous chit-chat and a drink when serious political problems had to be settled.

It was typical of Connolly that almost all his letters—even those to his oldest and most intimate friends—should start with the impersonal salutation, 'Dear Comrade'. Was this the result of his childhood in Presbyterian Scotland, of his years under British Army discipline, or was it inherent? Whatever the cause, it played an important part in the disruption and collapse of the Party.

At long last the invitation arrived from the Scottish District Council of the Social-Democratic Federation to give lectures in Edinburgh, Glasgow and other Scottish cities. Though the contract was not to begin until 1 May, Connolly left Ireland a month early, crossed to Edinburgh and there edited two issues of the *Workers' Republic*.

According to his colleagues, he also attended some classes in linotype operation given at a local technical college.

Connolly had not been working long for the Scottish District Council before it was rent by a dispute between supporters of H. M. Hyndman, founder of the parent Social-Democratic Federation, and the supporters of Daniel De Leon. The Federation was, in any case, an odd socialist organization: condemned by both Marx and Engels, deserted by William Morris and many other dissidents, afflicted by gigantic errors of opportunism and dogmatism, it was still the first modern organization of its type in Great Britain, and lasted long enough to train several generations of labour and socialist leaders.

At its Easter meeting, the Social-Democratic Federation more or less expelled the Glasgow branch, which promptly reconstituted itself as the Glasgow Socialist Society, and took over Connolly's contract of £1. 10s. a week—with payments frequently late.

Both Connolly and Matheson welcomed the new development, and both sought to build a new organization throughout Scotland that would resemble the Socialist Labor Party, even to the name. To that end Connolly devoted his best efforts, travelling through Scotland all through April and May 1903, and describing in detail the political blunders of Hyndman, whose character was to 'preach revolution and practise compromise, and to do neither thoroughly'.

From time to time, he drew on his American experiences, contrasting the clarity of the Socialist Labor Party with the amorphousness of the nascent American Socialist Party. He charged that the American Socialist Party had different policies in different states. In the east, where capitalism was highly developed, it paid lip service to the class struggle. In the midwest, where the petty middle class was a force, it stood for municipalization for the benefit of the taxpayer. In the far-west it argued that the basis of revolution was the farming class. Its periodicals reflected this inconsistency and sacrifice of principle. They represented the sentiment of the areas where they were published.

Connolly urged the new party in Scotland to adopt the name of the Socialist Labour Party since it would be called that anyway. The inaugural conference opened in Edinburgh, and was attended by delegates from seven Scottish cities. Formation of a branch in London was announced. Connolly took the chair, and congratulated the delegates on leaving the moribund Socialist-Democratic Federation. A manifesto was adopted. Connolly was appointed national organizer for the next three months.

The executive committee of the new party met on 13 June, when Connolly announced that the *Workers' Republic* had 'temporarily suspended' publication. He asked that copies of *The Socialist* be sent instead to its American subscribers, by arrangement with the ISRP, which was still breathing fitfully. The new Scottish organization felt strong enough financially to accede to this request, and arrangements were made to supply the Scots paper with Irish material.

Connolly threw himself into his work as national organizer with great energy, paying visits to Edinburgh, Kirkcaldy and Dundee, but concentrating on Glasgow. Here lectures by George Yates on Marx's *Capital* had drawn together a band of enthusiastic young socialists full of zest for knowledge but hazy on how to translate it into practice.

Against great odds Connolly performed wittily and energetically. In Glasgow he conducted a class for prospective Marxist tutors. When they entered the room, they found a large table with a chair upon it. Connolly sat in the audience with a bundle of current newspapers on his lap. The students were to apply their Marxist knowledge to some of the headlines. To overcome stage fright, they had to mount the table and chair before making their speeches. Connolly would pose as an opponent of socialism, throwing up awkward questions and emphasizing all the time that the test of an able lecturer was the ability to explain a subject in elementary terms. Those who laughed at the mistakes of others had to mount the rostrum themselves.

He found time to write the words for many proletarian songs. His 'Rebel Song', which appeared in the May 1903 number of *The Socialist*, was set to music by Gerald Crawford, one of his followers, but most of the other songs he wrote in 1903 and 1904—his prolific years—were set to such tunes as 'Come, send round the wine', 'The Holy City', 'Believe me if all those endearing young charms', 'Love's young dream', 'Pearla an Brollaig Bain', 'Wreathe the bowl', 'Seaghan O Duibir an Gleanna', 'One bumper at parting', and a Boer War song called 'Volkslied'. Titles of the songs were 'When Labour Calls', 'The Message', 'Shake Out Your Banners', 'The Flag', 'Freedom's Sun', 'Freedom's Pioneers', 'Hymn of Freedom', and 'A Love Song'—the object of the love being freedom.

One would guess from the number of times that 'The Watchword' was reprinted that it was the most popular of Connolly's songs. It appeared in *Songs of Freedom*, published in the US in 1907; in *The Irish Worker* of December 1913; in *The Legacy* and *Songs of Freedom*, published by the Socialist Party of Ireland in 1918, in *Connolly Souvenir*,

1919, and published separately, with music, by Whelan & Son, 17 Upper Ormond Quay, Dublin.

The chorus of this poem runs as follows:

> Then send it aloft on the breeze, boys!
> That watchword the grandest we've known.
> That labour must rise from its knees, boys!
> And claim the broad earth as its own.

This is bad enough, but some of the other poems are much worse. Connolly had no flair for expressing abstract ideas in concrete forms—which, if we are to believe W. H. Auden, is the whole task of the poet; he was addicted to the Victorian device of turning prose into poetry by reversing the usual word order; his idea of poetry was nothing more than rhymed exhortation to combat. He obviously thought that putting together a poem of twenty lines was no difficult matter for anyone capable of envisaging the overthrow of an entire empire and economic system. Some years later, he wrote a few plays, which proved that his ignorance of the playwright's craft was as complete as that of the poet's.

It must be said, however, that he could appreciate better verse than his own. He admired in particular the poems of Freiligrath, and translated Max Kegel's 'Sozialistenmarsch' from German into English verse. How he picked up his knowledge of German nobody knows.

In his street meetings, which often amounted to a dozen a week, he was convincing and pungent. His repartee became a byword, and many of his answers were long preserved. But how far they can be guaranteed original and how far they belong to the street speaker's venerable stock-in-trade it is difficult to determine. No doubt Connolly added his contribution to this traditional art.

In private conversation his sharp but playful wit delighted the rebels. Because De Leon wore a fresh white handkerchief each day instead of a tie, Connolly said, 'He suffers from an affectation of the throat.'

His humour is evident in his letters also, but there it appears rather lumbering and cumbrous. For instance, he started a letter to Matheson by saying: 'I am at a loss to know why you should heap such insults upon me. I would have you know, sir, that the miscreant who writes *verses* in the *United Irishman* and the genius who writes *poetry* under the nom-de-plume of "Spailpin" are not one and the same person, witness the signing of the name, its spelling and the reference to London. To say nothing of the internal evidence.'

It has been said that the young, humorous Connolly who left Dublin in 1903 never returned. It is true that his letters after that date bear few such touches. But he was thirty-five years old when he departed, and it is unlikely that his US experiences, unfortunate though they were, could have greatly altered his temperament at that late stage.

The new Scots organization—the Socialist Labour Party of Great Britain—never caught fire although *The Socialist* continued to appear regularly as its official organ for another half-dozen years. For most of those years it was edited by Matheson in Glasgow and published in Edinburgh.

In July 1903 Connolly announced formally that he intended to leave for the United States. He was in a mood of depression—not a rare circumstance with him—following a series of financially disastrous meetings staged by the Dundee branch. Connolly had to make good the losses personally.

He was emboldened to leave Ireland by a letter from his 'loving cousin' in Troy, Margaret Humes. She wrote to him on 29 June 1903:

I am glad you were candid and so long as you are determined to come here and bring your family and make this your home I will do all in my power to assist you and as the time is short and it would be a bad time for to wait untill October the sooner you get here the better I will send you a draft for your fare so you will have it by the 1st of August so you can make your arrangements and I am sorry you said anything to Mona about coming with you for I think we canot manage that at present and she will be disapointed, but with the help of God it may not be so long untill the family can come altogether.

Mrs Humes was a warm-hearted woman. She was grateful that Connolly had sent her information about her parents who were living in Scotland, but 'I would hate for you to settle in Scotland Ireland before that I wouldn't live there if they give me Holyrood Pallace'.

At the end of August he crossed once more to Dublin, and addressed two final open-air meetings at Foster Place. Relations between Connolly and his former comrades were still cool. Most of the members had vanished or entered other organizations. The remaining fragment proclaimed itself the Irish section of the Socialist Labor Party, but the American movement could no more provide a philosophy for these Irish socialists than the Social-Democratic Federation or the Independent Labour Party.

A few days before Connolly left for the US he received a touching letter from Matheson:

Just a short note to bid you goodbye and good luck. I am intensely sorry that you are going to leave us—but there's no use talking about it. I had looked forward to many years work along side of you for the cause and many years of your comradeship and friendship but destiny and capitalism have been against it. As I said before I feel pretty damned blue about it now that the time has come, but there's no use wasting words . . . Take good care of yourself old chap and get rich if you can, without being altogether a beast. Let's have your address as soon as you can. Yours in the Cause.

Leaving his family in Dublin, Connolly sailed for the US on 18 September 1903. It is a graphic picture of his isolation and defeat that, after seven years of work in Ireland, not one of his Irish comrades came to see him off. In later years Connolly often spoke of this discourtesy. The letter from Matheson compensated only in small measure for this neglect.

A few years after Connolly departed, there appeared in *The People* a communication by William O'Brien which gave the impression that the Irish Socialist Republican Party had made great advances since the departure of Connolly. Connolly commented on this piece in a letter written to John Mulray. The letter shows that Connolly still nursed his resentment against the Party, but was already wishing that he could return to Ireland.

Now about O'Brien's letter, of course I was glad to hear that the party in Ireland was doing well, although I did not agree with all that Bill said. I certainly thought that they might have told of their good fight to the readers of *The People* without going out of their way to tell how much better a fight they made than we had made before . . . But all that is hardly worth while disputing about. It is enough that they are doing well. If I was as satisfied that the propaganda is as clean and true to Socialist principles as I in my 'bullying way' strove to keep it in my time, I would be happy even in my banishment in this cursed country. For after all it is to Ireland all my thoughts turn when dreaming of the future. I suppose I will never see it again, except in dreams. But if Ireland and the Socialist cause therein ever find another willing to serve them and fight and suffer for them better or more unselfishly than him they cast out, who is now writing to you, they will be fortunate indeed. As to what O'Brien said about me going back, I do not know how the idea got about. Certainly I never wrote or expressed such ideas to anybody. I have spoken more freely to you than to anybody else about the matter, and you know that I always regarded such a thing as being outside the pale of possibilities. Handicapped as I am with a large family it is not an easy thing to move about the world. And at any rate I regard Ireland, or at least the Socialist part of Ireland which is all I care for, as having thrown me out, and I do not wish to return like a dog to his vomit.

IX

CONNOLLY'S FIRST move upon returning to New York was to seek work as a linotype operator with the New York Labor News Company on Reade Street, the firm which printed the newspapers and other publications of the Socialist Labor Party. He was turned down, Connolly wrote Matheson two years later, because he placed himself in the hands of a comrade, Frank Lyons, then manager of the Company, who 'succeeded in squelching my hopes of admission into the unions, and of sidetracking me until my chance was gone'. It was not until he found that Lyons had squeezed out of the printing firm all members of the Socialist Trades and Labor Alliance, the SLP affiliate, and manned it exclusively with men from the non-political, pure-and-simple printing unions called the Big Six, that he first suspected the quality of this advice. However, since Lyons enjoyed the full confidence of De Leon and other top SLP officials, Connolly dared not breathe his suspicions, 'lest it be thought I was sore on him on personal grounds alone'. More recently, Connolly was pleased to inform Matheson, Lyons had been expelled for swindling the party out of $200.

It was typical of Connolly to find political motives in what may have been quite unpolitical actions, but we need not go along with him. Other motives—some stated and some hinted at by De Leon's defenders—may have been more important. It was argued that the only printers who could set type in English were members of the Big Six; Connolly may have seemed unqualified; there may have been no vacancy; there was possibly a feeling that Connolly was unworthy of being given a position because he had deceived the Americans on his previous visit to the US by posing as an unskilled labourer whereas he was actually a skilled printer.

The net result was the same. No other printing shop would hire Connolly since he lacked a union card, and thus his hopes of working as a printer in the US were dashed.

In later years De Leon supporters attributed Connolly's hostility to De Leon to this failure to obtain employment with the Labor News Company. It is true that Connolly was bitterly disappointed; that he was always conscious of what he thought was mismanagement of the printing firm; and that he believed it paid exorbitant salaries: but to anyone acquainted with Connolly's make-up, the argument does not hold water. De Leon was doing inestimable damage to the SLP; to Connolly this was of far greater consequence than any misfortune that affected him personally.

After a disheartening spell in New York City, Connolly left for Troy where he lived with his cousins Margaret and Thomas Humes at 447 Tenth Street. There he obtained work as an insurance agent—actually a collector of premiums—for the Metropolitan Life Insurance Company. Troy, across the Hudson River from Albany, was then as now a dingy city specializing in the manufacture of Arrow shirts. It had attracted its share of Irish immigrants, some of whom had become socialists and set up a local branch of the Socialist Labor Party, with its own meeting rooms.

Connolly's cousins were friendly people and, though not radicals, willing enough to discuss politics and economics with him. On one occasion Thomas Humes accompanied Connolly when Connolly addressed a Socialist Labor Party meeting in Schenectady, New York. Connolly had a knack for finding audiences, even in a foreign country. Connolly here presented what he thought was the accepted Marxist theory of wages, only to find many in his audience strongly of the opinion that there was never any use in attempting to get wage increases; that, if gained, they were immediately and automatically nullified by an increase in prices. He was unable to convince these members that this idea, dating back to Ferdinand Lassalle, was in error.

Connolly decided that this question needed clarification among SLP members. He was troubled also by attitudes in the party on two other subjects—monogamy and religion. In March 1904 he addressed a letter to the *Weekly People* dealing with these three subjects. The letter, along with a reply by editor Daniel De Leon, was published on the first page of the 9 April 1904 issue.

Connolly's first point was this: if every rise in wages was offset by a rise in prices, why was the Socialist Trades and Labor Alliance, the trade union arm of the SLP, in existence?

On women and monogamy, Connolly wrote:

When touring this country in 1902, I met in Indianapolis an esteemed comrade who almost lost his temper with me because I expressed my belief in monogamic marriage, and because I said I still hold that the tendency of civilisation is towards its perfection and completion, instead of its destruction. My comrade's views, especially since the publication in *The People* of Bebel's *Woman*, are held by a very large number of members, but I hold nevertheless that they are wrong, and furthermore that such works and such publications are an excrescence upon the movement. The abolition of the capitalist system will undoubtedly solve the economic side of the Woman question, but it will solve that alone . . . men and woman would still be unfaithful to their vows and questions of the intellectual equality of the sexes would still be as much in dispute as they are today . . . Bebel's *Woman* is popular because of its quasi-prurient revelations of the past and present degradation of womanhood, but I question if you can find one woman who was led to socialism by it, but you can find hundreds who were repelled from studying socialism by judicious extracts from its pages.

Connolly was on familiar ground. In Edinburgh he had heard and criticized Bohemian socialists who had advocated free love; he had followed controversies on this subject in *Justice* in which Eleanor Marx and Belfort Bax had taken part; and he had read Lewis Morgan, and others.

On the third question Connolly wrote:

Theoretically every SLP man agrees that socialism is a political and economic question and has nothing to do with religion. But how many adhere to that position. The *Weekly People* of late . . . and the party are becoming distinctly anti-religious. If a clergyman anywhere attacks socialism the tendency is to hit back, not at his economic absurdities, but at his theology with which we have nothing to do.

Here again Connolly was on familiar ground. As a Catholic and Marxist he had necessarily thought long about his position. It can be stated in a few sentences. (1) Catholics and other religious people are concerned about the hereafter, socialists about the present. There is no necessary conflict if priests and ministers keep to their own field, and socialist leaders stick to theirs. (2) Socialism is exclusively concerned with material things, with improving the welfare of human beings, and establishing better relations between them. Religion is concerned with the state of the soul, with sin, guilt, and similar conditions. (3) Connolly felt that religion was outside the realm of Socialist thought. He meant what he wrote: 'We cannot undertake to correct all errors because we are not the possessors of all knowledge.' This kind of humility was rare among Marxists—then or now.

Connolly as usual avoided saying anything about his own beliefs. Did he personally believe in God and the Roman Catholic Church? In a letter to Matheson dated 30 January 1908, we find as explicit an answer as we shall ever get. When Matheson questioned Connolly concerning some remarks by the Pope on 'Modernism', Connolly responded:

Theoretically it was not *ex cathedra*, therefore was not binding. For myself, though I have usually posed as a Catholic I have not gone to my duty for 15 years, and have not the slightest tincture of faith left. I only assumed the Catholic pose in order to quiz the raw freethinkers whose ridiculous dogmatism did and does annoy me as much as the dogmatism of the Orthodox. In fact, I respect the good Catholic more than the average freethinker.

Connolly concluded his letter to the *Weekly People* by saying, 'I hold that mine is the correct SLP doctrine. Now will someone please tread on the tail of my coat?'

After deploring the 'flippancy' of Connolly's last paragraph, De Leon rolled up his sleeves and proved Connolly wrong on all three points. On the wages question, he quoted Marx at length. On the question of Women, he accused Connolly of 'projecting capitalist conditions into socialism', and declared that the 'monogamous family owed its origin to property'. Connolly's notion that only the economic aspects of marriage would be solved by socialism was unscientific, since it denied the 'controlling influence of material conditions upon any and all social institutions'. There would therefore be no such thing as jealousy or unrequited love under socialism.

On the question of religion, De Leon claimed that the free thinker Vandervelde, who had written in *The People* that the Belgian Catholic Church had converted itself into a political machine, was simply stating facts. That did not mean that the SLP accepted Vandervelde's reactionary political views. As for the argument that when priests attacked socialism, the socialist should rebut only the economic fallacies and not the theology, De Leon replied that he was working precisely on that principle. When a Cardinal had said socialism was un-American, he had replied that the Cardinal had taken an oath to the Pope, who was also non-American.

The opinion of Lenin on this precise subject may be of interest, particularly to those who take him as a guide. Writing in 1905, Lenin argued that any party founded on scientific socialism 'must necessarily explain the actual historical and economic roots of religion'. But he added significantly, 'We must not allow the forces waging a genuinely revolutionary economic and political struggle to be broken up for the sake of opinions and dreams of third-rate importance.'

A lively discussion ensued in the pages of *The People*, with many readers commenting. Eventually Passano, secretary of the Troy Branch, decided that the Branch should take disciplinary action against Connolly and invited De Leon to submit suggestions on procedure. De Leon evaded a direct answer, saying that the National Convention was being held in six weeks' time and he hoped Connolly 'would manage to be present'. The Lawrence, Massachusetts, branch reacted unfavourably and protested against the matter being debated at the Convention. It wrote:

If these debates take place, they will be circulated among the wage-slaves in order to make them more prejudiced against us. Comrades, be cunning and cute as the capitalists are. Don't bother yourselves with wages, marriage and the church.

Connolly sent J. Carstairs Matheson on 6 May 1904 an article for publication in the *Socialist*. In it Connolly attempted to refute De Leon's arguments by quoting contradictory statements made previously by De Leon. Connolly signed the accompanying letter, 'Once a staunch comrade but now a slandering misquoting capitalist tool.'

Matheson's reply that he would put the article on the front page 'nearly took my breath away', Connolly wrote on 26 May. 'I am glad *you* have not lost faith in me. By the time this letter reaches you I will have been tried by the Troy section, and if they decide against me I will be expelled. If they refuse to decide, then I will escape until the convention when, Dan says, the whole matter will be laid before the National Delegation.'

Connolly agreed with Matheson that 'the game is not worth the candle'—the candle being De Leon's friendship—but he intended nevertheless to put up a stiff fight, 'and I promise you all the wounds won't be on one side. I think Dan is up against a tougher proposition than he is aware of, to use an Americanism.' He said that other dissenters 'may have been so irritated at Dan's dogmatism and rather unscrupulous handling of their case, that they struck out too wildly and without premeditation committed something like treason'. But Connolly intended 'to fight the best I know how, but to fight so that when passion against me cools down no reasoning man can point to any act of mine to help the enemy'.

On 22 June 1904, Connolly wrote to Matheson that Troy had been converted and had sent his defence to the National Executive Committee of the Socialist Labor Party with the request that it be published in *The People*. He added:

At present you must excuse this short letter as I have just received word from Dublin that my wife is dangerously ill and may not recover, and my children have all had to be taken away in the homes of neighbours and friends.

The SLP National Convention was held 2 July, at the Grand Central Palace, New York City. Connolly described what took place there in a letter to Matheson postmarked 22 July. But first he noted with wrath that the Executive Committee of the SLP of Great Britain had apologized for the insertion of his defence in *The Socialist*; and observed bitterly, 'You are not the only person who differs from Dan, and is afraid to say so.' Connolly continued:

Dan played a very smart trick at the Convention. Of course I could not be present; was not a delegate, and had my nose too close to the grindstone of exploitation to attend, anyway. So Dan read my correspondence, paragraph by paragraph, *adding his own criticisms in between*, so that the delegates could not discern where I ended and my quotations began, and had lost sight of one sentence before he began to read the one that pointed its moral. As a result he had no difficulty in tearing me to pieces—and thus succeeded by this trick—worthy of a shyster lawyer—in preventing the publication of the letters, and in preventing the delegates and the party at large from having the opportunity of studying and calmly reviewing the evidence in cold print. It was a 'great victory'.

Connolly summarized:

> . . . neither in Great Britain nor in American can a Working Class Socialist expect common fairness from his comrades if he enters into a controversy with a trusted leader from a class above them. The howl that greets every such attempt whether directed against a Hyndman in England or a De Leon in America (excuse the comparison) sounds to my mere proletarian ear wonderfully alike, and everywhere is but the accents of an army not of revolutionary fighters but of half-emancipated slaves.

This feeling, first expressed here but often expressed later, was undoubtedly one of the facts that finally led Connolly to join the Industrial Workers of the World.

Connolly added that he had heard from his wife that she was out of bed for the first time in nearly two months, and was expecting to join him in the middle of August, on a boat leaving Liverpool on the fifth of that month.

Delegates to the convention wholeheartedly endorsed the views of the 'National Editor', namely De Leon, and the 'Connolly matter' was temporarily put to rest. There was no serious attempt to oust Connolly. In fact, during the following winter, at the invitation of various SLP branches, Connolly spoke in New York on 'Everyday Illustrations of Socialist Teaching'. on 'Labour Laws and Trade Unionism', and on 'The Unfulfilled Mission of Trade Unionism'.

Thanks to a price war between the White Star and Cunard Lines, the cost of transatlantic passage had gone down low enough for Connolly to purchase tickets for his family. It was high time. Connolly had been alone in the US for almost a year. The family was due to arrive on a Sunday. On the day before, Connolly travelled to New York from Troy to meet them. As he walked aimlessly through the city, he was surprised to meet Jack Mulray, the tailor. Jack was now working in New York. Having been one of the rebels in the ISRP, he had not dared to look up Connolly, but, in the surprise of the encounter, any embarrassment was forgotten, and Connolly stayed with his old friend overnight.

He stayed with Mulray much longer than he expected, meeting

boat after boat with rising anxiety. Finally he was summoned to claim his wife and children—but the oldest child was missing. On the very day the family was due to leave, Mona, then thirteen years old, had gone to take care of an aunt's house while the aunt helped Lillie with the packing. Lifting a pot from the stove with the aid of her apron, Mona set her clothes on fire, and ran out of the house screaming. She was so badly burned that she died in the hospital the next day. Consequently, the family sailed from Liverpool a week late, reaching Ellis Island in the middle of August 1904.

A year later Connolly, still brooding about the event, wrote to Matheson: 'I do not like the country, indeed my chief motive in coming here was to provide a better field for my girls than was open for them at home. But the girl for whose immediate benefit the change was made was stricken down by death on the eve of our departure, and the blow darkened my life, and changed all our hopes and prospects.'

The family now consisted of four girls and a baby boy. Nora, now the oldest, was a bright, imaginative child who astonished her teachers by her precocity. Aideen had more of her mother's placidity. Ina, chubby, angelic, and kittenish, was very much her father's girl. Then there was Maire, and the toddler Roderic.

The house in Troy which Connolly had obtained for them was at 76 Ingalls Avenue, only a stone's throw from where the Humes family lived. It delighted the family with its many rooms and its back yard with fruit trees. But hardly had they settled in when Connolly's job with Metropolitan Life came to an end.

Weeks went by without any signs of another job. By the end of November Connolly was forced to write Mulray to the effect that he thought the chances of getting another job in the insurance business were better in New York than in Troy and asking for help in finding a place to stay 'until I can get an exploiter. I will look after the grub part of it myself, but the bed item is one you cannot compromise on very well. One must sleep somewhere . . . Don't be afraid to write if you cannot do it'.

Mulray contrived to put him up in his own lodgings in Greenwich Village, where Connolly stayed for several months. Connolly grew desperate thinking about his family in Troy and how to find a few dollars to send them. For a brief period he worked as an insurance collector for the John Hancock Company but expenses exceeded income. Every time he obtained temporary work, Mulray would become unemployed, and vice versa. At scarcely any time were both employed. Jack Lyng had now settled in New York and kept open house, but he could not forgive Mulray for the stand he had taken against Connolly in Dublin and relations remained strained, even though Connolly had completely ceased to think about the débâcle.

Since Connolly could rarely get to his home in Troy, many weekends were spent walking with Mulray or the Lyngs in various sections of New York. Connolly and Mulray found restaurants where a meal could be had for ten cents. Connolly invented names for them; one was the Waldorf, another the Netherlands, another the 'coffee without onions' restaurant—so-called because a cup of coffee had appeared with fried onions in it. The next time he visited the place, he asked for 'coffee without onions' and laughed explosively when the waiter called out the order in those words.

Another incident streaked with the hysterical humour of the bitterly poor occurred when some visitors from Dublin looked up Connolly and Mulray. The pair ordered only a cup of coffee, while the visitors ordered a huge dinner, and did not realize until later that the visitors had intended to pay for the whole company.

1905

Early in April 1905 Connolly returned to Troy where there was supposedly an opening for an agent for a 'Sick and Accident Benefit Company'. To get a bond made out for this position, he had to clear his account with the John Hancock Company in the amount of $4·33. On 12 April Connolly wrote an urgent plea to John Mulray asking for the loan of this amount. Three weeks later he wrote to Mulray:

> You promised in your letter of reply to look after that matter, but I have heard no more about it, and as a consequence I was not able to get that job.
>
> I suppose you are in Easy Street now, but I am as bad as ever, and you would confer a favour on me I would never forget if you would send me that five by return post. Until I get that matter straightened out I will have poor chance of getting any decent job, and I am desperately anxious. Pardon me for bothering you, but this is the last time I will trouble you.

On 7 May he wrote contritely:

Your two letters with five dollars in all enclosed arrived safe. Now, John, there were two mistakes you made in reading my letter. I will tell you of them.

First: I only asked you for five dollars because I was under the belief that the Hancock money was not paid. I never dreamt of you going personally to the office and paying it. I thought you would not find time to do so.

I would never have dreamed of asking for any money if I had known that money was paid. So that mistake cost you five dollars, for of course I am still too hard up to return it once it gets into my hands. Your action in sending it was generous to a degree I shall never forget.

Second: I see you refer to my phrase about your being in 'Easy Street' and if it hurt you. If it did I heartily apologise, but I did not mean anything more than to express the fact that you had got out of the stage of life represented by the Netherlands and 'coffee without onions', while I was still in the rut.

I did not mean to hurt by this simple remark, but I have such an unfortunate knack, as you know, of saying things that turn my best friends into enemies, that it is possible the remark was offensive. If it was, John, let it go. After our recent experiences together and what I hoped was the firm comradeship born of those experiences it would be a pity to have any more misunderstanding.

The kind of contretemps described in this letter is all too frequent among the desperately poor; the admission in it by Connolly that he had an unfortunate knack for saying things that turned his best friends into enemies is rare.

Connolly remained unemployed until May when he was appointed representative in Troy of the Pacific Mutual Life Insurance Company. Regarding this appointment, Connolly wrote to his friend Mulray:

I am as deep in the mud as ever, although to judge by this paper on which I am writing it would seem to you that I have landed a soft place. But this job is only a commission job, and although in a year *if I can hold it so long* it will be one of the best jobs in the country, yet at present I cannot earn bread and butter. I have the right to employ agents and have a big enough margin of profit left to pay them more than they would get from most companies, but as the company is new to this district agents are hard to get. In a while, when the company gets better known, I will be on the warm side of the fence. At present I am taking side-leaps with the hunger, although to get on this job I had to represent myself as worth 3,000 dollars and get a bond for 2,000 dollars from the National Surety Company. I was playing the American capitalists at their own bunco game, and succeeded so far.

A strike of the shirt and collar manufacturing plants in Troy which began 14 May 1905 and lasted three and a half months made it the worst of all possible times to introduce a new insurance company. The blank pages of Connolly's books told their own story. But even under the best of conditions it is unlikely that Connolly would have made a success as an insurance agent. He lacked 'sincerity'—the ability to believe that self-interest was synonymous with the welfare of the buyer. In addition, he lacked the heart to press poor people, whose problems he knew so well, for payment of premiums. His instinct was rather to collect money for the strike fund—and to this he turned for a time.

Having decided that seeking another job in strike-paralysed Troy was hopeless, especially since he had a reputation as a socialist agitator, Connolly tried many other areas. He began by writing to the secretary of the Connecticut Socialist Labor Party concerning the position of organizer and literature agent for the region consisting of Massachusetts, Connecticut and Rhode Island. He was informed that the salary would be twelve dollars a week, plus the customary percentages on books and papers sold, but the position fell through.

Reverting to an earlier tactic, Connolly placed an advertisement in the *Daily People*. In response, the secretary of the Socialist Labor Party of Pennsylvania asked him if he would consider a position as organizer and literature agent for that area. Connolly. in desperate straits, responded by asking for a loan of fifteen dollars, and received it. On 2 August, the secretary wrote Connolly that the necessary financial support for the position could not be raised. The only other response to the advertisement, so far as we know, was a letter from an SLP member in Texas who said that he had heard that the editor of a weekly published in Globe, Arizona, was looking for printers.

It appears that Connolly did hold a position for a short time in Paterson, New Jersey, perhaps as a tile worker. But as the American style of job-hunting became clearer to him, his luck improved. He finally got a job in October 1905 at the Newark plant of the Singer

Sewing Machine Company. He did it by representing himself as a skilled machinist, and telling

a fairy tale about the places I had learned my trade in, and the places in this country I had worked in. It is a great joke to be passing myself off as an engineer, but I am doing the trick all right. Of course I have to study at night on the theoretical part of the work, and having a fairly good knowledge of geometry it helps me in drawing the designs, and I think I will pull it off.

Connolly had another problem; he was near-sighted, and employers (says Greaves) did not look favourably at men who had to bring blueprints close to their eyes to read them or who wore glasses. However, he was able to keep his job, and indeed improved it somewhat by transferring to the Singer plant in Elizabeth, New Jersey, to run a lathe. The task was now to move his family from Troy, where 'if a man was hard up everybody knew it', to New Jersey. The move was made in two stages. The family lived temporarily in New York City with the Lyngs, and in the autumn of 1905 moved to a house in Newark. Commuting from there to Elizabeth was fairly easy.

Typically enough, these personal matters occupied only two pages of a seventeen-page letter Connolly wrote to Matheson on 19 November 1905. The remaining pages concerned events taking place among left-wing organizations in the US.

Connolly reported that the Socialist Labor Party was weaker both financially and politically than it had ever been, but said he had lost none of his confidence in the party despite its dwindling voting strength. At the same time 'I have nothing but contempt for men who now, echoing De Leon like parrots, pretend that the vote is of no importance.' He denounced De Leon for his readiness to accept compromises in Europe of socialist parties with capitalist parties, and was astonished that De Leon's stand was being endorsed by the British and Australian sections of the SLP.

Matheson must have found rather novel Connolly's concept that: 'all actions of our class at the ballot box are in the nature of mere preliminary skirmishes, and . . . the conquest of political power by the Working Class waits upon the conquest of economic power and must function through the economic organisation'. The impetus for this idea came from the meeting in Chicago at which the Industrial Workers of the World was founded, and from the SLP itself, which was desperately seeking to become associated with the new movement.

As the year 1905 drew towards an end, Matheson wrote Connolly: 'The ISRP have that printing press that they bought three or four years ago. It's no use to them. Couldn't we purchase it from them and start printing our paper ourselves. What is to hinder your being the printer and business manager of the paper?'

Connolly responded that the suggestion 'that I return to Scotland and take up the printing for the party . . . takes my breath away'. He proceeded to explain in detail what printing the weekly involved, demonstrating in the process his hard-won knowledge of every possible economy that could be used. He concluded:

As far as the personal equation in the problem is concerned. At present I am earning an average of $15·00 per week—the average wage for most mechanics here—in New Jersey. I have emerged out of the depths, else I would not have written to you, and am only troubled by my health which is indeed giving me great trouble of late . . . My wife who was as enthusiastic about coming here as I was careless is now mad to get out of the country. But to shift a family across the Atlantic is no picnic, and to return home myself, and leave them in the United States is not as easy as it would have been to leave them in Ireland or Scotland and come here. Five dollars sent to them every week would keep the wolf from the door in Ireland, but in the United States it is a very small thing indeed. But let me know how your proposal was taken by the EC (Executive Committee) All I can say at present is that I am not averse to it.

His hopes of returning to Ireland were to be similarly raised and dashed many times during the coming years.

X

1906

THE YEAR 1906 was a busy one for James Connolly. Though his job with the Singer company occupied fourteen hours of each working day, door to door, he managed to become increasingly involved in affairs of the Socialist Labor Party and the Industrial Workers of the World, wrote regularly for the SLP newspaper, became a sort of adviser to an Italian radical group, and studied German and Italian.

Since the majority of the people in the department where he worked were Germans, and German was the principal language spoken, he asked Matheson to send him Hugo's *Simplified German Teacher*, 'thinking that I can do a little learning on the Berlitz system, whilst earning my daily bread if I only had a few books to teach me the rudiments'.

He was learning Italian so that he could work more effectively with the Newark branch of the Italian Socialist Federation, a small militant organization immersed in old-world feuds which held meetings on Sunday mornings to express its contempt for the Mass.

In the Socialist Labor Party he was gradually gaining recognition from his articles in the *Weekly People*, and from his efforts in New Jersey to win the Socialist Labor Party members towards support of the Industrial Workers of the World. This was an indigenous American organization, formed in protest against the low wages and frequent unemployment that were the lot of the manual worker at the time. The average annual salary was then four or five hundred dollars a year, the work week was six days of ten hours each, and the accident rate was shocking.

The hope of the IWW leaders—'Big Bill' Haywood, Joseph J. Ettor, Arturo Giovannitti, Vincent St John, Elizabeth Gurley Flynn and many others long forgotten—was to organize and unite the proletariat into industry-wide unions, thereby displacing the craft-organized American Federation of Labor. Eventually the workers, by downing their tools, would bring the capitalists to their knees.

Daniel De Leon, having found his Socialist Labor Party losing political influence, and membership of the Socialist Trades and Labor Alliance shrinking, cautiously welcomed the new organization when it was founded in Chicago on 27 June 1905. He saw in it the might to ensure that, when the decision for socialism was cast at the ballot box, the decision would be accepted by the capitalists.

Connolly saw the IWW in the same light. He could not possibly resist the appeal of the flat statement in the IWW constitution: 'the working class and the employing class have nothing in common'.

He soon developed the firm conviction that the IWW, by opening the way to industrial unity, would automatically eliminate the need for two separate socialist parties. He expected that the IWW would ultimately establish its own political party that would absorb the others.

The Chicago convention was an unqualified success. Though right-wing Socialist Party leaders such as Hillquit and Spargo remained unmoved, most socialists found the event earth-shaking. To discuss it, the Socialist Labor Party called a meeting in New York City with Connolly in the chair and De Leon as the principal speaker. The entrance of De Leon into the auditorium was typical of his flair for showmanship. Though only fifty years old, he entered the room from the back of the hall with the stooped, slow gait of a man of seventy. When he had gone two-thirds of the aisle towards the platform, one admirer noticed and shouted 'De Leon!' For the remainder of his walk to the platform, the hall rocked with cheers and applause. Connolly's voice was drowned in the tumult. Greaves reports that Connolly was nonplussed and angered by this exhibition of the 'cult of personality'—a term invented fifty years later.

In line with De Leon's hope that the national executive committee of the IWW would become 'the central administration of the nation', his Socialist Labor Party went to work organizing engineers, musicians, and workers of all nationalities into IWW locals.

In the weeks that followed Connolly threw himself into this work. His instrument was open-air propaganda; his helper was Patrick Quinlan, a man from Tipperary who bestowed on Connolly all 'the admiration he could spare from himself'. But despite Quinlan's flamboyant self-confidence, he was a hard worker and a good street orator, and the two men made the IWW known in Newark. (Quinlan eventually served a jail sentence for the part he played in the Paterson silk strike of 1913, but was released in time to meet James Larkin when Larkin came to the US in 1914.)

Those members of the Socialist Labor Party and the American Socialist Party who were working together for the IWW began to lose their mutual hostility. Soon the New Jersey sections of the two parties held a conference to discuss amalgamation. Quinlan, as the delegate from the Essex County SLP, upheld the position that support for industrial unionism should be exclusive and obligatory, in accordance with the idea that in this way a framework of socialism would be created within the shell of capitalism. The Socialist Party members, on the other hand, wished to leave the American Federation of Labor in possession of the 20 per cent of the workers they had organized, while urging the remaining 80 per cent to join the IWW. The agreement hammered out was near the SLP position; whereupon the Socialist Party referendum rejected it.

Meanwhile, an event took place in the west which rocked the labour movement. Three leaders of the Western Federation of Miners, the union which formed the backbone of the IWW, were arrested for complicity in the murder of Idaho Governor Studenberg. In February 1906 the men were deported from Colorado—illegally, many believed—and lodged in a Boise jail. At a meeting of the New Jersey Socialist Labor Party, which Connolly attended as delegate from Essex County, this token of 'impending legal murder' was hotly protested. The convention recognized Connolly's gifts as a publicist by appointing him to its press and literature committee. He and Quinlan organized a protest meeting which filled Kurz's Coliseum in Newark when De Leon came to speak there on 3 April. Since more than two-thirds of Newark's population were foreign-born (mostly Italians, Germans and Irish), speeches were made in Italian and German as well as English. The 'Newark Workingmen's Defense Committee' held several other indoor and outdoor meetings during the rest of the year.

Speaking with Connolly at one of these meetings was Elizabeth Gurley Flynn, then a schoolgirl of seventeen whose severely simple dress contrasted strangely with her forceful and sparkling oratory. On this occasion, somebody accidentally spilled a glass of water on Connolly's hat. He remarked with a grimace, 'I hope it won't shrink; it's the only hat I have.' In her memoirs she describes him as, 'Short, rather stout, a plain-looking man with large black moustaches, a very high forehead, and dark sad eyes—a man who rarely smiled. A scholar and an excellent writer, his speech was marred for American audiences by his thick, North of Ireland accent, with a Scotch burr from his long residence in Glasgow.'

One of the organizations represented at the IWW founding convention in Chicago was the Italian Socialist Federation, which had a branch in Newark. In order to win this group towards the SLP and the IWW, Connolly spoke at its meetings, translated articles from its organ *Il Proletario*, and published them, with prefaces of his own, in the *Weekly People*.

Elizabeth Flynn accompanied him to one of these early Sunday meetings of Italian socialists. She remembers asking him before the meeting started, 'Who will speak in Italian?' Connolly 'smiled his rare smile and replied, "We'll see. Someone, surely." After we had both spoken, they took a recess and gave us coffee and cake behind the scenes, a novel but welcome experience for us. Stale water was the most we got elsewhere! Then we returned to the platform, and Connolly arose. He spoke beautifully in Italian to my amazement and the delight of the audience who "viva'd" loudly.'

Her admiration of Connolly was reciprocated. He wrote of 'La Belle Flynn' to Matheson:

Like you I have a distrust of prodigies, but Lizzie is entirely free from the stereotyping characteristics. In fact the really wonderful thing about her is the readiness which she evinces a desire to learn, and to abandon her previous opinions when they are proven untenable. She started out as a pure utopian, but now she laughs at her former theories. Had she stuck by her first set of opinions she would have continued a *persona grata* with the Socialist Party crowd, which of course commands the biggest purse and the biggest audience, but her advocacy of straight revolutionary socialism and industrial unionism alienated them and now they hate her.

Under Connolly's influence, the Italian socialists in Newark began to hold more public meetings. The police, irked by their increasing activity, entered their headquarters on 18 March and removed the red flag flying from the window to commemorate the Paris Commune. On May Day, when the Italians were parading on Seventh Avenue, the police stopped them and seized the red flag they were flying.

To protest these actions, an open-air indignation meeting was held on 13 June at the corner of Seventh Avenue and Cutler Street. Speeches were given in both English and Italian, and the red flag flew unharmed.

In addition, a memorial was sent to the police commissioners of Newark protesting the police actions. Undoubtedly drafted by Connolly, the text is still available. Dated 16 July 1906, it described the acts taken by the police as 'violations of the constitutional rights of the citizens', requested the return of the flags to their proper owners, and 'instruction to the police to avoid such illegal practices in the future'.

According to Greaves, these actions 'created a tremendous impression on the Italians who had hitherto regarded themselves as a powerless minority who must suffer not without protest, but without redress'.

In July 1906 an editorial appeared in *Il Proletario* calling upon Italians to abandon their exclusive preoccupation with Italian affairs; to seek affiliation with the Socialist Labor Party to defend the immigrants immediate interests; to break down the anti-clerical prejudice which cut the Italian socialists off from their compatriots; and to unite all Italians within the IWW. Connolly believed, with some justice, that his translations and other activities had helped cause this change of mood among the Italians, and wrote to *The People* urging that it receive every encouragement. However, no welcoming gesture was extended by the SLP.

But this was only the least of the grievances against De Leon which Connolly was collecting. His wrath was mounting, but for the time being his only listener was in Scotland. On 10 June 1906, Connolly wrote to Matheson that he was in complete agreement with De Leon on his attitude towards the IWW, the American Federation of Labor, and everything else, but completely disagreed with his attitude towards the membership of the Socialist Labor Party:

> We are not treated as revolutionaries capable of handling a revolutionary situation but as automatons whose duty is to repeat in varying accents the words of our director general ... Scarcely any production of the pen of a comrade can get into *The People* ... Every kind of literary initiative is frowned down upon, as is every other kind of initiative ... I can write the foregoing without any personal feeling in the matter, because he has always published any articles or notes that I sent in on the question in general.

He condemned De Leon for failing to train and equip other comrades so that there would be scores ready to fill his place in case of death or removal in any form. But Dan's settled policy is the direct antithesis of this. His policy is to make himself so indispensable, so much the pivot on which the movement turns that in every dispute with a member of any point Dan will be sure to secure the victory because of the honour attaching to his name as the only author, writer, or tactician the party has been allowed to know about.

On other matters, Connolly predicted that no union of the Socialist Party and the Socialist Labor Party would take place, and gave his opinion that Eugene Debs was thoroughly honest. 'I base my belief upon the fact that although he has changed his position several times in the past every change was a move forward. In no case has he changed to go backward.' Connolly saw no reason why Debs should leave the Socialist Party and join the Socialist Labor Party since neither group had yet taken a stand on the IWW.

He concluded wistfully: 'I have had no word from Ireland for over a year, and then only a business communication. Good luck to you all.'

Early in November 1906 a Socialist Labor Party organizer named Bernine took his stand at the gates of the Singer plant in Newark, and held an open-air meeting. It was sparsely attended, but on the following day more listened. A literature booth was set up and an appeal was made for fifty men to picket the gates for trade unionism and the SLP. Connolly inevitably joined in this and succeeding enterprises, and immediately became a marked man in the factory. 'In the following months (says Greaves) his foreman was under continuous pressure to dismiss him, and finally Connolly resigned rather than jeopardise his colleague's appointment.'

This account (the only one we have) is too skimpy to be satisfactory. It leaves too many questions unanswered. One immediately wonders: what did his wife Lillie think of this noble gesture? How many months was Connolly out of work—and his family presumably out of food? Was it possible that he left Singer's because he found more interesting and more important things to do? If this was the fact, was he justified? Are we prepared to accept the idea that revolutionaries are entitled to live by a different code from the rest of us? Apparently their wives do. But whatever the circumstances surrounding it, Connolly's departure from Singer's left him free to engage in a great many activities which were much more to his taste than running a lathe.

XI

1907

WHEN THE national executive committee of the Socialist Labor Party held a meeting in New York City on 5 January 1907, James Connolly was present as representative of New Jersey. He had reached the zenith of his position in the party. One of the questions discussed concerned the powers of an executive sub-committee composed of members living in and around New York. This sub-committee had rejected an appeal for financial assistance from the Transvaal Labour Party, and the *People* had published word of this action during De Leon's absence from New York. De Leon and some of his followers had protested. In an attempt to clarify the matter, Connolly now offered a resolution empowering the sub-committee to have the same power to insert material into the columns of the *People* that the full national executive committee had. De Leon opposed this resolution. The Connolly–De Leon feud burst into flames. For months thereafter the debate over what seems at first sight to be a mere organizational trifle raged within the SLP and its publications. By the end of the year the conflict was being fought within the Industrial Workers of the World as well.

What lay behind it was a host of policy and personal disagreements. De Leon was jealous of his control over the party publications; he was opposed to the idea of ethnic groupings; he knew that the type of influence he was seeking to exert over the IWW was not the same that Connolly was seeking. He remembered Connolly's attempts to alter the attitude of the Party regarding monogamy and atheism. And he was particularly angry when Connolly said at the meeting what he thought everybody knew—that an employee had been able to defraud the Labor News Company of over $600.

Connolly's dislike of De Leon was equally vehement, and his charges equally voluminous. They are contained in several long letters he wrote to Matheson in 1907 and 1908. What bothered him most was to see an instrument—the Socialist Labor Party—so well fitted to emancipate the working class subject to the dictates of a single man, De Leon.

Here are some of Connolly's charges:

1. It was a mistake to elect so many SLP men to the executive board of the IWW. 'But that is De Leon's method, he can't trust the revolutionary working class movement unless it is in the control of his creatures.'

2. 'As an organising force he does not exist. Despite all the rosy reports in the paper as to our progress the cold truth is that the average circulation of the *Daily People* is between 2,000 and 3,000, never going higher than the latter although every member in the country from Maine to California subscribes to it . . . The only places where we gain adherents now is where sections are formed in new districts.' (In the same letter, Connolly wrote: 'I guess you are right about Debs. The truth is, I understand, that he is too fond of his "wee drappie",' and when half-cocked can be enticed into situations which he would at other times avoid, and when he shows up he accepts the result of his foolishness. He is in a strange fix; his instincts are all revolutionary; but he balks at swallowing De Leon, and the latter's followers insist that to accept the IWW in its entirety is to accept Dan.')

3. If De Leon had the same spirit of self-sacrifice as the rank and file of his party, he would not have continued drawing his $30 a week salary as editor of the *People*, or charging it up against the party, when party finances were running short. This salary was twice that received by the assistant editor of the paper, even though the latter kept office hours, as De Leon did not, and did most of the work. (This was the limited view of the 'proletarian', I suspect. If De Leon had wanted money, he would have long since left the party and worked at more profitable occupations.)

4. De Leon and his party discriminated against 'proletarians' in the selection of officers. The vaunted democracy of the elections was a fraud.

5. De Leon considered the IWW merely 'a recruiting ground' for the SLP and deferred its future 'as far off as the Christian Millennium' instead of considering it 'the organisation of the present as well as the future'. Later, Connolly was to charge that De Leon was not sincere in

expressing a desire to unite with the American Socialist Party for fear he could not dominate it.

During the same month that the eventful SLP national committee meeting took place, Connolly took a major step towards reconciliation with his Irish comrades. But even then he could not refrain from using the occasion to berate De Leon and his tactics. On 28 January 1907, Connolly wrote a lengthy letter to the secretary of the Irish Socialist Party to inform him that three former members of the ISRP—Connolly, John Mulray and Jack Lyng—would, he hoped, be directly affiliated with the movement in Ireland and not with any Socialist Party in America because:

> the best way to make the Irish in America listen to Socialist propaganda was and is to help the Irish Socialists at home to attain prominence. Also because from my experience of both countries I have come to the conviction that as revolutionists the Irish comrades are immeasurably superior to anything I have met in America. The Irish comrades were self reliant as Socialists—the Americans rely upon their leaders.

He went on to give as proof of De Leon's dictatorial grip upon the Socialist Labor Party the defeat of the motion to allow the national executive committee and its sub-committee the right to insert notices, communications, and correspondence in the *People*. The SLP has the correct position, Connolly wrote, but De Leon 'stifles all originality and initiative in the rank and file. His services are valuable, but he makes the revolutionary movements pay too high a price—the price of the surrender of its reliance upon the initiative of the Working Class.'

Connolly wrote off the Socialist Party of the USA—the group he would soon join—in a few words: 'Its leaders are for the most part corrupt and incapable, and attempting the impossible task of sitting on the fence of neutrality on the Trade Union question.'

In writing this letter to the socialists in Ireland Connolly was making the first of many attempts to restore relations with his former comrades, to build a bridge over the Atlantic which he might eventually be able to cross. He concluded this letter by asking the Irish Party to find out how much it would cost to publish two pamphlets in Ireland, which he would purchase and distribute in the US.

When the war with De Leon grew hotter, Connolly again sought support from the Irish movement. On 29 April 1907, he wrote to Owen G. Cullen, then secretary of the Socialist Party of Ireland, that De Leon had alluded to Connolly's 1902 trip to the US in the following words: 'The party yielded to his request to be allowed the opportunity to tour America in the interest of the British movement.' Connolly said that this was an attempt to slander the Irish movement by portraying it as a beggar seeking favours from the Socialist Labor Party of the US; and that the purpose of the trip was certainly not to aid the British movement, since the Socialist Labour Party of Great Britain was not in existence at the time. He described the details of the agreement between the two parties, and pointed out that only after all these had been ironed out was there any discussion as to what member would make the trip. Connolly noted that it was Henry Kuhn, national secretary of the SLP in the USA, who first suggested that Connolly be chosen.

He told the Irish comrades that he was resigning his position as a member of the SLP executive committee 'in order that I might be in a position to more freely protest against this calumny upon the Irish movement', and requested the Irish party 'to take steps as an organised body to refute this slander by placing the true facts before the Socialist comrades in as public a manner as you can devise'.

What action the Irish party took on this request is unknown. Very likely it took none. Many members were still out of sympathy with their former organizer. Others felt that the Irish party was having a difficult enough time staying afloat without engaging in a distant and complicated squabble overseas. Others, no doubt, had the good sense to realize that there was very little calumnious in the statement that the SLP yielded to Connolly's request to tour America on behalf of the British labour movement. By this time, it must be confessed, Connolly was blind with rage, using every instrument he could find to crush his *bête noire*.

Connolly's resignation from the national executive committee of the Socialist Labor Party was not easily accomplished. There seems to be a tradition in militant Marxist organizations to punish defectors, rather than to permit them to depart freely. Moved perhaps by this sentiment, the SLP national executive committee did not accept Connolly's letter of resignation; instead, it drafted a resolution condemning Connolly's recent actions and asked for approval of this resolution by the New Jersey sections.

The resolution was approved, and in a letter dated 6 June 1907,

Connolly was informed of the results. Connolly protested strongly that this vote was 'grossly irregular and scandalously unfair'. He pointed out that the SLP Constitution required that when any member was accused of performing an irregular action he should be informed of the specifications and permitted to defend himself. 'Instead, the Section making complaint against me kept me in ignorance of their intended action, moved on the matter, discussed it and condemned me in my absence and without a hearing.' In the second place, Connolly wrote, the executive committee 'in submitting this vote to the membership took care to quote in full the condemnatory resolution but neither notified me that such a vote was demanded, nor asked did I intend to make any answer. The Party Constitution . . . certainly never intended that condemnatory resolutions . . . should be submitted to the Party Membership without the accused delegate being even acquainted or asked if he had any defence to offer.'

Ignoring his protest, the sub-committee took a further step. It passed an additional resolution that approved of Connolly's removal from all national governing bodies on the grounds of 'double-dealing', 'persecution' of members of the New Jersey executive committee, and subsequent 'persecution' of the editor of the *People*.

It is a characteristic of organizational life that the right·hand often does not know what the left is doing. Even while these votes were being taken to condemn Connolly and expel him from the national body, he received a notification from Frank Bohn, national secretary of the Socialist Labor Party, informing him that he had been nominated a delegate to the International Socialist Congress to be held at Stuttgart, 12 to 18 August. 'Expenses will be met by the Party. Please inform me, *at once*, whether or not you will accept the nomination.' Connolly, not appreciating this characteristic of organizations, thought the notice was insulting and sardonic.

But in the main his interest in the Socialist Labor Party was ebbing rapidly. The regular elections to the SLP executive committee took place in October; Connolly not only failed to run for office but by that time had left the Party completely. It was his Irish magazine and the IWW that now absorbed him. But throughout he had no great desire for a career in America. He was lonely and dissatisfied. He did not seek the limelight, and often signed his articles with pseudonyms. Once, when a chairman introduced him with a succession of sugary compliments, he seized the man by the shoulders and bodily removed him from the platform.

He sought no further debate with De Leon. But circumstances did not permit him to evade it. In December 1907 the largest and bitterest confrontation between the two men occurred. Connolly was then trying to persuade an organization called Waterside Workers to join the IWW. It numbered 10,000 men—about a quarter of all the long-shoremen employed in Manhattan, Brooklyn and Hoboken. The men were mostly Irish and Italian, had been members of the Knights of Labor, and regarded the American Federation of Labor as a strike-breaking outfit.

To discuss the mass entry of such a large body, the General Executive Board of the IWW met in New York City instead of its usual meeting place, Chicago. It was two days before Christmas. On the first day of the meeting the matter was discussed and reasonable terms for affiliation were fixed.

Connolly had no idea that Daniel De Leon would appear on the second day of the meeting. He did not realize the depth of De Leon's fear that the mass entry of all these Irish and Italian Catholics would put an end to the final traces of Socialist Labor Party influence in the IWW. Had he anticipated such an appearance, he might well have feared another defeat at the hands of his arch-enemy. Only three weeks earlier, at a general SLP meeting held 7 December, almost the entire subject of discussion had been the criminal actions of James Connolly. In a letter to Matheson, he recounted some of these charges:

> I came and grafted upon them in America during my first trip and when they wanted me in Troy to speak two times in one day I refused because I was not paid by the lecture but only by the day; when I came back I wanted the party to support me but when they gave me a job in the People office I was found unfit, and when they tried me as a printer I was found incompetent. I was sore on De Leon because I wanted to be editor in his place, and I had founded the Irish Socialist Federation in order to become an editor, that the founding of that body was an insidious attempt to break up the working class and divide them . . . that I was an ignoramus but the slickest fakir that ever came along since I had secured the adhesion of veteran comrades . . . I disrupted the party in Ireland because they did not keep the American subs to the W. R. for me to graft upon.

Rather unnecessarily, Connolly told his friend that he had never worked 'a fraction of a second' either for the *People* or the Labor News

Company; and that, with regard to the Troy incident, 'I have an apology from Kuhn, an apology from the comrade who insulted me at that time, and an apology from the branch itself. Yet now five years after the event these lying slanders are hurled at my head and I am refused the opportunity to refute them. Great is Democracy.'

What took place at this meeting of the IWW General Executive Board is graphically described by Connolly in a letter to Matheson dated 30 January 1908.

But the second day of the session whilst I was absent—my sickness was just getting the better of me—who appears at the meeting but Dan, and asks that everybody be excluded from the room but G.E.B. [General Executive Board] members ... Dan opened out with the statement that when he heard of the proposed accession of the Longshoremen he had made up his mind to go to Chicago to the G.E.B. meeting to warn the members. He was therefore rejoiced that they met in New York. For Connolly was an agent of the Jesuit order who was employed to break up the labour movement, and Connolly's purpose in breaking in the Longshoremen was to carry out the wishes of the Jesuit order, as the majority of these Longshoremen were Irish Catholics, and there was a secret agreement between Connolly, the Longshoremen and the Jesuits to demoralise the I.W.W. He then dropped his voice and in a melodramatic manner, looking furtively round like a stage conspirator asked the members: 'What would you do if one of your organisers was a Jesuit agent working to destroy you?'

At this time, Connolly relates, one of the members named Cole left to go to the men's room, and Dan was told to stop talking during his absence. Outside, Cole was told by a number of the most active members, 'all white with rage' at these Star Chamber proceedings, that if De Leon could control the General Executive Board, all hopes of IWW growth in the area were doomed. Thus advised, 'Cole went back and as soon as Dan began to speak he rose and declared that he would not tolerate any more such star chamber proceedings, and if Dan said another word he would demand his fare back to Chicago.' The chairman, Robert Williams, ruled that 'the proceedings must stop, and Connolly be summoned to attend in the morning, and that the proceedings be public and open to all members. Dan did not like that but the chairman was inexorable.'

That night Connolly learned of De Leon's appearance before the IWW executive board but could get no details of what had taken place. Only later did he learn that members Trautman and Cole had been furious at being tricked into holding a secret session to try him; that Williams, an old SLP organizer, had come to New York deeply prejudiced against Connolly 'but the sight of Dan in action converted him. Of course nobody took the charges seriously. They only served to illustrate the depth of the malevolence to which De Leon had sunk. Well there were discussions and interviews galore until after three in the morning, and Trautman got the views of the men who support the IWW here before the chance to sleep was allowed him.'

At the meeting the following morning, all IWW members were admitted. De Leon spoke only a quarter of an hour before Cole rose to a point of order, stating that, since these were personal charges against a member, they should be submitted in writing to the member's local and district council before coming before the General Executive Board. Chairman Williams ruled the point well taken and was supported by all except a member named Katz. 'Dan made three separate efforts to get the G.E.B. to reconsider their position in vain, and finally slunk away with his tail between his legs.'

Several factors helped Connolly's cause: a general conviction that matters relating to the Socialist Labor Party and the Irish Socialist Republican Party which he had allegedly wrecked were 'political', and therefore irrelevant to the position of an IWW organizer; a memory by some that this 'Jesuit agent' Connolly and his Irish Federation had forced Monsignor Brann to retract his denunciation from the altar of a Haywood-Moyer release demonstration; and the desire of the members to be home for Christmas.

In any case the battle had gone against De Leon. Without a viable labour base the SLP would become in the end, as Connolly predicted, a sect, a 'church'. Connolly was quite right in attributing much of this failure to De Leon's personal characteristics; but since the same fate has overtaken the Industrial Workers of the World and the Socialist Party of the United States, it is difficult to believe that the future of the SLP would have been any different than it was, even if De Leon had been all that Connolly wanted him to be.

*   *   *

One of the causes of the split between De Leon and Connolly was Connolly's conviction that a man's national feelings could be used to draw him towards socialism; that they need not be overridden in the cause of international solidarity. Implementing this conviction, Connolly set about establishing a socialist organization composed 'of men and women of Irish race and extraction'.

A notice was sent around stating that the purpose of the organization was to develop a spirit of revolutionary class-consciousness among the Irish working class in America; educate its members regarding the historical development of the class struggle in Ireland; and 'spread a knowledge of, and help to sustain, the socialist movement in Ireland'. The statement said that the organization would be 'affiliated directly with the Socialist movement in Ireland'. Signers of the notice were Lyng, Mulray, Connolly, Elizabeth Flynn, Patrick L. Quinlan and M. P. Cody.

Connolly sent a letter (previously described) bearing the same information to the Socialist Party of Ireland, successor to the ISRP, at 35 Parliament Street, Dublin. He received from William O'Brien a reply dated 13 February 1907 stating that the members noted with pleasure 'the intention to form an Irish Socialist Club in New York, and we accept your offer to affiliate with our Party and also to assist in publishing literature'. The first link in the chain of circumstances that was eventually to draw Connolly back to Ireland had been forged.

On 3 March 1907 a preliminary meeting of the Irish Socialist Federation was held at the home of Elizabeth Gurley Flynn's parents in the Bronx. On 29 March a more formal meeting was held at 79 MacDougal Street, Manhattan. In addition to those who had signed the original announcement, there were about five others present, including a faithful and sympathetic Jewish friend, Sam Stodel. Because the group feared ridicule if a Jew were admitted as a member, Stodel was excluded from the business session. In the kitchen, he learned from Mrs Flynn that there was nothing for the group to eat, and so went around the corner to purchase ham, cheese, corned beef, beer and crackers to feed the doughty Irishmen before they went forth to battle.

Connolly wrote O'Brien on 15 April:

We have formed our organisation and are getting down to work. One curious result of our move is that it has created such a feeling against all race federations that the proposal to admit such into the S.L.P., although approved by the N.E.C. [National Executive Committee] will, without a doubt, be voted down. The Americans love us so much. They fancy we have no rights except to be their valiant soldiers, they to be the officers, we the rank and file.

He then went on to discuss the printing of literature in Ireland that the American group would pay for and distribute. Any pamphlets that were printed should advertise only the Irish Party; no mention should be made of the US group. *The New Evangel*, the first pamphlet to be printed, should have green covers.

To a query by O'Brien as to whether Connolly would consent to represent the Irish Socialist Party if he were attending the international meeting to be held in Stuttgart, Connolly wrote:

> Of course, as you must be aware by this time, there is not the slightest chance of me going to Europe as an S.L.P. representative to the International Congress. That was a grim joke. But the offer of your party gave me more pleasure than anything I have experienced since the unfortunate day we had our disagreement. I thank you.

Connolly concluded by asking particulars on the fate of his old comrades.

O'Brien, listing himself as 'Librarian', responded on 30 April by saying he would send this information later on; meanwhile, he reported that he had received a request from the Labor News Co. asking for a thousand copies of a pamphlet, *The Rights of Ireland*, by Brady. Thinking it strange to receive such an order at the present time, O'Brien had declined filling it.

On 20 May, Connolly gave his opinion that the Irish Party should supply any order, from any source. The important thing, he thought, was to get the Party and its literature known. He enclosed $15 for a thousand pamphlets. 'As to your question, whether we will want more than 1000, we undoubtedly will. From the look of things at present, correspondence from groups of enquirers, etc. it looks as if we would have a very large sale in this country.' He admitted, however, that the enclosed cash had been raised not from subscription lists but by diving down into their own pockets.

The Irish Socialist Federation, with Jack Lyng as secretary, held several indoor and outdoor meetings throughout the summer of 1907, generally in Irish neighbourhoods. The residents heard the socialist messages with astonishment, and looked wide-eyed at the large green and white banner bearing the Gaelic slogan, 'Faugh-a-Balach' (clear the way) surrounded by harps and shamrocks. At first some speakers at outdoor meetings were heckled, but after a while the meetings were held without incident. A German comrade who was a blacksmith built the Federation a sturdy platform that could not easily be upset. It had the further advantage that its iron legs could be detached in an emergency and used as shillelaghs.

Connolly was able to write to the Socialist Party of Ireland on 3 October 1907 that the Federation expected to issue a monthly publication, and would like articles from Irish socialists. But even as he worked to establish the organization in the US, he was filled with nostalgia for the Old Country, repeatedly asking his friends to send a long personal letter describing how things were with them. 'O'Brien promised one long ago, but he never kept his promise in that respect,' he wrote plaintively.

Connolly's appointment as an IWW organizer came at a providential moment, when he was low both in spirits and in funds. His salary came from the building trades and machinists, two unions in New York City which had formerly been affiliated with the Socialist Trades and Labor Association; hence their members could be considered as possessing some knowledge of Socialist Labor Party tactics and of revolutionary ideology in general. Connolly wrote to Matheson on 27 September:

> They asked me to take the job when the fight between Dan and I was at its height and when I believed I was utterly discredited in the party. Instead I found to my surprise that they had come to the conclusion that I had the real grasp of the revolutionary situation, and they were willing to attest their belief by their purses. So after some persuasion I accepted and I have now been about three months in their pay. 'Tis a world of surprises.

During his first months as an IWW organizer in New York, Connolly travelled daily between that city and Newark, spending the night with the Lyngs, when necessary. But the accumulation of evening meetings made this impracticable and towards the end of 1907 the Connolly family moved to Elton Avenue in the Bronx, occupying a fire-trap tenement only a few hundred yards from the Flynns. During the year, Fiona, Connolly's 'American' child, was born. Heedless of the class struggle, the Connolly and Flynn children had a good time on Elton Avenue. Once Patrick Quinlan left a bookcase with a glass door at Connolly's house. Connolly came home to find all the books on the floor and the children playing funeral, with one child beautifully laid out in the bookcase. 'Who's dead?' Connolly asked. The children, who did not like Quinlan, replied serenely, 'Quinlan.'

Connolly, now thirty-nine, threw himself enthusiastically into his work as an IWW organizer, revealing aptitudes which surprised even his friends. He was listed as secretary of the 'Building and Constructional Workers Industrial Union', but the IWW was flexible, and soon he was organizing trolley-car workers, garment workers, milkmen and dock workers. He made great use of outdoor propaganda, especially on the waterfront, among the Irish of Brooklyn and the Germans of Hoboken. As the New York correspondent of the *Industrial Union Bulletin*, organ of the IWW, he became nationally known.

For relaxation Connolly would meet his friends, either at the Flynn household, where all Scottish and Irish socialists were welcome, or in a little Irish saloon where men talked and sang the songs of home. Connolly, as usual, took only soft drinks. He was desperately poor; his $18 a week was paid irregularly. But he had little occasion to go far from home, and during this rare spell of settled family life he was able to do more work on *Labour in Irish History*.

Organizing for the Industrial Workers of the World was an arduous task. In the first place, the union was the target of an enormous, unrelenting effort by the newspapers and the magazines of the time to portray it as a monster dedicated to destroying all decent American institutions. In the end the IWW was destroyed (although one of its basic principles, organization by industry, not by craft, was revivified by the Congress of Industrial Organizations), and only the historians are left to deplore the vilification. How shameful and unprincipled that vilification was is made clear in several new scholarly works. In one of them,* the author remarks that the IWW was considered in its day 'as little better than a rabble, and its members as no better than work-shy tramps. But they were much more than a rabble or a mob. They were usually decent working men, more perceptive and spirited than most, who revolted against intolerable working and living conditions; migrants unable to find permanent jobs using the only weapons they had at hand to assert the dignity of their labor.'

* *We Shall Be All*, by Melvyn Dubovsky, Quadrangle Books, 1969.

A second problem for Connolly was a business slump that took place in the autumn of 1907. It led him to remark that the typical American institution was the bread line. A third problem was the refusal of many members of the American Federation of Labor to work with the Wobblies. When steel-erectors, bronze workers, and carpenters were organized into IWW Local 95, they were able for a time to use an AFL hall for their meetings, but this permission was eventually withdrawn. Connolly obtained a hearing before the AFL union that controlled the hall, but received no satisfaction. When the trolley-car workers in Yonkers struck, Connolly made a bid to assume leadership. He and the organizer of the AFL teamsters union both addressed the strikers. Because, in Connolly's words, the electricians and engineers had taken 'a firm grip on their union cards, and scabbed' on the trolley-car workers, he urged the latter to besiege them in their homes. If the electricians and engineers joined the strike, it could be won. The representative of the teamsters delivered a long invective against the IWW, to which Connolly replied measure for measure. Again the AFL won, and the following day the workers went back to work.

Even within the IWW itself, old craft traditions could linger. For example, Connolly discovered that a branch affiliated to Local 95 was exacting an 'examination fee' of three dollars for all new members. The workers were divided into three grades, with different rates of pay. When Connolly ordered an investigation, branch officials destroyed the books.

In addition to all his other activities, Connolly was active in defending a man named Preston who was charged with murder 'for shooting a hoodlum who drew a gun on him while he was picketing'. On 30 November 1907, Connolly called a conference of working-class organizations at his office at 60 Cooper Square, and established a defence organization. The green banner of the Irish Socialist Federation played its part in the ensuing campaign.

The year 1907 ended with the welcome receipt of a sixteen-page letter from William O'Brien, telling Connolly all that he had longed to know about the destiny of the Irish Socialist Republican Party and its individual members. O'Brien said the present Socialist Party of Ireland was formed in March 1904 by a fusion of the ISRP and the Socialist Labour Party. Once the new party was launched, it held 'some of the most successful propaganda meetings I have ever seen. We enrolled 20 new members in the first 3 months . . . In the following

November we arranged a debate with the Trinity College Philosophical Society; and Brady, Lyng, Loughran and myself as the Party speakers met with a very good reception from the students.'

O'Brien then recounted that Stewart and McLoughlin were expelled for supporting the candidature to the city government of a reactionary named Nannetti; 'Arnall was also thrown overboard for speaking in support of John Burns in London during the General Election. G. B. Shaw and himself were the only socialists that spoke in favour of Burns' candidature.'

O'Brien then described what had happened to each member. He considered it remarkable that Deering, Creede and several others had dropped out of the movement when the amalgamation of the two parties took place. 'Though very active while the division lasted, as soon as a united Party was secured, they seemed to lose all further interest in Socialist propaganda.'

From these thumbnail biographies, one is again reminded of the youth of the original members of the ISRP and of their native abilities. 'Peter Dolan is now a country publican, and an organiser for the Town Tenants League. John Shiels is Master of Naas workhouse.' Of the Cork branch, 'Horgan is a Professor in Ballinasloe College. Gallagher is an M.A. and passed an exam for the Research Dept. of the Indian Government, and is now stationed in the Malay Peninsula. Tobin is in one of the South American Republics. Cody is Editor of the "Cork Trades and Labour Journal", organ of the Trades Council.' O'Lyhane was 'now admitted to be one of the finest Socialist propagandists in England'.

O'Brien wrote: 'The Party is still confined in its activity to Dublin, but we have hopes of extending it in the near future,' despite gains being made by the Independent Labour Party. 'They are to bring over a bevy of M.P.s, including Hardie, Ramsay MacDonald, Pete Curran, and Victor Grayson to speak for them, and consider that we are already wiped out.' In the middle of this paragraph, he referred for the first time to a movement and a man destined to have profound consequences on the life of both O'Brien and Connolly. Unaware of the future, O'Brien mentioned 'the big Belfast strike of Dockers and Coal-carriers which you will doubtless have read of . . . The prime mover is the Dockers' Organiser—James Larkin—who was in charge of the strike in Belfast, and is now organising the Dublin Dockers. He is a Liverpool I.L.P. man, and tells me he knows you.' Larkin had never met Connolly; this kind of inaccurate talk was one of the factors that eventually made O'Brien a deadly enemy of Larkin's, and was to make miserable Connolly's life as one of Larkin's lieutenants.

In another passage, O'Brien noted that 'The Sinn Fein Policy is making considerable progress just at present, more by reason of the helpless position of Redmond & Co. than of any inherent virtues of its own. They held a big meeting in London a few weeks ago, and Con O'Lyhane created consternation at it by attempting to move an amendment to the official resolution.' O'Brien said that the Sinn Fein now had fourteen officials in the Dublin city government, of whom the most important were Aldermen Kelly and Cole, and Councillor P. T. Daly. This was the same Daly who, almost ten years before, had set type for the first issue of the *Workers' Republic*.

XII

1908

THE FIRST issue of *The Harp*, organ of the Irish Socialist Federation, appeared shortly after Christmas 1907 but was dated January 1908. It had twelve pages and carried as its sub-title a quotation from the Jesuits: 'In things essential, unity; in things doubtful, diversity; in all things charity.' A yearly subscription cost fifty cents.

The editorial in the first issue urged American socialists to be more solicitous about finding points they had in common and not exaggerate the points on which they differed. Had they followed this prescription, a great socialist party operating democratically might have been built long before in America. In an obvious reference to such leaders as De Leon, he jibed at those who would 'prefer a party of ten sycophants to a million who could think for themselves'.

In this and succeeding issues Connolly carefully avoided any appearance of entering into IWW–Socialist Party–Socialist Labor Party controversies. He was still known as a SLP member, and as such was bound not to publish a political magazine without the party's sanction. He did not wish to lose any SLP readers by going counter to SLP doctrine. In the outcome he avoided American issues so well that some of his American readers became dissatisfied because of the heavy stress on Irish affairs.

The owner and publisher of *The Harp* was a professional printer named J. E. C. Donnelly, originally from Donegal, who had been associated ten years before with the publication of Connolly's first work, '*98 Readings*. Donnelly's printing firm and *The Harp*'s address were both at 749 Third Avenue, New York City, between 40th and 47th Streets. From the correspondence between him and Connolly, it would appear that he took a deep and sincere interest in seeing that the paper was printed and delivered on time to those places where

Connolly spoke, and that he conducted matters in a businesslike manner. Unfortunately, his financial resources were limited; there were several months when *The Harp* failed to sound.

Connolly distributed the paper in any way he could. 'It was a pathetic sight,' writes Elizabeth Flynn, 'to see him standing, poorly clad, at the door of Cooper Union or some other East Side hall, selling his little paper. None of the prosperous professional Irish, who shouted their admiration for him after his death lent him a helping hand at that time. He had no false pride and encouraged others to do these Jimmy Higgins tasks by setting them an example.' It is doubtful if Connolly, then or later, ever felt 'pathetic'; he did feel abused and ignored by the white-collar opportunists and megalomaniacs who held leadership positions in the socialist groups, but he felt also that history would vindicate his principles and that it was an honour to be able to spread these principles abroad.

Early in 1908, to speed the course of history and to assist IWW recruiting by explaining industrial unionism, Connolly founded some IWW 'propaganda leagues'. De Leon promptly protested this action to Connolly's employer, the IWW outfit called the New York Industrial Council. De Leon demanded the immediate dissolution of the leagues and the dismissal of Connolly from his post as organizer. He termed Connolly a 'police spy', an insult no trade-union organizer could overlook. Connolly responded by lodging a complaint with De Leon's local and demanding his expulsion from the IWW for slandering one of its officials. Since neither IWW body took action, De Leon and Connolly both appealed to the national convention scheduled for September.

In a speech at McMahon Hall where Connolly proposed the formation of the propaganda leagues, Connolly described the revolution of working-class movements from its Luddite beginnings, and concluded that the most hopeful augury of the future was that trade unionism was falling into the hands of 'men actually engaged in the work of trade union organization . . . and not in the theories of any political party'. This speech was published in the Industrial Union Bulletin and is now available in the pamphlet, *The Axe to the Root*.

In the April 1908 issue of *The Harp*, Connolly envisaged the workers as seizing the organized industries through their economic organizations; the conquest of political power would come second. He went so far as to deny that political parties, in the world of the future, would have any usefulness at all. He wrote: 'Under socialism, states, territories or provinces will exist only as geographical expressions and have no existence as sources of governmental power, though they may be seats of administrative bodies ... the administrative force of the Socialist Republic of the future will function through unions industrially organized.'

This comes close to an expression of pure syndicalism—that form of trade unionism 'which aims at the possession of the means of production and distribution, and ultimately at the control of society, by the federated bodies of industrial workers'. In fact, Connolly readily described himself as a syndicalist during this period, but in his letters to Matheson he indicated that there was still room in his mind for political action. In April 1908, he put it this way:

If I were in your place I would insist upon the paramount importance of the *economic* organisation. But I would also insist that while that economic organisation is still gathering its forces, is still in the initial stages of its formation, it is good policy to encourage the formation of volunteer forces to wage war upon the political society of capitalism. The stronger the volunteer force (the SLP) and the better directed its attacks, the easier will be the work of the regular army (the economic organisation) when it moves up for the final actions.

In an odd way, the strength of his belief in the Industrial Workers of the World made it easier for him to drift towards acceptance of the Socialist Party, whose 'reformism' and opportunism he had attacked so long and so bitterly. These flaws would not matter in the long run, since the SP would eventually be absorbed into a new political party that the IWW was destined to establish. Other factors influenced Connolly. As one who prided himself on being a pragmatic, not a theoretical, socialist, he could not ignore certain events which seemed to indicate that the Socialist Party was the party of the future: the successful launching in May of the *New York Evening Call*, a socialist daily which proved as lively and popular as the *People* was dead and airless; and the sending of a railway train across America to boost Debs for president. Nor could he help being pleased by the willingness of the Socialist Party to allow him to air his opinions within it, even to the extent of setting up a special literature stand for displaying *The Harp* when the Party held its national meeting in the spring.

Still Connolly hesitated. The Socialist Party of America contained, after all, many reformists of a type he had known only too well in Europe. Finally deciding that the Irish Socialist Federation could not stand aside from the presidential contest of 1908, he published in *The Call* a 'Manifesto to Irish Wage-Slaves', urging them to join the party which tolerated the greater freedom of opinion. He argued that 'a political party must be catholic enough to tolerate differences of opinion among its adherents, provided they unite to face the common enemy'. Social revolution, he maintained, 'depends in the last analysis upon the growth of class-consciousness . . . and therefore the chief task of the socialist political party is to educate . . . by clearing the minds of the members, not by a process of weeding out'. Finally, he contended that 'since the political body does not accomplish the revolution, but only leads the attack on the political citadel of capitalism, there no longer exists danger in the unclearness of its membership'. In other words, social revolution proceeded basically from economic organizations; therefore, the Augean stable of political confusion did not need to be cleansed absolutely. Syndicalism and socialist politics could thus be made to live together.

In a letter dated 7 May 1908, Connolly told Matheson, almost casually, that 'I left the SLP two weeks ago'. But his entrance into the Socialist Party required more explanation, and he gave it in his letter of 27 September.

Now if before joining the S. P. I had to accept the compromising elements, and their political faith, I could never have joined it. But it is not necessary to do so. In the S. P. there are revolutionary, clear cut elements . . . and there are also compromising elements. I have read S. P. papers which branded Berger, Carl Thompson, *et al.* as tricksters, and compromisers, and other papers which sneered at their opponents as 'impossibilists', but both are loyal members of the party, and fight out their differences at their Conventions. Neither attempt to expel the other. Now it was a long time before I could believe this, but at last I made up my mind to join because I felt it was better to be one of the revolutionary minority inside the party than a mere discontented grumbler out of political life entirely. I would rather have the I. W. W. undertake *both* political and economic activity now, but as the great majority of the workers in the movement are against me in that matter I do not propose to make my desires a stumbling block in the way of co-operation with my fellow-revolutionists.

In writing for Irishmen, Connolly did not need to discuss such abstruse matters. To readers of *The Harp*, he maintained that the overriding need was for an independent republic, 'the only purely political change in Ireland worth crossing the street for'. He warned the Irish socialist against only two major dangers: one was that of isolating himself from other Irishmen, the other was that of submitting to clerical interference in secular (that is, economic or political) affairs.

Concerning the first point, he wrote:

The first result of the winning to socialism of a worker of the Irish race should be that he should become . . . a channel for conveying the socialist message to others of his race.

But this he could only do as long as his socialism did not cause him to raise barriers betwixt himself and his fellow countrymen and women, to renounce his connection with, or to abjure all ties of kinship or tradition that throughout the world makes the heart of one Celt go out to another, no matter how unknown. Yet this is precisely what their adoption of socialism has caused in the great majority of cases among Irishmen.

Led away by a foolishly sentimental misinterpretation of the socialist doctrine of universal brotherhood, or internationalism, they generally began by dropping out of all the Irish societies they were affiliated with, no matter how righteous their objects were, and ended by ceasing to mix in Irish gatherings or to maintain Irish connections. The results upon the minds of their fellow-countrymen were as might be expected . . .

We propose to show all the workers of our fighting race that socialism will make them better fighters for freedom without being less Irish.

In essence, Connolly's socialism was national in form, but international in substance. Religious scruples against socialism he was able to discuss with the ease of one born in the fold. He wrote:

To the average non-Socialist Irishman the idea of belonging to an international political party is unthinkable, is obnoxious, and he feels that if he did, all the roots of his Irish nature would be dug up. Of course, he generally belongs to a church—the Roman Catholic Church—which is the most international institution in existence. That does not occur to him as atrocious. In fact he is rather proud than otherwise that the Church is spread throughout the entire world, that it overleaps the barriers of civilization, penetrating into the depths of savagedom, and ignores all considerations of race, colour or nationality ... But although he would lay down his life for a Church which he boasts of as 'Catholic' or universal he turns with a shudder from an economic or political movement which has the same characteristics.

In another issue of *The Harp* he scoffed at the prediction that the final conflict would be between the forces of socialism and those of the Catholic Church.

As a matter of fact the Catholic Church always accepts the established order, even if it has warred upon those who had striven to establish such order.

To use a homely adage the Church 'does not put all her eggs in one basket', and the man who imagines that in the supreme hour of the proletarian struggle for victory the Church will definitely line up with the forces of capitalism, and pledge her very existence as a Church upon the hazardous chance of the capitalists winning, simply does not understand the first thing about the policy of the Church in the social or political revolutions of the past. Just as in Ireland the Church denounced every Irish revolutionary movement in its day of activity, as in 1798, 1848 and 1867, and yet allowed its priests to deliver speeches in eulogy of the active spirits of those movements a generation afterwards, so in the future the Church, which has its hands close upon the pulse of human society, when it realises that the cause of capitalism is a lost cause it will find excuse enough to allow freedom of speech and expression to those lowly priests whose socialist declarations it will then use to cover and hide the absolute anti-socialism of the Roman Propaganda. When that day comes the Papal Encyclical against socialism will be conveniently forgotten by the Papal historians, and the socialist utterances, of the von Kettelers, the McGlynns, and McGradys will be heralded forth and the communistic utterances of the early fathers as proofs of Catholic sympathy with progressive ideas.

In *The Harp* Connolly preached adamantly the doctrine that a man had the right to be an Irish patriot, a Roman Catholic, and a socialist or Marxist, without interference from British imperialists, Irish

Home Rulers, socialist internationalists, priests, or any other groups. He wanted no one to step beyond the line, the socialist not to meddle with theology, the priest not to interfere in politics. When Cardinal Logue, on a visit to New York in May 1908, pledged support for Irish autonomy 'consistent with the unity of the British Empire', Connolly refused to join others in congratulating him, firmly stating that 'he stepped out of place to interfere in secular matters'.

In view of the tiny amounts of money and forces expended, the monthly began to show a modicum of 'success'. A volunteer staff appeared to post issues to the growing number of subscribers throughout the US. The *Gaelic American*, a leading Irish-American newspaper, quoted from it, and Catholic periodicals offered exchange arrangements.

Connolly decided to make a lecture tour on behalf of *The Harp*. He was encouraged by its growing circulation outside of New York, and prodded by Donnelly, who told him that the monthly was incurring a loss which could be met only by increased circulation. An advertisement was printed which stated Connolly was available for lectures, and a few dates were obtained. Most of them were from Socialist Party branches.

A more important factor in his decision to make a tour was the decline in IWW recruiting. The depression was still on, unemployment was high, and IWW members, the organization of the oppressed and victimized, were the first to be fired. Connolly's salary of $18 a week was just not to be found, partly because the Socialist Labor Party had withdrawn its support. Other considerations were the opportunity to take part in the 'Debs for President' campaign, and to attend the Chicago convention of the IWW at the end of his trip. Connolly closed his office, forcing the Irish Socialist Federation to transfer its meetings to the Murray Hill Social Club, and went on tour.

During July, August and September 1908 he visited many cities in New England, Pennsylvania, upper New York State, and finally Detroit and Chicago. According to custom, he usually stayed at the homes of sympathizers, not at hotels. John D. Williams, with whom he stayed in Malden, Massachusetts, recalls him as a quiet, knowledgeable man whose mission met with too little success. Members of the Socialist Labor Party were resentful, and members of the Socialist Party were suspicious. Connolly received his best reception in Boston.

The fourth annual IWW convention was the first and only one Connolly ever attended. Convened in Chicago on 21 September 1908 it was rich in Wobbly sentiment and anarchist fervour, but completely without funds. There was no money to pay a stenographer to take down the minutes; and all delegates met their own travelling and living expenses.

Connolly's position was no different. He was able to get to the convention only because H. Traurig, a long-suffering official of the New York Industrial District Council, came up with the money at the last minute. He wrote to Connolly on 16 September:

About an hour ago I sent you a letter replying to your postal of the 15th inst.
I didn't have any money then hence I sent none. But I'm in Brooklyn now and I've met a friend from whom I've borrowed a five spot which I enclose.
Now the situation is this.
The $8.00 I sent you was from the League's treasury. The $5.00 bill which followed I advanced personally, and this, the enclosed $5.00 I am again advancing. That makes $10.00 in all that I have advanced, and I don't know I'll ever get this money back. I don't mind loosing $5.00 but I don't care to loose $10.00. Am therefore sending you the $5.00 extra with the understanding that if the League doesn't return it, that you will. Am adding this $8.00 to the $10.00 you already owe me. Hope this will be satisfactory to you. It will at least help to carry you to Chicago where you can keep to the dates you have made arrangements for.
Am making an attempt to raise money. It's tough business however. I nevertheless hope you'll not forget to drop me a line occassionally regarding the doings of the Convention. You owe me now receipts amounting to $18.00. Drop me a line immediately straightening out this tangle, and let me know whether youre on your way to Chicago.

Letters like this were only too common among those Connolly received. It appears that, in this case at least, Connolly managed to meet his obligations. The proof consists of the absence of any mention of financial obligations in a later letter by Traurig which asks Connolly to deliver a lecture at Brevoort Hall on 24 January 1909.

This IWW convention is famed as the one attended by hordes of migrant workers from the west who, in their desire to keep 'politics' from being forced down their throats, got to Chicago by stealing rides on freight cars. The convention's first action was to move to debar

De Leon from participating in the proceedings on the grounds that he was not a wage worker and therefore ineligible for membership. His credentials were further challenged because he represented an office workers' union instead of the printing and publishing local which, as editor of the *People*, he should have joined. After four days of wrangling, the convention ruled that he could not be seated. De Leon gave a spirited defence of his position, which included remarks about Connolly, but the delegates were not moved.

Writing from the convention hall on 27 September, Connolly wrote to his friend Matheson:

> Our side were in control from the first. Francis, De Leon's chief tool in New York, was thrown out by 42 to 7 for his pernicious activity in the New York District Council.
> De Leon himself was thrown out by 40 votes to 21 ... on the technical point that although he was engaged in the printing trade as editor of a paper he refused to join the printers I.W.W. local, but stayed in a local of store and office workers. But he shifted the discussion on to the proper grounds of the dispute of the past year and fought it out on that, and on that was defeated. St. John gave him the worst drubbing ever I saw a man get.

In a more thoughtful letter concerning the convention, written after the November 1908 elections in the US, he told Matheson that he would not term 'slum proletarians' those men

> who gave up their work and in order to save expense to their locals risked their lives jumping on trains and beating their way half across a continent to attend a convention in the interest of the working class ... Nor yet were they anti-political, as a whole. They held that the reference to political action in the old preamble had tended to confuse the workers by all sorts of suppositions as to what political party they favoured, and that it was best to cast that reference out ... I would have been as well pleased had the old preamble stood, but I do know that the wording of the old preamble did cause confusion.

In *The Harp* Connolly applauded the new preamble without reservation, but when asked if he approved its repudiation of political action, he laughingly replied, 'It will be impossible to prevent the workers taking it.'

There was little doubt about the convention's opinion of Connolly. His credentials were accepted, and his report on the propaganda leagues was approved, with accompanying congratulations. His appeal against the refusal of Local 58 to expel De Leon was upheld at first, but then referred back to the local.

Having irrevocably lost control of the IWW, De Leon demanded the return of the money paid by the Socialist Trades and Labor Alliance to publish the Industrial Union Bulletin. After the appearance of a few more issues, the paper succumbed. De Leon then led his much-diminished union locals out of the IWW. It was a sad ending; De Leon deserved a better fate. Connolly's sympathy for the fallen Marxist Pope was minimal. In his opinion the departure of the Socialist Trades and Labor Alliance locals would only leave the IWW 'free to progress and build up a revolutionary organisation of *workers*. Not an annexe to a political party.'

He thought that Debs' vote of a million was 'an exceedingly good showing. Debs talked good Industrial Unionism in every large centre he was in.'

He was delighted that the Socialist Labor Party had pulled so few votes in its campaign against Hillquit,

when the latter was engaged in fighting to wrest a seat from Tammany Hall. And bear in mind that the De Leon candidature involved drawing all the S.L.P. activities from all over New York into his own district. With what result? . . . the vote fell from over 5,000 to less than 2,000. Less than 2,000 in a city of 4,000,000 inhabitants where practically every male adult had the opportunity to cast a vote! How could it be otherwise when the very few men they did have were withdrawn from the work of attacking capitalism to the work of knifing Hillquit. Let Hillquit be what he may, and I do not know him at all, he was at least the representative of Socialism fighting Capitalism.

Connolly went so far as to say:

The belief is slowly growing in my mind that Dan has fooled me all along, and that he really is purposely doing the work of the capitalist class. It is hard to believe that any Socialist really thinks that the immigration question is serious enough to justify a Socialist in doing the dirty work of the capitalist class as De Leon has done in his campaign against Hillquit . . .

While in Chicago, Connolly established a branch of the Irish Socialist Federation. What was more important, through its secretary, Bernard MacMahon, he met the Kerrs, publishers of the *International Socialist Review* and of many socialist tracts. They offered to republish Connolly's articles on industrial unionism. Thus *Socialism Made Easy* appeared. It contained four expository articles, prefaced by 'Talking Points' extracted from the *Workers' Republic*.

This was the first pamphlet from which Connolly earned any money. A model of simple argument for the man in the factory, it made an immediate impact and spread far afield. In May 1910 Tom Mann, then in Australia, greeted it enthusiastically; and a section of the pamphlet was incorporated in the 1911 Year Book of the Australian 'One Big Union' movement. Distributed widely in Britain, the pamphlet helped to strengthen the idea of class struggle into trade unions and the Independent Labour Party, and was still being reprinted in Ireland in the thirties.

On his return to New York, Connolly found the Irish Socialist Federation without a secretary. Faithful Jack Lyng had succumbed to malaria. A man named Brady, who had written a pamphlet on the history of socialism in Ireland and had recently arrived from that country, became national secretary temporarily; Elizabeth Gurley Flynn's younger sister Kathleen, fifteen years old, became New York secretary. Elizabeth puts it, 'Connolly was strong for encouraging "the young people".' Connolly's own daughter Nora also began to help. So the work of the Irish Socialist Federation continued throughout the winter of 1908–09 with Quinlan, Walsh, O'Shaughnessy, Brady, Shanahan and Connolly speaking regularly in New York every Saturday; and with extensive mailings of *The Harp* and letters to Irish people residing in various countries.

Connolly remained on the move. One Sunday in December 1908 he spoke at Faneuil Hall in Boston upon invitation of the local branch of the Irish Socialist Federation. The following week he repeated the speech in New York, with William Mailley, manager of *The Call* and a member of the ISF, acting as chairman. At Christmastime, Brady relinquished the post of secretary. It seemed to be an auspicious time to make a move that Connolly had been contemplating for some months—that of moving the headquarters of the Irish Socialist Federation from New York to Chicago. Generally speaking, the Federation met with more favour in the west than in the east (perhaps it would be better to say it met with less resistance); prejudice against the Irish was less virulent, and branches of the Socialist Party more militant.

All told, 1908 had been a better year for Connolly than most. He had bested Daniel De Leon; had established an Irish Socialist organization in the US, complete with its own magazine; would soon have a pamphlet printed by Charles H. Kerr & Company, 'A Socialist publishing house owned co-operatively by over 2000 Socialist locals and individuals'; and was notified in December by J. Mahlon Barnes, national secretary of the Socialist Party, that he had been nominated as a candidate for membership to the Party's national executive committee. To people outside the working-class movement, these might seem trivial accomplishments and honours. To Connolly, who considered nothing important except the movement, these were great accomplishments in the US. But his desire to return to Ireland would not be assuaged.

Early in April he had received a letter from John Mulray, now back in Ireland, saying that (original punctuation):

we are greatly in need of you here it is a remarkable fact that while Ireland was never more ripe for Socialism than it is now the Party is nearly wiped out it was very strong, we are in great need of a good man to Infuse energy into the Members. the members are dropping away the Party is getting weaker some of the members asked me to ask you that if there was any Possibility of getting you to come over to live here if the members would Put you up in some Business would you be in favour of it

On 8 April 1908, Connolly passed on to Matheson this far-from-concrete information, and reminded him that he too had suggested that 'it would be good if I could get home. Well, you people are all contributing to make me homesick. I wrote to my Dublin comrade, saying that I had all the will and all the desire in the world to get home out of this cursed country, but I can't. The District Council owes me over 80 dollars back salary. I am now off the pay roll, and the misery and hunger now in New York are dreadful. I am simply frightened at the immediate outlook for the family and myself. How then get home.'

He implored Matheson:

Now I want to ask you is there anything in it? Give me your
opinion on this matter, so that I may either finally abandon hope of
repatriating myself, or else get something to hope for . . . I have a
hunger to get back amongst the parties I disrupted. If you take any
interest in this matter and care to write to my Dublin correspondent
his name and address is John Mulray 55 Jones Road, Dublin. But
be sure and write to me at your earliest, and let me know your
opinion as to its feasibility and desirability, and be plain. Do not be
afraid that the truth will hurt my feelings, or rather tell it, whether
it does or not.

Not long after that, he told the famous labour agitator Mother Jones
that he was tired of America and was awaiting an opportunity to return
to Ireland.

Connolly could see that new forces were at work in Ireland—the
revival of the Gaelic language and athletic games, the attempts to
create a Celtic literature, Larkinism, Sinn Fein (economic self-reliance)
—but could not determine which of them he could use to accomplish
his return to Ireland. He even knew many of the people involved—
Arthur Griffith, Yeats, W. P. Ryan, Standish O'Grady, Douglas
Hyde, and his old comrades William O'Brien, Tom Lyng and Maud
Gonne. When Maud wrote him about her separation from John
MacBride, Connolly replied, 'I hope you will now be Maud Gonne
again.' She never was, quite. Other names were new to him: youngsters named Padraic Pearse, Eamonn Ceannt, Sean MacDermott.

It seemed to Connolly that Griffith's Sinn Fein movement was
making the most progress. It was natural for him to ask: Could Irish
socialists join Sinn Fein with the principle of national self-reliance as
the common ground?

Connolly discussed this question in the January 1909 issue of
W. P. Ryan's *Nation*. Many of the Dublin radicals and socialists could
not accept Griffith's obvious lack of interest in the working class; they
knew that often the most vocal nationalists and Sinn Feiners were
'merciless grinders of the faces of the poor'; they rejected the concept
of national independence as a distraction from socialist tasks. In Belfast,
many who had learned socialism in the struggle against the shipyard
owners felt that a green flag was no substitute for higher wages; they

could see no connection between national independence and socialism. Connolly's suggestion was that all socialist sections should meet in conference and seek a common platform. From this base they could work out a decision on their attitude towards Sinn Fein.

XIII

1909

AFTER THE US elections of 1908 a one-page leaflet was issued to Socialist Party branches informing them that the results of the election demonstrated 'that the slow and systematic education of the working class between campaigns counts for more than any amount of hurrah work when the fervour of the campaign is on'; and that Comrade Connolly, the editor of *The Harp*, was available to provide this type of education. He would speak at any branch meeting for '$5.00 flat per lecture'.

The leaflet, signed by 'Manager, The Harp'—Donnelly, supposedly —said that Connolly had toured many states during the recent campaign, and that Socialist Party national headquarters had received from these states 'the most glowing reports of his abilities, and especially of his tactfulness in dealing with such delicate questions as religion. He makes a specialty of appealing to the Irish and the success of his paper, in that respect, has been sorrowfully admitted by capitalistic Catholic papers throughout the country. He is, however, equally entertaining and convincing on the broad question of Socialism in general.'

Appended were notices from newspapers regarding Connolly's speeches on his previous trip. The *Cleveland Plain Dealer* called him 'A forceful speaker—Well versed in the history and literature of his country, and in speaking draws from an abundant store of knowledge gained both from great study and wide experience.' The *Salt Lake City Tribune* called him 'An eloquent Irishman', and the *Boston Herald*, 'A man of pleasing personality. His manner is that of an orator and his language that of a scholar.' *Detroit Today* said that he gave 'a vivid, forceful, eloquent exposition of Socialism, and a well fortified defense of its principles . . . As he warms up to his subject, his delivery grows more animated until it fairly scintillates with eloquence.'

The appeal had limited results, and so did a letter sent out to Socialist Party branches by Comrade McMahon, of Chicago. But together they may have moved the national secretary of the SP, J. Mahlon Barnes, to take a hand. On 8 April 1919, he mailed out letters to the SP secretaries of New Jersey, Pennsylvania, Ohio, Indiana and Illinois, asking whether lecture assignments could be obtained for Connolly in those states. Barnes offered two alternative: one, that the secretaries themselves arrange for Connolly's visits to the locals within their states, beginning in May; two, that the national headquarters be given the right to seek assignments directly from the local branches. The states preferred the latter course.

Consequently, on 14 April, Barnes sent out letters to several hundred locals giving a brief biography of Connolly, and the price for his lectures—$5 for one meeting or $18 for three, 'the National Office furnishing advertising matter, free of cost'. Connolly was described as former editor of the *Workers' Republic* in Dublin, leader of the anti-Jubilee demonstration of 1897, Socialist candidate in the municipal elections in Dublin in 1902 and 1903, and editor in the US of *The Harp*. Barnes noted that Comrade Connolly was 'perhaps better fitted' than any other man they had to break down the notorious prejudice of Irish Catholics against socialism.

Within a few months matters had developed so far that Connolly was made one of the Socialist Party's six national organizers, with a salary of $21 a week, plus reimbursement of train fares and whatever profit he made from the pamphlets and books he sold at his lectures. His wages were paid meticulously, so that Connolly was relatively prosperous during his final year in the US.

The action of the Socialist Party headquarters in Chicago in hiring Connolly says much about its tolerance and courage. It should be remembered that Connolly was the object of hostility from many quarters; to the Socialist Labor Party he was a Jesuit and a renegade; to many Socialist Party members he was a syndicalist, a Wobbly; to the Wobblies he was too much of a socialist; to the Roman Catholic Irish he was an atheistic socialist; and to almost all left-wingers he was a curiosity—a man who wanted to free Ireland from British rule. It was typical of his status that on May Day 1908 he and his Irish Socialist Federation were not permitted by the New York section of the Socialist Party to march in the afternoon parade. A month later he was working for the Party's national headquarters.

In May 1909 Connolly left New York for a nation-wide tour, and did not return for eleven months. It was the usual rough schedule. After travelling all day, Connolly would address a meeting in the evening, and probably sit up half the night discussing ways of improving the work of the branch and discussing politics with his hosts and visitors. Nevertheless, he should have been content. He had achieved a degree of financial security, and was doing the work he wanted to do. He was proud of his pamphlet, *Socialism Made Easy*. Writing to Matheson from Crooksville, Ohio, on 10 June 1909: 'It is the first pamphlet advocating industrial unionism issued by a Socialist Party publishing house. I framed it up with that end in view, and was successful. It is on sale now all over America, in the meetings of the Socialist Party. I have sold about 500 myself from S.P. platforms.'

Though his feud with De Leon had taken its toll, he had achieved a certain degree of peace and philosophical certainty. To Matheson's statement that he was still obsessed by Dan, Connolly wrote:

> If you had been getting the *Harp* you would have known better. I never mention his party, and have not read a copy of his paper for about 10 months. My opinion is that he is not in the Labour movement, and I am not interested in him. I know or believe that the S.L.P. will continue to exist in name (in reality as an adjunct to the Labor News Publishing Co.) and that the large profits of the jobbing plant will probably keep alive the paper to scatter venom and poison broadcast, but that does not make Dan's outfit a part of the Labour movement.

Concerning the results of the work done by himself, De Leon, and Matheson during the past years, he had concluded

> that while our position is absolutely sound in theory, and might be sound in practice if adopted by men of large outlook, yet its practical immediate effects have been the generation of a number of sectarians, narrow-minded doctrinaires, who have erected Socialism into a cult with rigid formulas which one must observe or be damned. From whence I draw the further conclusion that our position . . . needs the corrective of association with Socialists of a less advanced type. In short, I believe that our proper position is in the general Socialist, or rather Labour movement, as friendly critics and helpers, rather than in a separate organisation as hostile critics and enemies. It is a bitter lesson to learn, but it is better to learn it than to persist

to the end in endeavouring to make statesmanlike Socialists out of a covenanting cliquer—with apologies to the covenanters.

Still, he could not be happy because 'most any one can do the work I am doing here, but . . . there is work to be done in Ireland I can do better than most any one'.

Just as he was beginning his travels, he was startled by a communication from William O'Brien asking him what salary he would require if he became editor of a weekly paper to be issued by the Dublin Trades and Labour Council. From Philadelphia he cabled a two-word message to O'Brien: 'Fifty shillings.' On the following day, 24 May, he wrote O'Brien that he had little hope of getting the position—that he had cabled as he did

more as a means of showing you that I am more than willing to be repatriated (I am extremely desirous for that end) than with any belief that you had found a means. I may confess to you that I regard my emigration to America as the great mistake of my life, and . . . I have never ceased to regret it.

From his studies of Ireland at a distance, he had become convinced that conditions were favourable for a forward move.

That thought has filled me with a burning desire to get back, but as an individual the position was hopeless. My family are growing, and their needs are pressing . . . If by any possibility you get that job for me, the task of raising the money for the passage would fall entirely upon the comrades in Ireland.

Also . . . owing to the terrible accident which blighted our last separation my wife would never consent to make the trip without me accompanying her. So that *if I go to Ireland I have to bring my family along with me*. To do that would require about 200 dollars, £40, and I do not see how in Heaven that money is to be raised.

He suggested, with bitter humour, that if the comrades could break into the Bank of Ireland when the cashier was not looking, and send him the passage money, he would set out for Ireland in a week or two. He concluded: 'I am dying to go to Ireland, but how? If you can answer that question future generations (of little Connollys) will rise up and call you blessed.'

Six weeks later, after he had learned that P. T. Daly had got the job as editor, Connolly was again chewing over the subject:

Well, you say in your letter that you hope the matter 'has not knocked me about in any way'. Well, it has. It has upset me entirely. It has aroused the Call of Erin in my blood until I am always dreaming of Ireland, dreaming of going back to the fight at home.

He now thought that, by saving the money from his tour, he could raise the passage money.

But I do not see my way to live after I once more set foot on Irish soil. And that part of the problem is the hardest, as of course I could not go into the Dublin slums again to live; one experience of that is enough in a life-time. My children are now growing up, and it is part of my creed that when I have climbed any part of the ladder towards social comfort I must never descend it again . . .

He knew that he would be lucky if he could get in Ireland half his present salary, but 'I am not satisfied here, have not near the enthusiasm for the fight that I had in Ireland, and want to get amongst a people with whom I feel I have more in common'.

In the same letter he wrote: 'We have at least the consolation that a much worse man than Daly might easily have got the place—one less susceptible to advanced ideas.' He was moved to learn that Tom Lyng 'appeared as my representative. It reminded me of the many fights in which Tom and I stood shoulder to shoulder before our cursed (Irish) hot-headedness made us mistake and misrepresent each other.'

He asked O'Brien if he knew a Miss Helena Molony. She had written him: 'I only wish it was in Ireland that you were publishing the "Harp". There is a great, a *very*, *very* great need for a workers' Journal in Ireland. The Trade and Labour Journal will not supply it, I am afraid.' Connolly added that he too wished he were publishing *The Harp* in Ireland. In a final paragraph, he wrote: 'Tell Comrade Larkin that I believe his Union to be the most promising sign in Ireland, and that if things were properly handled on those lines the whole situation in Ireland might be revolutionised.'

In his response dated 27 August 1909, O'Brien agreed with Connolly that once passage money was raised the real difficulty was: 'How are you to live when you are here?' He also agreed that the time was ripe for a forward movement, and that Connolly could do good work if he were in Ireland.

Therefore in this, and subsequent, letters I want to discuss ways and means as to that end. I showed that portion of yr letter referring to the Transport Union to Larkin and mentioned that you were anxious to come to Ireland, but the difficulty was to get you a suitable job. He said that if the Cork strike turned out anyway well his Union might be able to offer you something but I know the Union is not (and will not, for some considerable time) be in a position to employ any organisers. At the same time I believe Larkin wd be glad to assist you in any way he cd, but he's been doing badly since the Dublin Strike last Dec., and his Union has fallen very low in numbers.

Commenting on efforts being made to unify Irish socialists from various organizations into one new, broadly based Socialist Party of Ireland, O'Brien wrote:

I think it possible to weld all these parties into one body and to double the present membership if there was a man with the necessary tact and ability in the country, and I know of no one who wd more likely succeed than yourself. For this reason I intend to do all I can to enable you to come back here . . . Will you give me an idea as to what you expect us to do? You say you can see yr way clear to get to Ireland, but you do not see how you are to exist when you get here. Well, it seems to me that it wd be possible for you to organise a party of 400 to 500 if you were some time in the country and that it wd be necessary to retain you as organiser, but the difficulty is to arrange matters at the start. Suppose we cd get a *reliable* guarantee to pay yr salary for 6 months dont you think by that time a permanent agreement cd be come to. I was thinking that if you cd keep 'The Harp' afloat and that you transferred it to Dublin when coming yourself it wd be a good idea . . .

O'Brien then advanced the idea that the Irish socialists should in the future steer clear of such alliances as they had had in the past with the Socialist Labour Party of Scotland and the US, and shape their propaganda and policy to suit the peculiar needs of Ireland without bothering what socialists in other countries thought of them. He ended by saying he did not know Miss Molony but would look her up.

Writing from Springfield, Missouri, on 12 September, Connolly sent his best wishes for the success of the new party, and urged members to 'realise that it is better that differences of opinion should be discussed within the party, rather than form a number of small parties in which to ventilate said differences'. He was pretty sure now that he could raise passage fare. Unlike the other SP national organizers, he was going to be kept on through the winter, travelling all the way to the Pacific Coast and back. Thus, the money that he would ordinarily have used to supplement the earnings of the winter months he could save and apply to the purchase of tickets to Ireland. 'Although it is the best job I ever had in my life, I am willing to resign it if I can get a living at a tradesman's wages in Ireland.'

On the other hand, 'how to live when I get back is another question. And unless I can see some way to satisfactorily settle that, I would scarcely venture my family upon the chance.' Referring to the time that he had transplanted himself and his family from Scotland to Ireland, he wrote: 'It makes me shudder even yet when I think of the hard grind of those poverty-stricken years, of the hunger and the wretchedness we endured to build up a party in Ireland. And you know the outcome.'

Having had some experience with 'guarantees', Connolly was sceptical as to whether they could be obtained but said nevertheless, 'go ahead. See what you can do.'

He agreed with O'Brien that 'the less we interest ourselves in what other Socialist parties think of us the better for the movement in Ireland'. He asked if he would find out whether Sheehy-Skeffington, whom O'Brien had mentioned as one of the members of the new Socialist Party, would be willing to submit his manuscript, *Labour in Irish History*, to a London publisher. Connolly said that most American publishers, being 'ridiculously conservative', would not touch it; Kerr & Co. of Chicago would take it, but had only a socialist public; another publisher who had offered to handle it was new and might not make a go of it.

On 3 October 1909, Connolly wrote that he had been considering O'Brien's suggestion about moving *The Harp* from the US to Ireland, and now thought he saw a way of doing it.

I have proposed to Donnelly that he turn the paper over to me, that

I will print it in Dublin in two editions, an Irish and an American, and turn the American over to him, he to collect and retain all the American subs, and deliver to American subscribers, and pay me for printing the American editions. By this means we would be saved all the trouble of attention to the American end of it, and the arrangement would last at least long enough to enable us to get the paper on its feet in Ireland.

He asked O'Brien to take an issue of the paper to some Dublin printer, find out how much he would charge for printing it, and send the data back to him immediately. He should also contact W. P. Ryan's *Irish Nation* for the same figures, and if the *Nation*'s figures were moderately close, it should be given the job. The next steps would be to fix a date for the first Dublin issue of *The Harp*, and to inform all socialist bodies of its transfer. He concluded:

You see I am proceeding upon the idea that I am going back to Dublin. Perhaps I am doomed to disappointment. It would break me up completely if I was.

Let me know how you have succeeded with your end of the negotiations. And tell me if . . . you are representing any number of the party members, or only speaking for yourself individually. You see I am grown cautious. I do not want my family to do any more starving.

Connolly was told, apparently, that O'Brien would handle the manuscript of *Labour in Irish History*, for he wrote on 20 October: 'Will send on M.S. as soon as it is out of the hand of the typewriter', meaning typist. But he complained that 'you say not one word about the other matter, my getting to Ireland. Have you abandoned it, or found out the S.P.I. was not sympathetic? *Please* let me know, as it will have a great effect upon my plans to know whether I am destined for exile or for Ireland.'

O'Brien responded on 4 November that it was out of the question for the Irish socialists, who were trying to meet the heavy expenses incidental to the start of their new party, to be of assistance in financing Connolly's return. In fact O'Brien had not dared to raise the question. However, he now intended to hold a meeting to discuss the project within the next fortnight and would let Connolly know the result without delay. Connolly had not yet received this letter, apparently, when he wrote to O'Brien on 19 November, from Durango, Colorado, that he had sent as a present to the Socialist Party of Ireland 100 copies each of his pamphlet *Socialism Made Easy* and his song book, *Songs of Freedom*, published by Donnelly the year before.

After two more weeks of travel in the deserts and mountains of the far west, Connolly could wait no longer. Ignorant of the growing caution of his Irish comrades towards the project, he addressed a letter on 1 December to the manager of the *Irish Nation*:

> I am forwarding copy for the January issue of 'The Harp'. Comrade O'Brien has probably told you that I have resolved to give you the contract of printing it. I believe that we can be mutually helpful to one another. Some one appointed by the Socialist Party of Ireland will furnish you with the rest of the copy, and will receive the printed copies from you and arrange for its publication [Connolly meant distribution] in Ireland.

It was an extraordinarily precipitate step for Connolly to take. He had received no information from O'Brien about how much it would cost to print the magazine, and had received no promise that the Socialist Party of Ireland would supply any copy, appoint a sub-editor, or indeed take any interest in the project whatsoever.

In the same letter he went on to give directions about the size of the paper, and told the manager

> Run Mrs. Green's letter on first page, typewriter type, 'Notes from America' in place where 'Harp Strings' usually appeared. And put in full instalment of 'Labour in Irish History'. (By the way, what do you think of my prospects of getting that published in book form in Ireland?)
>
> Consult sub-editor appointed by Socialist Party for any difficulty . . .
>
> If Socialist Party of Ireland resolve to accept paper as their official organ make insertion accordingly.

However, he must have had a few scruples for he added as a P.S.: 'Aint this an unique way of editing a paper—at 5000 miles distance?'
Connolly wrote to O'Brien from El Paso, Texas, on 6 December:

> This is to notify you that I have sent in share of the copy for January

Harp to the Nation office. I trust that in conformity with my suggestions in a previous letter you have been able to get someone to act as manager and sub-editor.

It was a long letter containing observations on varied subjects. He would be glad when the paper was out of the hands of Donnelly. 'His production of it was as irregular as that of the '98 Readings, which, you will remember, Dan and I got out "fortnightly" every six months.' He had never supposed that the business of arranging for his resettlement in Ireland would be easy, and cautioned O'Brien about 'guessing what were another man's thoughts'. It had caused enough trouble in the past. 'My *last* recollections of the Dublin comrades are not happy ones. Please do not revive them. I only know that I would rather work in Ireland than anywhere else, *for the cause*. Apart from the cause Ireland has no attractions for me.'

He then proceeded to describe some major changes he hoped to see in Ireland.

If anybody asks you about my editorial for January, if I am desiring to abolish the Unions at present existing, say No. My idea is that all the Unions in Ireland should combine to elect an Executive Board, that such Executive Board should issue one label for all unions, said label to bear the words 'Made in Ireland by trade-union labour', that the organizations thus formed should be grouped together according to industries, the executive board to be composed of delegates from such industrial groups, and that the questions of closer organisation, dues, initiation fees etc. should be left to be worked out within the organisation and voluntarily adopted by the individual unions. This is, I think, as far as we dare go in Ireland at the present time until the ideas of solidarity nurtured by such a process shall bear their fruit.

My suggestion that such an organisation could settle the question of imported material for buildings, glass windows for churches, etc. by refusing to handle them or transport them, is calculated to knock the feet from under the Sinn Fein Bourgeois element and to appeal to the working class followers of that cult. I would accept the card of every working man who came from England or elsewhere to *live* in Ireland—accept it without question and enrol him at once as a member. But I would counsel our members to refuse to work with any man sent from another country for the purpose of doing any

167

work that could be done by men idle in Ireland. This policy would be more international and class-conscious in the first case than any Irish or English trade union pursues to-day, and in the second case would be defended on the grounds stated, viz: the necessity of the Irish working class organisation controlling the Irish market. I believe you will appreciate the force of this point in exploiting the feeling for things Irish—we must use it, but in such a way as to prevent sweated labour employers in Ireland from taking advantage of it. Hence the words on the label—'by trade union labour'.

Blithely proceeding, Connolly sent O'Brien the text of an advertisement announcing the transfer of *The Harp* to Ireland; O'Brien was to submit it to a half-dozen labour and socialist journals in Britain, with a request for publication in exchange for an advertisement of the same size from the recipient journal. The announcement stated that *The Harp*, after being published in New York for two years, was being transferred to Dublin, effective 1 January 1910, with the same editor, James Connolly. 'Price one penny. Monthly 1/6d. per annum post paid—or 9d per dozen for bundles paid in advance.'

With the advertisement went a suggested news item which added that Comrade Connolly was 'present National organiser of the Socialist Party . . . and will contribute a series of American notes, as well as the leading articles. Other contributions will be from men and women in the newly organised Socialist Party of Ireland, and will deal with every phase of the Socialist movement as it affects Ireland. This should be a good means of propaganda amongst Irish residents in Britain.' The Dublin address of the paper and the place to which orders should be sent were necessarily left blank.

The blow fell in a letter from O'Brien dated 30 November. Or rather, the blow would have fallen had not Connolly been moving so rapidly. The letter said that the project offering Connolly a position as organizer for the Socialist Party of Ireland

has fallen through at any rate for 12 mths. I placed the whole matter before a mtg. and although all agreed that you were just the man to deal with the present situation no scheme cd be arranged. I find it very difficult to convey to you a clear idea as to the conditions here especially as I have not none [sic] time to write you fully. With reference to the 'Harp', when I suggested transferring it to Ireland *when you were coming yourself* I did so because I thought it wd help solve the problem as to how you were to live here and that we cd devise some way to occupy yr spare time and at the same time it wd help in getting Belfast into line if we had an organiser and an organ. But transferring the paper *before* you come yourself is a totally different thing and every member I have consulted disapproves of it. Some of them say its a matter for you and does not concern the S.P.I. at all; but I dont agree with that view. You appear to assume that there is a demand for the paper here but you are mistaken, as for the present at any rate we think 'The Irish Nation' serves our purpose admirably. Therefore you cannot expect any assistance in running the 'Harp' from the S.P.I. Under these circumstances the paper cd not be made a success, and I wd strongly urge you to drop the project. I am glad I sent you that letter a couple of wks ago as it somewhat prepares you for this. The S.P.I. has not yet found its feet, and you must understand that out of its 80 odd members *less than a dozen* know you personally. If it were only possible for you to be on the spot and discuss the matter of yr coming here with the members I feel sure all difficulties wd be overcome, but the idea of taking you out of a good job and bringing yourself and family 3,000 miles frightens the most of the members. If I thought you wd be idle for a mth, or even less, after yr present tour, I wd make strenuous efforts to arrange a short tour to Dublin and Belfast, etc., but I suppose this is out of the question.

Another letter, now lost apparently, contained a blunt refusal to seek a sub-editor for *The Harp*, or to forward the advertisement for it.

From Tucson, Arizona, in a letter dated 18 December 1909, Connolly gave O'Brien his bitter reaction to this blow. He was astonished at the contents of the two letters. Either he was unable to make himself understood or his command of the English language was poor. He would try again. In the first place, he wanted *The Harp* published in Dublin even if the Irish did not buy a single copy of it, and even if the Socialist Party of Ireland did not want to have a single thing to do with it. Donnelly was not able to pay for it any longer, and he, Connolly, wanted to transfer it to Dublin because printing costs there were cheaper and because it would have more appeal coming from Ireland.

You tell me that the comrades say I will lose money on it. What the devil do they know about it? Do they know how many subscribers

I get per month or anything else, about the matter. I am old enough to know what I am doing, and my day for guileless trust in the comradeship of Socialists is long since over.

All he wanted was some comrade to add some local material to the paper and see that it got posted. It would not take three days of work for any man, and for this Connolly would pay a pound.

Connolly's idea in sending notices about *The Harp* to the English socialist papers was to work up a circulation for it in Great Britain so that he could get enough lecturing in that country to maintain his family in Ireland until he obtained a foothold there. If O'Brien had sent out these notices,

I could, I am certain, maintain myself between the two countries until things were ripe enough in Ireland. But to take a trip to Ireland to *beg* the comrades there to help me come back permanently —excuse me, friend, I ate that bread once and it was made very bitter. When I go back to Ireland my family will accompany me or I do not go.

Please help me to get that paper published in Dublin irrespective of whether I return or not, and I will for ever remember you in my prayers.

Ask the Nation people will they consent to handle it in Ireland if I pay printing of 1000 copies, and the mailing to our American subscribers.

Two days later Connolly wrote to O'Brien again, going over the same ground and trying desperately to elucidate his position. Ominous silence followed. Weeks and months went by without an answer. But the editor of the *Nation*, W. P. Ryan, took the matter as a straightforward business proposition, and in one way or another got the January issue of *The Harp* published. Ryan was listed in the magazine as technical editor and Nora Connolly as business agent in New York.

The Connolly pattern was again evident. (The psychiatrists tell us that it is the pattern, not the single action, that matters in analysing the psychology of the individual.) In the same precipitate way that Connolly deserted the British Army during the last few months of his enlistment, abandoned jobs, and left Ireland for the US, he was now seeking to return to Ireland. In each instance he displayed a remarkable degree of impatience, and a disregard for the advice of others that almost always led to disaster. The last time he would display these qualities would be on Easter Monday 1916.

*　　*　　*

Connolly's arduous travels on bumpy railway tracks, talks in draughty halls, and fitful sleep in the homes of comrades did not affect his literary output. During 1909, in addition to writing lengthy letters to William O'Brien and Matheson, he filled the pages of *The Harp*; completed the final draft of *Labour in Irish History*; and wrote two articles for the *International Socialist Review*, the magazine published by Kerr in Chicago. In one of these articles he tried to answer the perennial question: what if the people vote socialist in the polls and the capitalists refuse to accept the verdict? Connolly answered, use the strength of industrial unionism. In the other article, Connolly rejected the idea that anything could be accomplished by attempting to persuade the American Federation of Labor to take progressive stands; he called its craft set-up 'the most dispersive and isolating force at work in the Labour movement today'.

In *Labour in Irish History*, which is considered Connolly's masterpiece, Connolly put in all the information about the Irish past that he had gleaned since assembling facts for 'Mad' Gonne's banners at the anti-Jubilee demonstrations in 1897. It is a short book (only 168 pages in the edition I have) which examines such matters as the early peasant rebellions, social changes, the Irish Volunteers, the United Irishmen, the Emmet conspiracy and Daniel O'Connell from a rare viewpoint:

> Were history what it ought to be, an accurate literary reflex of the times with which it professes to deal, the pages of history would be almost entirely engrossed with a recital of the wrongs and struggles of the labouring people, constituting, as they have ever done, the vast mass of mankind.

Some of the best pages deal with the attempt made in 1831 by Mr Craig, of Manchester, to establish a socialist colony on his property at Ralahine, County Clare; and with analysis of the tenets of James Fintan Lalor, John Mitchel, Thomas Devin Reilly, and William Thompson. The descriptions of the 1845 famine and of economic conditions at various other times are vivid.

In essence, Connolly maintained that

the Irish question is a social question, the whole age-long fight of the Irish people against their oppressors resolves itself, in the last analysis, into a fight for the mastery of the means of life, the sources of production, in Ireland. Who would own and control the land: The people or the invaders; and if the invaders, which set of them—the most recent swarm of land-thieves, or the sons of the thieves of a former generation?

The extent to which various movements and leaders understood the importance of this fact, and sympathized with the oppressed, was Connolly's test for assessing the good and the bad, for dividing the sheep from the goats. In the process, he did a good job of showing that there was always a 'socialist' underground in the country, that many great Irish leaders acted in consonance with this trend while others considered equally revolutionary were actually minions of the British rulers.

XIV

1910

STILL roaming the inhospitable west, Connolly found himself in Butte, Montana, on 7 March 1910. On that date he made an attempt to re-establish relations with William O'Brien by writing a long and newsy letter on a variety of matters. What had happened to the labour journal that P. T. Daly was expected to edit? Had O'Brien found time to visit Miss Molony? He (Connolly) was worried that he might have to re-write the last three chapters of *Labour in Irish History* since they had apparently been lost on the way to the typist.

Connolly then got to the point. Upon reconsideration, he had decided that it might not be such a bad idea after all if he accepted O'Brien's suggestion and made a trip home by himself to look over the ground. He had been asked, he said, to take the job of editing a new weekly in the US that was being planned by some Socialist Party members who were sympathetic to the concept of industrial unionism; he decided that 'if once I became moored into a constant job of that kind I might bid farewell for ever to my dream of returning to Ireland. The work would be too engrossing. So I asked for time to consider, and in the considering your suggestion cropped up again. Write me fully.'

In a postscript Connolly added that he had just received a letter from a man named J. W. O'Beirne telling him that James Larkin had accepted the position of managing *The Harp*. 'Good,' Connolly wrote. Apparently Larkin had been impressed by the first Dublin issues of the magazine, and in turn the members of the Socialist Party of Ireland were now impressed by Larkin's approval. These circumstances formed the background for the Party's decision to sponsor a Connolly tour of Ireland. On 18 April 1910, O'Brien wrote:

I convened a mtg of members of the SPI and other Socialists to consider yr letter. It turned up 21 of them members of the SPI. Of that number Lyng Mulray McManus and myself were the only ones that knew you personally. The mtg approved of the suggested tour and opened a Guarantee Fund to assist you make a lecturing tour in Ireland this year. A sum of £10 was guaranteed at the mtg and a Committee appointed to work with the project generally. Having considered the financial aspect of the tour the Committee instruct me to state that they believe they can raise £20 inside the next 4 months. Are you prepared to come on that understanding? We assume you propose touring in England and Scotland also. We think this wd be a wise step. I suppose Dan Irving wd be willing to organise a tour for you. We think the Catholic Socialist Society wd be willing to take you up wherever they have branches. If you want to communicate with the C.S.S. write Wm Regan 14 Chapel St Rutherglen Glasgow. At the mtg, a discussion took place as to what yr relations with the S.P.I. wd be but no decision was come to. Write as soon as possible and if you decide to come let me know when you propose coming and any other information you think wd assist us such as length of tour what towns you think mtgs sd be held in etc. etc.

By the time Connolly received this letter, he had completed his travels for the Socialist Party, had rejoined his family in New York City, and had received a letter from James Larkin offering *his* services in arranging a tour of Ireland. It was a time for deep consideration, with Connolly 'torn between desire and fear', as he himself put it. After a lengthy discussion with his wife, Connolly wrote to O'Brien on 3 May 1910, that he had definitely decided to be in Dublin on the last week in July.

Concerning the questions O'Brien had raised as to where Connolly wished to go and his relationship with the Socialist Party of Ireland, he answered that he wished to go where he would do the most good, and that the tour committee might tell the party that it desired to place his services 'at the disposal of the S.P.I. as, say, National Organiser, whilst I am in the country. Then you could get the Party to arrange for meetings in such places as they have correspondents or chances of an organisation. I think a week in Belfast would be well spent.' He thought that he should spend at least a month in Ireland before going to Great Britain, thinking that he could thus establish a footing in Ireland for his return. On the whole, he would prefer Larkin to organize the tour, but if he couldn't, since he might soon be in jail, Connolly told O'Brien to write Regan in Glasgow to organize a tour for him among the branches of the Independent Labour Party as well as Regan's own Catholic Socialist Society; Regan should also ask the Liverpool or Manchester branches of the Independent Labour Party to undertake the same task in England. 'Between you and I and the wall,' Connolly added, 'I am not in love with a Socialist Society identifying itself with any religious creed, or irreligious propaganda.'

Always the organizer, Connolly told O'Brien to put an announcement in *The Harp* that he was 'open for engagements in Great Britain commencing—fill in the date yourself. Add to this advertisement the press notices enclosed, and an extract from the one I sent on to you from a paper in New Mexico. Also send a copy of this notice (enclosure) to whoever you ask to do the organising in Great Britain. Dan Irving is not available (nor desirable).'

In reply, O'Brien said that the Connolly Tour Committee, taking up Connolly's suggestion, would offer Connolly's services as national organizer to the Socialist Party of Ireland; the Party would hold a special meeting the following Tuesday to consider other details. O'Brien noted that there might be difficulties in the way of Connolly lecturing for the Independent Labour Party, since its Irish section did not favour a separate Socialist Party for Ireland. He said that he had sent the notices of Connolly's availability for speeches to *The Harp* and other socialist magazines. He saved the most important matter for his last sentence: 'Larkin has agreed to get the organising in England and Scotland done for you.'

Connolly's next letter to O'Brien was written from New Castle, Pennsylvania, where Connolly, shortly after his return to New York, had gone in order to participate in a fight for a free press. His assistance had been solicited by Justus Ebert, an important Socialist Party functionary. It was Connolly's last struggle in the US and, as he himself said, the most bitter one he had ever encountered. The tinplate workers at New Castle had been out on strike for almost a year. They were strongly supported by two local papers, the *New Castle Free Press* and *Solidarity*, and by both the IWW and the Socialist Party. The editors of the two papers were lodged in jail on the charge that they had failed to comply with some imprint regulations, although it was shown that another local paper, similarly guilty, had not been bothered. The collection of defence funds was started in New York and Chicago;

Big Bill Haywood joined his arch-enemy Justus Ebert on the scene. And Connolly was enlisted to edit the *Free Press* in the absence of its regular editor. He immediately issued a statement that the technical charge had been lodged only to obtain evidence for a charge of 'seditious libel'. He argued that, in any case, the offence of seditious libel did not exist in American law.

The government officials used every weapon to put the newspapers out of business and keep their staffs in jail. Customers of the jobbing plant which helped to support the *Free Press* were warned to discontinue their patronage. In order to prevent the prisoners from being able to consult with their attorneys, the Governor proclaimed a diphtheria epidemic and the county jail a quarantine area. Connolly, the very epitome of the 'outside agitator', found few friendly faces in New Castle as he went about his work.

The trial was held from 17 June to 20 June. The jury disagreed, and a new trial was announced for September, but on 29 June the judge suddenly announced that he would settle the case for a fine of $100. The staff of the *Free Press* accepted the offer, Connolly relinquished the editorship, and returned to New York City.

Connolly was still in New Castle when he sent O'Brien sixty-four dollars to pay for the cost of publishing the May and June issues of *The Harp*. At the same time he complained that he had not yet received a receipt for the previous sixty-four dollars he had sent, that no copies of the May issue had been received, and that 'no one in Ireland seems to think it worth their while to render me an account of subs expired or anything else. And the manner in which the paper has *not* been delivered to American subscribers has practically killed the hope of new subscribers . . . It is all very disheartening.'

In his reply O'Brien said that he could not understand why this letter and money order were sent to him, not to Larkin, the manager of the paper. He reported that Larkin was equally puzzled, and would forward a full statement of the paper's financial condition in a few days. From New York City, Connolly responded on 6 June that he had written to O'Brien instead of Larkin simply because of 'notices that all orders etc. had to be sent to "The Harp" office, 43 Belvedere Place, Dublin', and because of hints from Larkin that he might be in jail after St Patrick's Day.

As to the Belfast trip, Connolly said he would prefer to go there independently of the Independent Labour Party. He considered any Socialist Party that was against political freedom for Ireland 'a joke . . .

I am a bit of a humourist myself but that kind of a joke does not appeal to me ... The I.L.P. has frequently repudiated Home Rule; if I were asked upon their platform what my views upon that question were I would state frankly that I am a Separatist, and do not believe that the English Government has any right to Ireland, never had any right, and never can have any right. I can imagine the mess that would make of an I.L.P. meeting in Belfast.'

Connolly was never entirely doctrinaire. It was typical of him now to suggest that he appear three times in Belfast: first, under the sponsorship of the Socialist Party of Ireland; second, at a meeting where he could speak to members and supporters of the Independent Labour Party on behalf of a socialist party for Ireland, and where the two groups could argue out their differences; and third, at a meeting ending his Belfast trip. After mentioning other places where he could lecture, he said: 'Also it might be necessary to devote a night or two to personal visiting and discussion. That is often as fruitful as any other kind of organising—sometimes more ... perhaps it would be as well to reassure you that I do not mean to attack or fight the I.L.P. in any way than by a statement of our reasons for a separate Socialist Party for Ireland and to enlighten them on the true status of the clergy in matters national.' Becoming increasingly euphoric as the time for his departure neared, Connolly ended the letter, 'In joyous anticipation of our re-union.'

On 18 June, O'Brien wrote that the Socialist Party of Ireland had decided that the services of James Connolly should be offered to the Independent Labour Party of Belfast for the term of one week. O'Brien had received a letter from William G. Orr, the ILP organizer in Belfast, and in the face of this letter, could see no other alternative. He added that Larkin agreed with this course, and the money they might get would come in handy.

He enclosed a copy of a letter from the Honourable Cecil Spring-Rice, a subscriber to *The Harp*, which requested an opportunity to meet Connolly and discuss with him 'the Socialist outlook in Ireland'. It was an intimation of future events; the name would crop up again when his cousin Mary would be associated with a successful attempt to smuggle guns to the Nationalists. Spring-Rice was a unionist, that is, an opponent of Home Rule or Irish independence, living in the southern part of Ireland. O'Brien concluded by asking Connolly for a print of his portrait, to be used in advertisements of his meetings, and for the exact date he expected to arrive in Dublin.

These were normal problems connected with organizing a tour, but Connolly got an intimation of the brouhaha he was heading for when he received a letter from O'Brien (now lost) saying that Larkin had been sentenced to a year's hard labour on two charges of 'conspiracy to defraud'. The first charge was that he and some others had obtained fees and dues from dock workers at Cork although an officially established branch of the National Union of Dock Labourers had never been established in that city. The second charge was that the money raised had been used to support striking Dublin transport workers although it had not been contributed for that purpose.

On 24 June Connolly voiced his distress at the news, enquired as to whether Larkin had a family or not, and expressed a typical Connolly reaction—that the trade union and the socialists owed it to Larkin to keep the flag flying 'whilst he is in prison—that it fly all the more defiantly because of his imprisonment'. He reminded O'Brien that the twenty-pound guarantee would be almost entirely eaten up by the round-trip fare. The ten dollars remaining 'goes a very small way in America, particularly when one is paying 17 dollars per month rent. So that unless you hustle and get me good engagements in Great Britain to enable me to recoup myself in some way it will be a very dear trip to me. As it is I cannot see how I can avoid losing about 60 dollars on this tour'. For the sake of the cause he was prepared to lose that much but if he lost any more it would mean robbing his family. He told O'Brien that he was leaving New York on the *Furnissia*, of the Anchor line, would reach Londonderry on Monday morning, 25 July, and would get to Dublin the following day.

In a letter dated 4 July, O'Brien had two matters of importance to relate. One was that the printers of *The Harp* were being sued for libel. In the June issue Larkin, in describing certain events that had taken place at the recent meeting of the Irish Trades Union Congress, had dealt rather harshly with the activities of four people. These four had promptly informed the printers that they would institute actions for libel unless an apology was inserted in the next issue. In view of these circumstances, O'Brien had decided not to issue the July number until Connolly appeared.

Second, Larkin was eager to have a private talk with Connolly as soon as he arrived. It would have to be in jail, under the eye of the warden, and not later than Wednesday, 27 July. On that date his application for a new trial would be heard, and if it were not granted, Larkin would no longer be accessible to visitors. At present he was considered a 'remand' prisoner, entitled to receive only one visitor a day.

O'Brien wrote again almost immediately. Putting the libel suit and the Larkin matter aside, he was now greatly troubled by the financial aspects of Connolly's impending tour. The Tour Committee wished Connolly to know that, once the twenty pounds were raised, it considered its obligations fulfilled. Last Monday O'Brien had visited Larkin and asked him what he had done regarding Connolly's tour of England and Scotland. Larkin replied that he had written to George Dallas, secretary of the Independent Labour Party in Scotland,

> asking him to take on the job in Scotland, but had not rec. any reply. He had heard that Dallas was laid up. That was the only thing he had done. He asked me to again write Dallas, also to C. N. L. Shaw of London Sec Clarion Scouts asking him to take on the job in England; to an I.L.P. organiser in South Wales to do a few towns there, and to Victor Grayson to use his influence on yr behalf generally. I will write these letters tomorrow impressing on them that you are strongly recommended as a first class lecturer by Larkin. If these Comrades do what they are asked all will be well I think, altho the time is now short, but if they wont take on the work whats to be done?

O'Brien reported that a reunion party would probably be held on Friday, 29 July, and Connolly's opening talk would be at the Park on Sunday morning, 31 July. He concluded, despondently:

> I may tell you candidly there is no enthusiasm so far about the tour, and the S.P.I. seem to have taken the matter up in a very half hearted fashion . . . The S.P.I. is not in the flourishing condition it was up to 6 months ago financially or otherwise. All these things are troubling us as they must trouble you. We must only hope and work for the best.

He was quite wrong about Connolly's feelings. Now that the decision had been made, Connolly refused to be ruffled. He answered briefly: 'Your letter read. Cheer up, my boy, we never died of a winter yet. Be assured, whatever happens, no blame is put upon you for not being master of circumstances. I'm not kicking.'

On 14 July the Irish Socialist Federation held a farewell banquet at

Cavanaugh's restaurant in New York City. It can stand as a measure of what Connolly had achieved in the US that Frank Bohn and Justus Ebert, both noted socialists, were present. Again leaving his family behind, Connolly embarked on 16 July, as planned. On the boat home he wrote a poem called 'The Call of Erin', to be sung to the strains of 'Rolling Home to Bonnie Scotland'. The text of the poem and the authority for its place of origin are found in a typed collection of Connolly's poems in the National Library of Ireland. One stanza is sufficient:

> With the engines 'neath us throbbing,
>   And the wind upon our stern,
> Little reck we of the distance
>   That divides us now from Erin.
> For we hear her voices calling—
>   Sweeping past us to the West—
> Calling home to her the Children
>   She once nourished on her breast.

After arriving in Derry, Connolly sent a telegraph to O'Brien saying he would be in Dublin on Tuesday, 26 July.

* * *

During the months before his departure Connolly had been busy writing a rebuttal to a series of Lenten talks given in 1910 by Father Kane, SJ, at the Gardiner Street Church in Dublin. As Connolly says, the work 'grew on my hands', and eventually developed into a seventy-page pamphlet that, like *Labour in Irish History*, was published in Ireland only after he had arrived there. The edition of *Labour, Nationality and Religion* that I have was published in 1920 by the Socialist Party of Ireland, with headquarters at 42 North Great George's Street, Dublin. The back part contains advertisements for (1) *The Watchword of Labour*, then the official organ of the Irish Transport and General Workers' Union, edited by Cathal O'Shannon; (2) pamphlets on Irish labour; and (3) the James Connolly Labour College, President, Miss Nora Connolly.

The pamphlet is of continuing interest, particularly to Catholics aware of the present ferment in the Church. The Foreword reads as if it were written today, with its stress on

One point of Catholic doctrine ... the almost forgotten and

sedulously suppressed one, that the Catholic Church is theoretically a community in which the clergy are but the officers serving the laity in a common worship and service of God . . .

Should the clergy at any time profess or teach doctrines not in conformity with the true teachings of Catholicity it is not only the right, but it is the absolute duty of the laity to refuse such doctrines and to disobey such teaching. Indeed, it is this saving clause in Catholic doctrine which has again and again operated to protect the Church from the result of the mistaken attempts of the clergy to control the secular activities of the laity . . . it is entirely regrettable, that clergymen consecrated to the worship of God, and supposed to be patterned after a Redeemer who was the embodiment of service and humility, should in their relation to the laity insist upon service and humility being rendered to them instead of by them . . . they have forgotten or ignored the fact that the laity are a part of the Church, and that therefore the right of rebellion against injustice so freely claimed by the Papacy and the Hierarchy is also the inalienable right of the laity. And history proves that in almost every case in which the political or social aspirations of the laity came into opposition to the will of the clergy the laity represented the best interests of the Church as a whole and of Mankind in general.

In the remaining eight pages of the Foreword, Connolly ticks off at least fourteen instances where the Catholic laity took political action contrary to the express commands of the Pope and the Catholic hierarchy, and in which 'subsequent events or the more enlightened conscience of subsequent ages' justified the actions of the laity and condemned those of the clergy. It is a long and damaging list, which includes one item where the Catholic Bishop of Ossory, during the American Revolution, ordered the Catholics of his diocese to 'observe a day's fast and to humble himself in prayer that they might avert the divine wrath provoked by their American fellow-subjects, who, seduced by the specious notions of liberty and other illusive expectations of sovereignity disclaim any dependence upon Great Britain and endeavour by force of arms to distress their mother country'.

In the remaining fifty or so pages, Connolly quotes at length the charges against socialism made by Father Kane, and answers each charge *seriatim*. In the process, Connolly defends the principle that labour alone is the source of economic value; explains the economic interpretation of history; quotes such statements from the Founding

Fathers as St Chrysostom's aphorism that 'The rich man is a thief'; and answers the Jesuit's claims that socialism involves compulsory equality, state ownership of children, free love, the destruction of incentive, and obligatory atheism. The pamphlet still makes good reading. It may be used by some Protestants to lend substance to the charge that the Roman Catholic Church, as an institution, has always been an obstacle to progress and freedom; but it can also be used by enlightened Catholics to strengthen their demand for a 'renovated' church. There is not a word in it that overtly or covertly attacks Roman Catholicism as a religion.

XV

CONNOLLY'S FIRST action upon arriving in Dublin was to visit Jim Larkin in Mountjoy Prison. They had much to talk about. The prime subject was, of course, the task of getting Larkin released. The Dublin Trades Council had requested his release, and Larkin Release Committees were collecting signatures for a petition, but there was much more agitational work to be done.

Despite a similarity of background and views, the two men never took to each other. Both had been raised in dire poverty outside of Ireland—Connolly in Edinburgh and Larkin in Liverpool; both had endured a variety of jobs as youngsters; both had received a minimum of schooling; both were teetotallers, and married to non-Catholics; and both were committed revolutionaries. But the temperamental differences were enormous. Connolly by this time was forty-two, only eight years older than Larkin, but he seemed much older. Connolly was cool, calm, sober, always thinking ahead and planning; a veteran of numerous struggles with police and government, and a survivor of internecine fighting as well; a socialist theoretician and tactician. Larkin was fiery revolution incarnate; a man able to set crowds aflame while seeming to speak to each listener individually; a man contemptuous of logic or theory, who identified himself with the cause, and trod on other people's toes mercilessly. Connolly soon came to detest his ebullience and unpredictability; he squirmed when he heard him support sound courses of action with appallingly wrong arguments. Though he applauded publicly Larkin's courage and his ability to come down on the side of the angels, he doubted inwardly that Jim received his instructions directly from God.

Connolly's attitude towards Larkin is revealed in passing comments in his letters. On 9 January 1911 to Matheson: '*The Harp* has been suspended since June. There were *four* libel actions instituted against it over its last issue, and as the whole thing had been mismanaged since its transfer to Dublin I did not feel able to lose any more money upon it.' On 11 January 1911, again referring to *The Harp*: 'You will find it a very disappointing paper. Larkin edited it after I transferred it to Dublin whilst I was in America, and the result was sorrow but painful.' On 24 May 1911, to William O'Brien: 'As to what he says about me not taking part in the Union in Dublin, you know that he organised a dozen demonstrations in Dublin while I was there, and invited all sorts of hybrids to speak for him, but never invited me at any time. Did you notice that while in Glasgow, he claimed, at the May Day demonstration to be a member of the S.P.I.? The man is utterly unreliable—and dangerous because unreliable.'

After attending a reception held in his honour at the Antient Concert Rooms in Pearse Street, Connolly began the old round of itinerant propagandizing. He began with Dublin itself, then continued with Belfast, Cork, Liverpool, Glasgow and several smaller Scottish towns. In each city he preached on some aspect of socialism. Behind the scenes he continued to negotiate, through William O'Brien, with the Socialist Party of Ireland on ways and means of establishing a financial base in Ireland for himself and his family. In Dublin, at various outdoor meetings sponsored by the Transport Workers' Union, he urged the release of James Larkin.

In Belfast his goal was to establish a branch of the Socialist Party of Ireland. After a series of indoor and outdoor meetings, including addresses to two different branches of the Independent Labour Party, he accomplished his purpose. It was not easy. Many of those who fought him were as principled and obdurate as he himself was. A comrade named William Harrison, writing to William O'Brien, expressed the feelings of many:

I am really surprised that you seem anxious that we should form a branch of the Irish Socialist Party in Belfast. If we affiliate or form a branch of any political party I believe nothing short of the SLP would please our members. I saw an extract from a letter . . . from an Irish Socialist Party member wanting us to form a branch of the I.S.P. He said even Socialists could not afford to ignore nationality and he believed an Irish party could do more good than any foreign importation or words to that effect. To me this is distasteful from a working class standpoint. Being brought up myself in a mad-Orange atmosphere and having shaken myself free from the shackles that bound me I am now able to take a sane view of the situation. I have travelled a good deal through Ireland and am convinced that we must throw aside everything that savours of prejudice or bigotry among the masses and preach the class struggle. Ireland is now ripe for such a propaganda. Straight Socialism or nothing.

Despite such opposition the branch prospered. On 4 February 1911, Connolly wrote to O'Brien that the branch was 'doing nicely, getting lots of new members. I issued six cards on Sunday and got three more applications. And more coming.'

At Cork, Connolly met with the same success. At the first public meeting, held 20 August, 600 people attended. Another meeting was attended by 2,000 'earnest, eager working men and women', and 200 copies of *Labour, Nationality and Religion* were sold. After each meeting, members and friends repaired to a bar owned by William O'Shea, where Connolly sipped lemonade and answered further questions. O'Shea had been president of the Young Ireland Society which gave support to Con O'Lyhane in the gasworkers' strike of 1901. The branch of the Socialist Party of Ireland established in Cork consisted mainly of railwaymen; hence the Railway Servants Hall became branch headquarters. Founding members numbered 24.

During his next stay in Belfast, Connolly received a letter from O'Brien stating that the national executive committee of the SPI was willing to offer him the position of national organizer for a period of six months, at a salary of 35 or 36 shillings a week.

Connolly's rejection of the offer was buried in the middle of a long letter devoted to other matters. First, he expressed his hope that every effort would be made to encourage the new branches to grow and in their turn encourage the formation of other branches. Second, he stated that the Belfast people desired a conference be held in Dublin to enable both new and old members 'to take part and compare notes. I think this is a good plan', Connolly went on, 'and hope when it comes off that the Dublin comrades will give their new found comrades from the North and south cause to remember with pride and pleasure their visit to the Capital'. He ended by asking that literature be sent to various places in Glasgow, Manchester, Edinburgh and Liverpool.

As for the job offer,

I regret to be compelled to decline it on the terms indicated. It has been a struggle with me to come to this decision, as all my desires are in the movement in Ireland, and I honestly believe I could serve it to its satisfaction as well as my own. But a man with my responsibilities could not maintain life on less than £2 per week unless I went into the slums which I will not do. And the limitation of the offer to six months in the year, making possible as it does the complete lack of employment during the remaining six months makes the thing too much of a gamble—so much of a gamble that I would not dare to entrust the frail bark of my family fortunes to it.

As you cannot raise any more, and I cannot accept what you propose, I am afraid that I will have to bid a final adieu to Erin on this occasion. Unless some other plan can be conceived and worked out.

On 12 September 1910, Connolly wrote to O'Brien that the Belfast and Cork members desired the date of the conference to be 18 September, and reminded him that: 'First impressions are lasting and a very great deal will depend upon the show you make, and the reception you give your visiting comrades. Remember it will be the first conference of anything like a national character of Socialists in Ireland. You should organise something in the nature of a tea (like what you gave me) to start with, then get down to business after. Then if you have time wind up with a few songs etc.' In the same letter he reported that his meeting in Liverpool had been 'a rousing success'.

O'Brien responded on 14 September, saying that the time was too limited to arrange a proper conference, but since the Belfast men were coming in any case, the Dublin members would arrange for an informal discussion of propaganda, organization, and literature. O'Brien said that the party would pay Connolly's fare if he desired to attend the meeting.

Connolly, writing from Belfast on 16 September, wrote that he could not see his way clear to go to Dublin on the conference date. 'I feel that the conference can discuss certain subjects in my absence better than in my presence. Hence I do not want to be present, or in any way to influence the proceedings.' He was hoping that the conclave would accept a plan devised by Danny McDevitt of Belfast for hiring Connolly as an organizer. The idea was for the Socialist Party of Ireland to guarantee a specified sum for his wages, to be reimbursed in part by whatever funds Connolly raised in tours of Scotland and England.

The conference in Dublin was duly held, with Francis Sheehy-Skeffington presiding. O'Brien thought it was as successful as could be expected considering the hurried manner in which it was called. The members became acquainted with each other, exchanged views, and decided that a national executive committee should be formed composed of four members from Dublin, two from Cork, two from Belfast, and two from each new branch that came into existence.

Writing from Glasgow on 20 September, Connolly expressed his disappointment that the conference had declined taking responsibility for appointing him as organizer. He said that he was sure that the McDevitt plan would have worked, but since it had failed, he was planning to return to America. He asked if O'Brien could arrange enough meetings in Belfast, Dublin, and Cork so as to justify Connolly's returning by way of Queenstown instead of Derry or Glasgow. As for the possibility of getting a job with Larkin, 'I fancy that Jim will have enough to do to pull his forces together without bearing the responsibility of my sins. I was glad that I was able to initiate the move that lead to his release but dont want to demand a price for it.'

In a postscript, he gave a further explanation as to why he could not accept O'Brien's proposal. It would cost more to bring his family back to Dublin than the entire six months' salary he was being offered, 'to say nothing of the sacrifice of my furniture on one side and the stocking of a new home on the other. Thus I would be working six months for nothing, so to speak, and at the end of that period might be left idle altogether . . . I am afraid that I must resign myself to become an American for good or bad. This, I need hardly say, I regret.'

In his reply, O'Brien made no comment on the last remark. He noted merely that the executive committee was

unable to say just now whether they cd arrange mtgs in Cork Dublin and Belfast for you. We are in very low water financially. You did not mention the probable date you wd be passing through. I said I thought about Nov. 1st. Is that correct. If later it wd of course give us more time to work it up. I will write Cork and Belfast asking what financial support they are in a position to give. It wd help us to a decision if you wd let us know the total amt we wd be expected to supply for a visit of say 2 days each to Cork Dublin and Belfast. I'm afraid the Cork Bch [Branch] will never do without you or some other speaker being sent down occasionally.

The dickering went on. On 10 October, writing from Kilmarnock, an industrial town in Ayrshire, Connolly explained in detail how the party could raise funds for his wages as organizer. A statement should be issued

> on the lines of the enclosed to all your members and to sympathisers, asking for a statement of how much they can, or are prepared to give towards a National Organiser Fund, and enclosing a stamped envelope for reply. The Belfast and Cork secretaries to do the same, and get a short note put in the Irish Nation also. And I think that a note would also get insertion in the Forward Glasgow. When all the answers come in you would know where you are. I am sure that I can always get about three months in Scotland, and you can knock that off your liabilities. And if the Party allowed me to make the effort perhaps I could get an equal time in England, and return to the party the £2 per week pay the time I spent in that country. But I would like the Party to be my paymaster for the 9 months . . .

Connolly went on to explain that his expenses, including rail fares and board outside of Dublin, would amount to a total of one hundred pounds, but some of that would be defrayed by collections and profits from the sale of literature. He was willing to turn over to the Party the entire profit from his pamphlet, *Labour, Nationality and Religion*, while the arrangement lasted. The net result would be that the average cost per member per week would be only four pence, reckoning on the basis of one hundred members.

Returning to the possibility of a job with the Transport Union. Connolly thought 'that to ask them to engage me now would be a bad, a very bad move. But if I were in the country for a year as your representative, of the Party I mean, and incidentally helping them wherever I could it might be easily arranged afterwards. You can put that idea before Jim, who I hope is out by this time, and also give him my congratulations.' Connolly enclosed a draft for a suggested fund-raising circular.

This letter crossed with one of O'Brien's dated 3 October. It was a time of great excitement in Dublin. Larkin had just been released from prison after serving only three months of his year's sentence. During a long conversation, Larkin told O'Brien that he had received very little information about Connolly's activities in Belfast. He had not been able to assess the union's feelings about Connolly, and was therefore not in a position to make any promises about employing him until he could judge the situation for himself by going to Belfast.

Meanwhile, it would be a great pity if Connolly were not retained in some job in Ireland, and he was willing to do his part. O'Brien then advised Connolly to keep Larkin informed of his speaking engagements and other activities in Scotland.

O'Brien said that the processions and lectures held during the past weekend to celebrate Larkin's release had been tremendous. On the evening of his release, a gigantic torchlight procession in his honour traced its way through the streets of Dublin. Larkin addressed the crowd from the centre window of the union offices in Beresford Place. O'Brien wrote that the mass meeting held the following afternoon at the same spot was 'the largest labour mtg I've seen in Dublin'. Larkin's talk was preceded by one from Countess Markievicz, who preached militant nationalism: '. . . every Irishman ought to recognise that in regard to everything in Ireland, whether trade union or anything else, England was its foe. The great evil in this country was English influence. In this fight of Irish labour against English labour Mr Larkin ought to receive the support of every Nationalist minded person in Ireland, whether in the labour ranks or not.'

On 10 October O'Brien wrote to Connolly that the executive committee of the Socialist Party of Ireland had met and had decided that sixty-five pounds was the most that could be raised to hire Connolly as an organizer, that it was impossible for the Party to raise the additional two pounds a week that Connolly desired, and therefore the Party could not adopt his proposal. O'Brien thought there was some hope that a job with the Transport Union might yet develop, but it would be foolish to build on it.

O'Brien's letter rejecting Connolly's proposal reached Connolly just after he had met Jim Larkin. Larkin had come from Liverpool to Glasgow to confer with him concerning the position of national organizer for the Socialist Party of Ireland. In a letter dated 11 October, a confused Connolly wrote that Larkin,

> after due consultation with you people, was sure that there was no difficulty in the way; also that he had already deposited some money in the bank for that purpose. That he was making arrangement with some friends of his own for the purposes of creating the fund and assisting it. And all the time he was with me he was speaking of the fund as an actuality, and of my remaining in Ireland as a foregone conclusion.
>
> On the top of this comes your letter stating that your committee

refuses even to try and find out what funds are available, from which refusal I have no alternative to appeal to . . .

But what is the meaning of the Larkin visit to me, if the committee have no intention of going on with it?

Personally I would not dream of allowing Jim Larkin to push me upon the pay-roll of his Union, and thus make me the target for all the malcontents and reactionaries who hate him but fear his influence, and so would wreak their petty spite upon the paid official thus forced upon them from abroad. Nay, nay, William, that job would be far more valueless than any guarantee from socialist sources.

So at the bottom of this negotiation we will write the words FINIS—all off. Me for America.

After a few paragraphs concerning the management of funds obtained from the sale of his pamphlet, Connolly concluded in an elegaic tone:

In conclusion permit me to thank the Dublin comrades for their expressions of cordiality towards myself. As I *shall not likely visit Dublin again*, in view of your letter, I wish to take this opportunity to thank them. But allow me also to say that I am convinced that their work will be for ever sterile and unfruitful unless they summon up courage enough to fight elections. I hate to say it of Irishmen, but that is what is wanting in Ireland today—moral courage amongst Irish Socialists. Their lack in that respect is a discredit to the race.

Finally, whilst I feel humiliated by the refusal of your committee to make an effort to test the feelings of the comrades and sympathisers, I accept it as final.

A few points in this letter are worth underlining. The paragraph in which Connolly explains why he did not want to be put on the Transport Union's payroll could have been written only by a man of great moral stature. The belief that Connolly was an all-out syndicalist, uninterested in or opposed to political action, should be discarded once and for all in view of this admonition to his Irish comrades that their work would be forever sterile and unproductive unless they summoned up the courage to engage in political campaigns and to contest elections.

But Connolly was entirely premature in bidding farewell to Ireland.

In the face of Larkin's conversation with Connolly, the executive committee of the Socialist Party of Ireland threw caution away and accepted Connolly's proposal. On many subsequent occasions Connolly was to curse Larkin's bulldozing tactics, his tendency for taking action without consulting his colleagues, his propensity for exaggeration and inaccuracy, but at this time he could only feel grateful.

The party promptly issued an 'Appeal for Organisation Fund' along the lines Connolly had suggested. It noted that Connolly had established branches in Belfast and Cork, and had become widely known as a writer because of 'his able and striking reply to Father Kane which has obtained a large circulation and his just-published volume, "Labour in Irish History" (Maunsell and Co.), one of the most valuable contributions to democratic and Socialistic literature ever published in Ireland'. The proposal was to raise a fund of one hundred pounds 'so as to guarantee Comrade Connolly a year, this including travelling expenses'. This amount would be supplemented by Connolly's earnings as lecturer in Great Britain, 'where he is also well known and has established many ties with the Socialist movement . . .'

With this guarantee in hand, Connolly borrowed and scraped together the money to bring back his family to Ireland. People on the boat were so astonished to see an Irish family *returning* that they called them 'the millionaire's family'. 'You mean the madman's family,' laughed Connolly, when he heard of it. At the same time he assured Lillie that she was not returning to the misery she left. A party to welcome the family was held at the Antient Concert Rooms; of those attending, the children recognized only Jack Mulray. The family found a place to live in the Ballsbridge area.

Connolly's stay in Glasgow (during October 1910) proved productive in other ways. He made contact with John Wheatley of the Catholic Socialist movement, and, more importantly, with Thomas Johnston, editor of *Forward*. From that time on Connolly contributed articles regularly to this influential labour publication. Connolly's hand was also apparent in a manifesto issued about this time by the Socialist Party of Ireland. The manifesto opened with a statement blaming all the evils of modern times on the dependence of the working people on the owners of capitalist property, and the desire of these capitalists and landowners to keep the vast masses of people so subject and dependent. To remedy this condition in Ireland required that the Irish working class 'organise itself industrially and politically with the end in view of gaining control and mastery of the entire resources of the country'.

The method was for the people to elect 'representatives of Socialist Principles' to all the governing bodies of the country; eventually the political power of the state would be in the hands of those 'who will use it to further and extend the principle of common or public ownership'.

The Socialist Party of Ireland admitted to a degree of flexibility. Depending on conditions, it might run candidates of its own or elect any 'independent working-class candidates pledged to a progressive policy of social reform. We know that every victory won for progress today is a victory for Socialism, even when the victors most anxiously repudiate our cause.'

Rather inconsistently the manifesto went on to urge labour not to allow itself 'to be swallowed up in and identified with new political alignments, scattering and dissipating its forces instead of concentrating them upon Socialist lines . . .' What was meant, possibly, was that the socialists were to exercise considerable flexibility of tactics, support every democratic movement and every partial reform, while seeking to guide the entire people by the aid of socialist theory. More important is the absence from the manifesto of any demand for national freedom and the emphasis on political weapons. This did not indicate that Connolly had renounced either his nationalism or syndicalism. Like everyone else, he expected Home Rule to be achieved rather soon, and his syndicalism, as we have previously noted, never excluded the ballot box.

After his return to Ireland from Scotland, Connolly approached two women's organizations, the Women's Franchise League and the Daughters of Erin, the women's nationalist group founded by Maud Gonne a dozen years earlier, with the suggestion that a joint campaign be started to extend to Ireland the benefits of new legislation that provided for feeding needy children at school. This reluctance to extend welfare benefits to Ireland was characteristic of the entire relationship between England and Ireland, even though the needs in Ireland were consistently greater owing to its higher rate of unemployment and lower wage scale. To make things worse, it was precisely during this period, 1905 to 1912, that food prices in Dublin increased 15 per cent, much higher than they did in London.

Maud Gonne, though now living mostly in France, was still 'Mad', still indignant at the rural and urban poverty raging in Ireland. She willingly joined Connolly, and Miss Magee, of the Women's Franchise League, in bringing the case for feeding school children before the Dublin Trades Council. Larkin, as a member of the Council, strongly backed their position. The Council gave way before this amalgam of miniscule and despised socialist, nationalist, feminist and syndicalist forces, and agreed to urge the Lord Mayor to summon a conference on the subject. Although it required some additional pressure, the Lord Mayor eventually did hold such a meeting at the Mansion House on 12 December.

In the December 1910 elections, the Socialist Party of Ireland was unable to finance any candidates, but issued a statement on the elections signed by Fred Ryan as national secretary and Connolly as national organizer. Others named in the statement were two members each from Dublin, Belfast and Cork. The statement urged voters to ignore the advice of John Redmond's United Irish League to vote for the Liberal Party candidates, and instead vote for Labour candidates. Connolly gave the same advice in an article in *Forward*.

XVI

1911

AFTER THE elections Connolly moved his campaign for school-feeding to the south. As arrangements were being made to send a delegation to the Home Secretary in London, Connolly began a series of open-air meetings at Cork. The citizens of Cork found the language used at these meetings uncommonly strong, and opposition developed. But the real outburst took place at Queenstown (now Cobh), fifteen miles away, on 7 March 1911. Connolly once called this town 'that nest of parasites feeding upon parasites'.

The local authorities had granted Connolly's group the use of the city hall for an indoor meeting but at the last minute withdrew its permission upon the insistence of a councillor named Healy who had an interest in a local laundry where the girls were paid 2s 6d a week. Connolly thereupon decided to hold an open-air meeting. Among those attending it was Healy himself, with a group of his followers.

After the audience had listened to Connolly in silence, Healy asked, 'Did you write in a book that the Jesuits killed Popes?' To the sound of resentful murmurs, Connolly declared, 'This is an appeal to prejudice, but I will not be intimidated. My answer is that Father Kane the Jesuit denounced us in his Lenten lectures and I wrote a reply showing that the mud he had thrown at us could be more fitly thrown at him and his Order. The Jesuits and Dominicans were expelled from many countries for political intrigue.'

'What about free love?' a woman demanded. 'Up the Mollies!' came answering shouts from the crowd. (The Mollie Maguires were so named from an Eniskillen woman famed during the land wars for her extreme devotion to Catholicism.) The mob then charged, smashing the soap box Connolly had been standing on, and giving him and

Jack Dowling a hard time until the police arrived and warned them to get back to Cork as fast as possible. Connolly shouted, 'We'll be back on Thursday,' as the police escorted the two speakers to a hotel where they took refuge until rain dispersed the mob. The two men were then given police protection to the railway station.

On the following day all Socialist Party speakers and members in the area were visited individually by detectives and advised not to return to Queenstown. None took the advice. On Thursday, at the same stand, William Travers, who had recently been converted to the cause by Connolly, acted as chairman. He opened by reminding the audience that Young Irelanders had once been chased out of Limerick. Almost his only supporters were John Dowling and a man named Hartland, who worked at the naval base in Cork harbour. As it happened, it was the same base where Connolly, as a teenage British soldier, had once mounted guard over Myles Joyce, the man who was executed for an agrarian atrocity in a famous case of the period. The opposition forces at the meeting were armed with chair legs, stakes and pokers. They were led by Hennessy, chairman of the local board, and three other councillors. Fifty men of the Royal Irish Constabulary were present to keep order.

Dowling and Hartland spoke against the constant banging of tins and upturned buckets by crowds of small children. Interspersed were cries of 'atheists' and 'soupers'. As Connolly was speaking, Hennessy stepped forward. 'Are you against religion?' asked Hennessy. 'We are not,' Connolly replied. The crowd grew menacingly quiet as Hennessy approached nearer. 'Look here, my good man,' he said, 'the decent people of this town want neither you nor your doctrine. Let you take yourselves and your followers out of here or I'll not answer for what may happen.' Declining to move, Connolly tartly commented on Hennessy's resemblance to a codfish standing on its tail with its mouth open. A policeman plucked him by the sleeve, saying: 'Now, Mister Connolly, will you please go along with Mr Hennessy.'

Connolly roughly shook off the policeman's hand and answered, 'I'd die a thousand deaths before I'd go anywhere with a scoundrel like that.' After a few more exchanges of this sort, the crowd charged. The socialists abandoned their soap box and beat a hasty retreat through a shower of sticks, stones and other missiles. Shouting 'This way,' Connolly led them through an archway where a cart and driver were standing. He leaped up beside the driver and with a 'You'll be paid,' seized the reins. The others clambered aboard as the cart gathered speed, and it did not stop until it reached the railway station four miles away. No more meetings were attempted in Queenstown.

For Connolly, these outbursts of popular wrath at any gospel which seemed to conflict with that of the parish priest were expected and frequent. Behind them lay hundreds of years of identification with a Church which had shared their religious, economic and social persecution under British tyranny. That this Church had its own interests to preserve, interests which sometimes conflicted with its role of acting as a shield against British Protestant rule, was something difficult for them to comprehend. What the Irish masses felt when they listened to Connolly was comparable to what some construction workers today feel when they listen to a black militant or other kind of left-winger. Then as now, their reactions were not entirely spontaneous. In Ireland they were nourished by the Ancient Order of Hibernians, sometimes called a 'grand old Catholic society', but once denounced by Connolly as 'the foulest brood that ever spawned in Ireland'. Padraic Pearse condemned the organization for the 'narrowing down of Nationalism to the members of one creed'. This sectarianism contributed greatly to strengthening a corresponding Protestant bigotry in the North, to the detriment of both national unity and economic reform.

* * *

Back with his family in Dublin, Connolly became increasingly despondent. He was discovering how hollow his negotiating victory with the Socialist Party of Ireland really was; the members, no matter how well intentioned, simply could not pay his salary. They were too few and too poor. In addition, the Spring-Rice family, which had been making up some of the deficit, had withdrawn this support. There is no record, incidentally, to show that Connolly ever met any members of the family.

On 7 to 12 May Connolly attended a meeting of the Independent Labour Party for Lanark County, which includes Glasgow. He took the opportunity to visit Edinburgh and discuss his plight with his old friend and mentor, John Leslie. He told Leslie that he was thinking of settling in England. He now regretted that he had left the US, saying, 'My first mistake was to go to America; my second was to leave it.' Leslie urged him to remain in Ireland, insisting, with startling prescience, that he would yet find 'a niche in the temple of fame'.

Connolly returned to Belfast, where he did have some sort of niche—a corner in the home of Danny McDevitt at 5 Rosemary Street. Every rebel group met at some time or other in this establishment. He was soon joined by his oldest daughter Nora, who found work in a linen mill. She was surprised to find herself called 'a papish', and to learn how intricate was the system of craft snobbery which further divided the workers. Connolly wasted no time in joining the Belfast branch of the Irish Transport Workers Union. It was a paper outfit, for most of the Belfast dock workers were still members of the National Union of Dock Labourers. Only seven members were present when Connolly attended his first branch meeting. On the agenda was the election of a delegate to the Irish Trades Union Congress to be held in Galway. Connolly would have liked to win this appointment, but failed. He wished to support a resolution calling for the establishment of an Irish labour party separate from the Independent Labour Party or other British group.

When the Congress met, the debate on this question was bitter, but eventually the position of William Walker, who favoured support for the British Labour Party, was upheld by a vote of 32 to 29.

In an article published in the 27 May 1911 issue of *Forward*, Connolly said the debate was between those who believed that the socialist movement in Ireland should remain a dues-paying organic part of the British movement and those who held 'that the relations between Socialism in Ireland and in Great Britain should be fraternal and not organic'. His own opinion was that the two parties should operate by exchanging literature and speakers, rather than by attempting to treat the British and Irish people as one, since the Irish had 'for 700 years nurtured an unending martyrdom rather than admit or surrender its national identity'.

So far as the issue of 'internationalism' was concerned, Connolly felt that the concept of a 'free federation of free peoples', as preached by the Irish Socialist Party, was superior to a concept which seemed 'scarcely distinguishable from imperialism, the merging of subjugated people in the political system of their conquerors', as preached by the Belfast branches of the Independent Labour Party. Connolly concluded his article by proposing a convention at which the two groups would discuss the idea of nationalism as an absolute condition of socialist unity in Ireland.

It has been popular in some circles to consider that Connolly adopted Irish independence only in his later years, sacrificing his socialist ideas in the process. Such articles as this one quoted makes it clear that national freedom was always one of Connolly's prime goals; it was his misfortune, as he said lying in Dublin Castle before his execution, that his socialist comrades could somehow never remember that he was an Irishman.

William Walker replied to this article by pointing with pride to the progress of 'municipal socialism' in Belfast—ownership by the city of gasworks, waterworks, harbour works, markets, tramways, electricity, museums and art galleries. The debate in *Forward* continued with Connolly quoting Karl Marx who once wrote that, unless the British workers took the initiative in severing the bond with Ireland, they would remain forever dependent on their own rulers. The Irish question was more than an economic one; it was a democratic question, a matter of national independence. Walker, in his next reply, included an abusive personal attack on Connolly.

As this debate drew to its close, demonstrations took place against the coronation of King Edward VII and his impending visit to Ireland. Once again black flags flew in Limerick and Kilkenny. In Dublin, Countess Markievicz conducted a meeting outside the Sinn Fein office in Harcourt Street which the police broke up. Connolly spoke at his usual stand, Beresford Place on the Liffey. He also issued a manifesto protesting the visit and urging the workers to 'stand by the dignity of your class'. He called 'these parading royalties, all this insolent aristocracy, all these grovelling, dirt-eating capitalist traitors . . . signs of disease in any social state'. He urged the workers not to participate in any form in the visit, said that every man or woman 'should have an equal opportunity to attain to the proudest position in the land', and ended with a poem declaring

> That the Thinker and the Worker
> Are Manhood's only Kings.

For distributing this manifesto, Walter Carpenter, a member of the Socialist Party of Ireland, was sentenced to three months in jail.

During May 1911 Connolly spent some time trying to put his organizational and personal affairs in order. On 24 May he wrote to William O'Brien not to give up his position as president of the tailors' union and his membership on the Dublin Trades Council, but to give up enough tasks so that he could have time 'to spend on the movement proper. Else I foresee disaster. Do not make the mistake of underestimating the force of your good *or bad* example.'

He did not think that Francis Sheehy-Skeffington would accept the position of national secretary of the Party. He thought that Skeffington was not in favour of any national action against Redmond's United Irish League, although willing to fight against it in the municipalities. 'He wants it to rule the roost politically until we get Home Rule.' Connolly's own choice for secretary was Miss K. M. Shannon, otherwise known as Mary Devoy or Maire Debhoy. 'She has enthusiasm and business ability, and the S.P.I. is sadly lacking in both. Besides we must get that class of people to take an interest in the movement, and leave to us plebs to do the rough and tumble work. A good National Secretary would be of great service in urging the branches on.'

He had finally found lodgings in Belfast for himself and his family at I Glenalina Terrace at the head of the Falls Road. It was then, as now, a Roman Catholic residential area; Falls Road is mentioned frequently in current newspaper accounts of conflicts between Catholics and non-Catholics in Belfast. Connolly's wife and children moved in on 27 May.

He wrote to Richard J. Hoskins, treasurer of the Socialist Party of Ireland:

The whole affair had me nearly crazy. Between the railway fare of my family to Belfast, the transportation of my furniture and incidental expenses in taking the house it cost me about £4 to move to Belfast, and on the same week I had to raise the instalment on my loan—making a total of £9—exclusive of that interest, all to be paid inside of two weeks. Hence, my past and present anxiety about money . . .

I am under the impression that you imagine that I have been paid already, and Mrs Connolly is under the impression that when the Dublin comrades got us out of Dublin they left us to starve, as she has already been 3 days in Belfast, a strange town, without a penny to buy food, and I away in Scotland. Such an impression on *her* part makes *my* work in the movement rather difficult.

The reasons why Connolly made this move, why he felt that Belfast would be more hospitable than Dublin as a permanent home, are not entirely clear. It may be that Belfast provided more work opportunities for his children than Dublin, although Connolly felt justifiable indignation whenever some well-meaning comrade pointed out to him the advantage of having children of employable age. Or it may be that Connolly was gambling that Larkin would eventually appoint him as Belfast organizer for the Irish Transport Workers Union, a move that O'Brien and others had long been urging Larkin to make.

By the summer of 1911 the Transport Union was well able to afford a full-time organizer in Belfast. The fortunes of Larkin had taken a swift and miraculous upturn. Less than a year before he had seen his union on the edge of disaster, himself bankrupt, and facing a year in prison at hard labour. Now the union had over 5,000 members, the treasury had a balance, and Larkin had acquired, with the astute assistance of William O'Brien, domination over both the Dublin Trades Council and the executive committee (termed Parliamentary Committee) of the Irish Trades Union Congress.

Furthermore, Larkin had possession of the *Irish Worker*, the most effective and best-selling propaganda paper in Ireland. It was a weekly, started in July 1911, with a circulation per issue of 16,000 copies. In August its average circulation was almost 19,000, and in September 23,500. Thereafter it levelled off to 20,000 copies a week, an amazing feat for a paper in an area where *Sinn Fein*, for instance, averaged about 2,000 copies during its subsidized existence. It was a tempestuous, free-swinging sheet that exposed and denounced the numerous cases of labour sweating that flourished in Dublin, naming names and undaunted by the seven cases of libel that were brought against it during its first year of existence. As the first issue had promised, the paper gave 'ventilation . . . to any and every grievance'. The readers revelled at seeing the masters squirm, for Dublin, with a population of 300,000, was still much of a village, and almost every resident knew every person of consequence.

When a strike broke out that closed every port in Britain, including Belfast, Larkin could no longer evade the necessity of hiring every trained organizer he could find. Connolly was first in line. With the notice of his appointment came two weeks' pay. Both were extremely welcome.

In Belfast, four years earlier, James Larkin had led a magnificent organizing effort for the National Union of Dock Labourers. Hundreds of carters, dockers and coal fillers went on strike, but the deep-rooted religious differences, running through all phases of society, prevented any long-term success.

Nevertheless, Larkin had done so well that one of Connolly's problems, when he began organizing, was the loyalty of the men to the National Union of Dock Labourers. The Transport Workers' Union was so far from their minds that, when Connolly opened an office on

Corporation Street, they thought he must be recruiting on behalf of the Seamen's and Firemen's Union, the only rival of importance to the Dock Labourers. Connolly tacitly accepted this view by working closely with the Seamen's and Firemen's Union. He could do this comfortably enough since the SFU was not recruiting the same type of worker. The SFU itself had little strength, even lacking affiliation with the Belfast Trades Council, the association of all important unions in the city.

SFU members were on strike at the Head Line. Connolly proceeded to the lower docks and addressed the men from a conveniently placed barrel. On 19 July, he brought out 300 dock workers in sympathy, and marched with them to meetings at Garmoyle Street and the Custom House steps. There arrangements were made for picketing the boats which plied the English Channel. At the same time the workers put forth their own claims for increased pay, less speed-up, and fewer working hours.

Aware of the many and various weaknesses of the labour front, the employers responded to the sympathetic strike by the sympathetic lock-out; they issued notices that all men had to return to work by Monday, on penalty of a general lock-out. To their surprise, the employees stood firm. Part of the reason was Connolly's tireless ingenuity in keeping enthusiasm high. He obtained players from both Catholic and Orange (Protestant) brass bands and combined them into what became subsequently the 'Non-Sectarian Labour Band'. Using IWW techniques, he paraded through Belfast taking up collections for the strike fund. The Belfast Trades Council, coming to life, held a special meeting on 30 July, at which it pledged full support of the strikers, and invited the Seamen's and Firemen's Union to affiliate with it. With help from Dublin, Connolly was able to make strike payments of 4s. one week and 5s. the next.

All this furore drew attention to the docks. People became aware that men were being paid a penny for shovelling a ton of iron ore, whereas the rate in Britain was fourpence. Grain workers had to lift 100 tons a day for 5s. Hours of work were unlimited. If a winch broke down for fifteen minutes, a quarter of a day's pay was forfeited. So demanding was the pace that men could not stand it for more than three days a week. By straining 'every muscle to the breaking point' and exercising 'feverish recklessness menacing life and limb', they could contrive to earn 15s. a week.

The Burns Laird Line was the first to offer a settlement with their seamen, but the seamen refused to return without the dock workers. The employers grouped their forces by electing a committee to act on behalf of all companies using the port. Wild scenes took place, with coal, grain and flax carts being overturned, and their contents scattered over the cobblestones. But time was running out for the workers. Words, no matter how fervent, could not replace wages. About to leave the union office in order to address another meeting in front of the Customs House, Connolly hesitated, and, leaning on the railing, pondered his next step. It was then that a member gave him a copy of the evening paper. It reported that the employers had decided to offer a compromise settlement which included recognition of the union and a shilling a day extra for 100 tons.

Connolly's face lit up as he read the item. 'We'll accept. Better take what we can and avoid a prolonged struggle,' he remarked. He transformed the meeting into a victory celebration, and the next day issued a statement to the papers, calling attention to the employers' concessions and calling on the public to see that the promises were kept. Belfast remained the lowest paying port in the United Kingdom, but the wage increase averaged 3s. a week, and there was some easing of the pace of work.

As the wave of unrest on the docks ebbed, another wave succeeded it—this time sweeping spontaneously through almost every industry in all of Ireland. Beginning in August 1911 it ranged from Jacob's biscuit factory in Dublin to the bacon factories in Limerick, from the dock labourers in Belfast to the Urban Council employees in Cork. Newsboys, clothing workers, golf caddies, leather tanners, dairy and brewery workers, trolley car men, all clamoured for an increase in wages.

The employers attributed all this to the work of Larkin—an easy error to make as they watched him captivate thousands of workers every night at indoor or outdoor meetings. Over six feet tall, he was a powerful, natural orator, with a 'deep, dark, husky voice and an endless flow of words and sweeping gestures'.

O'Brien wrote to Connolly on 28 September 1911:

'Smash Larkin' is the battle cry in Dublin just now. All the papers—but in particular the Independent—are going for him bald-headed. The meeting of the Dublin Chamber of Commerce yesterday, and the decision to form an organization of Irish Employers, shows a determination to down the Transport Union at all costs. The mover of the resolution said: 'This railway strike is not a strike in the ordinary sense of the word; it is the beginning of a Social War, a Revolution . . . the thin edge of the wedge of Socialism . . . Force must be met by force and the Unions of the workers must be met by Unions of the employers to uphold public order.'

In Belfast as well, affairs remained disturbed. On 4 October 1911, a number of girls in the linen mills, striking spontaneously against a speed-up, asked Connolly for advice. Among them were the wives, daughters and mothers of the dock workers he had just organized. It was Troy all over again. Throughout the shops notices were posted announcing a system of fines for, among other things, singing, laughing, talking, or even 'adjusting the hair during working hours'. A girl who brought sweets or knitting needles into the mill could be instantly fired.

The Belfast Trades Council had previously sponsored the formation of a linen-workers union under the leadership of Miss Mary Galway. Typically enough, she had concentrated on recruiting the better-paid Protestant workers in the 'making-up' section, and had left most of the mill-girls unorganized. She now declined to assist them in their unofficial struggle against the new rules. When some of her own members joined the strikers and went to listen to Connolly's speeches, she held a counter-demonstration to denounce the strike. After holding several open-air meetings, Connolly addressed 1,500 women at St Mary's Hall. Here he advanced a claim for wage increases as well as demanding an end to the restrictive regulations. The band was brought out again and the collection boxes gathered enough to give each striker 2s. a week.

Belfast was thrown into a turmoil. Many Catholic priests denounced the strike. Connolly attended a Mass where he listened impassively through a diatribe against syndicalism, socialism, and Connolly. He probably attended it because he knew what was coming, and thought it important to face the charges. The mill owners stood firm and refused to negotiate. There were no more strike funds to be obtained, and Connolly had to advise the girls to return. But he also told them to disregard the rules. If one girl was reprimanded for singing, let all sing. If one was dismissed, they should all walk out. Fearing that production would be reduced to chaos, the supervisors thereafter allowed the rules to become a dead letter.

Connolly had not entirely lost. The strike had given the girls a unity of will which they had previously lacked, and the basis for organizing a textile workers section of the Irish Transport Workers Union. The new organization was founded at the end of November 1911, with Mrs Tom Johnson as its first secretary. Miss Galway did not let its formation go unchallenged. A week before Christmas, at a meeting of the Belfast Trades Council, where Connolly represented the Transport Union, she complained of interference and requested that Connolly be ordered to 'confine himself to the class of workers he was sent to represent'.

A sharp debate followed. Connolly repudiated the allegation of poaching, pointing out that 18,000 textile workers were unorganized. He reported that, when he was approached by the strikers, he had asked if they were members of Miss Galway's union and had been told, in rather rough language, that they were not. Connolly said the new organization now had offices on York Street, and he was not going to allow 18,000 women to remain unorganized just because the Trades Council had sponsored the Textile Operatives Society. To those who objected to his activities on the docks, he pointed out that he had recently won a rate of 6s. for an 80-ton day, and that by the end of the year every worker on Donegall Quay would be a member of the Transport Union. Against this kind of argument, Miss Galway could not make much headway, and she agreed to 'seek an amicable settlement'.

XVII

1912

IN JANUARY 1912 Connolly was sent to Wexford to see what he could do about settling one of the most bitter labour struggles in the history of Ireland. Wexford, the site of an historic bloodletting by Cromwell's troops in 1649, and of a month-long peasant uprising in 1798, was now being shaken by a lock-out and strike that was affecting all sections of the population, and drawing the attention of all Ireland.

The struggle had begun the previous summer when workers at three iron foundries followed the dock workers into the ranks of the Irish Transport Workers Union. The foundries immediately dismissed their employees. P. T. Daly, an unswerving and loyal supporter of Larkin's union from its earliest days, was sent from Dublin to rouse support, whereupon the dock workers made fresh wage demands and resumed their strike. Extra police were enrolled and charged a demonstration, resulting in the death of a worker. As a result, Daly assembled a 'Workers' Police' force, the first proletarian defence force formed in Ireland.

The strike afforded Arthur Griffith an opportunity to publish in the official Sinn Fein organ a blistering attack on Larkin. In a significant reaction, a strong Gaelic language partisan, Eamonn Ceannt, wrote to Griffith: 'You have no condemnation of the Employers' Federation, or is there one law for them and another for their servants?' When these pro-labour sentiments were adopted by such equally strong Republicans as Padraic Pearse and Sean MacDermott, the road to Easter 1916 was paved.

The employers declined offers from Wexford city officials to mediate, and brought in scab labour, first in driblets then in scores. This created an accommodation problem. Brushing aside the protests of the priests, who wanted to avoid an injection of heretics into their flocks, the employers sought lodgings for their new employees while urging landlords to evict Wexford men for non-payment of rent. The strikers received support not only from the Dublin Trades Council, and from Belfast comrades (at a meeting arranged by Connolly) but also from middle-class sources. The Oulart Trade and Labour League, an organization founded by Michael Davitt, voted funds. Shopkeepers provided credit. The Gaelic Athletic Association organized games in support of the strikers; when its members paraded with black flags, the traditional sign of dissent, the police assaulted them as freely as if they had been foundry workers.

When Connolly got to Wexford he found that Daly had been arrested and lodged in the Waterford—not Wexford—jail. He had been seized quietly, taken to an emergency court in the police barracks, tried in secret and, a true bill being found, taken out of town. When the workers learned of it, there was a protest demonstration at which more arrests were made.

Since Connolly's aim was to settle the strike, not widen it, he approached all the influential elements in the city—employers, clergy, shopkeepers, professionals—with a set of proposals designed, he said, to prevent any possibility that the iron industry so essential to the economy of Wexford would leave. To that end, he suggested that the employers be taken at their word. They had said they would accept any union but the local branch of the Transport Workers Union. He would therefore establish a new Foundryman's Union which would be affiliated nationally with the Transport Union in Dublin. As for the imported workers, most of them did not wish to stay. The Wexford men would return to work on the understanding that the imported workers be sent away as soon as possible. Nothing was said about increasing wages or improving working conditions. The proposals proved basically acceptable, and final terms were negotiated through the good offices of Cruise O'Brien, editor of the Wexford Free Press, who acted as intermediary between Connolly and the employers. 'A drawn battle,' commented Connolly in an aside, as he organized a victory demonstration.

Connolly remained in the area until early March in order to conduct a campaign to free Daly. He called the charge under which Daly was confined—'incitement to riot'— completely illegal, and demanded a public enquiry. Mr Field, MP, brought up the question in Parliament, and soon a compromise was reached. If Daly provided sureties for his good behaviour in Wexford henceforth, he would be released.

Connolly also spent time putting the new Foundrymen's Union on a stable footing, and strengthening other branches in the area. The branch at New Ross had suffered a decline, and Connolly went there to revive it. He was met by the local police chief who confidentially passed on to him word that some local hoodlums intended to attack the open-air meeting that was being planned. For his own safety, the chief said, Connolly should give up his notion of speaking in New Ross. An old hand at dealing with police, Connolly coolly replied, 'I'm not accustomed to being bluffed,' and held his meeting. The thirty-six policemen present formed a large part of the audience. However, a number of workers signified their desire to join the New Ross branch, and marched to its headquarters to fill out the application forms.

*   *   *

At this time, Connolly, like almost everyone else, anticipated the imminent passage of a Home Rule Bill. In his mind it was essential that the Irish Parliament to be established under its provisions should have in it representatives of a labour party qualified and eager to promote Ireland's transformation into a workers' republic. This party would be different from Redmond's Irish Parliamentary Party, with its record of opposition to extending school meals and other social benefits to Ireland; different from the eccentric Social-Democratic Federation, with its splitting tendencies and chauvinism at moments of crisis; different from the British-controlled Independent Labour Party.

Upon returning to Belfast, Connolly redoubled his efforts to bring such a party into existence. He had previously held innumerable conversations with Belfast branches of the Independent Labour Party, with members of the Social-Democratic Federation, and with his comrades in the Socialist Party of Ireland. Now he threw himself into plans for a conference that would bring such a party into existence. This was held at Easter at the Antient Concert Rooms in Dublin. Present were representatives from four Belfast branches of the Independent Labour Party; from the Dublin, Cork and Belfast branches of the Socialist Party of Ireland; and from the Belfast branch of the British Socialist Party. This last group was a fusion of left-wing elements from the Independent Labour Party and the Social-Democratic Federation. Its delegates refused to walk over a British flag that had been placed by a prankish Dubliner as a doormat, and hence their participation ended with startling speed.

The remaining delegates laughed off this contretemps and proceeded to vote into existence an 'Independent Labour Party of Ireland'. Its programme, as drafted by Connolly, was remarkable in that it accepted, and placed side by side, both social-democratic formulations and syndicalist formulations. Having had enough of both Hyndman's opportunism and De Leon's dogmatic ultra-leftism, Connolly emerged with a statement that called for labour organizations to form their own party and support its candidates for elective offices; and for wage earners to organize themselves by industry rather than by craft. The goal of the new party was to build an 'Industrial Commonwealth' based on common ownership of the land and instruments of production, distribution, and exchange. It was to be 'open to all men and women, irrespective of their past political affiliations, who desire to see the working class of their country organized upon the political field'.

The Belfast branch of the new party held a meeting in St Mary's Hall, where Connolly took the lead in denouncing various provisions of the Home Rule Act introduced by the Liberal Party on 11 April 1912. He accused the Redmondites of accepting partition without a struggle, and of placing financial obstacles in the way of Irish representation in the proposed new Parliament by opposing the payment of members. He demanded proportional representation, excision of the proposed Senate, and women's suffrage.

Participating, and notably present as always when good causes were discussed, was Francis Sheehy-Skeffington. Originally from County Cavan, he was smallish but wiry, with a reddish-brown beard, high-pitched voice, and dressed in tweed knickerbockers, long stockings, boots and cap. His opinions resembled those of G. B. Shaw, and his hero was Michael Davitt. He did not agree with Connolly's willingness to respond to injustice with violence, but had the knack of valuing a man at his worth, without regard to the man's opinions. Thus, he found no difficulty in recommending Connolly as a reporter for the *Manchester Guardian*. On 12 April 1912, he wrote to Connolly that the editor C. P. Scott had asked him for the name of

a capable and level-headed person whom we could ask to correspond for us from Belfast . . .

I have sent him two names, of which yours is one. I have suggested that your position as a Socialist and Trade Union official is a good qualification for a detached and 'level-headed' view of Belfast factions.

If you are inclined to take the matter up, it would be worth your while to run over to Manchester and see Scott. He is personally a very pleasant man to deal with, and a keen judge of men.

It was typical of Skeffington to think that a socialist and trade-union organizer could have a detached view of Belfast factions. It was equally typical of Connolly that he did not find time to pursue this lead.

But he did find time to write a long letter to Edward Lynch, a comrade in County Cork, giving his views on the uselessness of borrowing ideas from other countries, on political socialism and on syndicalism. Dated 23 May 1912, a few weeks before Connolly's forty-fourth birthday, the letter reads as follows:

I consider that the problem of the propagation of Socialism in Ireland is a big enough one for you, as it is for me, without taking sides in, or getting excited about, what is happening in a country 100 years ahead of us in political and industrial development. But there are some people in Great Britain who have saturated themselves with American Socialist and Industrial literature to such an extent that their conception of revolutionary work is to copy in Great Britain whatever happens in the American Socialist world. So if there is a split in America there should be a split in Great Britain, and the names taken by the factions in America should be adopted in Great Britain . . . If the Industrialist and 'political' Socialist go for one another's scalps in America instead of seeking to work together in harmony, then the industrialist and the political comrades are bound to seek one another's gore in Great Britain, instead of seeking to avoid the mistakes of the other country. This is the picture presented, to my mind, by the good comrades who are adepts in American Socialist literature in Great Britain.

Your letter seems to indicate that you are developing the same curious bent of mind in the South of Ireland. Instead of trying to develop a Socialist Party based upon the labour movement of Ireland . . . you are cultivating the mind and methods of a little religious sect quarrelling about points of doctrine. Political pro- grammes, political phrases and political parties unless they are the expression of the phase of economic development already arrived at in the country where they exist are but fantastic and unreal will-o- the-wisps luring their users to destruction. American programmes, phrases and parties are no more applicable to Ireland than the programmes, phrases and parties of Ireland are applicable to Timbuctoo. Hence, why get excited about them? When I was in America I took a very decided stand on one side, but if I was to meet in Ireland to-day a man who took the opposite side I would fraternise with him and forget about our feuds.

After recommending that Lynch read an article by Jean Jaurès dealing with the true relationship between syndicalism and socialism published a few weeks earlier in the *Irish Worker*, Connolly went on:

Syndicalism is simply the discovery that the workers are strongest at the point of production, that they have no force available but economic force, and that by linking the revolutionary movement with the daily fight of the workshop, mill, shipyard and factory the necessary economic force can be organised. Also that the revolutionary organisation necessary for that purpose provides the frame-work of the Socialist Republic. Upon that point all Syndicalists are agreed and nothing else is necessary to make a Syndicalist. All the so-called differences are simply a proof of the fact that this idea appeals to men and women of all temperaments and of every political bias. My conception of Syndicalism is in that book under the name of Industrial Unionism, which name I still prefer. Tom Mann is now anti-political in theory, so are many others. But as long as we agree upon the essential point why cavil about others? And the essential point is a belief in the wisdom of organising the economic power of the workers for the revolutionary act.

Soon afterward the Irish Trades Union Congress met at Clonmel. Connolly, carrying out a life-long dream, presented a resolution from the Belfast branch of the Irish Transport Workers Union that an Irish Labour Party be established. The proposition stated that 'amongst the objects of this Congress' should be included 'the independent representation of Labour upon all public boards'. One day at least should be devoted to this subject at future annual meetings. Affiliated unions should pay a levy of one shilling per year per member to defray the expense of political activity. As one point in his argument, Connolly said that the loss to Irish workers of the medical benefits of the British Insurance Act was directly traceable to the absence of a satisfactory labour party in Ireland.

The craft unions took the lead in opposing the motion. In rebuttal,

Connolly, who was becoming no mean diplomat, complimented his opponents on the form of their speeches and his supporters on their substance. The resolution to establish the Labour Party was passed by a vote of 49 to 18.

Passage of the resolution entitles Connolly to the position of a principal founder of the Irish Labour Party. It represents one of Connolly's greatest achievements, on a par with his studies in Irish history, his reorganization of the Irish Transport and General Workers Union after Larkin's departure, and his martyrdom. The party thus born went through many years of struggle before it reached maturity; it has still not gained power but few doubt that, as Ireland continues its course of urbanization and industrialization, it will some day have its turn at controlling the Irish parliament.

Few of the delegates at Clonmel paid any attention to the fulminations against the Home Rule Bill delivered during previous months by such Orange hot-heads as Edward Carson. One of England's most successful barristers, he had warned that, if the Bill was passed, Ulstermen 'would march from Belfast to Cork, and take the consequences, even if not one of them returned'. If Ulster won, there would be no Irish Parliament in which an Irish Labour Party could function.

Connolly, together with most of his colleagues, considered these the rantings of a fanatical few, and concentrated on the task of creating, by word and pen, a stronger and more mature working class equipped to take control of the country. This task involved attending innumerable meetings, addressing all kinds of audiences in outdoor or indoor meetings, and writing at great length for the *Irish Worker*.

Cathal O'Shannon, a devoted follower from the time of Connolly's return to Ireland in 1910, has described his talks as having

something in them different and apart from any I have heard anywhere. He was not exactly a great orator, although he could rise to oratory too. But he had a method, a style, a manner that exactly fitted and adorned the splendid material he used in his speeches. He was never slipshod, never flamboyant, but always earnest, simple and informative. He spoke as one who had carefully thought out what he was going to say, and before saying a single word he had obviously chosen just the right words that would convey his meaning and his message. His sentences came then freely and naturally enough, and every word told effectively. And in a single speech he was master of all the styles every aspect of his subject required. But he never played to the gallery. He always had respect for the intelligence of his audience, and he invariably suited the form of his address and the manner of presenting his argument to the particular audience before him. The result was that from Connolly you got a cogent, coherent and reasoned statement of a case, presented in the clearest manner, illustrated by the most telling allusions, with the argument marshalled in the coldest and calmest fashion, yet warmed with the burning fire of sincerity and sympathy. And it was always chock-full of good stuff, as informative and as educative as his writings, but never put in a schoolmasterly way and never above—nor yet below— the heads of those listening to him.

The effect of Connolly's oratory was remarkable. If it did not arouse the wild and whirling enthusiasm evoked by the outburst of a demagogue, it created enthusiasm of a different kind. It compelled assent as well as respect, it carried conviction and it aroused enthusiasm of the more lasting kind, a quiet, enduring enthusiasm which forced the hearer to act on Connolly's side rather than cheer his words.

For the *Irish Worker* Connolly wrote a series of articles dealing with housing and health conditions in the city of Dublin; the problems of the working class in Belfast; the condition of women in Ireland; the history of agricultural co-operatives; and the lack of decent schools and schooling in Dublin and Belfast.

These pieces were collected and issued in 1915 as a single book of some ninety pages under the title of *The Re-Conquest of Ireland*. Its underlying idea is to demonstrate the need for the Irish labour movement to reconquer Ireland, and what such a reconquest involves in modern times.

The first chapters are historical; they explain how Ireland was conquered and its Catholic residents subjected and despoiled by force; and how the early Protestant settlers were similarly robbed first by fraud and then by force. The middle section deals with conditions in urban Ireland in Connolly's time. The final chapter describes those elements which have the promise of reconquering Ireland: industrial unionism; public ownership of the means of production; political power in the hands of labour parties; co-operation from intellectuals; and a 'concert of action' between city workers and members of the new agricultural co-operative societies proposed by AE.

In a concluding paragraph, Connolly urges all worthwhile elements to support labour's cause as the way in which they can achieve their own ends. He put it this way:

The Gaelic Leaguer realises that capitalism did more in one century to destroy the tongue of the Gael than the sword of the Saxon did in Six; the apostle of self-reliance amongst Irishmen and women finds no more earnest exponents of self-reliance than those who expound it as the creed of Labour; the earnest advocates of co-operation find the workers stating their ideals as a co-operative commonwealth; the earnest teacher of Christian morality sees that in the co-operative commonwealth alone will true morality be possible, and the fervent patriot learns that his hopes of an Ireland re-born to National life is better stated and can be better and more completely realised, in the Labour movement for the Re-Conquest of Ireland.

Though the pamphlet lacks unity, the average reader will be impressed by its scholarly quality; the amount of data it presents on urban life in Ireland during the early twentieth century; the novelty of such ideas as the oppression of the Presbyterian settlers by the Episcopalian settlers; and above all by the obvious sincerity, integrity and high purpose of the author. These qualities, in addition to the author's special empathy for the plight of women, emerge clearly in such passages as this one:

Wherever there is a great demand for female labour, as in Belfast, we find that the woman tends to become the chief support of the house. Driven out to work at the earliest possible age, she remains fettered to her wage-earning—a slave for life. Marriage does not mean for her a rest from outside labour, it usually means that, to the outside labour, she has added the duty of a double domestic toil. Throughout her life she remains a wage-earner; completing each day's work, she becomes the slave of the domestic needs of her family; and when at night she drops wearied upon her bed, it is with the knowledge that at the earliest morn she must find her way again into the service of the capitalist, and at the end of that coming day's service for him hasten homeward again for another round of domestic drudgery. So her whole life runs—a dreary pilgrimage from one drudgery to another; the coming of children but serving as milestones in her journey to signalise fresh increases to her burdens. Overworked, underpaid, and scantily nourished because underpaid, she falls easy prey to all the diseases that infect the badly-constructed 'warrens of the poor'. Her life is darkened from the outset by poverty, and the drudgery to which poverty is born, and the starvation of the intellect follows as an inevitable result upon the too early drudgery of the body. Of what use to such sufferers can be the re-establishment of any form of Irish State if it does not embody the emancipation of womanhood.

Passage at Clonmel of the resolution for establishing a labour party did not automatically bring it into existence. Nor did the sense of shared victory bring about warmer feelings between Connolly and Larkin. When William O'Brien wrote to Connolly asking for a special article for the *Irish Worker*, Connolly replied on 29 June 1912:

. . . the first question that arises to my mind is: 'In what capacity do you make the request?' Is it made with Jim's authority and sanction? For, of course, I know that unless it is so made, there might be a doubt as to it appearing.

I may mention that I wrote to Jim stating that I had still two chapters of the 'Re-Conquest of Ireland' to write, and as there had been a suggestion, *originating with him*, that they might be published as a Labour Party Pamphlet, I would be obliged if he would let me know if that was his desire, as in that case I would phrase those two chapters accordingly. I have received no acknowledgment even of the letter; hence the non-appearance of the two chapters in question.

Connolly went on to ask if anything was going to be done about the labour party resolution. If the executive committee, otherwise called the Parliamentary Committee, of the Irish Trades Union Congress was to meet its usual number of times, arrange for the usual representations, 'and make no effort to rise up to the level of the new situation, it would have been better had we been defeated. The Committee has now the chance to create a great Labour movement on sound political lines, and should not hesitate to go out of the beaten track and create precedents instead of following old ones.' In particular, Connolly wrote, the committee should not have departed Clonmel without instructing its secretary to send notices to all trade unions asking for

involved in polemics with Catholic lay and clerical
question of whether the Catholic Church had ever been
olitical matters. The discussion, based on a review in
ald of Connolly's pamphlet, *Labour, Nationality and*
conducted in the columns of the *Catholic Times* of
e *Catholic Democrat*, and at an annual conference of the
 Society. Greaves reports that Connolly's handling of
controversy 'greatly enlarged his reputation among the
s who surrounded the *Daily Herald*, and brought him to
bate with Hilaire Belloc at the Irish Club in Charing
On this occasion the audience was astonished at the ease
Connolly trounced one of the leading intellectuals of

e end of 1912, Connolly ran for a seat in the Belfast
The ward he sought to represent contained the homes of
ort Union members, and Connolly received the official
Belfast Trades Council. In his election address, Connolly
abour needed more representation in the City Council
ouncil had certain duties to perform under the National
nce Act which otherwise might not be properly done. If
omised to help the City Council pay more attention to
; than to perpetuating the 'religious discords which make
vord among civilised nations'. His programme also called
ing of labour on city contracts, a union shop for city
minimum wage of sixpence an hour, the enclosing of
cars used by workers in the chilly morning and evening
 more democratic selection of the members of the
rbour Board.
nunicipal Socialism' with a vengeance, but Connolly did
eive the voters concerning his larger aims. He stated that
all-out socialism, a system to be achieved by the 'con-
se in the power of the working class'. It was as a socialist
of this class that he sought election. He also declared
dvocate of national independence for Ireland and a sup-
ne Rule. He favoured equal rights for women, including
ote.
ost part, Catholics, Nationalists, Socialists and trade
ed for Connolly in the January 1913 elections, although
with reluctance, thinking that votes for women were a
h. Others were unable to find any logical connection

action on the resolution, and to union associations urging them to hold public meetings in support of it.

The person at fault was not O'Brien, who had been working hard since the Clonmel Congress in May to get the Parliamentary Committee to implement Connolly's resolution; the fault was Larkin's. Elected chairman of this Committee, he had resigned in a huff at its initial meeting when other members disagreed with one of his rulings. He was adamant in his refusal to withdraw his resignation or to take the lead in forming the proposed Labour Party.

Connolly got the story in a letter from O'Brien dated 12 September 1912 (names of persons and organizations have been amplified to facilitate comprehension):

I assume David R. Campbell posted you about the proceedings of the last meeting of the Parliamentary Committee of the Irish Trades Union Congress and especially the attitude assumed by Larkin with regard to the arrangements about the public meetings in support of labour representation. Well, it seems he intends to persist in his resignation, as he has refused to attend the Conference held by the Dublin Parliamentary Committee members with representatives of the Dublin Trades Council to make arrangements for the inaugural meeting to be held in the Antient Concert Rooms on Monday next, and we have reason to believe that he will not even speak on that occasion. Those who are pushing the question of Labour Representation here are being vigorously denounced by Lord Mayor Sherlock and Co as 'enemies of Home Rule' and 'Socialists in disguise', and are being left severely alone by the old gang in the Unions, so that Larkin's defection at this moment puts us in an awkward corner. Without a speaker like Larkin, I'm afraid the appeal will fall rather flat . . . I'm terribly sorry that you are not to be one of the speakers.

Connolly's reply, dated 13 September 1912, is given in full:

Your very distressing letter just arrived. I begin to fear that our friend Jim has arrived at his highest elevation, and that he will pull us all down with him in his fall.

He does not seem to want a democratic Labour movement; he seems to want a Larkinite movement only. The situation will require the most delicate handling. I would have been in favour of cancelling the Antient Concert fixture, of informing Larkin that as he will not attend, you do not see your way to go on with it, and that pending and awaiting his co-operation, you feel it unwise to go further with the movement. This *seems* tame and slavish advice, and it is; but it is, I fear, the only way to get him on the move again. He must rule, or will not work, and in the present stage of the Labour movement, he has us at his mercy. And he knows it, and is using his power unscrupulously, I regret to say. We can but bow our head, and try and avert the storm.

It is impossible that I should be there. He would have too much of a grip on me, as he would be able to appeal to my own members against me, on the plea that I neglected my duty to go there against his wish. At present my strength in Belfast is that no one knows whether his influence counts for much amongst the Transport Workers here. There is a strong feeling against him in the phrase that 'He was a great fighter, but too reckless.' So a fight by him upon me would wreck the Branch again, and he is headstrong enough to make it. He knows he could not oust me, and save the Branch, but in the case of too flagrant a flouting of his position, he would not consider that.

I am sick of all this playing to one man, but I am prepared to advise it for the sake of the movement. In fact, the general inactivity since the Congress has made me sick and sorry I ever returned.

Connolly had learned at least one thing from his experience with De Leon. Egotists must be handled with care.

It was decided to hold the meeting in any case. Larkin did not take the chair but he did attend and speak. What he said was petty, nagging and pointless, and he was obviously upset. He later attributed this to illness.

For the next few years the movement for an Irish Labour Party was quiescent as other controversies flared up. The principal one concerned Home Rule. Orange and Catholic fervour grew at the same pace. In June 1912, members of the Ancient Order of Hibernians broke up a Protestant school outing at Castledawson. In response Orange workers at the Workman-Clarke shipyard beat up some Catholic workers. The disturbances spread to Harland and Wolff's huge ship-building yards, where Carsonite sentiment forced the 'Disemployment' of some two thousand Catholics, together with 400 Englishmen and Scotsmen who refused to co-operate with the Orange firebrands. Though stationed in Belfast, Connolly could steer clear of these

disputes for the time being because th
the Transport and the Textile Worker
Catholic and lived in a seamless Roma
he instituted daytime open-air meet
Textile Workers Union gradually rose
amount for those times. He also tried t
beginning with Irish dancing, but the g
Another difficulty arose when the
became sick and had to be replaced
from the suffragette ranks.

But Connolly was still able to sh
During July 1912, under the auspices
only union that allows no bigotry i
evening demonstration. Headed by the
the procession of dock workers and mi
at 122 Corporation Street and proceed
Connolly and others addressed them.
evening was missed. If Connolly was
place. 'Civil and religious liberty' was
frequent references to women's right t
controversial; many suffragette meetin
were being broken up at the time.

On 28 September 1912, Ulster senti
Bill reached a peak when a 'Solemn Lea
means which may be found necessary to
to set up a Home Rule Parliament' was
people. In December 1912, the signatorie
to fight for their beliefs by enlisting in t
applied to the magistrates for authoriza
received it.

Connolly, still convinced that the ru
strong majority and widespread support,
these fanatics was busy with other matters.
a manifesto *To the Linen Slaves of Belfast*,
mills to strike. It was, he said, the only
obtain the minimum wages of three pence
Sweated Industries Act but never applied t
that the spinning room held the key to th
special appeal to the reelers and spinners
some of our pious mill-owners spend week

He was al
leaders on th
mistaken in
the *Daily H
Religion*, wa
London and
Catholic Tru
his part in th
Catholic circ
London to
Cross Road.
with which
Britain.'

Towards
City Council
many Trans
support of th
argued that
because the
Health Insur
elected, he
school feedi
Belfast a by-
for direct h
employees,
certain tram
hours, and
important H

This was
not try to d
he advocate
tinuous inc
and membe
himself an
porter of H
the right to

For the
unionists v
many did
bit too mu

between Home Rule for Ireland and socialist doctrine. However, there were more than enough Protestants, Unionists and Orangemen in the ward to defeat Connolly, and he lost by a vote of 905 to 1,523.

During the election campaign, Catholic hoodlums prevented the socialists from holding meetings on Barrack Street. The threat of similar stonings by Protestant hoodlums kept the socialists from holding their meetings in Protestant areas. The socialists had to find refuge on Clonard Street, off the Falls Road, for their open-air meetings. It was a significant sign of a trend—the crushing of the Irish labour movement by religious bigotry. Connolly probably thought that this change of meeting place was merely a temporary intensification of the age-long religious division in northern Ireland.

The important events were taking place in Dublin. In January 1912 Jim Larkin had won a smashing victory for a seat in the Dublin city government. Debarred from taking this seat because of his previous conviction as a felon, Larkin was free to turn his enormous energies in the direction of organizing the Irish working class and imbuing it with the philosophy of the sympathetic strike and direct action. He completed organization of the docks by detaching the stevedores from the shipping firms and persuading them to enter a new organization affiliated with the Transport Workers Union. At the same time he was busy organizing the general, miscellaneous and casual workers employed in small factories which had never been reached before by a trade union. To cap it all, he made plans for organizing the most difficult employees of all—the agricultural workers of County Dublin —and in 1913 successfully carried out these plans. Meanwhile, Larkin's sister Delia founded an Irish Women Workers' Union. The membership figures for the Transport Workers Union tell the tale: in 1911, something less than 4,000; in 1912, about 8,000; in 1913, about 14,000. A growth of three-and-a-half times in two years.

XVIII

1913

DURING THE early part of 1913, while the Ulster Volunteers began training to combat Home Rule by force, Connolly was deep in matters of union administration. The Irish Transport Workers' Union had registered as a society 'approved' for disbursing funds under a National Insurance Act, and it was necessary for Connolly to hire and train clerks so that government requirements would be met. Connolly was in favour of the Act, writing to Matheson on 6 June 1913 that 'the people who are howling out against compulsory contributions, and about the worker being robbed of the awful sum of 4d or 3d are playing right into the hands of the reactionaries'.

His task was complicated by the fact that Jim Larkin, who legally controlled the funds, was a careless administrator in every sense of the word. Connolly scarcely had time to answer any letters because, he wrote to O'Brien, 'Jim withholds all books etc. until the day after the last legal minute. With a result that we have to do in a day what ought to be done in the course of a whole week.'

Nor was Larkin averse to raiding the insurance funds in order to pay strike benefits, forcing Connolly on occasion to go to Dublin to thump on Larkin's desk in protest. By summertime Connolly was ready to resign, writing to Larkin on 15 July 1913:

> On the occasion of your last visit here you asked me for a statement of our expenditure which was furnished you on July 1st.
>
> Since that time I have on more than one occasion asked for a statement that we might start this quarter clear. Everything here is in arrears, our clerks' salaries atrociously so. But no notice is taken of my appeal.
>
> Last week I asked Mr. Casey for £25, which he promised to

send, but only sent £20, and as I had to pay Insurance Benefits to the extent of £28. 12. 2. I consider this response to my appeal if not designedly insulting, has at least all the appearance of it.

Under these circumstances I can only conclude that you are dissatisfied with my conduct of the Insurance Section, perhaps with more than that, and as I can take a hint as well as anyone I must ask you to come through here this week, or send some one through to re-organise.

I propose absenting myself, on holiday, from the offices from Wednesday, July 16. Whether I ever resume office or not will of course depend upon the report of your agent. All the books of both sections, trade union and Insurance, will be left in the hands of Miss Carney and Mr. Flanagan, in their respective positions.

Larkin responded by asking Connolly to come to Dublin to straighten out matters. After the meeting, Connolly wrote to William O'Brien that he didn't think he could stand Larkin as a boss much longer.

He tried to bully me out of the monies due to our branch for administration benefit of the Insurance Act, and it was this that brought me to Dublin last week. He did not succeed, and had to pay £37 which was due my staff as wages. I told him that if he was Larkin twenty times over he could not bully me, that I was charging for not one cent he had not contracted to pay for, and that I was not going to hire clerks and leave them without their wages to suit him . . .

I would formerly have trusted to his generosity in financial matters, now I would not trust him at all.

The two men were also at odds about the speed with which Connolly was organizing the Belfast dock workers. In the same letter quoted above, Connolly wrote:

He is for ever snarling at me and drawing comparisons between what he accomplished in Belfast in 1907, and what I have done, conveniently ignoring the fact that he was then the Secretary of an *English* organisation, and that as soon as he started an Irish one his union fell to pieces, and he had to leave the members to their fate.

He is consumed with jealousy and hatred of anyone who will not cringe to him and beslaver him all over.

Connolly found much relief and pleasure in his work with the linen mill girls, even though he had to pay his salary of 5s. a week as its organizer from his own pocket. Though the union made little progress (only the dances, now making no educational pretences, held it together), working with it was important. For Connolly, it was a matter of principle as well as pleasure. On 6 June 1913, he wrote to Matheson:

I am unfeignedly glad to hear that you are on the right side in this Woman's business. The attitude of most Socialists, including the chief Socialist press, in that matter is just beneath contempt. All glory to the women, say I! Their hearty rebellion is worth more than a thousand speeches of the doctrinaires with which the Socialist movement . . . is infected. I am with the militants, heart and soul.

The girls, all pious Catholics, were not offended by Connolly's indifference to religion. When a friend, Danny MacDevitt, pointed out to him that it might be politic to raise his hat when he passed a church, he lifted it, looked at Danny quizzically, scratched his head, and replaced it. The girls ignored his dreadful book against Catholicism, unsold copies of which lay around the union office. Connolly told a strong Catholic supporter, James Grimley, that he had 'long ceased to practise religion'. But the girls also sensed that he meant it when he told Grimley, 'I would die for the Irish Papist.'

Connolly made few demands on his mill-girls. Lively and high-spirited, they playfully threw snowballs at Countess Markievicz when she came to speak to them at the gates. But they read and understood his new manifesto 'To the Linen Lords', when it appeared in March 1913.

The 'flax roughers' were not members of his union, and on one occasion tried to break up a meeting of the Textile Union. But in mid-April, when these workers struck for their own demands, Connolly gave them unconditional support. On 2 May, he and others spoke by invitation before the flax roughers, and all speakers called for one big union for the linen trade. This meeting was held on Falls Road, in the Irish area. The day before it had been possible to hold the May Day meeting on the Custom House steps only because of a show of overwhelming strength. The appeal of Connolly, Malcolm of the railwaymen, and others for working-class solidarity rang hollow in this period of increasing religious bigotry.

O'Brien, in Dublin, was worried about the forthcoming Irish Trades Union Congress. Larkin was still sticking to his decision not to resume chairmanship of the Parliamentary Committee, and was threatening not to attend even as a delegate. O'Brien, conscripted to take the position, lacked time to write the customary presidential address. On 9 March 1913, he wrote to Connolly asking if he would write the speech for him.

It was a long letter in which he confided other worries. A record number of conservative delegates were coming from Cork, supposedly intent on ousting such militants as himself, Daly and Larkin. It was important therefore that Belfast send as many delegates as possible. O'Brien thought that it might be a good idea to run Connolly for a seat on the Parliamentary Committee if Larkin remained obdurate, and that Connolly should prepare for the Congress a few resolutions 'that will give you an opportunity of giving a good lead'.

The fight in Dublin against Larkin and his union was growing keener every day, O'Brien wrote

> The misrepresentation in the press is cruel, and has a bad effect on his members, I greatly fear. Scarce a day passes but the 'Independent' contains an attack of some kind, and the 'Telegraph', which up to 9 months ago was not so bad, is even worse because it has ten times the influence of Murphy's rag. How it will all end 'tis hard to say. Larkin is looking and feeling bad lately, and if the strain is not eased soon, I fear he will break down mentally and physically. He must be made of iron to stand it so long. He is despondent too, which is most unusual with him, and told me a week ago, and a number of us last night, that if this fight with the City of Dublin [Steam Packet Company] was over that he would resign and leave the country altogether.

This letter has special interest as indicating that as early as March 1913 Larkin was contemplating departure from Ireland.

O'Brien concluded by stating that the Independent Labour Party of Ireland was in the doldrums; 'but the lectures are kept going and the landlord is, with a struggle, placated somehow or other each month, so I suppose we must be satisfied, and hope for better times.'

The Irish Trades Union Congress met at Cork from 12 May to

14 May 1913. Connolly was present as a representative of the Belfast transport workers. William O'Brien delivered the presidential address (presumably drafted by Connolly) which spoke confidently of the growing power of labour. It was basically accurate; though the movement in Belfast was fighting a rearguard action, labour elsewhere was making important advances.

The Congress took a long step towards making the proposed Irish Labour Party more than a pious hope by adopting a resolution (proposed by a special committee consisting of Connolly and others) for setting up a permanent committee to draft a constitution for it. This permanent committee would also attempt to give effect to political decisions of the Congress; examine all legislative measures affecting labour in Ireland; indicate any legal actions required; obtain labour representation on public bodies; and support the British Trades Union Congress in all matters affecting the United Kingdom as a whole. The committee would meet four times a year, and its sub-committee would meet every month.

At the Congress, Connolly spoke at various times attacking the gerrymander implicit in the Home Rule Bill, still not doubting that it would become law; denouncing the Liberal Government's use of coercion against suffragettes; and supporting the extension to Ireland of the medical benefits contained in the Insurance Acts. A report was heard from a deputation that had gone to London to ask the British Labour Party to insist on proportional representation in the Home Rule Bill. When a delegate asked, 'Was sending a deputation to London an innovation?' Connolly responded, 'Everything we do is an innovation.' It was better, he thought, to appeal to their own class across the water than to their enemies in Ireland.

The people in Cork who disliked economic unrest and who followed Redmond and his United Irish League were not pleased at the invasion of their city by the Irish Trades Union Congress. The United Irish League *Examiner* did not hesitate to publish such slogans as 'Keep Larkin out' and 'refuse hospitality'. But thanks to the strengthening of trade unionism under Larkin's magic touch, they could not make much headway in discouraging the invasion. At Daunt Square two large meetings were held without incident. The first was sponsored by the Congress, the second by the Irish Transport Workers' Union. Speakers at both included Connolly and Larkin, the latter having showed up in Cork after all. On one morning Connolly and Ellen Gordon travelled to nearby Blackpool, addressed the workers at a

224

local linen mill, and organized a branch of the Textile Workers' Union forthwith. That evening, together with Larkin and O'Brien, they spoke again at a meeting sponsored by the Independent Labour Party of Ireland. The audience was friendly, making amends for its behaviour towards socialists of two years earlier.

Soon after Connolly returned to Belfast, he found that working-class militancy was growing, but that opposition to it was growing even faster. On 6 June 1913, Connolly wrote to O'Brien (finally addressing him as 'Bill') that

I am in the midst of strife and tribulation here, a strike on in the brickworks, 300 men out, a strike in Larne, the same number out, and a rival union established on the docks to fight us—the Belfast Transport Workers' Union. This is an Orange move, fostered by the employers, and directed by a Councillor Finnigan, an Orange leader. I see ahead the fight of our life.

For years the workers at the aluminium plant in Larne, north of Belfast, had been dissatisfied with their seven-day week, twelve-hour day schedule. Almost all were Protestants, but some had not been able to get to church on a Sunday for years. Feeling the whiff of fresh air being blown from Dublin, 300 aluminium workers and a number of dockers joined the Irish Transport Workers' Union, and promptly went on strike.

All the Protestant clergy sent out notices to the strikers, inviting them to come to church on 15 June, the following Sunday, since they were now free to do so. Then every minister delivered a sermon against the strike, representing it as a devilish Fenian and Papist plot. The strikers were told that it was their Christian duty to go back to work and rely on the generosity of the management for satisfaction of their grievances. The workers took the advice, providing a classic example of how 'religion' could support exploitation. Connolly commented bitterly that it was Ulster, not the southern provinces, that was the clergy-ridden part of Ireland.

The same Protestant clergy gave ardent support to the Orange rebellion against Home Rule. They were joined by such eminent persons as Andrew Bonar Law (leader of the Conservative Party), Walter Long, Lord Esher, Lord Curzon, F. E. Smith (later Lord Birkenhead), Lord Milner, Viscount Halifax, Rudyard Kipling and Sir Edward Elgar. At Easter 1912, in Belfast, Bonar Law took the salute from 100,000 Ulster Volunteers marching past him in formation. Guns poured into Ulster and military manoeuvres became part of the Ulster landscape.

When the time came for the Orangemen to celebrate the Battle of the Boyne, all Connolly could do for the young republicans who came to him for assistance in frustrating the celebration, was to write an historical note informing the Orangemen that they were really celebrating a papist festival; that Te Deums were sung in Rome when news of King William's victory reached the Vatican. Printed on adhesive paper, this document was plastered on the route when the Orange lodges held their usual processional on 12 July.

Connolly described the situation in a letter to William O'Brien dated 29 July 1913:

> Our transport members here are not near so good a class as they have in Dublin, and the feeling of the city is so violently Orange and anti-Irish at present that our task has been a hard one all along. But we have gained for them more substantial advantages than even the Dublin men have gained. But as a consequence of all the rival unions and sectarianism here our expenses have always been higher than other branches. Our fight is a fight not only against the bosses, but against the political and religious bigotry which destroys all feeling of loyalty to a trade-union.

The growing Carsonite terror against nationalism and labour found an easy target in Connolly's textile and transport unions. The opportunity came in August when the unions held a joint outing to Portrush, travelling by rail. On their return, the members were almost mobbed by a crowd of ten thousand Orangemen from the shipyards who had assembled at the railway terminal. While waiting, they had entertained themselves by firing pistol shots and singing patriotic songs. The union members ran a terrifying gauntlet of sticks and stones as they left the railway station under a simulation of 'police protection'.

Despite the unfavourable climate, Connolly managed during the month of August 1913 to negotiate a contract for the labourers working for 'G. & G. Burns Ltd. Shipowners'. Its provisions show what it was like to work in Belfast at this time. The dock labourers worked six days a week, ten hours a day. Their salary was one shilling an hour, £3 a week. The company could spread the daily ten hours in any manner it chose between the hours of six in the morning to seven at night. However, no man was to be released from work with fewer than four hours of labour recorded. The men were given two hours off each day for meals. Overtime was granted for work on Sundays and holidays—but Christmas Day was the only holiday. The Transport Union was recognized as the official bargaining agent.

Hardly was this agreement signed when Connolly received, on 29 August, a telegraph summoning him to Dublin to take part in the general strike or lock-out (either term can be justified) of 1913, one of the greatest labour struggles in West European history. It lasted some five months, and affected over 20,000 workers. These men, with their families, comprised one-third of the entire population of Dublin.

XIX

THE STRUGGLE began in August 1913 when Larkin began to organize the men who distributed the *Irish Independent*, the Dublin daily published by his arch-enemy, the slight, seventy-year-old capitalist, William Martin Murphy. On the 18th Murphy dismissed forty men who refused to resign from the Irish Transport Workers' Union. On 21 August Murphy ordered the workers on his trolley-car system to sign a pledge to continue working if the union called a strike. On the morning of Tuesday, 26 August, the drivers and conductors responded by stopping their cars and abandoning them. This occurred during Horse Show week, the height of Dublin's fashionable season.

At a giant meeting held at Beresford Place, Larkin announced that a demonstration would be held on O'Connell Street the coming Sunday, and, 'by the living God, if they want war they can have it'. On the morning of 28 August, five Labour leaders, including Larkin, were arrested for 'seditious conspiracy' and for raising 'discontent and hatred' between 'the working classes of Dublin, the police forces of the Crown and the soldiers of the Crown . . .'

The *Daily Herald*, the London Trades Council, the British Socialist Party and the Dublin Trades Council demanded Larkin's immediate release, and issued an appeal for funds. Within hours of his arrest, Larkin and his colleagues were released on payment of bail.

Connolly reached Dublin on the evening of Friday, 29 August, in time to participate at another meeting in Beresford Square. Before the 10,000 people assembled, Larkin burned a proclamation banning the Sunday demonstration, and vowed that he would be on O'Connell Street Sunday 'dead or alive'. As Larkin discreetly vanished, Connolly took the rostrum. He said that, even if the meeting were banned, he saw no reason why people should not be permitted to take a stroll through O'Connell Street to see if a meeting were being held there or not. The King of England hardly had the right to prevent Dubliners from gathering in their principal thoroughfare. The police finally broke up the meeting.

The Government was not slow to react. Connolly and William Partridge (for the second time) were promptly arrested on Saturday afternoon, 30 August, and given a swift hearing by a magistrate appropriately named Swifte. Connolly told the magistrate that he did not recognize the ban on the meeting because 'I do not recognise English Government in Ireland at all. I do not even recognise the King except when I am compelled to do so.' As for the proposed O'Connell Street meeting, he had advised the people not to 'hold a meeting', but merely to 'be there'. He reminded the judge that 'the only manner in which progress can be made is by guaranteeing the right of the people to assemble and voice their grievances'. He refused to give bail as a pledge of good behaviour, and was sentenced to three months' imprisonment. It was not a bad start. Twenty-four hours in Dublin and he was already in Mountjoy Prison. Larkin, informed that a warrant was out for him also, made his way secretly that Saturday afternoon to the home of Countess Markievicz, Surrey House in the Dublin suburb of Rathmines. The Count and Countess held a dance there that evening which effectively put detectives off the track.

With tempers inflamed, fights broke out between strikers and police at a football game at Ringsend, and between strikers and scabs on Pearse Street. In a wild baton charge on Saturday night near Liberty Hall, a 'bright and promising' young worker, James Nolan, was clubbed to death by the police, and James Byrne was fatally injured. It was charged that the police had been drinking. In the face of such disorders, with Larkin missing and Connolly in jail, William O'Brien did what he considered the sensible thing. He ordered that the demonstration planned on Sunday be transferred from the heart of the city to Croydon Park, the recreation area in Clontarf owned by the Transport Union. This action was countermanded by Larkin, but it explains why so few strikers were on O'Connell Street that Sunday afternoon when Larkin dramatically stepped out on the balcony of the Imperial Hotel, another of Murphy's properties, and addressed the pedestrians below. His arrest was followed by a riot in which four hundred persons, mostly inoffensive churchgoers, were bludgeoned by the police.

During September 1913 the number of men dismissed for refusing to sign the Murphy pledge (not to join the Transport Union or leave it if he already belonged) rose to 25,000. Among them were the workers in Jacob's biscuit plant, the coal trade, the construction industry, timber and cement workers, and even farm workers. The month was further marked by emotional funeral parades for Nolan and Byrne, by a vain attempt of emissaries from the British Trades Union Congress to work out a settlement, and by the beginning of a flow of money from trade unions and labour periodicals to the Dublin Lockout Committee, for which William O'Brien, the clubfooted tailor, acted as secretary. The only instrument that might have won the battle—a sympathetic strike on the part of all British labour—never won the approval of the top leaders. The refusal to handle 'tainted goods' by Liverpool dockers and railway workers in Birmingham, Yorkshire and South Wales was not enough.

Immured in Mountjoy Prison, Connolly became increasingly discontented—not by the squalor and bad food, which he had expected—but by the lack of news about the progress of the strike. The first days had not been unpleasant; he had been visited by Danny McDevitt from Belfast, who promised to bring him a grammar so that he could begin the study of Irish; by William O'Brien, Richard Hoskins, Sheehy-Skeffington; and by Keir Hardie, 'the grand old man of British Socialism'. Connolly and Hardie, their doctrinal differences of a dozen years ago forgotten, discussed only ways of winning the current labour struggle. Hardie went on to Belfast where he succeeded in obtaining the support of the Trades Union for the strike.

Connolly implored each visitor to arrange with a news dealer to supply him daily with the *Citizen, Herald, News* and either the *Evening Telegraph* or *Freeman's Journal*. When his requests were ignored, he wrote, passionately and at length, to O'Brien: 'It is hard to hunger for news and get none. I dont expect people to come up with papers every day, but it is a simple thing to arrange with a newsagent. Please for old times sake see that the little is granted to Yours fraternally, James Connolly.'

Two days later, on Sunday, 7 September, Connolly went on a hunger strike. Too much was going on outside for him to remain idle in jail. It happened to be a good time to protest, since it had been disclosed that magistrate Swifte was a substantial stockholder in the Dublin United Tramway Company. Though the authorities tried to keep Connolly's action secret, word leaked out, and added fuel to the continuing mass protests against the incarceration of Larkin and Connolly. The protests worked. On 12 September, Larkin was released on bail, although a true bill was found against him. Connolly was released two days later, on the seventh day of his fast. Weak and feverish, he was quietly taken out of the prison and driven in a government vehicle to Madame Markievicz's home.

While resting at Surrey House, Connolly wired Nelly (Ellen) Gordon that his return to Belfast should be used to stimulate solidarity in the north. When he got off the train, he was greeted by the music of the Non-Sectarian Labour Band and an assembly of dockers and linen-mill workers. Flanagan delivered an attack on religious sectarianism, and Nelly made some welcoming remarks.

Connolly recuperated for a few days more in Belfast, then returned to Dublin to assume command while Larkin went barnstorming through England and Scotland in order to obtain support for the Dublin workers. To the unprejudiced eye (which few possessed at the time), intimations of the final result could already be discerned. J. H. Thomas squelched the railwaymen's sympathetic strike. British labour leaders and labour papers extolled the judicial approach and condemned Larkin's extremism, expressed in a passage like this: 'I am out for revolution. What do I care? They can only kill me, and there are thousands more to come after me.' The movement by labour not to handle tainted goods was being supplanted by a campaign to send foodstuffs to Dublin.

The first foodship *Hare* arrived in Dublin on Saturday, 27 September. The food was unloaded and taken to Liberty Hall where preparations were made for its distribution. On the following Saturday the *Fraternity* arrived with another cargo of food. Liberty Hall became a vast warehouse and welfare centre. Food parcels were made up and food tickets were issued to the men when they collected their strike pay. Clothes were also distributed to the needy. Soup kitchens were formed and meals were served. Delia Larkin, head of the Irish Women Workers' Union, founded in September 1911 as an affiliate of the Transport Union, and Countess Markievicz were in charge of these welfare operations.

The Countess had gone far since her birth forty-five years earlier as Constance Gore-Booth, daughter of one of the largest landowners in western Ireland. Sir Henry's home, 'Lissadell', in County Sligo was a showplace. Tiring of tea parties, dances and horse meets, she went off to Paris at the age of thirty where she met and married a pleasure-loving Polish count named Casimir Dunin-Markievicz. In Dublin the couple became leaders of Dublin's artistic and theatrical set, but at the age of forty Constance found the cause that won her restless, seeking spirit: Irish freedom. Her mentor was Bulmer Hobson, a capable Sinn Fein organizer. The following year, 1909, she founded a nationalist youth organization called Fianna na Eireann, and became acquainted with the Fenian Tom Clarke and Padraic Pearse, the young headmaster of St Enda's school where the Irish language and culture were taught.

After hearing James Larkin speak in 1910, she expanded her definition of national freedom to include economic liberation of the Irish masses, and by 1913 was ladling soup in the kitchens of Liberty Hall, in a dress composed of green, gold and purple lozenges. Connolly admired her ability to keep up the spirits of the volunteer workers as they peeled thousands of potatoes in the damp old basement during the Dublin winter; he could readily see that her altruism and dedication surpassed her liking for the limelight and the dramatic gesture; and he appreciated the way she had turned her suburban residence, Surrey House, into a resort for boys on manœuvres, patriots in hiding, and labour leaders like Larkin and Connolly resting up between jail sentences. The house became known as 'Scurry House'. It was eventually Connolly who won her wholehearted devotion. She first met him and his family in December 1911, when she appeared in Belfast with a theatrical group she sponsored. She stayed with the Connolly family on two occasions. On the second, as she left, she said to Mrs Connolly, 'I hope I wasn't too much bother to you.' 'Oh, no more than one of the children,' Lillie replied, patting her affectionately on the back.

After Connolly's execution, she wrote to her 'Hero-love' a poem resembling a widow's lament. It reads in part:

> You died for your country and left me here
> To weep—No! my eyes are dry
> For the woman you found so sweet and dear
> Has a sterner destiny—
> She will fight as she fought when you were here
> For freedom I'll live and die.

On the basis of this poem, the long periods of time Connolly lived at Surrey House (from 1914 to 1916) while his family stayed in Belfast, and the way Constance worked for the rest of her life to bring about the workers' republic Connolly had sought, it is possible to deduce that Constance and James were more intimate than was proper. All three biographers of Constance's life agree that such a conclusion would be wrong. They were both in their forties when they met; both subscribed to a code of honour that barred such liaisons; and both were by temperament more passionate about causes than about individuals. In these liberal days the question of whether their affection was ever expressed in physical terms has become of no consequence to anyone; what does matter is that, after Connolly was executed, Constance continued to pursue his cause of a workers' republic in Ireland with a devotion, idealism and passion that transcended any physical relationship and that lasted until the day of her own death in 1927, at the age of fifty-nine. During her last years she presented the perfect picture of a widow bereft.

The general lock-out was a month old when the Government announced that the Board of Trade would make an official examination of the struggle. The court of inquiry opened on 29 September, with T. M. Healy, long a dominant figure in Irish politics, presenting the case for the employers, and Harry Gosling of the British-based National Transport Workers' Federation presenting the labour side. Larkin did most of the cross-examination.

The brief for the workers was drawn up by Connolly. In it he made his stand clear; 'the ultimate tribunal to which we appeal is not this Court, but rather the verdict of the class to which we belong'. He admitted the employers' contention that 'for the past five years there have been more strikes than there have been since Dublin was a capital. Practically every responsible man in Dublin today admits that the social conditions of Dublin are a disgrace to civilization. Have these two sets of facts no relation?' To the argument that the Irish Transport and General Workers' Union could not be trusted to keep its agreements, he pointed out that the majority of shipping firms in Dublin were still in operation, 'with perfect confidence in the faith of the I.T.G.W.U.'. He answered the employers' complaints about sympathetic strikes by calling attention to the sympathetic lock-out being suffered by the United Builders Labourers Union.

The official report of the court of inquiry, as issued on 6 October, declared that 'No community could exist if resort to the "sympathetic" strike became the general policy of Trade Unions'. The report stated, on the other hand, that the conditions which the workers were being required to sign were 'contrary to individual liberty', and no workman or body of workmen could reasonably be expected to sign them. As a new basis for negotiations, the court proposed reinstatement of the workers without the requirements of a pledge not to join Larkin's union. However, the workers would have to promise not to use the sympathetic strike for a period of two years unless the employers rejected conciliation.

These terms were not unfavourable to the union. Its cause was further strengthened by the publication in the 7 October issue of the *Irish Times* of the now-famed open letter by George Russell (AE) in which he told the Dublin employers that 'your insolence and ignorance of the rights conceded to workers universally in the modern world were incredible, and as great as your inhumanity'. He termed the masters 'blind Samsons pulling down the pillars of the social order', and warned them that they were destined to meet the fate of other aristocrats 'if you do not show that you have some humanity still among you'.

The employers refused to accept the report of the court of inquiry as a basis for negotiations and demanded that the Transport Union 'be reorganised on proper lines' with 'new officials who have met with the approval of the British Joint Labour Board'. In other words, they would not deal with James Larkin, although they hinted delicately that they might be able to do business with Connolly. A group of prominent citizens seized upon the report in an attempt to mediate in the struggle. The 'Peace Committee', in a meeting with the executive committee of Dublin Trades Council, was told by William O'Brien that the workers had never rejected any peace overtures, and by Connolly that the proper type of intermediary might be able to bring both sides together. Since both the Protestant and Catholic Archbishops declined that honour, the committee's efforts failed.

The lock-out had started on 26 August. As the anniversary of the second month of mass starvation approached, the war intensified, with some battles being won by labour, others by the employers. Foodships were arriving at weekly intervals, with the third arriving on 13 October. Larkin went on a tour which took him to Glasgow, Hull, Birmingham and London. His talk in London was typical. He attacked Labour Party and trade union officials as being 'about as useful as mummies in a museum. The weapon that was wanted was the sympathetic strike used in a scientific manner. There were hypocrites who told them they must not have sympathetic strikes because they caused inconvenience to the public. The officials of the Railwaymen's Union pleaded that there were agreements and contracts. To hell with contracts. The men were far in advance of the leaders, and they would tell their leaders to get in front or get out.' Blunt attempts like this to induce the union members to break away from their leaders did not serve to increase the affection of union executives for Jim Larkin.

At Nottingham, Larkin was taken ill and could not attend a meeting scheduled for Aberdeen. Newspapers were not slow in pointing out that there was a 'responsible' successor in case Larkin was permanently indisposed, but Connolly dashed their hopes by declaring that the position was unchanged, and by organizing a procession through the streets of Dublin on 15 October. Some 4,000 persons marched with banners and bands to show their support of the workers.

At the meeting which concluded this demonstration, Connolly announced that evictions of the strikers had begun, and told the workers to pay no rent. Many, of course, could not do so if they wished. He told the crowd of the case of a worker who had been ordered to leave his lodgings. When men of the Royal Irish Constabulary were sent to eject him, they refused, feeling that this was not the kind of work they were supposed to do. There was a limit to the brutality of the RIC, said Connolly. But the Dublin police were not so squeamish. They broke open the door and forcibly threw out the man, his wife, and four children.

Liberty Hall was a centre of activity, with food being unpacked and distributed, and with the soup-kitchen running full blast. Both Irish and British suffragettes rallied to the cause. Committees were set up everywhere, encouraged by the *Daily Herald* and the *Glasgow Forward*. The London Gaelic League, established to foster the revival of the Gaelic language, forgot its non-political character so far as to establish a special committee to raise funds for Dublin. The Dublin Trades Council acted as the general clearing house for raising and distributing the funds. Even in Belfast sympathy was rising, with workers from several mills applying for membership in the Transport Union. Cathal O'Shannon, Nora and Ina Connolly held out collection boxes at church doors. The Gaelic League of Belfast joined in the movement.

At the same time there was an invisible undertow. Secondary effects of the strike began to appear, as small businessmen closed down through lack of materials. Civil service workers, shopkeepers, and small landlords began to feel the pinch. Many of these read Arthur Griffith's *Sinn Fein*, which described the labour struggle as a nefarious plot to advance British exports over the ruins of Irish trade.

A group of London sympathizers—suffragettes connected with the Daily Herald League—now committed a grave tactical error. Under the leadership of Mrs Dora Montefiore, they devised a plan for placing the children of Dublin strikers in the homes of British workers. Their announcement brought a number of applications from parents eager to spare their children the miseries of Dublin. Foster-parents were found in London, Edinburgh, Plymouth and Liverpool. Later the scheme was extended to the outskirts of Dublin and to Belfast. Larkin and Connolly failed to weigh all the implications of this scheme. Larkin was busy with his legal defence; and Connolly was preparing for a round of speeches in Scotland. Connolly spoke at Leith, where students tried to break up the meeting; then at Dundee, Glasgow and Kilmarnock, places he remembered from his earlier and, in retrospect, tranquil period of socialist preaching.

The lock-out was two months old when Connolly returned to Dublin, to find a host of problems facing him. The day before, Larkin had been convicted and sent to Mountjoy jail for seven months. In his final talk at Phoenix Park, Larkin cautioned the workers against accepting any settlement that was disadvantageous to them and announced that Connolly would act as union leader while he was in jail.

'Free' labour was steadily trickling in, and two British labour leaders, Gosling and Seddon, were about to visit Dublin to seek a settlement, on terms that might exclude the Transport Union. To cap it all, the Archbishop of Dublin had condemned the idea of removing children to foster homes in Britain, calling it a scheme to convert Catholics to the Protestant faith. Priests had picketed boats embarking for England; and Mrs Montefiore had been arrested on the grotesque charge of kidnapping.

Though confirmed in his opinion that, in times of crisis, the Catholic Church invariably placed its own interests as an organization above the interests of its parishioners, Connolly knew a lost battle when he saw one. He first ordered the plan of transporting strikers' children to foster homes be abandoned. Then he suspended the free meals at Liberty Hall, telling his supporters, 'Go to the Archbishop and the priests. Ask them for food and clothing. They are loud in their professions. Put them to the test.'

Catholic relief and charitable organizations were immediately flooded with demands for aid. Archbishop Walsh responded: first, by publishing in the daily press a pastoral letter calling for the formation of a committee to provide food and clothing for those helpless victims of the strike, the children; second, by sending a circular letter to all parish priests asking for subscriptions to the Dublin's Children's Distress Fund, and stressing the urgent need. None had the temerity to enquire why the need had become urgent so suddenly. Having made his point, Connolly ordered the free meals at Liberty Hall to be again resumed.

Concerning the visit of Seddon and Gosling to negotiate a settlement, Connolly told a British labour paper that 'we heartily accept the co-operation of our comrades across the water as *our allies*. The moment they are anything less than that we are ready to dispense with their co-operation. If we are to judge by the capitalist press, some of our English comrades are susceptible to the blarney of soft-spoken Dublin employers, but we are giving them the credit of not being easily wheedled out of their allegiance to the working class.' To his Dublin followers, he was more outspoken. 'If the trade union leaders from across the water are prepared to accept peace at any price and threaten to withdraw their foodships and support . . . then I would say, "Take back your foodships for the workers of Dublin will not surrender their position for all the ships on the sea." ' He rejected out of hand any suggestions that he oust Larkin and become leader himself, though, according to his own testimony, he was 'subject to influences that none could imagine', particularly from across the channel.

When the two British leaders arrived, the terms they proposed to the Dublin Trades Council for settling the strike did exclude participation by the Irish Transport Union, and the Council promptly rejected them.

Early in November Connolly travelled briefly to London to participate in a gigantic meeting in the Albert Hall to protest against the jailing of James Larkin. George Russell (AE) said: 'If the courts of justice were courts of humanity the masters of Dublin would be in the dock charged with criminal conspiracy. Their crime was that they tried to starve out one-third of the people of Dublin.' George Bernard Shaw, equally indignant, suggested the necessity for respectable people to arm themselves in order to put a decisive stop to police brutality. Other speakers were Delia Larkin, Ben Tillett and Mrs Montefiore. The most practical programme for obtaining Larkin's release was proposed by Connolly. He asked that, in the forthcoming by-elections, everyone vote against the Liberal Party, even though it was sponsor of the Home Rule Bill. There, and elsewhere, he argued: 'It doesn't matter whether it is a Labour man or a Tory that is against the Liberal. The immediate thing is to hit the government that keeps Larkin in jail.' 'Dublin working men are as firm as ever for national self-government. But they are not going to allow the government to bludgeon them and jail their leaders and comrades and place all the machinery of the law, police and military at the disposal of the employers without hitting back.' 'The government must go if Larkin stays in.'

These arguments no doubt influenced some people. Even some Liberals were annoyed that the Government should jail Larkin for seditious libel while Sir Edward Carson remained free to spout out-right treason and armed revolution. The result was that the Liberal Party was defeated in elections at Linlithgow, Reading and Keighley. Rockets were fired from the roof of Liberty Hall in celebration.

Heartened by the size of the Albert Hall protest meeting, Connolly hastened back to Dublin to lock horns with the City of Dublin Steam Packet Company. The only cross-channel company operating between Dublin and British ports, it was considered invulnerable because, during the previous May, it had signed an agreement with Larkin that the men who worked for it would not participate in a sympathetic strike. When threats that 'the streets of Dublin would run red with the blood of the working class', and mass picketing of the quays failed to halt the company operation, Connolly ordered all members of the Transport Union to cease handling goods for any ship of the Steam Packet Company. Though Larkin, on his release, supported Connolly for taking this action, even though it broke a hard-won agreement, it was probably a blunder. The employers vigorously renewed their cries about 'broken agreements' and some employers, who had tried to keep clear of the dispute but were using the facilities of the Steam Packet Company, were now involved against Larkin whether they wanted to be or not.

The Liberal Government would be moved neither by lost by-elections nor by the mounting campaign, now joined by two influential Liberal newspapers, to release Larkin from jail. The Government sensed that most of its followers could not tolerate the remarks for which Larkin had been jailed—seditious, free-swinging utterances which expressed his contempt for royalty, the British Empire, and those who lived on rent and profit. The Government did not need to concede anything; it knew that the ravages of starvation and the steady influx of scabs—fifty from Manchester on 29 October, and a hundred from Liverpool on 5 November—would in time dispose of the Larkinite madness.

In an article published in the 8 November issue of the *Irish Worker*, Connolly ordered that all individual picketing throughout Dublin be superseded by mass picketing. In the same article he flayed the hypocrisy of those who 'prostituted the name of religion' by insulting men and women who offered children shelter and comfort but allowed English blacklegs to enter Dublin without a word of protest. He warned the employers: 'If they think they can carry on their industries without you, we will, in the words of the Ulster Orangemen, take steps to prevent it.'

In proportion as labour was running out of weapons, its rhetoric became more violent. The authorities had more specific ways of replying. They put arms in the hands of the scabs, sent infantry to protect the strike breakers at Jacob's biscuit factory, and raised the pay of the police, whose main occupation now was dispersing massed pickets.

November 1913 has a special place in Irish history. During that month, some patriotic Irishmen decided that negotiations, whether for Home Rule or labour peace, worked best when assisted by military organizations: one, the Irish Volunteers; two, the Transport Union Citizen Army (otherwise known as the Irish Citizen Army or simply Citizen Army). On 11 November, at Wynn's Hotel in Dublin, eleven men met to consider the idea of forming an organization either to offset the influence of the Ulster Volunteers or to join with it in opposing England. Their names were Eoin NacNeill, Bulmer Hobson, Padraic Pearse, Sean MacDermott, W. J. Ryan, Eamonn Ceannt, Sean Fitzgibbon, James A. Deakin, Piaras Beaslai, Joseph Campbell and The O'Rahilly. They all knew each other as ardent nationalists. Some shared another bond; they were also members of the Irish Republican Brotherhood, a secret organization that most people considered defunct. Actually, it had been kept alive in America with American money and members living in America. In recent years its Irish forces had been strengthened by the return to Ireland of the Fenian Tom Clarke and an infusion of new members.

The following evening, on 12 November, another small group met in a room at Trinity College, bastion of Protestant higher education. It had formerly been the Peace Committee which had unsuccessfully attempted to mediate the labour struggle. In the process its members had developed a bias for the workers, and it now reconstituted itself as the Civic League seeking to assist them. One of the speakers was Captain Jack White, a former officer in the British Army, and son of a famous Boer War general. Captain White proposed, to general approval, that a drilling scheme be started as a means of bringing discipline 'into the distracted ranks of Labour'. A newcomer to Dublin, his sympathies for the strikers had been aroused by the words of AE. Short-tempered, a commanding speaker, versed in military matters, he gave lavishly of his knowledge, time and money to the Citizen Army when it was formed. On the following evening, 13 November, the Civic League held its first public meeting, and the formation of the Citizen Army was announced.

At noon of the same day, 13 November, Larkin was released from jail. Public pressure had shortened his sentence from seven months to seventeen days. He looked 'well and strong, but his voice did not carry as far as usual', *Freeman's Journal* reported. Larkin announced that in a few hours he was going 'to light a fiery cross in England, Scotland and Wales . . . and he promised the employers of Dublin that they were going to sup sorrow with a long spoon'.

Connolly's words were just as tough. 'We have got our leader back, and you must now demonstrate and picket as you have never picketed before, and see if the police will clear us off the streets as they threatened. If they attempt to do so then the present strike in the port of Dublin will be nothing to what is to come.'

That night, at a huge welcoming demonstration (Larkin did not attend because he was indisposed), Connolly wound up the proceedings in Beresford Place by saying (according to a report in the *Freeman's Journal*):

Listen to me, I am going to talk sedition, the next time we are out for a march, I want to be accompanied by four battalions of trained men. I want them to come with their corporals, sergeants and people to form fours. Why should we not drill and train our men in Dublin as they are doing in Ulster? But I don't think you require any training (laughter).

He asked every man willing to join the 'Labour Army' to hand in his name when he drew his strike pay at the end of the week. He had competent officers ready to instruct and lead them, and could get arms any time they were wanted.

On the following day, 14 November, Larkin and Connolly issued a 'Manifesto to the British Working Class'. It described the situation in Dublin, with workers, both men and women, being jailed every day and given 'ferocious' prison sentences, while scab labourers were being imported by the hundreds. The manifesto announced that the port of Dublin was closed, and appealed to British trade unionists to help keep it closed. 'We propose to carry the war into every section of the enemy's camp. Will you second us?'

The manifesto hinted at more than it said. One labour paper commented grumpily: 'In certain quarters a cry goes up for a general strike of British workers in aid of Dublin Labour. So far the proposal is urged in vague and superficial terms, and the details and consequences have clearly not been thought out.' Larkin's speech in Manchester before 4,000 people, with another crowd of 20,000 outside, was similarly militant and ambiguous. Connolly reported to this audience, 'The working class of Dublin is being slowly murdered.'

He was not far wrong. Though railways unions in Liverpool, Birmingham, London, Leeds and a dozen places had voted not to handle 'tainted' goods, the movement received no support from the national officials. A steady trickle of scabs were keeping many Dublin factories open. And what did it matter if the port of Dublin were closed if the ports of Derry and Belfast were still open?

On 18 November, Larkin, Connolly and some other delegates from the Dublin Trades Council met with the Parliamentary Committee of the British Trades Union Congress. The request of the Dubliners was becoming more specific. They wanted the Congress to 'take steps to prevent the further importation of non-union labour into Dublin, and should also isolate the Dublin employers by holding up the transit of goods to that city'. They dared not ask as yet for a sympathetic strike. Most members of the Congress were opposed to any extension of the action beyond the support then being given to the Dublin strikers, but, owing to pressure from the rank and file, were reluctant to say so. Instead, after some hesitation, they took the unprecedented step of calling a special session of the Trades Union Congress for 9 December, in three weeks' time. Not publicized at the time was the fact that the conference participants would consist only of paid officials, not of lay delegates.

On 19 November, Larkin and Connolly spoke at the Albert Hall in London, where students with capitalist sympathies, after attempting to disconnect the lighting system, swarmed over the balconies interrupting the speakers and creating pandemonium until they were ejected by a group of burly workers led by Con O'Lyhane.

On the same evening, in Dublin, the Civic League held another meeting. By a strange coincidence students were involved here also, but this time on the side of the strikers. The day before, Provost Anthony Traill, thinking the meeting was about Home Rule, forbade the students at Trinity College to attend. Reacting as might be expected, about 100 students appeared and expressed their approval of what the meeting was actually about, a protest against police brutality and the refusal of the employers to negotiate with labour. In addition, Captain White read a telegram from Sir Roger Casement, who had been knighted for his revelations concerning exploitation in Africa and South America, expressing his support of the movement to 'drill and discipline Dublin Workers ... I hope it may begin a widespread national movement to organize drilled and disciplined Irish Volunteers to assert Irish manhood and uphold the national cause in all that is right.'

In the 22 November issue of the *Daily Herald*, James Larkin started a campaign to ensure that the decisions to be made at the 9 December meeting of the British Trades Union Congress would be in his favour. He told the workers:

Tell your leaders now and every day until December 9, and raise your voice upon that day to tell them that for the future they must stand for Trade Unionism, that they are not there as apologists for the shortcomings of the Capitalist system, that they are not there to assist the employers in helping to defeat any section of workers striving to be free, nor to act as a brake upon the wheel of progress.

He considered it necessary as part of that campaign to name those trade-union leaders who were impeding, he thought, the progress of labour. At Sheffield he called J. H. Thomas 'a double-dyed traitor to his class'. He referred to both Thomas and J. H. Wilson as being 'too big for their boots'. In London, referring to Wilson and Philip Snowden, he said, 'I am not going to allow these serpents to raise their foul heads and spit out their poison any longer.'

Although his language was less picturesque, Connolly shared Larkin's views. He anticipated Larkin's appeal to the rank and file by announcing in Beresford Place that the 'labour leaders who were attacking them in England were only old fossils, and were willing to sell the pass any time'. On the night that Larkin spoke in Sheffield, Connolly denounced Wilson by name, and denied that the sympathetic strike had ever been used recklessly in Dublin.

On Sunday, 23 November, enough men to form two companies appeared in Croydon Park and applied to Captain White for admission to the Citizen Army. In an Albert Hall speech, Connolly had referred to 'a citizen army of locked-out men' and this may have been the genesis of the name. Soon the Citizen Army was regularly drilling with hurley-sticks and wooden shafts (sometimes 'shoed' with metal) at Croydon Park. It was essentially a labour defence force (though the speeches by Connolly and Captain White, and the telegram by Casement showed intimations of a larger destiny), and as such lacked the appeal of the Irish Volunteers.

The avowed purpose of the Volunteers, formed on 25 November at a huge meeting held at the Rotunda Rink, was a general one—to obtain and maintain the rights and liberties of all the people of Ireland. It appealed to all who felt the need for balancing or opposing the Ulster Volunteers in some fashion or other, and it drew no class distinctions. Hence the Irish Volunteers grew and quickly outnumbered the Citizen Army. Within a month it had 3,500 members as compared to the Citizen Army membership of 500. The Citizen Army hindered its own growth by placing age and size restrictions on applicants for membership; it wanted only grown men, not boys.

Though there was some hope and enthusiasm among the new militiamen, to the strikers, now entering their fourth month of unemployment, it seemed a long and unusually dreary winter. Usually, Dublin winters are marked by an endless procession of dark and over-cast days: the nights too are gloomy, with the streets badly lit, and the frequent pubs seem reluctant to provide passers-by with any illumination. This year the winter was unusually cold. By Christmas the ponds in Dublin were frozen and there was ice-skating in Phoenix Park. The locked-out workers looked forward to Christmas with no relish. As the time approached for the fateful 9 December meeting with the British Trades Union Congress, attacks on Larkin from both the 'responsible' labour press and the spokesmen for the capitalist establishment increased in frequency and virulence. Even while one labour paper hinted that Larkinism was a Catholic plot to discredit trade unionism, Church authorities attacked Larkin for declaring at a meeting, 'We want none of these sky-pilots; we can pilot ourselves.' Feeling the heat of the attack, Larkin refused to speak at a meeting in Grimsby when he discovered the proposed chairman was a divorced man.

At this point Archbishop Walsh made an attempt at mediation. With Larkin incessantly on tour, it fell on Connolly's shoulders to be the principal spokesman on behalf of the Transport Workers' Union. At the conference, which opened 4 December, the workers agreed to relinquish the weapon of the sympathetic strike, but demanded in return that all men be reinstated. The employers refused on the grounds that it would be unfair to the men who had replaced them, and that at the present stage of their business they could not absorb all the men at once. The workers felt that this argument was a cover for victimizing their most militant leaders, and refused to accept the employers' terms without some form of guarantee to protect them. On this rock of reinstatement the conference was shattered.

The long-awaited special meeting of the British Trades Union Congress was attended by 600 representatives from some 350 unions. The Congress had two choices: (1) to increase the funds it was sending to Dublin, and do nothing otherwise; (2) to boycott the handling of Dublin goods and, if necessary, call a general sympathetic strike.

The first order of business concerned the recent negotiations of Seddon and Gosling. Connolly admitted that there had been 'too much recrimination on both sides', but pointed out that the negotiations had ultimately failed, not because of the stubbornness or perversity of the Dublin workers, but because the employers were unwilling to make any concessions with regard to reinstatement. When the employers agreed to take on only as many of their former employees as they could make room for, they were acting, in essence, as if there were no trade unions in existence at all. The British delegates applauded this point. They were less happy when Connolly noted that the 'Irish delegates were not withdrawing any criticism they had made'; they were not going to allow criticism 'to draw them aside from the contemplation of the fact that they were that day fighting for liberty for at least 100,000 people in the city of Dublin'.

The crunch came when important British leaders introduced resolutions condemning the Irish leaders for 'unfair attacks' on trade-union leaders; accusing Larkin of sowing dissension in the ranks of the British railway workers; and pointing out that 'Murphyism'—personal dictatorship—existed in the trade-union movement as well as among the employers.

Larkin was not surprised. At first glance, he had noted that all those present were paid union officials, not branch delegates in any true sense; and had sensed that the Congress was intent on putting him on trial, with a loaded jury. Now there was no holding him. Overworked and exhausted, he sprang to his feet and thundered against the 'foul, lying attacks' being made against him. 'Not a man in this hall has been elected,' he declared, and demanded the boycott of Dublin goods.

Then followed a welter of other resolutions. The significant one, to call a boycott, was overwhelmingly defeated after being described by one delegate as 'silly' and after another had pointed out that the rank and file had given no mandate for a national stoppage. Hopelessly out-manœuvred, and worn out by the constant heckling, Larkin was speechless with indignation. It was Connolly who found words—moderate ones—to sum up the Irish sentiment.

We are 'under a deep sense of humiliation', he said. 'It would have been better for the conference to have first endeavoured to try and settle the Dublin dispute and afterwards wash their dirty linen. The reverse has however been the case.' Although he thanked the British unions for the help they had given, he warned: 'We in Dublin will not necessarily accept all the resolutions passed at this conference.'

The struggle was lost as soon as the Congress rejected Larkin's proposals. The employers knew it, and the workers began drifting back to work. Connolly fought the trend, J. H. Bennett, of the National Seamen's and Firemen's Union, wrote to Connolly that the captain of a Head Line ship had asked for a union crew and that 'if we do not give him a crew the ship will go away without them, and the officers of the other Head boats will take her to her coaling Port'.

Connolly, writing on 13 December, refused to grant permission, since the Head boats were working with scab labour both in Dublin and Belfast, and since 'Messrs Palgrave Murphy have decided that any settlement affecting the Head boats had perhaps better wait on a general settlement I think it would considerably weaken our hands if any signing on that boat were done now.' Connolly's decision was not accepted. When members of the Transport Workers' Union refused to handle Head Line cargo, they were informed that the men from the Seamen's and Firemen's Union would take their places. A consignment of Guinness was shipped to Sligo because Dublin men refused to handle it. Connolly was able to get the Sligo men not to touch it, but the consignment was shipped by rail to Derry where members of British-controlled unions loaded it, took it to Liverpool, and unloaded it.

As the dreary winter dragged on, aching hunger, cold and family necessity forced the men back to work at the factories, mills, docks and shops, to seek their own individual reinstatement. There were rumours of dissension between Larkin and Connolly; Connolly's return to Belfast before Christmas was attributed to this cause. It was a Christmas of hunger and heroism—'Dublin lies in the grip of the power of the purse,' Connolly wrote—but the union managed to provide a meal for 20,000 children at union-owned Croydon Park, and Wicklow venison was provided for 2,000 men. Larkin could cry, 'The struggle is not half over,' but the sympathizers were beginning to feel otherwise. Funds from the British Trades Union Congress and from the subscription lists in the labour papers were rapidly dwindling.

Connolly spent Christmas in Belfast putting together for publication in a pamphlet the various articles which make up *The Re-Conquest of Ireland*. But he was back in Dublin on 4 January 1914, to speak together with Larkin at the funeral of a young girl who had died after being shot by a scab. The two men simultaneously issued a manifesto affirming their intention of continuing the struggle, and calling for increased aid from both Ireland and Britain.

After returning to Belfast, Connolly took to his bed suffering from what he called 'a relapse of ulcerated sore throat'. He now had the time to consider the situation in a more realistic light. The task, he decided, was to salvage something from the general disaster, and to put the best face possible on the concessions that had to be made. He communicated these thoughts secretly to Larkin. To William O'Brien in an undated letter (probably written 15 January 1914), he wrote what his advice had consisted of.

My advice was: to announce that as the Cross Channel unions (in Great Britain) had definitely resolved not to assist us in fighting the battle against the Dublin sweaters in the only way they could be fought, viz: by holding up their goods, and as these unions were now handling all sorts of traffic loaded in Dublin by scabs, and the Seamen's and Firemen's Union supplying crews to man ships against us and against their own Dublin members, and as any traffic we do hold up in Dublin gets away by other ports and is handled across channel by trade unionists, we are now prepared to advise a general resumption of work and the handling of all goods *pending a more general acceptance of the doctrine of tainted goods by the trade union world*.

But having completely foiled the attempt of the employers to crush our union or to dictate to us our unions affiliations, we reserve to ourselves the right to refuse to work with non-union labour where such labour has not formerly been employed, or to withdraw our labour again if within a reasonable period, varying according to the nature of our work, we find that any of our members have been victimised, or left unemployed without a satisfactory reason.

Connolly thought that action along these lines would

> put the sole responsibility for our temporary check upon the cross-channel unions and also leave every employer free to act as he thought best, and I do not believe that the Murphy gang would be able to hold them in any longer.
>
> It would also save us from the danger of being compelled to sign an unsatisfactory *general* settlement.

On 18 January, the Transport Union held a closed meeting where Connolly's face-saving plan was adopted. It included the provision of refusing 'to work with non-union labour where such labour has not formerly been employed'. But the winter was too hard and children were hungry. The death knell for the locked-out men was sounded on 1 February when the Builders Labourers Union, 3,000 strong, promised the employers no members would remain or become in the future a member of the Transport Workers' Union, participate in a sympathetic strike, or take note of the union affiliations of other employees.

On 11 February 1914 the Dublin Relief Fund sponsored by the British Trades Union Congress was officially closed. In the 7 February issue of *Forward*, Connolly wrote: 'And so we Irish workers must again go down into Hell, bow our backs to the lash of the slave driver, let our hearts be seared by the iron of his hatred, and instead of the sacramental wafer of brotherhood and common sacrifice, eat the dust of defeat and betrayal. Dublin is isolated.'

Deeply shaken by this lost battle, Connolly licked his wounds in various *Forward* articles. What had gone wrong? Why had the British unions failed to respond to the call of class solidarity? He avoided the vulgar nationalist pitfall of blaming them because they were British, though it is doubtful if he ever again had much confidence in the British labour movement. He continued to insist on the need for industrial trade unions to conduct 'direct action', for a labour party to channel the votes, and a socialist party for conducting propaganda. But he now saw that in the process of amalgamation and federation that had produced such organizations as the Transport Union something had happened; there had occurred a loss in militancy, 'a freezing up' of the fraternal spirit. He concluded that 'Fighting spirit is of more importance than the creation of a theoretically perfect organization'. The way to maintain that spirit was by choosing officers 'from the standpoint of their responsiveness to the call for solidarity'.

This prescription was neither adequate nor practical. In another article he did better. Taking a cool, dispassionate look at what had happened, he decided that the struggle had been lost because

It was not practicable to enforce the policy of tainted goods in Dublin whilst the goods so held up could be transported from other ports and handled across channel by other unions. The executives of other unions failing to sanction the co-operation of their members, the enforcement of this policy became an impossibility. Hence I submit that the main difficulty in the way of the success of this policy is in the multiplicity of unions and executives. Every union not immediately engaged in the conflict is a union whose material interests—looked at from a narrowly selfish point of view—are opposed to being drawn into the struggle. Therefore, every executive naturally aligns itself in opposition to the policy of the sympathetic strike, except when it is its own union that is immediately concerned.

Connolly was describing what is now a well-known characteristic of organizational life—the tendency of each bureau in a department, of each office in a bureau, of each desk in an office, to think first and foremost of its own survival, of its own immediate best interests. But again Connolly's remedy falls short. It urged the men, in addition to working 'for industrial unionism in some form', to 'work for the abolition and merging of all these unions that now divide our energies instead of concentrating them—and for the abolition of all those executives whose measure of success is the balance sheet of their union, instead of the power of their class'. It was a commendable goal—and one that many officials in both American and Irish labour organizations are still trying to achieve.

Connolly could not face the terrifying possibility—one that haunts all socialists, communists, radicals, reformers—that there is something inherently corruptible in the nature of man and the organizations he builds; that once a leader is chosen he often falls prey to the delights of power and glory; that the masses themselves find the temptation irresistible to accept temporary and immediate gains in lieu of broader and more lasting achievements. America supplies some cogent examples. Many trade-union officials, executives, and members have failed to facilitate the admission of black members or to fight war expenditures that provide work.

One more question can be raised. How decisive was the defeat the workers suffered? It was certainly a grievous one. The struggle had accomplished nothing in the way of raising the wages of the strikers, in improving their working conditions, or establishing their right to organize, much less boycott tainted goods or indulge in sympathetic strikes. But gains there were—some intangible, some whose consequences could not be known at the time, some difficult to define, but present. The long struggle revealed to the world the feudal nature of life in Dublin. It led to the formation of a Citizen Army. It gave a handful of ardent nationalists—to Padraic Pearse in particular—a greater appreciation and understanding of the workers' cause. Pearse already believed that 'the great enemy of practical Christianity has always been respectable society'. Now, in the October 1913 issue of *Irish Freedom*, he wrote:

> I do not know whether the methods of Mr. James Larkin are wise methods or unwise methods (unwise, I think, in some respects), but this I know, that there is a most hideous wrong to be righted, and that the man who attempts honestly to right it is a good man and a brave man.

He accepted Larkin's son as a student at his school, and, as the months went by, came to accept Connolly's ideas on the emancipation of women, the virtue of Fintan Lalor's thought, and the necessity of freeing the working masses as part of the liberation of the Irish nation. Says the historian Giovanni Costigan, Connolly was 'the last considerable influence' on the thinking of Padraic Pearse.

The greatest gain was an intangible one. For the first time Dublin's urban workers had asserted their rights in a large and concerted way. It had been a true 'revolt from below'. Never again would the employers dare treat their workers with the casual brutality and indifference that had marked their actions in the past. The slaves had proved that, pushed hard enough, they could and would act like men.

A second Cathleen ni Houlihan (the maid who symbolizes Ireland as Uncle Sam symbolizes the US) had emerged from the 1913 labour struggle. Sean O'Casey had the words to describe her: 'coarsely dressed, hair a little tousled, caught roughly together by a pin, barefooted, sometimes with a whiff of whiskey off her breath; brave and brawny; at ease in the smell of sweat and the sound of bad language, vital, and asurge with immortality'. During the last week of April 1916 she dwelt in the General Post Office, Dublin.

XX

1914

DURING the early part of 1914, the struggle for Home Rule was encountering the same kind of disaster that the workers' struggle for the right to organize had encountered. Sir Edward Carson and his friends conducted a gun-smuggling exploit at Larne on the night of 24 April that netted the Ulster Volunteers 36,000 rifles. In Parliament, Devlin and Redmond, leaders of the Irish Party, accepted an amendment to the Home Rule Bill which provided that any county wishing to be temporarily excluded from operation of the Act might do so on a simple majority vote of its electorate. Carson wanted more; he announced that, unless four counties were permanently and immediately excluded, the Ulster Volunteers would seize arms stored in military bases around Belfast. When troops were ordered north from the Curragh to meet this threat, fifty-seven officers resigned their commissions rather than obey. The Government capitulated, the troops did not move, and the officers were accepted back.

To Connolly and other militant nationalists, all this seemed evidence of black collusion between Carson, the Prime Minister Henry Asquith, Redmond and Joe Devlin. In the 14 March 1914 issue of the *Irish Worker*, Connolly urged labour in Ulster to fight to the death, if necessary, to prevent enactment of any scheme that would enable a county to stand outside the provisions of Home Rule. In *Forward* the following week he said that 'such a scheme would destroy the labour movement by disrupting it'.

Meanwhile, the numbers and enthusiasm of the Citizen Army were waning. Its pretentious name was almost an embarrassment. Sean O'Casey believed that a new and tighter organization was required. Captain White thought men were not attending drills because they had inadequate clothing and footwear. Some leaders blamed the lack of interest on natural depression following defeat in the great labour struggle. It is always easier for men to appreciate the need for obtaining food for their families than the importance of guerilla tactics in obtaining revolutionary goals.

O'Casey drew up a new constitution and a public meeting was held on 22 March for the workers to ratify it. Captain White, his head bandaged from a fracas with the police during a hunger march, was chairman. The constitution affirmed that 'the ownership of Ireland, moral and material, is vested of right in the people of Ireland'; that the Citizen Army would be 'open to all who accept the principle of equal rights and opportunities for the people of Ireland'; and that one of its objects was 'to sink all differences of birth, property and creed under the common name of the Irish people'. At the request of Jim Larkin, Constance Markievicz added a clause that somewhat contradicted the army's open admission policy. It stated, 'Before being enrolled, every applicant must, if eligible, be a member of his trade union, such union to be recognised by the Irish Trade Union Congress.' A governing committee was chosen, but Connolly was not made a member of it. It was understood that he was tied to his work in Belfast; some had the wisdom to understand that Larkin did not welcome too many visits to Dublin by Connolly.

How labour-minded the Citizen Army should be remained a constant source of friction. It prompted Captain White to leave it in May 1914; and created quarrels between O'Casey, the Citizen Army secretary, and the Countess. Captain White concluded that it was impossible to draw together the labour and national elements. 'A common emotion of patriotism cannot reconcile a concrete and fundamental antagonism of interest and objective.' In May 1914 Tom Clarke wrote to John Devoy in the United States that Liberty Hall's verbal attacks on the Irish Volunteers inspired 'by a disgruntled fellow named O'Casey' had made it 'a negligible quantity here'.

The meeting of 22 March increased Larkin's interest in the Citizen Army. He appealed to every union affiliated with the Irish Trades Union Congress to establish a company; and during the spring and summer of 1914 he held recruiting meetings throughout County Dublin.

In Belfast, Connolly booked St Mary's Hall, a large red-brick structure in a crowded shopping area, for a meeting to protest the agitation for partition. Although the newspapers refused to accept his advertisement for the meeting, the hall was packed to capacity, mainly by people from the Falls Road (Catholic and working class) area. Chairman William McMullen was impressed by the difference in the way the speakers were received. Captain White was given a vociferous reception and an attentive hearing during the course of a short, hesitant speech. Connolly, who made a much better speech, was received tepidly and had to shout to make himself heard above the hum of conversation. The reasons, as given by McMullen, were that White, son of a Unionist family and of a general famed for his defence of Ladysmith, had forsaken the traditional politics of his family and had come over to the nationalist side. Connolly, on the other hand, had alienated many moderate nationalists by denouncing John Redmond, Joe Devlin and their entire Irish Parliamentary Party for agreeing to sever from Ireland that portion which had been the cradle of republicanism in previous years. Another reason for the lukewarm reception was the fact that Connolly was the only Catholic among the speakers that evening; it is well known that a prophet is without honour in his own country. Connolly, no stranger to cool audiences, was 'quite jubilant' when the resolution condemning the exclusion of Ulster from the Home Rule Bill was passed unanimously.

As a Catholic trade-union organizer, in a city dominated by industrialists and beleaguered by Orange forces, Connolly was, of necessity, grateful for little. Nor is it to be wondered that he occasionally lost his sense of balance. At another meeting held in Belfast about this time, a visiting Dubliner gave a long and rambling account of the time when a parish priest was endeavouring at the Amiens Street railway station to prevent children of Dublin strikers from being sent to homes in England. According to the speaker, one of the parents asked this parish priest, 'What business is it of yours where the children are going, since they don't belong to you?' McMullen says:

> The latter portion of this remark, which was capable of either an innocent or a slighting interpretation was given the latter construction by Connolly, who rose to his feet in a white heat of indignation, passionately denouncing . . . the speaker for daring to speak so slightingly and so disparagingly of a parish priest and thundered that he considered the remark not only irrelevant but irreverent as well and one that should not be made at a meeting of that kind.

Those members of the audience who had read Connolly's *Labour, Nationality and Religion* were naturally at a loss as to why he should have become so indignant about a remark which, though in bad taste perhaps, did not seem worth such attention.

During this period, Connolly issued an appeal to the working class as the sole reliable force to prevent the exclusion of Ulster from the Home Rule Bill. He wrote: 'As the officers of the Curragh have stood by their class, so let the working class democracy stand by its class. Let it be heard and understood that Labour stands for the unity of Ireland . . . ' The appeal fell on deaf ears. Labour members in the British Parliament followed the line of their Irish colleagues.

To Connolly, this meant that British labour, having been guilty of betraying the Irish workers on the industrial field, was now betraying them on the political field. He wrote bitterly of the 'tired feeling' that Irish socialists experienced when they witnessed British labour representatives lovingly embrace 'our deadliest enemies', the members of the Irish Parliamentary Party. 'It will not help on a better understanding between the militant proletariat of the two islands.' It will be noted that the British and Irish capitalists were taking second place as targets of his proletarian wrath.

In his bitterness at British labour, Connolly rejected an invitation to speak at the 1914 May Day meeting in Glasgow. In the Glasgow *Forward* he told the Scottish workers: 'I cannot this May Day felicitate you or the working class of the world in general on the spread of working class solidarity. Instead of it I see much mouthing of phrases, much sordid betrayal of our holiest hopes.'

He summarized the feelings of the Irish worker-radicals towards the British in a quatrain:

> Aye, bitter hot, or cold neglect
> Or lukewarm love at best
> Is all we have or can expect,
> We aliens of the west.

Though driven by defeat to despondency and untypical musing, Connolly did not relinquish his abiding faith in the eventual success of the working class. In an article entitled 'Changes', published in the 9 May 1914 issue of *Forward*, he gave one of the most thoughtful expressions of his faith. His theses ran as follows:

1. The revolutionary class cannot take power until it is able to do the work of the class it seeks to destroy, and do it more efficiently.
2. When it has reached that stage, nothing can stop its march to victory.

3. The new socialist society must be built within the capitalist shell.
4. The only way this can be done is on the industrial foundation that capitalism itself has constructed, that is, through industrial unionism.
5. He is therefore heart and soul an industrial unionist, but because he knows that the capitalist class is unscrupulous, he proposes to compete with it on the political field as well.
6. He does not restrict his convictions to such theses alone, for all time, since he realizes that

> human nature is a wonderful thing, that the soul of man gives expression to strange and complex phenomena, and that no man knows what powers or possibilities for good or evil lie in humanity, I try to preserve my receptivity towards all new ideas, my tolerance towards all manifestations of social activity.

On 25 May 1914, the Home Rule Bill was given its third reading in the House of Commons. All that was now required to put it into law was the Royal Assent. Prime Minister Asquith procrastinated, feeling heavy pressure from British chauvinists, particularly King George V, who wanted the six northern counties entirely removed from the provisions of the Bill.

This subject was inevitably discussed at the Irish Trades Union Congress when it met in Dublin on 1 June. On the evening before, Connolly for once broke his resolve never to oppose Larkin in any respect, however trivial. At a rally in Phoenix Park, speeches from two platforms were scheduled to start simultaneously. Larkin, too impatient to wait for the signal, began speaking ahead of time. Connolly took offence at this, and refused to say a word, even though some men had come from Cork specially to hear him. Larkin, sensing that something was amiss, loudly praised his colleague, asking rhetorically who in Ulster could face Jim Connolly. Connolly's ill-temper was shortlived. By the time he came to write up the affair in *Forward*, he said simply, 'Jim was never in better form.'

As chairman at the Congress sessions, Larkin was his usual flamboyant and unpredictable self. His eccentricities in the chair caused much amusement and goaded William O'Brien into unconcealed fury. But Connolly and most of the delegates recognized that Larkin was a completely incorruptible man, head and shoulders above the opportunists who infested the labour ranks.

Connolly played a leading part in the deliberations of the Congress, and was elected to its national executive committee. He proposed the motion condemning partition, and pointed out that labour was the only force in Ireland consistently campaigning against it. There were only three dissenting votes. He also proposed a resolution condemning a factory in Ulster for introducing a 'no union' pledge and for allowing Ulster Volunteers to drill on its premises. In addition, he supported a resolution demanding that women be given the right to vote.

The meeting discussed ways to persuade British labour to oppose partition; to combat the gerrymandering of Irish constituencies as proposed in the Home Rule Bill; and to support extension of medical benefits and school feeding to Ireland. Subsequently, deputations were sent to Ramsay MacDonald and Arthur Henderson urging them to introduce such amendments to the Home Rule Bill, but they refused to move. Much correspondence and a protest meeting held in O'Connell Street failed to change the response.

While he was attending the Congress meetings in Dublin, Connolly apparently heard rumours that Larkin was again thinking of going off to America. Writing from Belfast on 8 June, Connolly told O'Brien: 'It seems to me that there is hope that the Congress might act as a tonic on Jim and get him to act with vigour again. In that case it is to be hoped that he will still remain in Dublin.'

A week later Larkin told Connolly over the phone that he, Larkin, was corresponding with Big Bill Haywood, of the Industrial Workers of the World, concerning a tour of the US. Connolly wrote to O'Brien that he thought this was a foolish idea since 'Haywood's crowd have no money at all. But in any case he seems bent upon a tour. I was in hopes that the Congress would pull him together again, but if things are as you say, then possibly the tour would be beneficial.'

The evidence was certainly clear that Larkin needed and wanted a change of scenery. In the 27 June 1914 issue of *Forward*, Connolly suggested that

the price Jim had paid was that he had broken down physically, run down mentally, and almost worn out. Hence he did not realise himself that what he needed was a rest . . . If he were to go to America and raise funds for the new Irish Labour Party it would recuperate him, and he would be back in seven days if needed.

It is easy to imagine Connolly's mixed feelings at the prospect of Larkin's departure. To be free of Larkin's unpredictable vagaries would be an inestimable boon; and there were many changes he would like to make if, as he expected, he became Larkin's successor as general secretary of the union. But at the moment there was no substitute for Larkin's courage, his magic way with the workers, and his capacity to feel his way to 'correct' decisions. The cause required Larkin, and for Connolly this was always the determining factor.

Finally Larkin announced that he was resigning from his post with the Transport Union and leaving Dublin for good. The union was thrown into a state of 'chassis'. A general meeting was hurriedly summoned to induce Larkin to change his mind. At the meeting, held on 21 June, Connolly, William Partridge and P. T. Daly all spoke to the same effect concerning Larkin's state of physical and mental exhaustion; and blamed it on internal forces who were taking advantage of the disorganization following the lock-out. It was suggested that, since Larkin did seem to need a rest, it was possible that he might go to the US to take it, and incidentally collect funds for the union. The meeting unanimously refused to accept Larkin's resignation.

Larkin himself was not present. Together with the Citizen Army, he was attending memorial services for past Irish patriots held each year beside Wolfe Tone's grave in Bodenstown. Since the Irish Volunteers were also present, there was hope for some degree of collaboration in the future. When Larkin returned from Bodenstown, he was met by three bands and escorted in a huge procession to a Croydon Park rally. There he delivered an hour's speech, complaining of 'interference' by other union officials. They had indeed secretly withheld some £7,500 from the strike fund so as to complete the purchase of Liberty Hall. Larkin, though no accountant, suspected things of this sort were going on. At the end of the speech, the union members declared they would camp all night on the grounds unless he agreed to attend a general meeting to be held next day at the Antient Concert Rooms.

The meeting was duly held, and was filled with praise of each other by Larkin and Connolly. Larkin said that he had been urged to re-pudiate Connolly's actions in fighting the Liberal Party's Home Rule Bill and in closing the port of Dublin during his imprisonment. 'I tell you here and now that I endorsed all Connolly did,' he said. Connolly replied, 'I stand for Jim because I believe he is the best man our class has turned out in Ireland. I am with him as a comrade, and I believe he accepts me as such.' He asserted that the closing of the Dublin port would have won the strike if the British unions had not been restrained for fear of diminishing their treasuries. Though ignorant of what had recently been taking place in Dublin, he believed that Larkin would yet thank God that he had produced men capable of criticizing him. He thought that Larkin was overstrung during the past few weeks, and that the union's executive committee, perhaps in a blundering way, was only trying to save him from doing too much. He advised Larkin to do less routine work. Whatever trivial objections had been raised by Larkin's opponents, he, Connolly, was not going to support them. He ended his speech, which was punctuated by cries of 'hear, hear,' from Larkin, by offering a resolution assuring Larkin of the continued fidelity of the union members to his leadership.

The motion was approved, and a union official set a match to Larkin's written resignation amid scenes of 'indescribable enthusiasm'.

On 3 July 1914, Connolly brought Larkin to Belfast to present gifts to two Dublin girls who had been active in the lock-out and were now in Belfast. Two days later Connolly spoke in Limerick at a labour demonstration held in support of members of the United Carmen's and Storemen's Society who were on strike. Limerick was noted for its narrow-mindedness and obscurantism; newspaper dealers there were afraid to stock not only the *Irish Worker* but such innocuous periodicals as *The Sketch* and *Reynold's News*. To Connolly's surprise, the demonstration was large and enthusiastic.

The stresses following the lock-out slowly eased. Larkin received medical advice for his nervous exhaustion, and, typically enough, ignored it. During the summer, Connolly busied himself with union problems in Belfast. The more important events were taking place elsewhere. In June 1914 Redmond demanded that twenty-five persons named by him should be placed on the executive board of the Irish Volunteers. This would give him control of the organization. In the interests of national unity, the executive committee (called Provisional Committee) of the Irish Volunteers agreed, though with great reluctance. The Irish Republican Brotherhood, which held key positions on the committee, thought that this would mean more funds and rifles for the Volunteers. It also feared that, if a split occurred, the militants might be the greater loser, since the Volunteers, in their rapid growth, had recruited many Redmondites. One newspaper estimated that the Irish Volunteers at that time had 128,500 members as contrasted with fewer than 1,000 in the Citizen Army. Of that 1,000 only a third were active at any given time.

In July the Irish Volunteers matched the gun-running exploit of the Ulstermen, but the event had an unforeseen and bitter aftermath. On 26 July, about a thousand members of the Dublin Battalion marched out to Howth several miles away on the sea. They thought they were on a normal Sunday route march; instead they were loaded down with rifles and ammunition that had been brought there on Erskine Childers' trim white yacht, *Asgard*. On their return, they were intercepted at Clontarf by a body of 200 policemen and a company of the King's Own Scottish Borderers. A scuffle ensued, and a few shots were fired. While a parley was going on, most Volunteers broke ranks and got away over the fields with the weapons.

When the British soldiers marched back to the city, they were jeered and stoned by the crowds in the streets. In Bachelor's Walk, near O'Connell Street, they halted and fired on their tormentors. Three people were killed instantly; one died several weeks later; and thirty-five persons were treated at Jervis Street Hospital for wounds.

One week after the funeral for the Bachelor's Walk victims, the United Kingdom of Great Britain and Ireland entered the war. The following month, on 18 September, the Home Rule Act received the Royal Assent and was placed in the Statute Book. It carried a proviso excluding the Province of Ulster. On the same day, the Commons passed legislation postponing implementation of the Home Rule Act until the war was over.

It is generally accepted today that the principal reason for the war was the competition between the nations for markets and colonies. What the people of the United Kingdom were told, and believed, was that German aggression was the sole cause of the war; and their duty was to defend civilization and helpless Belgium against the brutality of the Hun. The great majority of the Irish people accepted this fiction. At the outbreak of the war, John Redmond, chief of the Irish Party in Parliament, promptly proposed that all British troops be removed from Ireland and sent to France. He promised that the Irish Volunteers would defend Ireland against Germany.

Thousands of Irish (Catholics and Protestants) enlisted in the British Army. By the end of the war they numbered 250,000. Of these 50,000 died; and thousands more were crippled. To be sure, it was not always love of England that persuaded them to join the army. With some, it was desire for adventure; with others, it was to avoid poverty at home. The remittances sent by the soldiers to their families back home provided, incidentally, a strong motive for these relatives to resist republican propaganda.

On 20 September, John Redmond, in a speech at Woodenbridge, took a further step, and urged young Irishmen not to confine 'their effort to remaining at home to defend the shores of Ireland from an unlikely invasion', but to prove their gallantry by fighting 'wherever the firing line extends, in defence of right, of freedom and religion in this war'.

This open recruiting for the British Army proved too much. On 24 September, the Provisional Committee of the Volunteers (with members of the Irish Republican Brotherhood in the lead) declared that Redmond was 'no longer entitled, through his nominees, to any place in the administration and guidance' of the Irish Volunteers. At a convention held on 25 October, the Volunteers pledged themselves to continue resisting conscription and to remain faithful to Professor Eoin MacNeill, the Gaelic scholar, who headed the organization. By that time the Irish Volunteers had shrunk to a membership of 10,000 men. Most of these men did not seek to overthrow the British Empire in its time of difficulty; they stood for neutrality.

Before the war, millions of socialists in Europe had sworn to uphold various resolutions on war passed at international congresses. A typical one required all socialist parties and organizations to intervene promptly in favour of ending any war that arose between nations, and 'to utilize the economic and political crisis created by the war to rouse the masses and thereby hasten the downfall of capitalist class rule'. This very resolution had been printed by Connolly in the *Harp*.

With the outbreak of World War I, all socialist groups scrapped this resolution except the Bolsheviki led by Lenin, the Serbs and the Irish. Connolly was in large part the reason why the militant Irish workers, speaking through the Irish Trades Union Congress on 10 August, could say that 'a European war for the aggrandisement of the capitalistic class has been declared'.

From the beginning Connolly opposed the war with every resource at his command. For this alone he deserves some place in European history. Why did Connolly not defect from his socialist convictions as so many of his comrades did? The answer, I think, lies mainly in the circumstance that he was an Irishman, and hence slightly immune from British propaganda about the defence of small nations. Since many Irishmen *did* accept the propaganda about the defence of small nations, we must add that Connolly was a special kind of Irishman, a socialist Irishman—obstinate, cynical and deeply versed in the history of British imperialism. Perhaps we can put the matter in another way. The 'Marxist searchlight' often (not always) brilliantly illuminates some dark corners. But the person using it must hold it steady and firm. Connolly had the necessary rock-like quality.

He presented his position on the war in every publication that would give it space, on every platform that would permit him to speak. As soon as war was declared, he wrote in the *Irish Worker*:

What should be the attitude of the working-class democracy of Ireland in the face of the present crisis? I wish to emphasize the fact that the question is addressed to the 'working-class democracy' because I believe that it would be worse than foolish to take counsel in this matter from any other source.

I know of no foreign enemy in this country except the British Government. Should a German army land in Ireland tomorrow, we should be perfectly justified in joining it, if by so doing we could rid this country once and for all from its connection with the Brigand Empire that drags us unwillingly to war.

Should the working class of Europe, rather than slaughter each other for the benefit of kings and financiers, proceed tomorrow to erect barricades all over Europe, to break up bridges and destroy the transport service that war might be abolished, we should be perfectly justified in following such a glorious example, and contributing our aid to the final dethronement of the vulture classes that rule and rob the world.

Connolly's pragmatic proposal was that the labour movement should stop the export of foodstuffs from Ireland, if necessary through 'armed battling in the streets'. Starting thus, he said, 'Ireland may yet set the torch of a European conflagration that will not burn out until the last throne and the last capitalist bond and debenture will be shrivelled on the funeral pyre of the last war lord.' Opportunities for Connolly to express such ideas were closing fast. He was constantly being urged by his comrades to moderate his statements. Connolly said of these timorous colleagues: 'They seem to have a curious idea of what constitutes working-class propaganda. They don't seem to think that I ought to express an opinion on the greatest crisis that has faced the working class in our generation.'

The Belfast Branch of the Independent Labour Party of Ireland believed that the city would no longer accept anti-war propaganda and voted to discontinue its open-air propaganda meetings on Library Street. In a letter to O'Brien dated 22 August 1914, Connolly described the situation in the following way:

Principally through the machinations of [Daniel] McDevitt there has been a cabal against me holding meetings during the war, and last night it was decided to abandon them. The interruptions of about a dozen young Orange hooligans were magnified into an awful danger, and the majority decided against me. Indeed, I had only three supporters . . .
[David R.] Campbell spoke and voted against my amendment, and [Thomas] Johnson neither spoke nor voted on either side.
Campbell and Johnson and McDevitt have always been on that style. Ready to cheer every stand made in Dublin, but always against any similar attempt in Belfast . . .

He concluded his letter with a passage remarkably reminiscent of those he wrote in Dublin in 1903, and during many of his years in the United States:

I have spent myself pushing forward the movement here for the past three years, and the result of this is that my activity is labelled as a desire for 'cheap notoriety'. I am sick, Bill, of this part of the Globe.

The significant pattern was again appearing—the need to break out against restrictions no matter what the cost, no matter how reckless the deed.

When Connolly wrote a manifesto on the war, it had to be issued under the name of the Irish Citizen Army of Belfast, a non-existent outfit, and distributed by a 'don't care-a-damn' brigade of young socialists, suffragettes, and republicans. After predicting (erroneously) that the war would mean more unemployment and less wages for the workers, the document called the war 'utterly unjustifiable and unnecessary . . . We have no foreign enemy except the treacherous government of England—a government that even whilst it is calling on us to die for it, refuses to give a straight answer to our demand for Home Rule.'

Dublin was not under as heavy pressure from Protestants and British patriots as Belfast. Consequently, a second manifesto could be issued under the name of the Dublin Branch of the Independent Labour Party of Ireland. Its message was just as explicit: for Irish workers 'to take up arms in anger to kill any of the poor driven workers of another nation at the order of our rulers is as clearly an act of murder as any crime of violence ever committed . . . Has Germany ever harmed Ireland? No. Has England harmed Ireland? Yes.' Even Larkin was not quite ready to accept such strong language. During this period he toyed several times with the idea of offering Irish support to Dublin in return for a guarantee of dominion status, but he published Connolly's articles in the *Irish Worker*, and gradually swung around to his colleague's position.

At a meeting held in Beresford Place to commemorate Byrne and Nolan, Connolly launched a bitter attack on the Redmondites, saying that they had not merely 'sold' the people of Ireland, 'they have given you away'. He told his audience that the duty of an Irish worker was to his class, not to the Empire. He would be glad to see the Empire in a bottomless pit. While thus propagandizing, Connolly began to beat the bushes for allies among organized nationalist groups. In Belfast, as soon as war was declared, he tried to make contact with local members of the Irish Republican Brotherhood. Everyone knew that this group could be relied on to continue its fight against England, no matter what happened. At an executive committee meeting of the Dublin Trades Union Council, held 30 August 1914, he was told by William O'Brien that the people he had reached were of no importance, and that nothing could be done without Tom Clarke and Sean MacDermott.

On 1 September, less than a month after the war began, Connolly attended a meeting at which both of these men were present. Also participating were Padraic Pearse, Sean T. O'Kelly, Major John MacBride, Thomas MacDonagh, Eamonn Ceannt and Arthur Griffith. Which of these men were members of the IRB and which were not, Connolly did not know. But all agreed that the time had come for organizing an insurrection and for seeking military support from Germany. Two sub-committees were to be appointed, one to establish an open organization for propaganda purposes, the other to make contact with Germany. The first, if organized, never became active. But there is evidence that the second sub-committee, intended to negotiate with Germany or give her information, did come into being; that it consisted of Clarke, MacDermott, Countess Markievicz and Connolly; that it sent Nora Connolly on a secret mission shortly before Christmas. Nora was told by her father that discovery of her mission would mean that charges of treason would be placed against these four.

A possible second instrument for opposing the war was the Citizen Army. But its health was still precarious; Connolly, from his base in Belfast, could have little influence on it; and it was undergoing a mini-crisis. Sean O'Casey, secretary of the Council of the Citizen Army, tried to have Madame Markievicz expelled. The charge was that she was active in the women's group that was attached to the Irish Volunteers, and friendly with other leaders of this group which was, 'in its methods and aims, inimical to the first interests of Labour . . .' O'Casey's motion lost by one vote, whereupon he resigned. Trying to make peace, Larkin called another meeting of the Council. O'Casey repeated his charges and embellished them, winding up with assertions that Madame was a spy for the Irish Volunteers and, irrelevantly, that he was afraid of no man there. He pointed to Larkin and added, 'Not even of him.' Larkin came to his feet with a bellow of indignation. Larkin versus O'Casey was no even match, and Sean left the Army for good.

Connolly participated in another attempt to weld together the nationalists of different outlooks in a stand against the war. Called the Irish Neutrality League, it was formed in Dublin with Connolly as president, Sean T. O'Kelly as secretary, and Thomas Farren as treasurer. It had a short life—one public meeting on 12 October 1914, with Connolly in the chair, and speakers consisting of Arthur Griffith, Major John MacBride, Constance Markievicz, William O'Brien, Sean T. O'Kelly, Sean Milroy and J. J. Scollan. O'Brien described it later as an organization of leaders without members. It will be observed that the Irish Republican Brotherhood did not participate.

While he was in Dublin, Connolly also spoke at a demonstration called by the Independent Labour Party of Ireland to demand once more the extension of the school-feeding act to Ireland. Under the stress of war the government complied, and the Dublin authorities got to work to see that the children were fed. The Belfast officials were slower to accept their responsibilities. At the same time they tried to exclude trade unions from participating in administering the act. To induce them to see the folly of their ways, Connolly held a number of open-air meetings, under Transport Union auspices, in Belfast.

When it was announced that Asquith was to address a meeting in the Mansion House in Dublin on 25 September to encourage recruiting, some discussion took place on the advisability of seizing the Mansion House the night before and holding it long enough to make the meeting impossible. The idea was dropped when it was discovered that only eighty Irish Volunteers and forty Citizen Army men could be made available. Connolly wrote to O'Brien that he feared that the people who were sponsoring the Irish Neutrality League

> have not got sufficient dash and desperation to deal with the matter. The meeting for Asquith will be a military affair, and the City will be in the hands of the military to carry it through. In a sense all our future is on the cast of that die. I am ready for any call.

In the outcome, on the day of Asquith's visit, Connolly, Larkin, P. T. Daly and Countess Markievicz led a procession of a hundred rifle-carrying soldiers of the Citizen Army from Liberty Hall to St Stephen's Green, where anti-recruiting speeches were delivered.

In September, the differences between Larkin and the other members of the Transport Union's executive committee flared up again. Connolly sent a card to O'Brien saying,

> The fat is in the fire at Liberty Hall. All the Committee have resigned including Foran, and a general meeting is called for Sunday. I have told Jim that I wont mix in it at all, nor attend the meeting. He says it is a branch affair and is very sore on Foran. I think I had best keep out of it.

At the meeting, a majority of the executive committee agreed to let Larkin go to America, but some members felt that Larkin should not go as a representative of the union. Connolly was one of them; he feared the union would be embarrassed by Larkin's speeches in America.

Larkin did not leave Ireland without giving Connolly a final headache. Jim visited Belfast on 5 October, said that he was definitely leaving for America, and that he was recommending that P. T. Daly be chosen as the new secretary-general of the union. Connolly would be left in charge of the insurance section and the paper. Connolly told Jim he hated the insurance side of the work, expressed no opinion about Daly, and wrote to O'Brien the same day:

But you know as well as I do that such an arrangement would be unbearable and unworkable. For one thing, we could never hope to maintain an understanding with the Nationalists if Daly was in command of the Transport Union. They would not trust him, have him, or co-operate with him, and the Transport Union would become a mere dues-collecting Union if a man with the character of Daly for evading difficulties was in charge. Other reasons you will readily see. I think you should at once get hold of Foran and tell him Jim's proposition, and get him to see that the Committee makes it clear that they will not agree to any such proposal. The danger is that Larkin will *publicly* announce it *first*, and that would make it as difficult to alter as it would be to carry out. The Committee could avoid this by meeting immediately and raise this *among other questions* before any public announcement is made.

Two days later Connolly wrote again to O'Brien, saying that he doubted if he could serve under Daly, even if it meant losing his job with the union; and that the election of Daly would kill the position of the union 'as the one labour organization aggressively active on the true Nationalist side'. He added:

That the control of the Insurance Section should be left to *me* is incomprehensible, except on the supposition that it was given me in order to concentrate upon me the *unpopularity* which that nasty job entails.

I shall anxiously await word from you of the intentions of Foran and the Committee.

After two more days of reflection, Connolly, on 9 October, sent a letter to Jim Larkin expressing, in the mildest terms possible, his objections to the proposed new arrangement of the union. It was precisely the kind of controlled, rational letter that Larkin, in similar circumstances, could never have written.

I have been seriously considering your proposed division of labour in the Union during your absence, and I am afraid that it would not work out as satisfactorily as you imagine. I have looked at it in every possible way, and from every possible angle, and cannot come to any other conclusion. And the objections are serious.

First. We are at present in a very critical stage for the whole of Ireland as well as for the Labour movement. One result of this is that we have an opportunity of taking the lead of the real Nationalist movement, and a certainty of acquiring great prestige among Nationalists outside of the Home Rule gang, provided that our own movement is in charge of somebody in whom the Nationalists have confidence. They have not that confidence, nor any confidence, in Daly. In fact they would not touch any movement in which he had control. What the basis of their attitude is I do not know. But that it is a fact is indisputable. Hence I conclude that his leadership means the loss of all power and prestige to the Transport Union amongst the outside public, a price I think far too high for his services. *You* could afford to disregard outside prestige to some extent, he cannot.

Second. During the very critical period of last year's fight you placed me in charge, and to bring me to Dublin now and put me in a position subordinate to Daly would be equal to announcing to the public that you had come to the conclusion that I was not fit to be trustee.

I do not think that I deserve this, and it would help to convince a good many that you had been influenced by the attempts of your enemies to sow dissention amongst us, and had fallen headlong into their trap. Rather than that our enemies should have this public proof that they had succeeded in fooling you, I should, if you will allow me, prefer to stay away from Dublin entirely.

Third. As I have no confidence personally in Daly's ability to manage the Union I should not like to be in a position where I should share the responsibility of the failures without the power to avert them.

I trust that you will consider these points in the spirit in which I have offered them.

Connolly sent a copy of this letter to O'Brien, who showed it to Thomas Foran, general president of the Transport Union. Since there was to be a meeting of the executive committee that same day, Foran promptly spoke to several members and persuaded them to support Connolly. When Larkin proposed that Daly should take over the union in his absence, these members argued that Connolly would be the better choice, and after much discussion Larkin finally said, 'Have it your own way.'

Larkin left Ireland on 24 October 1914. His assertion in the *Irish Worker* that he was going to America to raise funds for the union and the new labour party was far from the truth. He needed time to rest and think, for he was emotionally and physically depleted. But he chose the wrong country. In America his amalgam of nationalism, socialism and Catholicism did not harmonize with popular sentiment (particularly during the time of the Palmer raids and red hysteria) nearly as well as it had in Ireland. After associating with the Industrial Workers of the World, a dying body, he became active in a left-wing element of the Socialist Party. For publishing its manifesto calling for a dictatorship of the proletariat, Larkin spent two years and eight months in a Federal prison.

He returned to Ireland on 30 April 1923, having been away almost eight and a half years. He attempted to regain control of his old Transport Workers' Union, which, under the tutelage of O'Brien, Daly and Foran, had grown from 5,000 members in 1916 to 100,000. Failing in this effort, he established the Workers' Union of Ireland. It started with 16,000 Dubliners who split from the Transport Union. From then on, Larkin suffered a slow, remorseless decline in popularity and power. He died in 1947, at the age of seventy, leaving his son Jim, an able socialist and astute administrator, in charge of the Workers' Union. The son, shortly before his own death in 1970, started negotiations to lead the union back into the mother body.

When Connolly became head of the union as 'acting general secretary', he found its affairs in a deplorable state. The treasury was still depleted as a legacy of the lock-out; the insurance fund was in such a chaotic condition that the Government was threatening to withdraw the union's status as an approved society; and membership was low, both in number and spirits. Connolly rolled up his sleeves and started working on the books. He reorganized the offices in Liberty Hall, streamlined the administration, earned extra money by renting superfluous rooms to friendly organizations, gave the building a coat of paint, and visited the branches outside of Dublin.

But his purpose was not simply to create an efficient trade union; it was to create an organization which, together with its Citizen Army and publication, would convince all of Ireland that it was indeed the 'anchor and foundation of any real nationalism this country can show'. He drastically altered the paper, eliminating many of the personal attack and space-wasting fulminations, and adding Citizen Army material and nationalist propaganda. Across the front of

Liberty Hall, he had a banner stretched reading 'We serve neither King nor Kaiser but Ireland'.

He tried other ways to demonstrate his convictions. When the Irish Volunteers held a convention at the Abbey Theatre on 25 October 1914, Connolly headed a deputation from the Citizen Army to propose that his organization be allowed to affiliate with them, and have two representatives on their executive committee. The Volunteer leadership, still reeling from the shock of losing so many members after Redmond was expelled, declined the proposal. The leaders were in no mood to lose any more middle-class elements by merging with the Citizen Army.

Connolly, still unaware of the Irish Republican Brotherhood faction ensconced within the Volunteer executive committee, took the rejection as a sign that the revolutionary will of the Irish Volunteers was weakening. Nevertheless, he sent a unit of the Citizen Army to join a parade of Volunteers that was marching to St Stephen's Green. There, an anti-war meeting was held. Connolly presided, with Countess Markievicz, P. T. Daly, and Padraic Pearse sharing the platform. Pearse's appearance signified his growing sympathy with labour. Connolly noted without surprise that the head of the Irish Volunteers, Eoin MacNeill, did not appear.

Connolly's lack of confidence in the Irish Volunteers appears again in an incident that took place in mid-November. The authorities dismissed Captain Robert Monteith, the Volunteers' best military instructor, from his government post, and ordered him to leave Dublin. When Monteith came into Liberty Hall to tell Connolly the news, Connolly rumbled, 'If I had the handling of this matter, I would put you in position in Dublin, turn out every Volunteer in the city, and say to the Government, "Now come and take him." Tell Bulmer Hobson this and if necessary I'll turn out the Citizen Army. That would stop all these deportation orders.' (Hobson ran the day-by-day operations of the Irish Volunteers.)

Before Monteith left, eventually to organize Irish Volunteer brigades in the south, Connolly showed him a poster advertising a meeting to be held 13 November to protest the deportation. The two men never met again, but in his old age Monteith used to repeat that the one man of 1916 who must never be forgotten was James Connolly.

The meeting, held again at St Stephen's Green, was well attended considering that a heavy rain was falling. William O'Brien presided.

Speakers were Connolly, P. T. Daly, Countess Markievicz, Sean Milroy and The O'Rahilly. O'Rahilly represented the large nationalist sentiment outside the labour movement. Connolly proposed a resolution pledging all those present never to rest until Ireland was a free and independent republic among the nations.

Angered by these anti-war demonstrations, even though the numbers participating in them were insignificant, the government took to censoring or suppressing dissident publications. The *Irish Worker* appeared on 5 December with a blank space where the leading article should have been. The banned article was published as a separate leaflet on 19 December 'while the censor wasn't looking'. With the war only five months old, Connolly had no practical policy to offer in the leaflet; he could only threaten the authorities with what he hoped was the sentiment of the Irish working class: 'If you leave us at liberty we will kill your recruiting, save our poor boys from your slaughter-house, and blast your hopes of Empire. If you strike at, imprison or kill us, out of our prisons or graves we will still evoke a spirit that will thwart you and, mayhap, raise a force that will destroy you. We defy you! Do your worst!' No doubt, most of Connolly's friends and foes considered this empty bluster. It took Easter Week of 1916 to prove that it was not.

XXI

1915

CONNOLLY WAS a busy man in 1915. As 'acting general secretary' of the Irish Transport and General Workers' Union, he naturally had to perform many administrative duties, conduct strikes, negotiate contracts, attend union gatherings and conferences. As Ireland's most extreme radical, most articulate spokesman for economic and social change, most vehement apostle for immediate action to free the Irish nation, Connolly was busy on many other fronts. He spoke at meetings protesting against the recruiting or conscription of Irishmen for the war raging in France; at commemorations of dead Irish heroes; at political rallies; at meetings supporting the right of women to vote; at military musters of the Citizen Army. He wrote voluminously for the union's own weekly newspaper, and for other publications as well, including a Christmas annual put out by the Fianna na Eireann, the patriotic youth organization founded by Constance Markievicz.

A listing of his activities during the year gives the impression that he was accomplishing a great deal. Connolly would have been the first to deny that. He was only too painfully aware of what little effect he was really having in reducing the power of the British Government and the Irish Parliamentary Party over all aspects of Irish life. A single circumstance was proof enough: the continued heavy drainage of young Irishmen into the British Army or into the labouring ranks of foreign countries.

He was alternately bitter or despondent when he saw how ineffective or dilatory the activities were of those organizations (including his own) which were supposedly committed to the obstruction or overthrow of the ruling political and economic establishment. Though he occasionally co-operated with these nationalists—the Irish Volunteers, the groups fostering the revival of the Irish language, sports and music—he often berated these same organizations for postponing endlessly the day of rebellion.

With equal vigour Connolly would have denied that his activities were too scattered or diverse to be effective. To him they were but different aspects of a single struggle—the struggle for a republic independent of England and controlled by the working masses. If the account given in this chapter of Connolly's activities during 1915 appears episodic, he would have attributed it to a failure of the narrator, not to the actual nature of the activities.

After spending Christmas of 1914 with his family in Belfast—his daughters were all becoming young ladies now—Connolly crossed over to Glasgow where he induced some of his old friends to agree to print the *Irish Worker* on a press owned by the Socialist Labour Party of Scotland. Under conditions of wartime censorship, no commercial Irish printer would accept this assignment any longer. The first issue of the revived paper was shipped to Dublin in boxes labelled 'glass', but in a few weeks the police caught on and the entire issue of 20 February 1915 was confiscated as it was being taken off the boat.

Connolly decided that his only recourse was to purchase a printing press of his own and set it up in Liberty Hall under Citizen Army guard. He searched for one in Liverpool, but in vain. During this visit he discussed with some comrades the possibility of making a revolution in Ireland. One Liverpool comrade asked, 'But is the time ripe?' Connolly answered coolly, 'If you succeed, the time is ripe. If not, then it is not ripe.' This perhaps tells as much about his reason for participating in the Easter Rising as dozens of paragraphs might.

Connolly did not give up his search for a press. He considered it as important to the revolutionary cause as a machine gun. That he also had a strong psychological need of an outlet for his writings was something he probably did not comprehend.

Finally Connolly found in Dublin a second-hand printing press that seemed suitable. Though it had to be propped up on bricks, it was motor driven and capable of turning out in one hour 1,600 copies of a small weekly. When a union member protested that printing of illegal matter might lead the authorities to close Liberty Hall, Connolly replied that the machine was 'only a little one', and won the argument. The first issue of the paper appeared on 29 May 1915. It was now called the *Workers' Republic*—a significant change of name from the *Irish Worker*.

Connolly took advantage of wartime prosperity and a growing shortage of manpower to demand and obtain higher wages for the various types of workers enrolled under the banner of the Transport Union. In a speech to the Cork branch of the union, he was able to report that the stevedores had won an increase of a penny a ton; both the deep-sea dockers and the casual cross-channel workers a shilling a day; the workers at the Dublin and General Company 4s. a week; the dock labourers 3s. 6d. a week; the workers at Ross and Walpole 2s. a week. The transport workers also won 2s. a week.

These economic advances did little to increase political militancy or interest. While in Cork, Connolly booked a hall for a meeting of the Independent Labour Party of Ireland. The Party was now a dying body, in part absorbed by the Labour Party proper, in part gone pacifist as a protest against the war. When Connolly arrived for the meeting, he found the door locked and nobody to be seen. Apparently, the members had not been notified or thought the meeting not worth attending. When a member finally showed up, apologizing profusely for the mischance, Connolly answered quietly, 'It's all right. I'm used to that.' He was right on both counts; such rebuffs had happened hundreds of times before and he had become accustomed to them. The only novelty is that there exists a record of the mischance and of his reaction to it.

Nevertheless, Connolly persisted in trying to expand the industrial struggle into a political and revolutionary one. When the union held its annual Labour Day meeting at Phoenix Park on 30 May 1915, he bypassed any mention of economic demands in his speech, preferring to attack the war and advising men to join the army—the Citizen Army. The meeting hailed the appearance on the day before of the first issue of the *Workers' Republic*, and extended fraternal greetings to the workers in every country 'who are striving for the emancipation of their class'. At the moment these workers were few; the great majority were busy dying for King, Kaiser, Tsar, Emperor and whatever ruling class was in power.

In June, when Devlin requested the support of the Dublin Trades Council and the Transport Union for a Nationalist candidate in a by-election, Connolly vehemently spoke in favour of labour running its own candidate. Four days before the election the Transport Union did put up its own man but he was defeated by a large margin.

On 12–13 June, the Transport Union staged an Irish musical and athletic carnival at its recreational centre, Croydon Park. One Gaelic enthusiast remarked that this was the 'sanest' attempt yet made to identify the working population with the Irish-Ireland movement.

At the annual pilgrimage to Wolfe Tone's grave at Bodenstown, County Kildare, on 20 June, the guard of honour consisted of equal numbers of Citizen Army men and Irish Volunteers, despite the disproportion in their membership. Connolly must have had some deep thought about the changes since last year's demonstration, when Larkin was being urged to remain in Ireland.

When Sean MacDermott and Sheehy-Skeffington were arrested for making anti-recruiting speeches, Connolly was one of the speakers at a protest meeting held at Beresford Place. Others were William O'Brien and Mrs Sheehy-Skeffington. On 13 August, in hostile Belfast, Connolly reaffirmed his opposition to the war and attacked the provisions controlling employment in the Defence of the Realm Act as barriers to trade-union recruiting. He also denounced the jailings and deportation of Volunteer leaders as unwarranted infringements of political liberty.

On 21 June the railway workers struck in order to obtain an increase in wages. When the funds available at Transport Union headquarters for strike benefits became exhausted, Connolly had to write to each branch to send in 'at *once* a sum equal to half your balance . . . ending July 3rd, 1915'. The men had been on strike for a month when Connolly told the workers that he could not raise another week's strike pay, and advised them to return to work. Luckily, a loan from another union came through, and on 14 August the employers granted an increase of 2s. a week.

In the pages of the *Workers' Republic* he commented on a much larger strike then taking place in the mines of South Wales. When it started, he feared that the British workers 'are crying out too late; the master class are now in possession of such impressive powers as they have not possessed for three-quarters of a century'. When the miners won, it proved to him 'that the only rebellious spirit left in the modern world is in the possession of those who have been accustomed to drop tools at a moment's notice in defence of a victimised or unjustly punished comrade'.

He repeated this theme in a speech before the Dublin Trades Union Council. The miners' strike was, he said, 'another signal proof of the strength and invincibility of Labour when united'. The miners had stood up against a government vested with extraordinary wartime powers, and, by stopping production, had proved that 'they were more powerful than all the mighty civil and military forces arrayed against them'. If the soldiers recruited from the working class in 1914 had shown the same amount of courage, if they had said to the diplomats 'that they would not march against their brothers across the frontiers . . . there would have been no war, and millions of homes that are now desolated would be happy'.

On 18 July 1915, Connolly held a huge anti-conscription meeting outside Liberty Hall, where he warned that attempts would be made to introduce conscription piecemeal, beginning with the Ulster districts. Conscription was a threat facing the country from 1915 on that touched on a sensitive nerve in Ireland. That it was never imposed was in part the result of the campaign waged against it by Connolly and other militant Nationalists.

In July 1915 Jeremiah O'Donovan Rossa died in his lonely exile in America. In 1865 he had been condemned to life imprisonment by the British Government for his Fenian activities. John O'Leary was sentenced to twenty years at the same time. Arrangements were made to have Rossa's body returned to Ireland and buried at Glasnevin. Since nothing in Ireland excites such enthusiasm and fervour as the funeral of a patriot, a broad committee was established to make the arrangements and to conduct a great republican demonstration in connection with it. Connolly represented the Transport Union on the committee. He published Bulmer Hobson's letter announcing the arrangements, but balked at writing an article for the official programme. 'When are you fellows going to stop blethering about *dead* Fenians?' he asked. 'Why don't you get a few live ones for a change?'

He finally gave in, but the article he wrote could have given little comfort to the moderates on the committee. He considered it questionable whether any amount of blood-letting 'could be as disastrous as a cowardly acceptance of the rule of the conqueror'. He doubted the right of the moderates to have any part in honouring a man whose 'very title to honour lies in his continued rejection of that which they have accepted'. The Citizen Army, on the other hand, was entitled to honour O'Donovan Rossa 'by right of our faith in the separate destiny of our country, and our faith in the ability of the Irish Workers to achieve that destiny'. The Volunteers and Citizen Army joined forces again for the processional to the Glasnevin burial grounds on 1 August.

Padraic Pearse's graveside oration was brief. In the gloom of a rainy late afternoon, he stood impassive and serious, as heavily built as Connolly but much taller, a slow, thoughtful speaker, an introverted man. 'They think,' he said, 'that they have foreseen everything, provided against everything but the fools, the fools, the fools!'—his hand cleft the air—'they have left us our Fenian dead, and while Ireland holds these graves Ireland unfree shall never be at peace.'

The younger generation, represented by the Fianna na Eireann, listened with particular attention. They had recently been reorganized under strictly military lines, and the character-building elements replaced by drill and musketry. It was now the outright tool of the Irish Republican Brotherhood and Madame's title of President had become honorary. She did not resist the change; it was entirely in line with her own thinking.

From such moments of high drama, Connolly had to swing to more mundane matters, requesting help from the Dublin Trades and Labour Council in obtaining money that had been raised in Great Britain for victims of the labour struggle of 1913–14. This money, Connolly wrote on 29 August 1915, is

> still in the funds of some of these cross-channel Trade Unions. As this Union has had to bear a very large proportion of liabilities for that dispute we would like if some effort could be made to secure the disbursement of these funds, now so uselessly tied up.
>
> One item alone of our bill—Legal fees for the defending of prisoners arrested during dispute—amounts to over £1400. As this was incurred in defending every arrested person whether a Transport Worker or not, we think that some effort should be made to share this burden with us.

As the year progressed, Connolly became sure that the Irish Volunteers under the leadership of Eoin MacNeill and the other moderates would never take action, that the Volunteers would follow in the footsteps of other patriotic organizations by talking big and doing nothing. He wrote to his daughter Nora that MacNeill should be removed. He even suspected that his group had played a part in trying to keep the Citizen Army from participating in a drilling competition held in June in Tullow. The Citizen Army won, indicating a modest degree of competence had been achieved. On the other side of the ledger, he could see in the pages of Padraic Pearse's new book, *From A Hermitage*, evidence that Pearse was becoming sympathetic to labour's cause.

If the Volunteers would not act, the Citizen Army would. The situation was summed up in a remark by Connolly: 'I can always guarantee that the Irish Citizen Army will fight, but I cannot guarantee that they will be in time.' Various ways of tightening discipline and improving training were initiated by Connolly and the army's chief of staff, a silk weaver named Michael Mallin. He was a British Army veteran, whom Connolly considered a 'great soldier'. A miniature rifle range was installed at Liberty Hall, and a standing reserve was formed from men who could not attend regular musters.

The *Workers' Republic* devoted considerable space to Citizen Army education. The back page of each issue summarized various insurrections and drew optimistic conclusions about the lessons to be learned from each. Rebels, after all, should know the history of revolt. The first lesson was devoted to the Moscow insurrection of 1905, which Connolly thought established the fact that, even under modern conditions, civilian revolutionaries in a city can do well against professional soldiers. In other issues he analysed the lessons of the Tyrol in 1809, Belgium in 1830, Paris in 1830 and 1848, and Lexington in 1775. About the 1821 defence of the Alamo, he wrote that it 'was one of those defeats which are more valuable to a cause than many loudly trumpeted victories'. Its similarity to the Dublin Rising of 1916 is apparent.

Some members of the Transport Union did not take in their stride this emphasis on military, political and nationalist activities. The organization had all it could do merely to survive as a trade union, they thought. There was dissension also in the union's female auxiliary, the Women Workers' Union; as a result, Delia Larkin resigned and returned to Liverpool. To replace her, Connolly tried to hire Miss Louie Bennett, but she declined since she did not believe in combining political and patriotic (separatist) sentiments with trade union ones. Connolly then installed some rank-and-file girls in the front offices of Liberty Hall, held a reorganization meeting on 10 August, and, together with Partridge, beat down all opposition to the trend the union was taking. But the grumbling continued, and even increased as time went on.

Then it was back to more normal trade-union combat. When the Government announced that it was imposing special taxes to pay for the war, Connolly held a public meeting on 26 September, and suggested: 'Before they were asked to pay the bloodtax of the war, it was surely right that the Irish race should have been asked to consent to waging war at all.' The way for the working man to pay the increased taxes, he said, was to demand more wages.

A rash of labour struggles followed. During the next two weeks the shipping lines, the Coal Association, and other employers were confronted with wage demands from several unions of dock and other workers. The Coal Association conceded the higher wages without ado, but the Burns-Laird Line, after offering an increase, withdrew it. Now it was the employers who were saying to hell with contracts, Connolly commented. It is likely that the employers were under pressure by the Government not to accede to the wage demands, since that would nullify the effects of the war budget.

But the trade unions were having their difficulties too. About 9 October Connolly again wrote the Dublin United Trades and Labour Council, pointing out that 'this Union has now a very big and important strike on its hands, involving many hundreds of men', and repeating its request for 'the sum of money lately received from England in connection with the 1913–14 lock-out'. It is not known what the final action of the Dublin Trades Council was, but in any case a settlement of the strike was reached three weeks later. Wage increases were also won in Sligo and Belfast.

Taking advantage of the favourable tides, Connolly visited Kerry at the invitation of the Tralee Trades Council, and recruited 160 men into the Transport Union. When the vice-president of the Council was dismissed from his job following this meeting, a large campaign to win reinstatement was conducted throughout the county. In succeeding months union branches were established at Killarney, Listowel and Fenit.

The Citizen Army remained prominent in Connolly's mind. When the dock workers were on strike and it became possible for them to participate in Citizen Army drills, Connolly twitted the employers on the good work they were doing for the organization. Discipline grew tighter. A peremptory notice in the *Worker's Republic* instructed those who were not prepared to participate in Sunday parades to hand in their rifles, since others were waiting for them. For the first time midnight exercises were held; one of them was based on the assumption that the insurgents had captured Dublin Castle and were attempting to prevent British troops from relieving it.

On 15 November 1915, the Dublin Trades Council appointed Connolly and Farren to discuss with the Irish Volunteers joint action against conscription. As a result, a large protest meeting was held at the Mansion House; its size held up all traffic on Dawson Street. Speakers in addition to Connolly and Farren were Bulmer Hobson, Arthur Griffith, Eoin MacNeill, Padraic Pearse and Thomas MacDonagh.

Lord Aberdeen, Lord Lieutenant in Ireland, responded by urging employers to 'facilitate enlistment' as much as possible. He was in essence politely asking employers to dismiss some workers so that, having nothing else to do, they might join up. This form of 'economic conscription' met with hostility on the part of many who otherwise supported the British Government and its war. Many moderate Irish, including the younger clergy, drew the line at conscription, but were willing enough to let recruiting flourish.

In addition to sharing a platform, Connolly tried to display in other ways his willingness to co-operate with the Irish Volunteer leaders. He wrote to Austin Stack, one of these leaders,

> It is not our purpose to disrupt but rather to increase and strengthen the true national movement, and in a town the size of Tralee there is no necessity for any other military body than the Volunteer Corps which has stood out so splendidly by the true Irish ideal . . .

But as 1915 drew to a close, Connolly felt more than ever that he was shouting into the wind. He saw the slaughter on the western front continuing; the blood of deluded working men, from all countries, being spilled endlessly in a war which netted gains only for the capitalists; Ireland continuing as a poor house appendage to Britain, unable even to gain Home Rule; and Irish 'patriots' mouthing calls for national freedom while finding on each day new pretexts for inaction.

Week after week in the pages of the *Workers' Republic* Connolly thundered, pleaded, protested against this stalemate. He begged the Irish Volunteer leaders to 'break through their refined distrust of the mob' and swing into action. He cited previous cases of men who, 'having all their lives sung the glories of the revolution, when it rose up before them they ran away appalled'. The revolutionaries of 1848 had been held back by talk of 'premature insurrection'; on the other hand, 'the Fenians of Manchester rose superior to all the whines about prudence, caution and restraint', and as a result only two of their countrymen were executed. He applauded Pearse's lecture on John Mitchel because it showed 'the nature of the forces which destroyed Mitchel'.

'Should the day ever come,' he wrote, 'when revolutionary leaders are prepared to sacrifice the lives of those under them as recklessly as the ruling class do in every war, there will not be a throne or a despotic government left in the world.' Instead, the people were being politely invited to struggle against conscription much as they would organize a cattle-drive. Was conscription to be fought with phrases or 'do you action on the resolution, and to union associations urging them to hold public meetings in support of it.

The person at fault was not O'Brien, who had been working hard since the Clonmel Congress in May to get the Parliamentary Committee to implement Connolly's resolution; the fault was Larkin's. Elected chairman of this Committee, he had resigned in a huff at its initial meeting when other members disagreed with one of his rulings. He was adamant in his refusal to withdraw his resignation or to take the lead in forming the proposed Labour Party.

Connolly got the story in a letter from O'Brien dated 12 September 1912 (names of persons and organizations have been amplified to facilitate comprehension):

I assume David R. Campbell posted you about the proceedings of the last meeting of the Parliamentary Committee of the Irish Trades Union Congress and especially the attitude assumed by Larkin with regard to the arrangements about the public meetings in support of labour representation. Well, it seems he intends to persist in his resignation, as he has refused to attend the Conference held by the Dublin Parliamentary Committee members with representatives of the Dublin Trades Council to make arrangements for the inaugural meeting to be held in the Antient Concert Rooms on Monday next, and we have reason to believe that he will not even speak on that occasion. Those who are pushing the question of Labour Representation here are being vigorously denounced by Lord Mayor Sherlock and Co as 'enemies of Home Rule' and 'Socialists in disguise', and are being left severely alone by the old gang in the Unions, so that Larkin's defection at this moment puts us in an awkward corner. Without a speaker like Larkin, I'm afraid the appeal will fall rather flat . . . I'm terribly sorry that you are not to be one of the speakers.

Connolly's reply, dated 13 September 1912, is given in full:

Your very distressing letter just arrived. I begin to fear that our friend Jim has arrived at his highest elevation, and that he will pull us all down with him in his fall.

He does not seem to want a democratic Labour movement; he seems to want a Larkinite movement only. The situation will require the most delicate handling. I would have been in favour of cancelling the Antient Concert fixture, of informing Larkin that as he will not attend, you do not see your way to go on with it, and that pending and awaiting his co-operation, you feel it unwise to go further with the movement. This *seems* tame and slavish advice, and it is; but it is, I fear, the only way to get him on the move again. He must rule, or will not work, and in the present stage of the Labour movement, he has us at his mercy. And he knows it, and is using his power unscrupulously, I regret to say. We can but bow our head, and try and avert the storm.

It is impossible that I should be there. He would have too much of a grip on me, as he would be able to appeal to my own members against me, on the plea that I neglected my duty to go there against his wish. At present my strength in Belfast is that no one knows whether his influence counts for much amongst the Transport Workers here. There is a strong feeling against him in the phrase that 'He was a great fighter, but too reckless.' So a fight by him upon me would wreck the Branch again, and he is headstrong enough to make it. He knows he could not oust me, and save the Branch, but in the case of too flagrant a flouting of his position, he would not consider that.

I am sick of all this playing to one man, but I am prepared to advise it for the sake of the movement. In fact, the general inactivity since the Congress has made me sick and sorry I ever returned.

Connolly had learned at least one thing from his experience with De Leon. Egotists must be handled with care.

It was decided to hold the meeting in any case. Larkin did not take the chair but he did attend and speak. What he said was petty, nagging and pointless, and he was obviously upset. He later attributed this to illness.

For the next few years the movement for an Irish Labour Party was quiescent as other controversies flared up. The principal one concerned Home Rule. Orange and Catholic fervour grew at the same pace. In June 1912, members of the Ancient Order of Hibernians broke up a Protestant school outing at Castledawson. In response Orange workers at the Workman-Clarke shipyard beat up some Catholic workers. The disturbances spread to Harland and Wolff's huge ship-building yards, where Carsonite sentiment forced the 'Disemployment' of some two thousand Catholics, together with 400 Englishmen and Scotsmen who refused to co-operate with the Orange firebrands.

Though stationed in Belfast, Connolly could steer clear of these disputes for the time being because the members of his two unions—the Transport and the Textile Workers—were almost entirely Roman Catholic and lived in a seamless Roman Catholic world. In May 1912 he instituted daytime open-air meetings where collections for the Textile Workers Union gradually rose to 12s 6d per day, a considerable amount for those times. He also tried to introduce some social activity, beginning with Irish dancing, but the girls preferred ballroom dancing. Another difficulty arose when the secretary, Mrs Tom Johnson, became sick and had to be replaced by Winifred Carney, a recruit from the suffragette ranks.

But Connolly was still able to show his libertarian sentiments. During July 1912, under the auspices of the Transport Union, 'the only union that allows no bigotry in its ranks', he organized an evening demonstration. Headed by the 'Non-Sectarian Labour Band', the procession of dock workers and mill-girls left union headquarters at 122 Corporation Street and proceeded to Cromac Square where Connolly and others addressed them. From then on, not a Sunday evening was missed. If Connolly was in Dublin, another took his place. 'Civil and religious liberty' was the usual topic discussed, with frequent references to women's right to vote. All three topics were controversial; many suffragette meetings in London and elsewhere were being broken up at the time.

On 28 September 1912, Ulster sentiment against the Home Rule Bill reached a peak when a 'Solemn League and Covenant' to 'use all means which may be found necessary to defeat the present conspiracy to set up a Home Rule Parliament' was signed by more than 219,000 people. In December 1912, the signatories were given the opportunity to fight for their beliefs by enlisting in the Ulster Volunteers. Carson applied to the magistrates for authorization to arm these men, and received it.

Connolly, still convinced that the ruling Liberal Party, with its strong majority and widespread support, would disregard the wishes of these fanatics was busy with other matters. In November 1912 he issued a manifesto *To the Linen Slaves of Belfast*, urging the girls in the linen mills to strike. It was, he said, the only means by which they could obtain the minimum wages of three pence an hour as laid down by the Sweated Industries Act but never applied to the Belfast mills. Realizing that the spinning room held the key to the whole industry, he made a special appeal to the reelers and spinners whose wages were 'less than some of our pious mill-owners spend weekly on a dog'.

He was also involved in polemics with Catholic lay and clerical leaders on the question of whether the Catholic Church had ever been mistaken in political matters. The discussion, based on a review in the *Daily Herald* of Connolly's pamphlet, *Labour, Nationality and Religion*, was conducted in the columns of the *Catholic Times* of London and the *Catholic Democrat*, and at an annual conference of the Catholic Truth Society. Greaves reports that Connolly's handling of his part in the controversy 'greatly enlarged his reputation among the Catholic circles who surrounded the *Daily Herald*, and brought him to London to debate with Hilaire Belloc at the Irish Club in Charing Cross Road. On this occasion the audience was astonished at the ease with which Connolly trounced one of the leading intellectuals of Britain.'

Towards the end of 1912, Connolly ran for a seat in the Belfast City Council. The ward he sought to represent contained the homes of many Transport Union members, and Connolly received the official support of the Belfast Trades Council. In his election address, Connolly argued that labour needed more representation in the City Council because the Council had certain duties to perform under the National Health Insurance Act which otherwise might not be properly done. If elected, he promised to help the City Council pay more attention to school feeding than to perpetuating the 'religious discords which make Belfast a by-word among civilised nations'. His programme also called for direct hiring of labour on city contracts, a union shop for city employees, a minimum wage of sixpence an hour, the enclosing of certain tram-cars used by workers in the chilly morning and evening hours, and a more democratic selection of the members of the important Harbour Board.

This was 'municipal Socialism' with a vengeance, but Connolly did not try to deceive the voters concerning his larger aims. He stated that he advocated all-out socialism, a system to be achieved by the 'continuous increase in the power of the working class'. It was as a socialist and member of this class that he sought election. He also declared himself an advocate of national independence for Ireland and a supporter of Home Rule. He favoured equal rights for women, including the right to vote.

For the most part, Catholics, Nationalists, Socialists and trade unionists voted for Connolly in the January 1913 elections, although many did so with reluctance, thinking that votes for women were a bit too much. Others were unable to find any logical connection prefer the method of that Catholic priest who recently advised his people to send a deputation of their ten best shots to meet the conscriptors? We believe in constitutional action in normal times; we believe in revolutionary action in exceptional times. These are exceptional times,' he wrote.

In response to a letter inviting him to address an anti-conscription meeting in Glasgow Connolly wrote on 23 November that he would be unable to accept, but sent this message instead:

Tell them that we in Ireland will not have conscription, let the law say what it likes. We know our rulers: we know their power, and their ruthlessness we experience every day. We know they can force us to fight whether we wish to or not, but we know also that no force in their possession can decide for us *where* we will fight. *That* remains for us to decide; and we have no intention of shedding our blood abroad for our masters: rather will we elect to shed it if need be for the conquest of our freedom at home.

In urging immediate uprising, Connolly was not accepting Pearse's concept of it as a mystical blood-bath required from each succeeding generation as a method of rejuvenating the national spirit. He was thinking of military action as a necessary step towards the conscription by a democratic republic of all the resources of the nation with 'men and women, all co-operating together under one common direction that Ireland may live and bear on her fruitful bosom the greatest number of the freest people she has ever known'. After the rising, the property of the wealthy classes 'who have so shamelessly sold themselves to the enemy' should immediately be seized. The railroads, canals, and farm land stolen from the Irish people in the past and not since restored should be made the property of the Irish state. The factories and workshops owned by people who did not swear allegiance to the new republic promptly after it was declared should be confiscated and used for the benefit of the loyal Irish community.

When Padraic Pearse spoke at the John Mitchel commemoration services under the chairmanship of Arthur Griffith, Connolly was confirmed in his belief that behind the failure of 'fervent advanced patriots' (meaning Arthur Griffith, Eoin MacNeill, Bulmer Hobson and Padraic Pearse) to put forward a minimum social programme, to state political aims, or put aside their prejudice against trade unionists, there lay a sheer lack of courage and integrity. On Wednesday,

19 January 1916, he wrote an editorial for the *Workers' Republic*, stating that he and his colleagues had created a movement that was willing to 'do more for Ireland than any other trade movement in the world has attempted to do for its national government'. Had it not been 'attacked and betrayed by many of our fervent advanced patriots; had they not been so anxious to destroy us, so willing to applaud even the British Government when it attacked us', this trade movement would now have the power to resist 'every offensive move of the enemy against the champions of Irish freedom'. It 'could at a word have created all the conditions necessary to the striking of a successful blow whenever the military arm of Ireland wished to move'.

Entitled 'What is Our Programme?', this editorial summarized Connolly's position on social progress and the philosophy of revolt. He claimed that anyone who insisted at this time that his first allegiance was to his country, and not to any leader or executive committee was being promptly stigmatized as a disturber, a factionalist, a wrecker. Reminding his readers that ever since 1896 he had held to the dictum that 'our ends should be secured "peacefully if possible, forcibly if necessary",' he asked, 'what is then our programme?'

In times of peace it

was to gather into Irish hands in Irish trade unions the control of all the forces of production and distribution in Ireland ... In times of peace we should work along the lines of peace to strengthen the nation, and we believe that whatever strengthens and elevates the working class strengthens the nation. But we also believe that in times of war we should act as in war ...

While the war lasts and Ireland is still a subject nation we shall continue to urge her to fight for her freedom. We shall continue, in season and out of season, to teach that 'the far-flung battle line' of England is weakest at the points nearest its heart; that Ireland is in that position of tactical advantage ... that the time for Ireland's battle is NOW, the place for Ireland's battle is HERE ...

In commenting on Easter 1916, Lenin agreed. 'A rebellion in Ireland has a hundred times more political significance than a blow of equal weight would have in Asia and Africa.'

When this editorial appeared in the *Workers' Republic* of Saturday, 22 January, it was out of date, overtaken by events. Connolly had been 'kidnapped' by the patriots he had condemned.

XXII

1916

THE REVIVAL of the Irish Republican Brotherhood dates from 1907, when Tom Clarke returned from the United States and began recruiting into it a number of young men who were active in organizations sponsoring Gaelic culture and in Sinn Fein. Clarke was fifty-seven, ran a cigar store and looked the part of a Dublin tobacconist. But underneath his mild exterior there was an acute intelligence. He did well in selecting as junior leaders such men as: Padraic Pearse, thirty-six, a schoolmaster, playwright and poet; Eamonn Ceannt, thirty-four, who worked in the city treasurer's office and whose marriage ceremony had been conducted entirely in the Irish tongue; Sean MacDermott (Sean Mac Diarmada), thirty-one, former bartender, tireless organizer, and a great charmer despite the fact that polio incurred five years earlier had left him with a limp; Thomas MacDonagh, thirty-seven, the poet, assistant professor of literature at National College, Dublin, married, father of two children; and Joseph Mary Plunkett, twenty-eight, poet, editor, critic, bearer of a name that has mattered in Irish history for six hundred years. Always frail, Plunkett underwent throat surgery only three weeks before the rising. A few hours before his execution he was married in a midnight ceremony to the sister of Mrs Thomas MacDonagh.

The formation of the Irish Volunteers was the I.R.B.'s first achievement. When the war broke out they assessed their position and decided to throw out the Redmondite representatives in the governing body of the Irish Volunteers, and eventually stage an insurrection while England was in difficulty. They would take the second move only if the British passed and enforced a law to conscript Irishmen into the British Army or if a German landing in force took place.

For many months the relations between Connolly and the Irish

Republican Brotherhood were, in the words of Pearse, in a state of 'armed neutrality'. As late as December 1915, Pearse told a friend that Connolly was two-faced in saying publicly that the world war was forced on Germany, while privately saying that the Germans were just as bad as the British. 'As for his writing in his paper, if he wanted to wreck the whole business, he couldn't go a better way about it. He will never be satisfied until he goads us into action, and then he will think most of us are too moderate, and want to guillotine half of us. I can see him setting up a guillotine, can't you? For Hobson and MacNeill in particular. They are poles apart. What can he do anyway just now? Riot for a few days.'

This attitude dissolved as the conspirators became convinced that Connolly would not wait much longer; that he actually intended to throw the Citizen Army into a precipitate and unilateral revolt. Such an action would force the Irish Volunteers either to join the fray or be forever condemned as cowardly ranters. It was under these circumstances that the so-called 'kidnapping' took place. The story, as developed fifteen years after the event, was full of drama and authentic-sounding detail. It told how Connolly, on the afternoon of 19 January 1916, was waylaid by Padraic Pearse, Joseph Plunkett and Sean MacDermott, and forced at the point of a gun into a taxi. How Connolly was driven to a private home near Chapelizod and detained there for three days until he consented to co-operate with the Military Council of the Irish Republican Brotherhood. How he was returned to Surrey House late Saturday evening, 22 January, but would reveal to his followers, who had been greatly alarmed by his mysterious long absence, no information about where he had been. To one, he said only that he had been 'through hell'; to another that he had walked forty miles during his absence; to a third, playfully, 'That would be telling you.'

Recent disclosures have removed much of the romance. They have eliminated the element of force, altered dates, and added details, but have not negated the fact of the meeting or its importance. It was not a kidnapping at all; it was a secret meeting attended by Connolly and the IRB conspirators to iron out their differences about the insurrection that each was planning. The meeting did take place in January, but a week or more before 19–22 January. Though it did not last three days, it extended long enough to disturb his followers, particularly Constance Markievicz. She was sure that Connolly had been abducted or killed and wanted to retaliate by ordering the Citizen Army to attack Dublin Castle.

By design or otherwise, Connolly was met at Beresford Place by Ned Daly, Frank Daly and Eamon T. Dore, acting as messengers for the IRB Military Council. They informed Connolly that Padraic Pearse wished to have a meeting with him. Connolly retorted, 'There's no man in Ireland I'd rather meet. When can I see him?' 'Now,' they replied, and drove him off in a rented car to a private house on Crumlin Road, owned by the head of the Crumlin brickworks.

Here a lengthy dialogue took place. Pearse told Connolly that a rebellion would definitely take place on the evening of Easter Sunday; that Sir Roger Casement was in Germany recruiting a brigade composed of Irish prisoners of war; that the US headquarters of the Irish Republican Brotherhood were acting as intermediary with the German Government and supplying money for the rising; that Germany had consented to send arms and ammunition to support it. According to detailed plans drafted by Joseph Plunkett, five thousand men were expected to rise in Dublin, and another five thousand in the provinces. The conspirators did not, however, anticipate an overwhelming success. Their hope was that, by proclaiming the existence of an Irish Republic and by presenting it as a nation in being for a certain period, Ireland would be assured of a place at the peace conference along with other small nations for whose right to independence the world war was ostensibly being fought.

Connolly was astonished and delighted by these revelations. They showed that the Irish Volunteers—or at least the conspiratorial band at its head—meant business; that they had scrapped their preconditions for revolution (a German landing or conscription); and that they were willing to associate with trade-union extremists for the common cause. But it still took a 'terrible mental struggle' (Connolly's own words) before he could agree to associate himself with the IRB conspirators. The barriers were both major and minor. He had no taste for secret societies (as he once wrote to J. Carstairs Matheson, he always preferred the direct and open approach). He could not be sure that the majority of Volunteers would follow the conspirators' orders when the time came. He feared that Easter Sunday was too far away; Germany might collapse before that date, or the British might swoop down upon the leadership, turning plans into waste paper. And there was always the ultimate question: would the trade unionists be spilling their blood for a middle-class, white-collar revolution that would end by giving them no better life than they now had?

These were difficult decisions that Connolly had to make. Presumably, it was while pondering them that he walked his forty miles—either indoors, pacing through the rooms of the house, or outside, walking alone on country roads. Eventually he became aflame with enthusiasm, sending a message to his wife, 'I have been beaten on my own ground.' Ultimately, he could hardly be persuaded to leave. Plunkett said later that he had never talked so much, never been so tired in his life, and never enjoyed anything so much as his long duel of words with Connolly.

Proof (to insiders) that an agreement was reached is contained in an editorial in the *Workers' Republic* for 29 January. It ran as follows:

The issue is clear, and we have done our part to clear it. Nothing we can say now can add point to the argument we have put before our readers in the past few months; nor shall we continue to labour the point.

In solemn acceptance of our duty and the great responsibilities attached thereto, we have planted the seed in the hope that ere many of us are much older, it will ripen into action. For the moment and hour of that ripening, that fruitful blessed day of days, we are ready. Will it find you ready too?

Another proof is the fact that Piaras Beaslai was dispatched on 23 January to Liverpool where he met with a steward on a trans-atlantic liner. From the steward the Clan na Gael in New York learned on 5 February that on Easter Sunday, 28 April, a rising of the Irish people would take place.

Connolly did not become a member of the Irish Republican Brother-hood, but, formally or informally, did become a member of its Military Council. During the first week of February 1916 this group met at Eamonn Ceannt's home on Herberton Road. Others present were Pearse, Clarke, Plunkett and MacDermott. Connolly was in high spirits and on excellent terms with all those present. He had completely forgotten what he had once told his son Roderic: the Irish Volunteers would fight only if they were given steam-heated trenches.

It cannot be stressed too strongly that this agreement was not between minorities but between fractions of minorities. It was between Connolly (and his military clique in the Transport Union) and the IRB conspirators within the Irish Volunteers. The rank and file of the trade union and practically all the Irish Volunteers might have been equally shocked at the thought of armed uprising. As for the great masses of the Irish—those without trade-union ties, clerks, the middle class in general—there is no question that they supported the British Empire and the war.

Connolly, with great bitterness, admitted as much in an editorial published in the 6 February 1916 issue of the *Workers' Republic*. He recalled that he had previously said that the working class was the only one for whom the term British Empire and all its symbols held no appeal. Now it was becoming impossible to name a single class or section of the population not affected by the bonds of avarice that had previously bound only the capitalist and landlord classes to the Empire.

The only section that had not furnished 'even one apostate to the cause it had worked for in times of peace' was the one consisting of 'militant Labour leaders'. Despite this, and granting all possible excuses, the facts were 'horrible and shameful to the last degree'.

Speaking from faith rather than knowledge, Connolly insisted, nevertheless, that the 'great heart of the nation remains true. Some day most of these deluded and misled brothers and sisters of ours will learn the truth, some day we will welcome them back to our arms purified and repentant of their errors.' In a passage reminiscent of some words of Padraic Pearse, Connolly called the degradation wrought upon the Irish people 'so deep and humiliating' that only a

red tide of war on Irish soil will ever be able to enable the Irish race to recover its self-respect, or establish its national dignity in the face of a world horrified and scandalised by what must seem to them our national apostasy.

Without the slightest trace of irreverence but in all due humility and awe, we recognise that of us, as of mankind before Calvary, it may truly be said 'without the shedding of Blood there is no Redemption'.

But Connolly was still far from becoming a mystic. The old practical socialist, the man who, within the limitations of strongly felt principles, constantly tried to build bridges between disparate groups, was still in evidence. In the *Workers' Republic* of 29 January 1916, he described a talk given by Father Lawrence to the Dublin Trades Council:

Here we had a great meeting of working men and women, overwhelmingly Catholic in their religious faith, gathering together to discuss problems of social life and national aspirations with a priest whom they held in affectionate esteem, but insisting upon discussing these problems in the spirit of comradeship and equality ... the lesson of France has not been lost ... The Church recognises that if she does not move with the people, the people will move without her.

It is generally recognised in Dublin that the editor of this paper represents the most militant, and what is called the most extreme, type of the labour movement. We are glad therefore to be able to say in all sincerity that we could see no fundamental difference between the views expressed by Fr. Lawrence and those views which we ourselves never hesitate to express ... We accept the family as the true type of human society ... Every man, woman and child of the nation must be considered as an heir to all the property of the nation ... We hold that the sympathetic strike is the affirmation of the Christian principle that we are all members one of another.

He concluded with a statement that shows how far he had drifted from the syndicalist abhorrence of politics: 'Recognising that the proper utilisation of the national resources requires control of political power, we propose to conquer that political power through a working-class political party ...'

During these days, Liberty Hall was the bustling centre of two separate enterprises. Connolly headed each one. On the ground floor, the normal trade-union business of the Irish Transport Union was conducted. Dues were collected, strike benefits were paid (there was at least one union somewhere on strike), committees met, local politics were discussed. The so-called national question—the matter of separating Ireland from the British Empire—was not even mentioned.

In the basement of Liberty Hall quite a different type of business was being conducted. Here great quantities of arms, ammunition and medical supplies were being stored. Metal tubes and gelignite were brought into an improvised bomb factory. Efforts were made to manufacture a kind of machine-gun. The military atmosphere was increased by the presence of Connolly's body-guard. His followers had insisted upon it, following the 'kidnapping'. They feared that he might be assassinated by the British authorities, or at least be seized and deported to England.

Ordinary members of the union were not encouraged to stray into the basement of Liberty Hall. Safety as well as security required such a policy. From time to time accidents occurred which could have ended in catastrophe. Once somebody lit a fire which might have ignited thousands of live cartridges hidden between the firebricks in the wall. At another time some gunshot went off which barely missed the gelignite stuffed in the pockets of a Citizen Army man. Two men were spattered with fine shrapnel when a faulty detonator exploded. Such incidents brought Connolly on the run from his office. Possibilities of danger were reduced when the business of making and testing bombs was transferred to Padraic Pearse's school, St Enda's.

The carnage on the European continent and the apparent desire of some Irish organizations to stage similar enterprises at home were both viewed with the utmost distress by Francis Sheehy-Skeffington, a devoted pacifist. At a meeting of the Irish Women's Franchise League, with Connolly in the chair, he urged the benefits of an early peace. Connolly did not dispute this stand; he simply expressed his admiration for Skeffington as a man who proved what he (Connolly) had always maintained—that it was possible to be an advocate of advanced social reform and at the same time to be intensely patriotic: 'It was those who had the strongest desire to secure social freedom who could best be trusted to fight for national freedom.' This sentence expressed in capsule form one of Connolly's deepest convictions.

The meeting ended by sending a message of approval to Henry Ford's Peace Crusade. Constance Markievicz dissented. She did not want to see the war ended until the British Empire was smashed and Ireland liberated. This led to a public debate between Sheehy-Skeffington and Constance, held on 15 February. To Miss Louie Bennett, the Countess showed no 'powers of debate. She reiterated the same few points in various wild, flowery phrases, and talked much of dying for Ireland.' After a warmly contested duel of words, just before the vote was taken, Connolly got up from the back of the room, and entered the fray. His strong speech for immediate action during England's difficulty swung sentiment around. After it was over, when Skeffington mildly reproved him for intervening, Connolly replied, 'I was afraid you might get the better of it, Skeffington. That would never do.'

The day set for the rising was now only two months away. As it approached, Connolly's words grew steadily bolder. At a meeting held 4 March to commemorate Robert Emmet, and another on 6 March to commemorate the Fenians, his theme was the same: all previous insurgents had waited too long. 'To us a glorious opportunity has come.'

St Patrick's Day was warm and bright. Some 1,600 Irish Volunteers—armed for the first time with bayonets on their rifles—lined up opposite the dignified bank building that had once housed Grattan's Parliament. The Irish Citizen Army of two hundred marched to Dundrum and Booterstown to drill. Connolly spoke to them as an Irish patriot: 'In this hour of travail, Ireland cannot afford to sacrifice any one of the things this world has accepted as peculiarly Irish.'

The British people were now bogged down in a bloody stalemate that resembled not at all the kind of war that had been anticipated. Their establishment could no longer accept these demonstrations and treasonable speeches. On 24 March the police visited various places to confiscate some seditious papers, particularly *The Gael*. One of them was the shop of the Workers Co-operative Society, located next door to Liberty Hall and connected to it by a door. Hastily summoned, Connolly went through the door and found policemen looking through the stacks of newspapers. Connolly demanded a search warrant (although none was necessary under wartime defence regulations), and when the police could not produce one, Connolly pulled out a revolver. 'Then drop those papers or I'll drop you,' he said. The police left, but it was obvious that they were going to return.

This readiness to use force was as much a recurrent part of Connolly's personality as his diligence in writing, his moods of despondency, his willingness to embark on bold and even reckless ventures in times of extremity, and his impatience with colleagues.

Connolly feared that when the police returned they would seize the press in Liberty Hall on which the *Workers' Republic* was printed, and possibly discover the store of arms in the basement. His only recourse, he thought, was to summon the Citizen Army. He returned to his office and told his daughter Nora (in Dublin on a visit from Belfast) and Constance Markievicz (alerted by seeing the police raid the office of the *Gaelic Press*), 'It looks as if we are in for it and as if they are going to force our hands.' He sat down and began to sign 250 orders mobilizing each worker while Nora and Constance filled in the names. Bearing these orders Citizen Army men on duty at Liberty Hall promptly set out at high speed to the railway yards, docks, barges, workshops and other places where Transport Union men toiled.

When the police returned, somewhat greater in number, Connolly again demanded a warrant. Observing some Citizen Army men now lounging about, Connolly still holding his automatic, and Madame toying with a large Mauser pistol, the police again withdrew. During their absence, Madame and the girls in the store looked for the new issue of *The Gael* which had set off the commotion and found that none had been received as yet.

The next contingent of police to arrive was headed by Inspector Brannon, who produced a warrant empowering the police and military to enter the shops of news dealers and seize copies of the offending newspapers. Connolly then allowed the police to search the shop, but warned them against entering the side door to Liberty Hall. The Inspector declared that he would never dream of doing such a thing. The search consisted of examining the newspapers on the counter, after which the police left.

While Connolly and the Countess were congratulating each other, the results of the mobilization summons became apparent. From all over Dublin, within an hour, 150 workers poured into the building. The *Workers' Republic* of 1 April reported with glee the shock received by 'staid middle-class men in the streets, aristocratic old ladies out shopping, well-fed Government officials returning from lunch' as they 'beheld the spectacle of working men with grimy faces and dirty working clothes rushing excitedly through the streets with rifle in hand and bandolier across shoulders, on the way to Liberty Hall'.

Stimulated by the confrontation, Connolly addressed the men and declared that henceforth Liberty Hall must be under armed guard day and night. He moved a bed into his office, and slept on the premises each night. Some other Citizen Army men started living there as well. Madame took to dropping in almost every afternoon with a bag of biscuits for their tea. She remarked one day that her bank account was in arrears and 'if this bally revolution doesn't take place soon I don't know how I'm going to live'.

But rebellious fervour did not sweep away Connolly's practicality. He learned that, though the police had dismantled the machinery on which *The Gael* had been printed, they had overlooked some frames of type. On the afternoon of the Friday following the raid, he sent some Citizen Army men to the office of the *Gaelic Press* with a hand cart. They were dressed in working clothes but carried small arms. Though police were on guard, they did not interfere when the men loaded the frames on the cart and took them back to Liberty Hall. Connolly had always bragged about his ability to maintain a printing establishment on the most meagre of funds. He was proving his point.

From his service in the British Army, Connolly had learned the value of parades, bands, ceremonies, pageantry, songs, flags, costumes. After he became chief of the Transport Union, a concert or play was given almost every Sunday evening in Liberty Hall. Weekdays were filled with recitations and mass singing. The emphasis now was on rebel songs, not the music hall songs of the Larkin period. One Citizen Army man recalled later: 'Connolly was a singing man. The Citizen Army didn't have many guns but they had lots of songs.' The favourite numbers on route marches were 'O'Donnell Abu', 'Step Together', and 'Wrap the Green Flag Around Me'.

At Liberty Hall the attraction on 26 March, and again on Palm Sunday, 16 April, was a drama written by James Connolly and presented by the union's dramatic group. The three-act play, called *Under Which Flag*, dealt with the dilemma in Fenian days of a young man who had to choose between joining the British Army or the Irish Republican Brotherhood. He chose to join the Brotherhood and Connolly made amply clear the wisdom of his choice. In the United States Connolly wrote another play called *The Agitator's Wife*. If nothing else, these plays testify to Connolly's diligence, his willingness to use all forms of literature to convey his message, and his love for the drama. Connolly is said to have had a passion for Shakespeare but never once had the money to see a Shakespearean play performed.

The leading role in both performances of *Under Which Flag* was played by Sean Connolly, who died on the night of Easter Monday, one of the first casualties of the rising.

The conversion of Liberty Hall into a military base, the stress on the words and deeds of Wolfe Tone, Fintan Lalor and John Mitchel, the presence of men in uniform at trade-union meetings, the songs, all these increased the perturbation of those trade unionists who saw in such incitements to rebellion a diversion from the true business of the Transport Union, namely, obtaining higher wages and better working conditions. Their feelings came to a head when the 8 April issue of the *Workers' Republic* announced that on Palm Sunday, 16 April, the 'Green Flag of Ireland', the very symbol of defiant Ireland, would be hoisted over Liberty Hall.

On 12 April the executive committee of the Dublin branch (No. 1), which also acted as the standing committee of the national union, voted seven to five to hold another meeting the following day to 'consider Connolly's action'. Connolly was not a member of this body. Thomas Foran persuaded them to talk first with their general secretary.

Accordingly, on Thursday, 13 April, Connolly met with the dissenters and discussed the matter. Only by threatening to sever his connection with the union did he win the committee's assent to the raising of the flag. In addition, he was compelled to promise that the Citizen Army would shortly leave Liberty Hall and 'probably never return'. Since the rising was only ten days off, he could easily make that promise.

The clash is significant as evidence of a basic ideological divergence. Had the rising been postponed longer or never occurred, it is conceivable that Connolly might well have ended in the same position as Larkin eventually found himself—outside the union he had helped to found, put there by persons more interested in obtaining economic gains for their members, and in achieving efficiency and stability for the union, than in creating a revolution.

The clash is equally significant as indicating a continuance of Connolly's personality pattern. Because he would not bend, ideologically or personally, to woo his colleagues, he had been forced out of Ireland in 1903; now he was being forced out of the Transport Union for the same reasons. An incident that occurred about this time sheds additional light on Connolly's personality. Mrs Sheehy-Skeffington happened to meet Connolly on the street and he indicated to her in veiled terms that a rising was imminent. While they talked, it crossed her mind that she was speaking to a man who might soon be losing his life. As a free-thinker who had thought herself out of Roman Catholicism and still retained a speculative turn of mind, she found herself saying to Connolly:

'Tell me, Jim, have you ever any hope of anything on the other side?'

He replied, 'The British Labour Party? Oh, no, they won't lift a finger to help us.'

Mrs Sheehy-Skeffington laughed, and explained what she had meant. At this he threw back his head and roared, 'Oh, no. I'm afraid I haven't time to be thinking about all that kind of thing just now.' This anecdote was contained in a letter written to me by the late Senator Owen Sheehy-Skeffington.

The authorities were becoming more vigilant. Liam Mellows, who had been delegated to lead the rising in the western part of the country, was suddenly arrested and deported to England. Connolly was consulted by Sean MacDermott on how to obtain his return. It was decided that Herbert Mellows, Liam's brother, should go to Belfast, there pick up Nora Connolly, and both would go by a circuitous route to Staffordshire where Liam was staying. Herbert would remain there posing as his brother while Liam, disguised as a priest, returned to Ireland. The substitution was successfully made and by 15 April Liam was hiding in Dublin, at St Enda's.

Palm Sunday, 16 April 1916

The ceremonies held on Palm Sunday to accompany the first raising of the Green Flag of Ireland over Liberty Hall were impressive. The Citizen Army drew up in formation in front of the hall. Positions within it were occupied by the Women's Section, the boy-scout group under Captain Walter Carpenter, and the Fintan Lalor Pipers' Band. A colour guard of sixteen uniformed men accompanied young red-haired Molly Reilly as she carried the flag to a pile of drums in the centre of the square. After inspecting the troops, Commandant Connolly, in uniform for the first time, took up his position in front of the drums with Vice-Commandant Mallin on his left, and Lieutenant Constance Markievicz (in her green uniform but feminine black hat with feathers) on his right. After the bugles, drums, pipes and salutes, the young colour-bearer, radiant with excitement, mounted an inside stairway to the roof of the building, and 'with a quick graceful movement of her hand unloosed the lanyard and the flag fluttered out'.

The *Workers' Republic* reported that 'as the sacred emblem of Ireland's unconquered soul fluttered to the breeze, the bugles pealed their defiant salute, strong men wept for joy, and women fainted with emotion'. The flag was composed of a golden harp (without a crown) on a field of green. It was not the new tricolor because this might have betrayed the compact Connolly had made with the Irish Republican Brotherhood. Neither was it the starry plough flag which had first appeared at a Citizen Army parade held two years earlier.

After the ceremony, Connolly gave a talk on street fighting. Some Irish Volunteer officers were in the group listening. But his remarks to the Citizen Army alone that evening were much more significant. He said that there would definitely be a rising, and that the odds would be a thousand to one against them. 'If we win, we'll be great heroes; but if we lose we'll be the greatest scoundrels the country ever produced.' He then enjoined his listeners: 'In the event of victory, hold on to your rifles, as those with whom we are fighting may stop before our goal is reached. We are out for economic as well as political liberty.' These words alone, delivered only a week before the rising, should end all charges that Connolly betrayed international socialism by taking up the fight for Irish national freedom. He then gave anyone who wished to withdraw the opportunity to do so, without recrimination. No one did.

During the week, the same internal dissension, individual errors, excessive secrecy, sloppy communications and sheer bad luck that had brought previous Irish rebellions to disaster ended any hope of success for this one. Indeed, they almost kept it from starting entirely. The only difference from previous rebellions was that this time there was no informer in the ranks.

The train of misadventures began when John Devoy, chief Irish conspirator in the US wired Berlin that the *Aud*, the German ship bringing arms to Ireland, should delay its arrival at Tralee from 20 April to Easter Sunday, 23 April. Since the ship had no wireless, it could not be notified of the change in plans. When no one met it on the twentieth, it sailed away and soon, under the threat of seizure by the British, was blown up by its own crew.

On Thursday, 20 April, two Irish Volunteer officers overheard a conversation that indicated that the manœuvres were going to be more than routine. They communicated their suspicions to Professor MacNeill, and the three went to St Enda's school where Pearse confessed the truth.

On Good Friday the submarine bearing Sir Roger Casement, Captain Robert Monteith of the Irish Volunteers, and 'Daniel Bailey', the pseudonym of one of the few prisoners from Germany who had joined Casement's Irish Brigade, reached the Kerry coast and discharged its passengers. Monteith, seeking help, announced their arrival to an Irish Volunteer named Mullins. Happening by chance to meet a Transport Union official named W. P. Partridge, Mullins was persuaded to convey his information to James Connolly in Liberty Hall. At a conference held that evening in the union headquarters, Pearse and Connolly conferred about the significance of Casement's arrival and arrest, and about the absence of the arms ship.

On Saturday MacNeill learned that the *Aud* was actually lost, decided that it was not too late to cancel the manœuvres, and issued an order rescinding all activities scheduled for the following day, Easter Sunday. By midnight The O'Rahilly and others were busy delivering this order to Irish Volunteer detachments in all parts of the country. Travelling by bicycle, MacNeill himself brought the notice to the Sunday *Independent*.

But in Liberty Hall that Saturday evening there was no discussion, no dissension, no talk of cancelling troop movements. Instead there was much bustling and preparation, with William O'Brien, Winifred Carney (Connolly's devoted secretary), and Constance Markievicz busy writing out mobilization orders and officers' commissions. A friend of Madame's was visiting her and concluded that the drama group was getting ready to produce a play. 'Rehearsing, I suppose,' she said to Madame. Constance replied in the affirmative. 'Is it for children?' inquired the visitor. 'No,' said Madame, in one of her rare bursts of humour, 'it's for grown-ups.'

The mobilization orders called for the Citizen Army to report to Liberty Hall at 3.30 Sunday afternoon with full equipment.

Easter Sunday, 23 April 1916

Easter Sunday in Dublin was bright and sunny, beginning a week of excellent weather. But those who had hoped for a rebellion to start that day were disappointed by reading on the front page of the Sunday newspapers such headlines as 'No Parades. Irish Volunteer Marches Ca..celled. A Sudden Order.' If they had connected this story with other items on the front page, they would have been even more dejected: 'Arms Seized. Collapsible Boat on Kerry Coast. Man of Unknown Nationality Found.' And 'Three Drowned. Tragic Motoring Affair in Kerry. A Wrong Turning.'

During the morning the IRB Military Council—Sean MacDermott, Tom Clarke, Pearse, Connolly—sat at a table in Connolly's bedroom (and office) and examined the chaos around them. Tom Clarke was for carrying out the original plan—revolution that night—relying on the Irish Volunteers to respond spontaneously. The others were more cautious, fearing that the combination of disasters—the sinking of the *Aud*, Casement's arrest, MacNeill's countermanding order—had made the rising impossible.

Certainly there was no longer any hope of real success. The questions were: if they took up arms, how bloody would the British suppression be? If the rising was ordered, would it not be so puny as to end in comic disaster, like so many previous Irish rebellions? If the rising were cancelled, would it not end for another century all hopes of a rising and stamp the present generation as cowards and idiots?

By 1 p.m. the decision was made. The rising would be held, despite all obstacles. But there was one major change in the plans. It would not be held that evening but at noon the following day.

Connolly's mood is indicated by a few remarks he made during the morning's discussion. 'If we don't fight now, all that we have to hope and pray for is that an earthquake will come and swallow Ireland up.' When someone mentioned the responsibility of letting people go to their death when there was so little chance of victory, Connolly said, 'There is only one sort of responsibility I am afraid of and that is preventing the men and women of Ireland fighting and dying for Ireland if they are so minded.'

There were, to be sure, some elements of good sense in the decision. A British swoop on the organization and its leadership might be more dangerous than all the risks of a hurried, partial rising. The public notice that the manœuvres were cancelled might lead the British to believe that the danger was over; it might cause them to relax their vigilance or delay their responses. Connolly thought, mistakenly, that capitalist armies would not destroy their own buildings, and hence the rising could be maintained long enough to prove that an Irish Republic existed and should have a seat at the peace table ending World War I. There was always the possibility of a popular, patriotic response extending further than might rationally be expected. Finally, Fintan Lalor, in words which Connolly well knew, had said: 'Somewhere and somehow and by someone, a beginning must be made, and the first act of armed resistance is always premature, imprudent, and foolish.'

Since the Citizen Army had been mobilized for Sunday, it seemed advisable to stage a drill of some kind to give the illusion that all was normal. Hence the men were marched, with Connolly and Mallin at the head, on a circular route to City Hall, Dublin Castle and the Four Courts. Constance Markievicz was particularly resplendent, in her 'dark-green woollen blouse with brass buttons, dark-green tweed knee-breeches, black stockings and huge heavy boots. Around her waist was a cartridge belt; from it on one side hung an automatic pistol, from the other a convertible Mauser rifle; a bandolier and haversack crossed on her shoulders.'

Back at Liberty Hall Connolly made a speech reiterating some old themes—the Citizen Army would stand in arms until the claim of the Irish Republic was heard at any future peace negotiations—but the real work was going on in the basement. On the same rickety press that produced the union weekly, three members of the Dublin Typographical Provident Society were printing copies of a document proclaiming the birth of an Irish Republic. A Citizen Army guard under William Partridge stood by. Thomas MacDonagh asked, 'Are the men sworn in?' 'They don't need to be,' Connolly answered. Owing to the shortage of 24-point type, the proclamation had to be printed in two operations, and even then type from another fount had to be used. .

MacDonagh went off to alert the Dublin brigade of the Irish Volunteers to the new time of the rising. Some Volunteers looked at him as if he were mad. Others had already tossed their rifles aside and burned their uniforms. Still others laughed, and continued their plans to spend the day at the races. Some 700 Irish Volunteers (of a possible 10,000 in the country, half of them in Dublin) accepted the message. So did all of the Citizen Army—some 120 men—who could be reached.

With this force, said the proclamation, Ireland 'strikes in full confidence of victory'.

XXIII

THE RISING lasted from Monday noon to Saturday noon. The weather was singularly good during most of this period, though some rain fell on Tuesday. Monday was especially pleasant, with the sky a brilliant blue. There was a feeling of holiday in Dublin, with most people looking forward to lavish meals after the Lenten fasts, a visit to the horse races, or family gatherings.

At Liberty Hall the mood was different. Military bustle filled the air as the 'Irish Republican Army' assembled for its first operation. There was a sense of purpose in the air but it was not founded on great hopes of victory. It was probably with a sense of hoping against hope that Connolly, while walking down the steps of the building, remarked to William O'Brien, 'We are going out to be slaughtered.'

'Is there no chance of success?' O'Brien asked.

'None whatever,' Connolly responded, cheerily. His happiness was genuine. He had long since finished with argument about when, why, where and with what chance of success. The important thing was to act. Any rising was better than none.

At 11.35 a.m., the first contingent of rebels left to occupy the Harcourt Street railway station. Next to leave was a contingent of sixteen men led by Sean Connolly, fresh from his successful appearance as the hero of *Under Which Flag*. The aim of this contingent was to seal up Dublin Castle by seizing the City Hall, the guard room in the upper part of the castle yard, the *Evening Mail* office, and other buildings facing the castle gates. The guard room was successfully seized. The entire castle could have been taken just as easily, since it was as unprotected as Pearl Harbor in 1941. Unfortunately, no one could have guessed that it lay so open.

The next contingent was much larger. Led by Michael Mallin and 'Con' Markievicz, it numbered over a hundred men and fourteen women, most of them members of the Citizen Army. Their task was to occupy St Stephen's Green. The first step consisted of digging trenches in the lovely Victorian park.

The final group to leave Liberty Hall was evenly divided between Irish Volunteers and soldiers of the Citizen Army. James Connolly, in his dark-green uniform with slouch hat, held the position of honour in the centre. He looked strong and confident, with his head and neck resting solidly 'on a broad sturdy trunk of a body, and all were carried forward on two short pillar-like legs, slightly bowed, causing him to waddle a little in his walk . . .' So wrote Sean O'Casey.

Joseph Mary Plunkett, with unsteady step, joined Connolly on one side. With his frail, emaciated body, pale face, sloping nose, and rimless glasses, he looked the very image of a garret scholar and poet. Then one saw the white bandage around his throat, protecting the wound from a recent glandular operation, the bangle on his arm, and the huge antique rings on his fingers, and concluded that he might also have aspirations to be the strategist of a Byronic guerilla war.

Padraic Pearse also was in uniform, wearing a long green coat, military boots and felt hat. As he strode to take his place on Connolly's other side, one of his four sisters ran up to him and grabbed his sleeve. 'Come home, Patrick, give up all this foolishness,' she pleaded. Pearse showed no emotion. Only a man with his monumental gravity could have ignored her as completely as he did. Connolly smoothed over the situation by calling his men to attention and quickly marching them off.

It was a raggle-taggle army. Some men wore full uniform, others part of a uniform, and many no uniform at all, only their working clothes with a yellow armlet on the left sleeve. All the men were dangerously and incredibly overloaded with an assortment of weapons and implements: shotguns and rifles, sledge hammers, picks, pikes, haversacks, ropes, shovels, crowbars, grenades and first-aid kits. Two trucks, a taxicab and a Ford passenger car brought up the rear. The vehicles were as burdened as the men, with rifles and pistols (Mausers, Schneiders, Lee Martins, Lee Enfields), shotguns, explosives and crude bombs fashioned from tin cans and lengths of pipe.

In the contingent were Tom Clarke, son of a career sergeant in the British Army, and an occupant of British jails for over fifteen years; and the polio-stricken Sean MacDermott. An unexpected feature of the parade was the presence in the Ford of its owner, Michael O'Rahilly. For the past half-dozen years he had insisted on being called The O'Rahilly, traditional name for the head of his clan; being a person of some substance, he was able to make the name stick. A genial, sandy-haired man with a handlebar moustache, he lived with his American wife and four sons in the fashionable suburb of Ballsbridge. Long an enthusiastic supporter of Sinn Fein and the revival of the Irish language, he was a founder of the Irish Volunteer organization and was now its Director of Arms.

During the past week he had helped to persuade Professor MacNeill that a rising Easter Sunday was premature, and that the countermand should be issued. He had spent the entire weekend travelling through Ireland to make sure that no Irish Volunteer took part in such a demonstration. Now, awakened Monday morning by the news that a rising was going to take place nonetheless, he had joined what he considered a hopeless, crack-brained enterprise. W. B. Yeats explained it all later: 'Because I helped to wind the clock/I come to hear it strike.'

The men marched over Lower Abbey Street and up O'Connell Street as far as the General Post Office, a low stone building built in the Greek classical style, with many columns. Its great size and dignity are difficult to see because the structure is so compressed between other buildings. Here Connolly ordered his men to halt, then barked, 'Left turn. The GPO—charge!' For a few seconds the men looked puzzled. Then a subordinate officer called out, 'Take the post office.'

Suddenly exultant, the amateur troops broke ranks and began a race for the doors of the Palladian structure. Several arrived at the door simultaneously, and hence entered with some difficulty. At Connolly's command to 'Smash the windows and barricade the doors', they broke the glass windows with their rifle butts, and brought in sandbags to festoon the window frames.

For the next few minutes Connolly went from post to post, exhorting the men to hasten their work and saying the British might attack at any time. Some of the younger rebels looked astonished; they had not anticipated that the project of freeing Ireland would start with moving furniture and carrying bags of sand. Meeting Pearse in his rounds, Connolly smiled reassuringly at him as if to say, well, we've lasted the first fifteen minutes. You see, it's not so bad after all.

After the bewildered clerks and customers had been evicted, Winifred Carney calmly seated herself at the main counter behind a huge typewriter and began typing instructions to the various snipers who had peeled off from the main contingent as it marched. Noticing little Sean T. O'Kelly standing idly behind her, Connolly sent him off to Liberty Hall to pick up some flags. They had been wrapped in brown paper but forgotten. 'Isn't it grand?' commented Connolly as he looked up at the flags flying in the breeze—one green with a gold harp in the centre and the words 'Irish Republic' (in Gaelic) emblazoned on it; the other consisting of a green stripe to represent the South, an orange stripe to represent Ulster, and a white stripe between them. This was the tricolour, inspired by Arthur Griffith, still the official emblem of the present Irish Republic.

Then Connolly hastened to stand beside Pearse and Tom Clarke on the portico of the post office while Pearse, pale and stony-faced, read to a puzzled, indifferent group of bystanders the document proclaiming the birth of the Irish Republic as a sovereign, independent state. Connolly's influence can be seen in its appeal for support from women as well as men, and in the following sentences:

We declare the right of the people of Ireland to the ownership of Ireland, and to the unfettered control of Irish destinies, to be sovereign and indefeasible . . .

The Irish Republic is entitled to, and hereby claims, the allegiance of every Irishman and Irishwoman. The Republic guarantees religious and civil liberty, equal rights and equal opportunities to all its citizens, and declares its resolve to pursue the happiness and prosperity of the whole nation and of all its parts, cherishing all the children of the nation equally, and oblivious of the differences carefully fostered by an alien government, which have divided a minority from the majority in the past.

The document says nothing about the need for overthrowing capitalism or for seizing the means of production from the ruling class. It does not even promise the ten-hour day, old-age pensions, or the end of child labour. The municipal socialism advocated by the Fabians was radical in comparison to these vague words about the 'ownership of Ireland'. This document gives colour to the argument that Connolly renounced socialism in favour of nationalism when he took up arms during Easter Week.

The proclamation was signed on behalf of the Provisional Government by Thomas J. Clarke, Sean MacDiarmada, P. H. Pearse, James Connolly, Thomas MacDonagh, Eamonn Ceannt, and Joseph Plunkett, all of whom were later executed. Disregarding the cool reception and perfunctory cheers, Connolly said to Pearse and Clarke, 'Thank God we have lived to see the day.'

The rising started with a smashing victory over the first attempt of the British to crush it. About one o'clock a company of Lancers galloped down the north end of O'Connell Street. They had been dispatched from Marlborough Barracks at the same time as troops were ordered from Portobello, Richmond and Royal Barracks to reinforce Dublin Castle. As the Lancers reached the Nelson Pillar, the insurgents fired, killing three of them and fatally wounding a fourth. The Lancers fled in disorder. With true Colonel Blimp thinking, they had believed that their spirited horses, handsome uniforms and glittering sabres would be enough to send the rebels scattering. One Irish Volunteer remarked with astonishment that if the British thought they could attack buildings with cavalry, there was still hope for Ireland.

Inside the post office all was bustle and activity as the broken windows were barricaded with boards, filing cabinets, anything at hand. Connolly kept up a continuous flow of messages to other insurrectionary centres: to Eamon de Valera, then a thirty-one-year-old mathematics teacher who had taken over Boland's mill, the Westland Row railway station, and other key points on the southern approaches to Dublin; to Thomas MacDonagh, who had occupied Jacob's biscuit factory; to Commandant Ceannt, who had taken over the South Dublin Union, a group of hospital and poorhouse buildings near one of the Liffey bridges and close to the Richmond Barracks; and to Edward Daly, who occupied a large area around the Four Courts, site of the legal institutions. As it turned out, it was at these places that the real fighting occurred. For the men in the post office it was a matter of constantly reinforcing the building, of building barricades on adjoining streets, and of tense waiting.

Nevertheless, Connolly seemed to draw new life from each moment. He ordered that a barricade be erected across Lower Abbey Street to help protect the post office from British troops who might come that way from the Amiens Street railway station.

He dispatched Sean T. O'Kelly on another errand—to put up copies of the proclamation around the city.

'Where do we get the paste?' O'Kelly asked.

'Go to hell and make it,' was Connolly's reply.

O'Kelly found in the basement of the building some buckets, brushes, ladders, handcarts and a sack of flour with which to make paste. Thus fortified, he proceeded to obey orders.

Connolly ordered a Volunteer to improvise a telephone line between the first floor and the roof of the post office building, so he would get an early warning when the British marched. At the same time he sent some commandeered vehicles to Liberty Hall with orders to evacuate all supplies and ammunitions stored there and transfer them to the post office. Since latecomers were arriving in some number, he was able to augment MacDonagh's force at Jacob's biscuit factory and the pocket garrison occupying Gilbey's distillery on Fairview Strand.

When things went wrong, he might wax sarcastic for a moment but showed no other signs of disappointment. When some men sent to reinforce the group holding City Hall returned with word that gunfire from the telephone exchange building had kept them from performing their mission, he was only temporarily shaken by this evidence that a major error had been made. No one had remembered to seize the telephone building; hence British communications with all military and civilian centres outside of Dublin were intact.

When an officer in charge of a position near the post office insisted on sending him a new dispatch every minute, he commented wryly, 'If that man were standing on his right foot, he would send me a dispatch to inform me that he planned shortly to put down his left foot.'

As commanding officer of all rebel troops in Dublin, Connolly concentrated on these military matters, ignoring such affairs as the stiffness between the Citizen Army proletarians and the Irish Volunteer white-collar workers; the embarrassment shown by Pearse and his co-conspirators when they met The O'Rahilly, one of the men they had deceived for so long; and the near-riot that took place at the side door of the post office when the women whose husbands were serving in the British forces failed to receive their weekly 'separation money'.

He also tried to ignore the looting that started up in the nearby stores—something none of the patriots had anticipated—but was forced to take action after a flow of golden oratory from Sean Mac-Dermott had failed to stop the looters from disgracing the fight for Ireland's freedom. He sent Sean O'Kelly, accompanied by a dozen men armed with rifles and police sticks, to drive them out of Clery's where the greatest of all imaginable sales was taking place—'everything free'. The insurgent squad roughly ejected everyone out of the store and moved on to the next shop, but when they looked back they found Clery's store again overrun. O'Kelly had never seen such industrious Irishmen in his life. He reported back to Connolly that the job couldn't be done even with two hundred men.

'Did you shoot anybody?' Connolly asked.

'Only over their heads.'

'That will do no good at all,' Connolly replied. 'Unless a few of them are shot, you'll never stop them. I'll have to send someone there to do the job right.' Having said that, he did nothing further. Somehow, this problem was one that all previous Marxist writers on insurrection had failed to recognize, much less solve.

A rumour reached Connolly that British troop trains were arriving at the Amiens Street railway station, quite some way east of the post office. Connolly remembered that, with Abbey Street barricaded, the British soldiers might reach the post office by way of North Earl Street. Following a consultation, Pearse selected an Irish Volunteer named Brennan Whitmore to head a group of ten Citizen Army soldiers to build a barricade there. Connolly reviewed the soldiers, who, in addition to their arms, were burdened with crowbars, hatchets, saws, hammers and whatever other tools they had been able to find, and told Whitmore, 'Take these men over to Tyler's boot shop and prepare to defend the place. But first I want you to build a strong barricade across Earl Street.' Looking hard at the motley crew, he added, 'You will defend the position to the last.'

The men left and completed their mission. The only problem that arose came from the greed of the onlookers. When material used in constructing the barricade was just lying around, it seemed to have no value, but as soon as it became part of the fortification, the looters promptly took it away. Brennan Whitmore was touched, however, by the eagerness of many onlookers to assist in building the barrier, and by the request of some to join the insurgents. He had to refuse because the orders were strict: only Irish Volunteers and Citizen Army soldiers were eligible.

As the day ended, Connolly was in an expansive mood, feeling that the rebellion had got off to a good start. The Irish Republic had been declared. Insurgents occupied so many key positions in many parts of Dublin that it could be said that they controlled the city. In many of these positions they were well entrenched. In their few encounters with British troops, they had come off victorious. A Citizen Army man came to Connolly with a report that made him smile. 'The Citizen Army has captured King George and Lord Kitchener'—he paused—'in the Henry Street waxworks museum.'

When the laughter died down, a Volunteer standing near asked, 'But, sir, what are our chances of winning?' Connolly replied quickly, 'Oh, they're beaten. I tell you we've beaten them.' Connolly had not changed his mind. He still believed the chances of success were nil, but, as commanding officer, he had the responsibility of keeping up the morale of his men.

Only one insurgent had been lost—Sean Connolly. He had been shot by a British sniper, and now his body lay lifeless on the roof of City Hall. There was a certain logic to his death, since Sean had been the first to kill. At noon he had shot down a policeman who tried to bar his way to City Hall. The same kind of tidy logic animated the amateur theatricals in which Sean loved to perform.

Tuesday, 25 April 1916

On the second day of the rising, Connolly got up at four in order to inspect the men at their posts and give them an encouraging word. Remembering that the rebels' only chance for success lay in risings flaring up in all parts of the country, he sent a man to Wexford in the south east to make sure the Irish Volunteers there knew about the Dublin fighting.

Dawn broke grey and sultry, with rain in prospect. Some Citizen Army men approached him and asked permission to leave the building because 'the holidays are over and we have to go back to our jobs'. It was something to make even Connolly's faith in the working-class waver. It may have reminded him of the conversation he had had several months before with Bulmer Hobson, the thoughtful and educated Quaker from Belfast. Connolly said, 'The Irish working class is a powder magazine. If you drop a match, it will go up.' Hobson had said in return, 'Since you must deal in metaphors, Connolly, I'll tell you what the working class is—it's a wet bog. You drop a match and it will land in a puddle.' Since that time Connolly himself had written that 'self-interest' was undermining proletarian fervour. But to go further in questioning his socialist faith would have meant denying the significance of his entire life.

At 8 a.m., Connolly again sent out a contingent of men to help the besieged garrison at City Hall. They were back in a half-hour, having encountered heavy British firepower at the Exchange Hotel on Parliament Street. Connolly, sensing the ring closing in on the post office, could not understand why the British were so slow to attack.

It made no difference. There was always work to be done. Anticipating a return of the looters, he sent a detail of men to roll some barbed wire across O'Connell Street at each end of the post office. He thought it would at least clear the looters from the area directly in front of the building, and prevent the parade of curious people. Next he sent men to bring to the GPO whatever guns and ammunition were stored in secret places throughout Dublin. Some women too were assigned to this task. They were members of the Cumann na mBan, the women's auxiliary force affiliated with the Irish Volunteers, who had felt it necessary to join Winifred Carney in the GPO.

Fearing that the post office could not withstand a siege, he had huge rolls of newsprint pushed across O'Connell Street from the *Irish Times* warehouse on Lower Abbey Street, and set up to protect corner windows and other vulnerable places. The sound of gunfire from the City Hall area was so frequent that he could not imagine that the British would wait much longer before attacking the post office. Then he left the building to inspect the Earl Street barricade. Shocked by its flimsy appearance, he asked Brennan Whitmore, 'What's the good of this thing? Schoolgirls could knock it over.'

Whitmore smiled. 'If you think so, try it,'

Connolly gave it a kick, then grabbed hold of a chair leg protruding from it, and yanked with all his strength. The barricade didn't budge.

'It's interlaced with wires.' Whitmore pointed out.

Connolly examined the barricade more closely, beamed approvingly, then pointed to the shoe shop on the opposite corner. 'Have you occupied that building?' he asked.

'I don't have enough men,' Whitmore responded.

Connolly could have answered that this was the general situation, but merely said, 'Good luck' and returned to the post office.

Inside, he stopped to dictate some orders to his secretary, Winifred Carney. One to the officer in charge of the Dublin Bread Company building went as follows:

The main purpose of your post is to protect our wireless station. Its secondary purpose is to observe Lower Abbey Street and Lower O'Connell Street. Commandeer in the D.B.C. whatever food and utensils you require. Make sure of a plentiful supply of water wherever your men are. Break all glass in the windows of the rooms occupied by you for fighting purposes. Establish a connection between your forces in the D.B.C. and in Reis' building. Be sure that the stairway leading immediately to your rooms is well barricaded.

Miss Carney was a woman with a sharp eye and tongue. Totally devoted to Connolly, she tended to compare the other rebel leaders unfavourably with him. She now told him, probably not for the first time, that she considered the appearance of Joseph Plunkett over-dramatic, a bangle on his wrist and large antique rings on his fingers. Nor did she think he was going to be able to handle his responsibilities, what with the bandage on his throat and his increasing weakness. Connolly disagreed, saying, 'Joseph Plunkett can do and wear what he pleases. And as for military science, he could teach us all a thing or two. He's a clear-headed man, and he's a man of his word.'

At noon hordes of people from the slums began to pour into O'Connell Street. In the shops food was no longer plentiful, and neither were goods, but there was plenty of liquor available and the mob took advantage of it.

Reports reaching the General Post Office were turning gloomy. The insurgents occupying St Stephen's Green had been driven out of the park by machine-gun fire from the Shelbourne Hotel. They were now occupying the Royal College of Surgeons on the west side of the green, but it was questionable whether they would operate effectively from this position. In any case, they were cut off from the post office—and so were the garrisons in the South Dublin Union and Jacob's biscuit factory—by the British seizure of Trinity College. The pressure on Boland's mill and the Four Courts was becoming heavy. The rebel leaders were becoming uneasily aware that the British strategy was first to eliminate the outposts and then to apply massive, irresistible force on the headquarters in the General Post Office.

The looters, out now in full force, had developed a sort of barter and sales system, selling watches for a shilling and shoes for a few pence a pair. Some were travelling in packs, swarming into a shop, then trailing out, one after the other, with their arms full. One Irish Volunteer, irked by the sight, sent a messenger to Connolly asking for permission to deal drastically with them. 'Leave them alone unless they attack you,' was Connolly's reply.

The early promise of rain was being fulfilled, but the looters disregarded it, having discovered some fireworks in Lawrence's large photograph and toy store on Upper O'Connell Street. They heaped sky rockets, Roman candles, and other devices in the middle of the street and gleefully watched them go off. The vandals topped this effort by setting off more fireworks in the store itself. Soon the whole building was ablaze. Efforts of the Irish Volunteers and firemen to extinguish the flames met with little success.

Connolly was told that the British had finally taken control of City Hall and the *Daily Mail* buildings, though they had lost twenty dead in the attempt. At 4 p.m., more bad news became apparent when the detachment in Westmoreland Street, just south of O'Connell Bridge, retreated into the post office.

An attempt was made to reopen a wireless school and use its equipment to establish communications with the outside world. Though the receiver battery was found dead beyond recharging, the transmitter was operative. At 5.30 p.m., over this transmitter went a message declaring that an Irish Republic had been founded, that a Provisional Government had been established in Dublin, and that the Republican Army was in possession of the city. The message was composed by James Connolly and delivered by Fergus O'Kelly. It was a 'first'.

As darkness fell, there was much wonderment as to whether the British would attack in the rain, but the question became academic when the storm ceased. Pearse now emerged from the post office building, walked with an escort to Nelson's Pillar and read in his slow, intense voice, a second proclamation from the Irish Republic. It stated that the republican forces were holding their lines, that Ireland's honour had already been redeemed. It urged citizens to help defeat the British by putting up barricades, and not to indulge in looting. Even before he had finished, some of the listening populace wandered off in search of new stores to rob.

On the evening of this second day, Francis Sheehy-Skeffington, who had been making vain efforts to stop the looting, was arrested and taken to Portobello Barracks. On the following morning he was shot by a firing squad acting under orders of a British captain mad with fear of German troops landing in force, with religious bigotry, with political rancour—or all three.

Wednesday, 26 April 1916

It was the third day of the rising. Soon after midnight, a group of sixty-six men, routed by the British from the suburb of Fairview, arrived at the post office for reassignment. Pearse told them that 'Dublin, by rising in arms, has redeemed the honour it had forfeited in 1803 when it refused to support the rebellion of Robert Emmet'. After getting some food, the men were divided by Connolly into three groups. One was dispatched to the Imperial Hotel directly across the street, the same hotel from which Jim Larkin had made his most memorable and shortest address; the second was sent to the Metropole

Hotel just across Prince's Street; the third remained in the post office.

The man whom Connolly designated to lead the Metropole detachment was reluctant to go, saying that he was not qualified for the job. Connolly stared at him fixedly, and said, 'Is it enough that I tell you you're qualified?' The man saluted and marched the group away.

There was little sleep that night. First came a rumour that the British were planning an airplane attack. Unlikely as the possibility seemed, Connolly and Tom Clarke decided to put more riflemen on the roof. Then came the report that the British were nearing Parnell Square, not far above the post office. Connolly called a full alert, and for hours the men waited, with rifles or grenades in hand. As dawn approached, two hundred exasperated, sleepless men were still watching from the GPO windows, waiting for the first sight of khaki.

At 7 a.m. Connolly ordered that the Plough and Stars flag be raised over the Imperial Hotel. It was the beginning of another fine, sunny day. At eight in the morning the rumbling sound of artillery reached the men in the post office. A British gunboat had come up the River Liffey as far as Butt Bridge and was lobbing shells into Liberty Hall. One Irish Volunteer turned to another and said, 'General Connolly told us that the British would never use artillery against us.' The second Volunteer answered, 'He did, did he? Wouldn't it be grand, now, if General Connolly was making the decisions for the British?'

Connolly went up on the roof to see what he could see. Connolly was as ready as the next man to discard a theory, reinterpret it, or devise a new one. 'Nothing to be frightened of,' he told the alarmed men. 'When the British government starts using artillery in the city of Dublin, it shows they must be in a hurry to finish the job. There are probably some forces coming up to help us.'

By the time he got downstairs he had convinced himself that the use of the big guns indicated that the British expected German intervention momentarily and were trying to quell the rebellion before the Germans arrived. This he told William 'Willie' Pearse, Padraic's younger brother. Willie was a tall, quiet man, a sculptor by profession. He taught modelling at St Enda's, and was also interested in the theatre. Though quite unpolitical, Willie had followed his older brother into the General Post Office without a murmur.

Other rumours multiplied. One of them stated that martial law had been declared in Dublin. An insurgent who was still indignant about the looting declared it was about time. 'We've had no law around here for the last two days.' During the morning, rifle and machine-gun volleys replaced the sporadic sniping of the previous days. The barrage of British fire from the Amiens Street area, from Parnell Square, and from the direction of Trinity College, south of the Liffey, intensified. The insurgent riflemen on the post office roof became much more careful in their movements, and even the looters were impressed. They retired to the side streets where there were still many shops that required their attention.

By this time Connolly knew that the garrison around Dublin Castle and City Hall had been eliminated; that the contingent in the Royal College of Surgeons had been neutralized; that Edward Daly's men at the Four Courts were pinned down; that the men at the Mendicity Institution were surrounded and under such heavy pressure that they could not hold out much longer. He had heard that British soldiers were arriving at Dun Laoghaire harbour and were marching along a route that would bring them face to face with De Valera's Mount Street and Northumberland Road outposts. Connolly thought that De Valera should be warned, but also knew that it was not likely that any of the men could get through. He sent instead two Cumann na mBan girls in civilian clothes, but knew very well that De Valera needed reinforcements, not messages. Ah well, he reflected, it would show that headquarters had not forgotten them.

Another conclusion he reached was that the British would soon shell the tower of the Dublin Bread Company on the other side of O'Connell Street. Fearing that the snipers in it would be torn to bits, Plunkett sent a message to Fergus O'Kelly, the man in charge, that the tower be evacuated immediately. The message as delivered called for the entire building, one of the cornerstones of the post-office defence, to be evacuated. The order was obeyed with great and under-standable reluctance, and the men began their slow and perilous trip to the post-office building.

When Connolly learned of this mischance of war, he erupted in fury. But by that time Plunkett had got the story from Fergus O'Kelly and sent the contingent to retrace its perilous journey.

The British, moving up carefully from Great Brunswick Street and College Street, placed a nine-pounder gun at the juncture of D'Olier and College Streets. At 2.30 p.m. it began lobbing artillery shells up D'Olier Street, across O'Connell Bridge, into the upper portion of Kelly's gun shop. The first explosion was so fierce that some men in the post office, two blocks away, thought that a bomb had gone off in the cellar. After an hour of shelling, the Kelly building was so battered that the men in it realized that their situation was untenable. So did Connolly, who ordered them to retreat to the Metropole Hotel.

During the day British shells began to zero in on the building of the Dublin Bread Company, the Imperial Hotel, and on the post office itself. Fires began to spread through the buildings on Lower Abbey Street and O'Connell Street. The decline in morale of the insurgents became obvious.

O'Rahilly found another cause for concern when he detected some shadowy figures moving on the rooftops of some buildings on Henry Street, west of the post office. When he aroused Connolly, who was having his first sleep in twenty-four hours, and said that the British were skulking on the rooftops, Connolly merely muttered, 'They are not,' and went back to sleep.

Soon after, a resident of the area, a boy too young to be a soldier, made a mockery of security precautions by slipping into the building and running over to Connolly to complain that the whole neighbourhood was out of food. 'The shops is empty, ye can see that. How can anybody eat if there's no food?' Connolly calmed the boy, told him to tell the people to keep their spirits up, and then tried to return to sleep but couldn't.

He got up finally from his cot and went around talking to the men. They were now becoming exhausted and frightened and could think only of the imminent assault against them. After looking into their unshaven faces, Connolly suddenly burst into the rousing strains of a favourite marching song, the song that would one day become the Irish national anthem. The men listened, dumbfounded at first, then slowly joined in until the building was filled with the strains of 'The Soldier's Song':

> Soldiers are we, whose lives are pledged to Ireland . . .
> 'Mid cannon's roar and rifle's peal
> We'll chant a soldier's song.

Michael Collins, who had proved himself one of the best fighters in the insurgent army, could no longer sleep against the roar of fifty voices. He murmured bitterly to Winifred Carney, 'If this is supposed to be a concert, maybe they'll want the piano in the back room.'

Thursday, 27 April 1916

During the early hours of the morning, there was a lull in the gunfire, but with the dawn machine guns opened up on the General Post Office with new fury. By mid-morning the din of gunfire was constant and ear-piercing. About ten o'clock a shell struck a building on Lower Abbey Street which housed the reserve print shop of the *Irish Times*. In a short time the building was shrouded in smoke.

Connolly now expected that the British infantry would move straight across O'Connell Bridge and up the broad thoroughfare to the post office. It would be a man-wasting frontal assault, in a British tradition that was not entirely obsolete. On the previous day wave after wave of British soldiers had been mowed down attempting to rush insurgent positions near the Mount Street Bridge. To prepare for the attack, Connolly gathered a detail of twenty men, marched them across the narrow, sheltered width of Prince's Street, and turned them over to Lieutenant Oscar Traynor in the Metropole Hotel, which protected the south side of the post office and also commanded Middle and Lower Abbey Streets.

Connolly then strode on to Middle Abbey Street, scornful of sniper bullets, assessed the prospects there, and ordered a barricade built in front of Eason's bookshop. The work was soon discontinued when an artillery shell opened a hole in the building a few feet away from Connolly, convincing him that it was too late to build a barricade there.

This was the day—the fourth day of the rising—when the fires took hold. The fire in the *Irish Times* print shop spread to all the stores on the block, ignited the frail barricade the insurgents had built Monday afternoon, and started licking the walls of Wynn's Hotel. Following a heavy artillery bombardment, the buildings that housed the Hopkins and Hopkins store and the Dublin Bread Company also started burning. The insurgents occupying them had no recourse but to huddle in the basement of one of the buildings, completely isolated from the post office by the roaring flames.

About noon a belated patriot reached the Prince's Street gate of the post office and pleaded for a chance to join the rebellion. Connolly, summoned for a decision, listened to the man's story, shook his head sadly and said that it would be foolish for anyone at such a late hour to join such a hopeless cause. 'No, you'd better go home. There's nothing you can do to help here.' It was a small but significant event. Connolly had conceded defeat.

At 3 p.m. the insurgents were lined up on the ground floor of the post office to listen to a new proclamation and to receive Pearse's assurance that, if they did not win this fight, they at least deserved to win it. 'But win it they will although they may win it in death.'

Always active, Connolly led some of the rebels to man sniping posts in the Prince's Street area as far west as Liffey Street. A few hours later he decided to strengthen the area by occupying the *Irish Independent* building. He called for thirty volunteers and led them out of the Prince's Street gate of the post office. They had not gone more than a few yards when Connolly stopped them short, and sent them back into the post office to find materials for building a barricade on Prince's Street.

Connolly hurried the men along in their work of piling machinery, barrels, stacks of paper and O'Rahilly's Ford on the street. He warned them to stay under cover, although he himself stomped back and forth in the open, acting like a man who could not wait to become a martyr to the Irish cause. In the midst of this activity, he stopped short, winced, then continued for a few more minutes with his flow of directions. Assuring the men he would be back directly, he went into the post office with his normal quick stride.

There he found Jim Ryan, a medical student who was in charge of the improvised hospital. 'Is there a private place where we can talk?' Connolly asked. Behind a green folding screen, he took off his coat and displayed a flesh wound on his arm. After Ryan had dressed his wound, Connolly prepared to leave but said first, 'Not a word about this to anyone. I don't want garbled reports floating around. I don't want people to think I've actually been hurt.'

Returning to the men in Prince's Street, he inspected their barricade, and then led them through an alley to Middle Abbey Street. He ordered twenty men to occupy the *Independent* offices and the other ten to occupy the Lucas lamp and bicycle shop directly opposite. As the men trotted down the pavement, close to the buildings for whatever protection they might offer, Connolly himself stood out in the open, encouraging them. Only when he was satisfied that they had reached their destinations did he start back towards the post office.

He had not gone more than a step or two when a bullet hit the pavement beside him, ricocheted, and shattered his left ankle. Connolly went down as if someone had knocked his legs out from under him. On his hands and one knee, he dragged himself out of the street and into the alley; then, despite the intense pain, inched his way to Prince's Street where he fell flat in the gutter, unable to move any further. One of the rebels saw him there, and, with others, carried him into the post office building. By the time he was lifted on to a hospital table, his pain was so severe that he was soaked with sweat.

After some fumbling by Jim Ryan and Dan McLoughlin, both medical students, a captured British Army doctor named George Mahoney took over the treatment. He extracted the bone fragments from Connolly's leg, ligatured the blood vessels and applied a splint with a foot piece attached. He also sent out a man to get hold of some morphine. All the man could find was some mixed with distilled water, but Mahoney was able to inject it and give Connolly some relief from his pain. Connolly told Mahoney, 'You know, you're the best thing we've captured this week.'

As news of Connolly's injury became known, morale in the post office visibly wilted. His way of making a simple request sound like a direct order had given them pride and strength. He had reprimanded them, scolded them, cheered them on when they showed proper courage, lifted their spirits by leading them in song. Now they felt exposed to the enemy. One young Volunteer went to Connolly's bedside and began to cry. Then he pulled himself together, realizing that if Connolly found him there blubbering, he would catch hell for it.

With Connolly disabled, command functions fell upon the tobacconist Tom Clarke, polio-crippled Sean MacDermott, and The O'Rahilly, who had opposed the rebellion in the first place. Pearse was temperamentally unsuited for command functions, and Plunkett was now so weak that he seldom arose from his cot.

That evening a warehouse containing oil and chemical supplies was hit by an incendiary bomb. Its flames ignited the Imperial Hotel, occupied by some eighty insurgents, many of them refugees from other positions. With Brennan Whitmore still in command, the insurgents left the hotel, some managing to get back to the post office, though not without casualties, others finding cover in a tenement building. The latter were discovered by some British soldiers early the next morning, and marched off to the Custom House.

Now it was the turn of the men in the post office to consider evacuation. The building would soon be aflame. The best suggestion offered was to burrow a tunnel under Henry Street. This hope faded when they became aware that the rebellion would be long over before they could dig their way through the thick subterranean walls. No decision was reached.

Connolly could take no part in these deliberations because he was suffering such intense pain from his shattered ankle. He was plied with successive injections of morphine, but, as each injection wore off, he would awaken from his fitful sleep and grip the sides of his bed in agony. On one of these occasions, Harry Walpole, a Citizen Army man who had been his orderly since the 'kidnapping', stepped closer to the bed, thinking Connolly might want something, but Connolly only shook his head and said, 'Oh, God, did ever a man suffer more for his country?'

Friday, 28 April 1916

It was the day before the end. After an agonizing night, Connolly was sufficiently himself again to demand that he be transferred to a bed with castors so that he could be moved from the hospital area and mingle with the men. Brushing aside objections from his 'medical staff', he was soon rolling past the rebels standing at their stations and exchanging cheering words with them. He ended up dictating to Winifred Carney an account of the progress of the rebellion. This done, he settled back against the pillows, and began a detective story offered by one of the rebels. When Harry Walpole arrived on the scene, Connolly looked up from his book and smiled. 'What do you think of this?' he said. 'A morning in bed, a good book to read, and an insurrection, all at the same time. It's revolution de luxe.'

When The O'Rahilly came downstairs to visit him, Connolly asked him to read his message. O'Rahilly gathered the men together in the main hall and in a loud, clear voice, read the document from the 'Commandant-General, Dublin Division'. It listed the areas controlled by Commandants Daly, MacDonagh, De Valera, and Kent (Ceannt), and declared in each case that they were holding their own. It added that Dundalk had sent two hundred men to march on Dublin, and that forces were rising in Galway, Wexford, Wicklow, Cork and Kerry. It ended:

Courage, boys, we are winning, and in the hour of our victory, let us not forget the splendid women who have everywhere stood by us and cheered us on. Never had a man or woman a grander cause; never was a cause more grandly served.

The facts were in error but no fault could be found with the sentiment.

With British fire bombs and artillery shells still failing to work any major damage on the stalwart post-office building, it became possible for Pearse to give the men, an hour later, another helping of the same sustenance. Pearse's new message admitted that headquarters was isolated, but asserted that they were 'determined to hold it while the buildings last'. He paid tribute to the gallantry of his soldiers who had 'during the past four days been writing with fire and steel the most glorious chapter in the later history of Ireland'. The only individual he named was Connolly who 'lies wounded but is still the guiding brain of our resistance'.

He was satisfied that, even if no more was accomplished, Ireland's honour had been saved. More could have been done had not the fatal countermanding order been issued, but of this 'I shall not speak further. Both Eoin MacNeill and we have acted in the best interests of Ireland.'

As the morning advanced, British gunfire intensified. Shortly before noon Pearse and Connolly decided it was time to evacuate some of the women. Some of those performing nursing duties were allowed to remain. Two others who were managing the kitchen refused to accept the order, and so did Winifred Carney, who looked at Connolly as if he were insane when he suggested she leave. After bitter protests, twenty girls finally walked out of the Henry Street door under the slim but adequate protection of a Red Cross flag, and were taken into custody by British soldiers before they had gone far.

During the afternoon the artillery bombardment increased, and incendiary bombs finally began to take effect on the building. Water hoses were ineffectual, and the upper two storeys were abandoned to the flames. At six o'clock, with beams crashing and burning fragments falling from the ceiling of the ground floor, Pearse, MacDermott, Clarke, Plunkett and O'Rahilly gathered around Connolly's bed and decided to work out an evacuation plan. Since the sewer proved to be impenetrable, the only recourse seemed to be to take over the large stone building that housed the Williams and Wood soap and sweet factory, and use it as a new base of operations. The building was on Parnell Street, quite a long way north, and would require an assault contingent to advance up Moore Street in the face of British guns to capture it. O'Rahilly quietly said that he would be willing to lead this party when the time came, and went back to fighting the fires. Despite O'Rahilly's initial conviction that the rising was a stroke of madness, four days in the company of Pearse, Connolly, MacDermott, Clarke and Plunkett had convinced him that this madness was inspired and would somehow lead to Irish independence.

The deliberations were constantly interrupted by the explosion of abandoned ammunition on the second floor, and the snapping of floorboards. Into the dust, smoke, and flames came dashing the men from the Metropole Hotel garrison, adding more congestion to the crowded courtyard. Plunkett took advantage of one of these interruptions to seek out Winifred Carney—of all people—and entrust her with an envelope, his filigree bangle, and one of his large antique rings. Anticipating that he would be shot, and expecting the insurgent women would not be, he asked Miss Carney to deliver these items to Grace Gifford, his fiancée. She had been cut off from her Protestant family because of her engagement to Plunkett and her conversion to Roman Catholicism. The envelope contained a short note to Grace and a will bequeathing her his considerable estate.

By eight o'clock the decision was made to break up the entire force into three parts. The first group, consisting of twelve women, and sixteen wounded men, would be led by Desmond Fitzgerald to Jervis Street Hospital. Dr Mahoney was a member of this group. Left behind were two nurses and Winifred Carney. Also left behind was James Connolly, who said, 'I'm not going out with the wounded. My place is with my men.'

This group managed to reach the Coliseum theatre through a tortuous route, when Lieutenant Mahoney was summoned back to the main body of men. One of them had fallen over Connolly's foot and smashed the cradle splint on his shattered ankle. Mahoney repaired the damage while Connolly clenched his teeth to avoid crying out in pain. After finishing his chore, Mahoney, still technically a prisoner, stepped through the hole in the rear wall of the post office and made his roundabout way back to the Coliseum.

Through a rear door of the theatre, this group reached Prince's Street and eventually Middle Abbey Street. The British recognized the Red Cross flag (actually a Red Cross nurse's apron on a pole), took custody of the straggling party of girls and wounded men, and brought them into Jervis Street hospital.

The second group, consisting of thirty men who were to move up to Moore Street to clear the way for the rest to take the Williams and Wood factory, had not gone far when they were blasted by machine-gun fire and pinned down. O'Rahilly was one of those wounded.

At 8.40 p.m., Pearse told the remaining group what the objective was, and they started dashing across Henry Street into Henry Place. British snipers soon saw what was happening and opened fire. Connolly was carried across on a stretcher, as fast as his bearers could run with such a heavy burden. A young Fianna Eireann lad ran beside Connolly's stretcher to shield him with his body. Remembering this later in the hospital, Connolly told his wife, 'We can't fail now. Such lads will never forget.' Winifred Carney, equally willing to defend him with her life, ran on the other side.

As the main body turned north into Moore Lane, an alley parallel to Moore Street, heavy machine guns opened up on them. The bullets came from behind a barricade at the top of the lane and from the roof of the Rotunda Hospital at the corner of Parnell and O'Connell Streets. Men were falling in agony and scattering in confusion. Plunkett ordered a van dragged across the mouth of the lane, and under its protection some men were able to continue their flight in the direction of Moore Street and take refuge in some doorways. What they would do thereafter nobody had yet decided. O'Rahilly's squadron had stirred up enough gunfire to make Moore Street impassable.

To O'Rahilly it seemed that the only way he could take the pressure off his comrades pinned down in the doorways was to overrun the barricade. Bringing himself to his feet, he grasped his Mauser, ordered a new assault, and stepped out firing at the barricade as he ran towards it. He was supported by a handful of followers who answered machine-gun fire with pistol shots. O'Rahilly had almost reached the corner of Sackville Lane when he was hit again, this time fatally. His followers scattered.

These and other stragglers collected together in a yard at the rear of Cogan's grocery store, on the corner of Henry Lane and Moore Street. Adjoining the yard was a small cottage occupied by Mr and Mrs Thomas McKane and their ten children. When an insurgent found the door locked, he opened it by shooting the lock. The bullet hit and killed one of the children, a girl of sixteen, and wounded the father. The insurgents piled into the cottage.

Another group of insurgents led by Sean MacDermott and Joseph Plunkett arrived. When Mrs McKane was asked by MacDermott who had shot her daughter, she said that it was an accident, then turned away and cried out, 'My husband is dying! I must get a priest.' Before anyone had a chance to stop her, she went dashing out into Moore Lane.

Next to arrive at the cottage was Connolly, carried on a stretcher and accompanied by Winifred Carney and nurses Farrell and Grennan. When he saw the room full of wounded men and the dead body of the McKane girl, he reacted in untypical fashion, perhaps because he was losing touch with reality. 'We need a priest,' he said. 'If only there were some way to get one.' When he was told that the woman of the house had gone out after one, he sighed with satisfaction and muttered that he wished he could have a cup of tea. There was none, but one of the men had some Bovril on his person and Winifred Carney hastened to prepare it for him.

Mrs McKane returned unharmed. With her was a priest whom she had met on the street near the Rotunda Hospital. The priest stared in disbelief at the bleeding men crowded together, and at the dead body, then went down on one knee, said a prayer for all of them, and then began going from man to man, administering the last sacraments. Connolly took Mrs McKane's hand. 'You're a brave woman,' he said.

Last to arrive was Padraic Pearse, who went into conference with MacDermott, Clarke and Plunkett around Connolly's stretcher. Someone said, 'Where do we go from here? We're surrounded.' The only answer came from one of the older McKane daughters. She suggested that they knock holes in the houses and in that way move on up the street.

This suggestion was adopted. Soon a hole was punched in the common wall of the McKane cottage and the neighbouring one. The men crawled through it, and then started another hole in the next house. Repeating this process, they eventually reached halfway to the corner of Sackville Lane. Pearse set up a headquarters of sorts in Cogan's grocery shop, and posted sentries in the various occupied houses. Connolly tried to settle down for the night but, with the excitement of the post office evacuation gone, his pain increased, requiring attention from Ryan.

Saturday, 29 April 1916

At three o'clock in the morning the fires in the post office reached the stores of gunpowder and gelignite in the cellar. The resulting explosion rocked the area, and awakened some of the men, but only briefly, because they were too exhausted, too weak, or too despondent to pay attention to anything.

Again, the dawn came up sunny, promising an excellent day for strolling through St Stephen's Green or visiting a beach. For the insurgents it signalled only more house-to-house burrowing up the east side of Moore Street. Pearse and MacDermott decided that a more secure place for their headquarters was the middle of the block they occupied, not one end of it; hence, during the morning Hanlon's fish market at 16 Moore Street became the gathering place of the leaders. To get Connolly to the new headquarters was a harrowing experience. His shattered ankle had now turned gangrenous, and in order to get him through the narrow holes, his bearers had to transfer him from his mattress to a sling of blankets, which offered his leg no protective padding.

Again the leaders conferred around Connolly's bed: Plunkett, with his face as white as his scarf, despite his need for a shave; Sean Mac-Dermott, his gaiety gone and his eyes red; and Tom Clarke, as always his gentleness covering an iron resolve. Only one desperate possibility remained—for the men to go west along Henry Street and link up with the insurgents in the Four Courts. This would require a diversionary charge by two dozen men, who would certainly lose their lives; others would die attempting to reach their destination; and so would many civilians in the houses occupied by the insurgents, as the British discovered which houses were involved and got the range.

Pearse and MacDermott could not stand the idea of any more bloodshed. Connolly was in no condition to offer any suggestions. After a final discussion, MacDermott walked over to nurse Elizabeth Farrell, and asked if she could find a white flag. A handkerchief was produced, and, a little past noon, Nurse Farrell stepped out into Moore Street, waving the flag in front of her. The British soldiers did not fire; and she was eventually taken to Brigadier General H. M. Lowe. The meeting was held in a building on Parnell Street that the British had commandeered for the emergency. By a strange coincidence, it housed Tom Clarke's tobacco shop.

To console Nurse Julia Grennan, who was worried about the safety of her friend, Connolly said, "They won't shoot her. They may blindfold her, and take her to their commandant, so she may be away some time, but they won't shoot her.' Julia noticed that his smile faded rapidly after consoling her; he could not restrain for long his own grief at the lost venture.

It was 2 p.m. when Elizabeth Farrell returned with a note to Pearse demanding that he surrender unconditionally. He was instructed to walk under a white flag, accompanied only by Miss Farrell, up Moore Street to Parnell Street, to meet General Lowe.

There was one exchange of messages. Pearse wanted to know what the terms would be. Lowe returned word that the surrender must be unconditional, and that Connolly should follow on a stretcher. There was no bargaining power left in the 'provisional government' of

Ireland. As Pearse departed, Winifred Carney rushed into the room that Connolly occupied and pleaded, 'Is there no other way?' Connolly shook his head. 'I cannot bear to see all these brave boys burn to death. There is no other way.'

Connolly summoned Jim Ryan and asked for his help in getting ready to travel. While Winifred Carney and Julia Grennan re-dressed Connolly's wound, washed his face, and combed his hair, Ryan obtained a stretcher and appointed four men to carry it. As the men were placing him on the stretcher, Ryan asked in a low voice, 'Have you any idea what terms we can expect?' Connolly reassured him: 'Don't worry. Those of us who signed the republican proclamation will be shot. But the rest of you will be set free.' The four bearers picked up his stretcher and, under a white flag, walked slowly up the streets to the British barricade. A section of it was set aside and Connolly was carried through.

Shortly after four o'clock Elizabeth Farrell was presented with typewritten copies of a surrender order that she was to distribute to all insurgent groups. In it Pearse ordered all his men to lay down their arms 'In order to prevent the further slaughter of Dublin citizens, and in the hope of saving the lives of our followers now surrounded and hopelessly outnumbered . . .' A codicil signed by Connolly read: 'I agree to these conditions for the men only under my own command in the Moore Street District and for the men in the Stephen's Green Command.'

The hungry and unwashed rebels, following instructions, marched to the Parnell statue, spent a cold, sleepless night in the yard of the Rotunda Hospital opposite, and in the morning proceeded to a detainment compound at Richmond Barracks. A few of the leaders—MacDermott, Plunkett, Willie Pearse, and Tom Clarke—were given the honour of being interred in historic but damp Kilmainham Jail.

XXIV

On Saturday, 29 April, the day of surrender, Connolly was removed on a stretcher to the complex of administrative buildings known as Dublin Castle and placed in an infirmary room attached to the officer's quarters. One soldier guarded each door to the room, and another was stationed inside it. A white-haired civilian surgeon named Tobin, who later said that he considered Connolly one of the bravest men he had ever seen, came in to treat his wound.

On the following day, Connolly was visited by a Capuchin friar, Brother Aloysius. At the request of General Lowe, he asked Connolly to confirm his signature on the surrender document. Connolly promptly did it, adding that he had surrendered 'to prevent needless slaughter'.

On Monday, May Day, Connolly was in great pain, unable to sleep even after successive morphine injections. He feared that gangrene had set in. He asked that the friar be summoned, and that the guard be removed while they were together. The military hesitated, possibly fearing that some political document, or even instructions for continuing the fight, might be smuggled out, but then granted Connolly's request. Brother Aloysius was summoned, and gave Connolly absolution. Except for a few Sunday visits to church, this was the first religious duty Connolly had performed since his marriage.

The causes for this step are open to argument. The pious will maintain that, like many others, he 'saw the light' on his death bed. The rationalist will argue that he was in a weakened mental condition. Others will say that he was moved by a desire to be closer to his comrades; that he was influenced (like Constance Markievicz, who decided during the rising to convert to Roman Catholicism) by the Catholic fervour exhibited by Padraic Pearse, Joseph Plunkett and The O'Rahilly.

It is unlikely that Connolly underwent any kind of mystical experience; or that, at the age of forty-eight, he abandoned his life-long belief in Marxist materialism and regained his childhood faith in organized religion. It is interesting to note that three other non-practising Catholics who signed the proclamation of Irish independence —Tom Clarke, Sean MacDermott and Thomas MacDonagh—also returned to the Church before their execution.

When Brother Aloysius told Padraic Pearse that Connolly had been given Holy Communion, Pearse replied, 'Thank God, it is the one thing I was anxious about.' On the following day, Wednesday, 3 May, he was executed, along with Tom Clarke and MacDonagh, in the yard of Kilmainham Jail.

On Thursday 'Willie' Pearse joined his brother in death, as did the poet Joseph Plunkett and two others. On Friday, Major John MacBride, the estranged husband of Maud Gonne, was executed. A fighter against the British in the Boer War, he had only by chance come across the detachment digging in at Stephen's Green on Easter Monday afternoon, and could not resist the temptation to resume the fight.

On Monday, 8 May, Michael Mallin and Eamonn Ceannt faced the firing squad. On Tuesday, it was the turn of Thomas Kent, of Fermoy, who had shot a policeman in one of the few risings attempted outside of Dublin.

Connolly, propped up in bed, was court-martialled the same day. He had been in almost constant pain during the week, but responded vigorously to the charge that the insurgents had mistreated their prisoners. He then went on to assert that the purpose of the rising—to establish an Irish Republic—was nobler than any other call that had been issued in connection with the world war. What had the rising accomplished?

We succeeded in proving that Irishmen are ready to die endeavouring to win for Ireland those national rights which the British Government has been asking them to die to win for Belgium. As long as that remains the case, the cause of Irish freedom is safe.

Believing that the British Government has no right in Ireland, never had any right in Ireland, and never can have any right in Ireland, the presence, in any one generation of Irishmen, of even a respectable minority, ready to die to affirm that truth, makes that Government for ever a usurpation and a crime against human progress.

I personally thank God that I have lived to see the day when thousands of Irish men and boys, and hundreds of Irish women and girls, were ready to affirm that truth, and to attest it with their lives if need be.

No doubt a splendid 'statement at the dock', but it seems hardly appropriate for a hardened socialist, syndicalist, or labour organizer. All the statement stressed is the right and duty of the Irish people to seek national freedom and to expel the British Government from Ireland. Not a word about freeing the working class from capitalist exploitation, about lightening the burdens of the toiling masses, about bringing a better and happier life for the impoverished Irish labourers. In a similar situation there is no doubt what other socialists and radicals—Lenin, Bukharin, Daniel De Leon, Jim Larkin, Emma Goldman—would have said. Eugene Debs did say it. When he was tried a few years later for agitating against the same world war, Debs was quick to tell the jury that he was being tried only because he wanted to do away 'with the rule of the great body of the people by a relatively small class', and because he was seeking to establish in the United States 'an industrial and social democracy'.

Desmond Greaves answers the question implied here by stating that Connolly was not delivering a political statement, merely answering specific charges brought against him at a private court-martial. It was not the time or place to speak about his socialist convictions, and his failure to mention them does not imply that he had shed them. Greaves's argument is not entirely convincing, for Connolly thought the statement important enough to warrant slipping a copy of it to his daughter Nora when she and her mother visited him after the court-martial.

During the past few weeks Lillie had been suffering as much mental torment as her husband had been suffering physical torment. During the rising she had stayed in the Markievicz villa in the suburbs, seeing smoke and flames rising from the city, knowing her husband and her sixteen-year-old son Roderic were both involved in battle, and cut off from all reliable information. On Thursday of Easter Week she almost collapsed when she read an erroneous newspaper report that her husband had been killed. About the same time she learned of the murder of Sheehy-Skeffington, a matter everyone refrained from telling to Connolly.

Matters brightened somewhat when she was told that James had survived, though wounded; and that Roderic had been released by his British captors because he was under sixteen and because he had informed them that his name was Robert Carney. Furthermore, Lillie's friends kept telling her that the British would not execute a wounded man.

Connolly had been a captive for more than a week when Mrs Connolly was told she could visit him. On Monday, 8 May, she did so, accompanied by her youngest daughter, Fiona. On the following day, she was accompanied by her daughter Nora. It was immediately after the court-martial, but no decision had been rendered. Connolly, pale, feverish and talking in a low voice, suggested to his wife that she ask Francis Sheehy-Skeffington to collect some of Connolly's proletarian and patriotic ballads and have them published. With difficulty, Lillie kept her secret.

When told that Roddy had been imprisoned for eight days, Connolly commented, 'Imprisoned for his country and not yet sixteen. He's had a great start in life, hasn't he?'

After extolling the way the insurgent men and women had fought in the rising, he asked Nora whether she had seen any socialist papers. She had not. 'They will never understand why I am here,' Connolly remarked. 'They all forget that I am an Irishman.'

On Wednesday Brother Aloysius found Connolly exhausted and running a high fever, but on the next day he was feeling much better. For the first time since leaving Liberty Hall, he had had a natural sleep. At 11 p.m. he was awakened with the information that the court-martial had reached a decision—he would be shot at dawn. At midnight a British officer visited Mrs Connolly. He said that her husband was very weak and wished to see his wife and eldest daughter, and that an automobile was waiting outside to bring them to the castle.

Connolly's head turned as Lillie and Nora entered the small hospital room. 'Well, Lillie, I suppose you know what this means,' he said.

Lillie, kneeling by his bed, sobbed, 'But your beautiful life, James. Your beautiful life.'

'Hasn't it been a full life, Lillie, and isn't this a good end?'

In the ensuing conversation, Connolly told his wife to take the family back to America where they would all be better treated. He cautioned her, 'Don't allow Larkin or Lehane to exploit you in America.' Con Lehane (sometimes spelt O'Lyhane), a native of Cork, had been active in London socialist circles before migrating to America in 1901, and was at this time associated with Larkin. William O'Brien, the source for this story, detested both Lehane and Larkin, but it is hard to believe that he would invent such a story.

Connolly mentioned that he had finally learned of the death of Skeffington, whereupon Nora gave him the names of others who had died in battle or been executed. Nora sensed that he was shocked—that he had somehow expected that he would be the first to face the firing squad.

Brother Aloysius arrived, heard Connolly's confession and administered the last rites. He remained at his side when soldiers removed Connolly from his bed, placed him on a stretcher, and drove him in an ambulance to Kilmainham Jail. When the ambulance reached the back entrance to the jail yard, Connolly was lifted out and transferred from his stretcher to a chair. The Capuchin asked, 'Will you say a prayer for the men who are about to shoot you?'

'I will say a prayer for all brave men who do their duty according to their lights,' Connolly replied, gripping the sides of the chair to steady himself and holding his head high to await the volley.

Earlier that morning the firing squad had executed Sean MacDermott, polio-victim, IRB organizer, and charmer, whose insouciance had hardly flagged at all during the week of the rising. The date was 12 May. Connolly would have been forty-eight years old within a month. Within that same month his brother John, who had helped James find his way to socialism, died in Glasgow. By ironical circumstance, John was buried with full military honours as an honourably discharged veteran of the British Army.

(The sixteenth and last insurgent leader to die was Sir Roger Casement. After a public trial, he was hanged on 3 August 1916. Attempts to save his life were made by many leaders in other countries but their fervour was weakened after the British Government showed them some pages allegedly taken from Casement's diary which indicated that Sir Roger had been a homosexual.)

The dead were buried in quicklime in Arbour Hill barracks, a place to be commemorated ever since in Irish patriotism. That should have been the end of it. A desperate, scatter-brained attempt had been made 'to free Ireland', and the rebels had been duly punished. Not counting the sixteen executed, only sixty-four insurgents had been killed. But they had caused the death of 130 military and police, and of 260 civilians. Many of these civilians had been the victim of their own reckless curiosity. During the week of the rising, local doctors and hospitals tended some 2,600 injured persons. A large part of the central city had been burned out, with 179 buildings wrecked. Damage was estimated at 2·5 million pounds. Public relief had to be given to 100,000 people, about one-third of Dublin's total population. The great majority of the Irish—and certainly all of the English— were shocked and outraged by the senselessness of the revolt.

What happened next was, in the words of Desmond Ryan, 'one of the most interesting and indubitable examples in all history of the triumph of failure'.

During the first days of the rebellion, the Dubliners, anticipating that it would be promptly suppressed, casually filed through barricades to buy bread and other groceries, and carried on with their everyday duties. The pubs were closed by government proclamation on Tuesday, but it was not until Thursday that the rebellion became a nuisance. By that time buses had stopped running, theatres and cinemas were shut, postal services were suspended, and no food could be found in some areas. With banks closed, people ran short of money, and even those who had a few shillings had difficulty in finding stores that had not been sold out or looted. Since few newspapers were being published, rumours ran rife. Connolly was reported dead on four occasions. Some people believed that the Germans had landed in Kerry; others were convinced that the men firing on British soldiers were Germans or at least in the pay of Germany.

Those who had relatives fighting in France and elsewhere for Britain were particularly bitter at this 'stab in the back'. Their number can be estimated from the fact that some 150,000 Irish were serving as volunteers with the British Army; another 115,000 were serving in such para-military organizations as the Royal Irish Constabulary. In contrast, the number of Irish Volunteers was not much more than 10,000; and the Citizen Army was only 300 at most. In other words, for every Irish Volunteer there were sixteen men serving with the British. The Irish Volunteers were themselves split, as has been described. Half of the headquarters staff, including Eoin MacNeill, chief of staff, opposed the rising. It was planned and conducted by 'a minority of a minority of the minority'.

Most of those Irish who had no relatives in the British forces still believed in the British promise of Home Rule after the war was over, and feared that the rising would only serve to prove that Ireland was not ready for it. All sections of the British and Irish Establishment, including the press and the hierarchies of the Protestant and Catholic churches, reflected and fanned these sentiments. The newspapers of

8 May carried a letter from the Protestant archbishop of Dublin calling for stern punishment of the rebel leaders. 'This is not the time for amnesties and pardons, it is the time for punishment swift and stern,' he wrote. The Roman Catholic bishops, had they not been taken so completely by surprise, would certainly have issued a statement condemning the uprising. As it was, Cardinal Logue telegraphed the Pope, 'Insurrection happily terminated'; according to *Freeman's Journal*, the Vatican 'greatly praised' the Irish clergy for the zeal with which they supported government efforts to restore law and order; and the Bishop of Raphoe demanded action against the 'new paganism' of the Huns.

On Friday of Easter Week the *Cork Examiner* attributed the 'lamentable outbreak' to Larkin, Connolly and other syndicalists. William Martin Murphy's *Irish Catholic* described the rising as criminal and insane, Pearse as a 'crazy and insolent schoolmaster', and the insurgents as 'an extraordinary combination of rogues and fools'. Murphy's other paper, the *Irish Independent*, was equally bitter. When a lull occurred in the series of executions, before Connolly's turn, it said editorially, 'Let the worst of the ringleaders be singled out and dealt with as they deserve.' The same issue contained a photograph of Connolly lying in Dublin Castle. Thanks in part to the conspirators' own passion for secrecy, miscomprehension of rebel goals characterized all the newspapers. Almost unanimously, they held Sinn Fein responsible.

Public bodies in many parts of Ireland joined in the clamour for revenge. The Ballyclare Urban District Council called Pearse and Connolly 'traitors of the meanest and most cowardly type'. Naas officials dwelt upon the 'wickedness and insanity of the rebels'. Tralee officials 'deplored with horror the outbreak which brings the blush of shame to every honest Irishman'.

Socialist and labour leaders were equally unsympathetic. A leader of the Social-Democratic Federation, a Swiss named Jeanneret with whom Connolly occasionally stayed during his visits to Edinburgh, wondered how the great socialist agitator could have 'got mixed up with that Sinn Fein business'. John Leslie, prostrate with grief, bitterly reproached himself for helping Connolly to settle in Ireland in the first place. An attempt to hold a protest meeting in Birmingham was a complete failure.

In the United States, the eminent socialist, Victor Berger, could not understand why Connolly should go down in a 'skirmish'. The

Socialist Labor Party, now more than ever a sect rather than a party, but still vocal, stigmatized Connolly as a convert to the madness of nationalism.

Other labour and socialist groups reacted in similar fashion. The Independent Labour Party declared itself as much opposed to the militarism of the insurgents as to the militarism of the capitalists. The September 1916 issue of *Socialist Review* said, 'We do not approve of armed rebellion or any other form of militarism and war.'

The Irish Trade Union Congress and Labour Party, meeting at Sligo in August 1916, made no protest against the execution of Connolly and Mallin. The keynote of Thomas Johnson's presidential address was that 'this is not the place to enter into a discussion as to the right or wrong, the wisdom or the folly of the revolt'. The delegates, with fine impartiality, stood in tribute to the memory of both those who fell in the rising and those who died on the European battlefields.

Though the delegates did not seem to know it, the tide was already turning. The bloodthirsty traitors were becoming martyred patriots. The patriotism which had not been kindled by the rising was lit by the successive executions of the rebel leaders; by the mass arrests of many persons guilty of nothing but mild nationalist sentiments; by the harsh attitude of British soldiers towards their prisoners and the general populace; and by the realization that hundreds of badly armed men had waged a gallant struggle for Irish freedom against tremendous odds.

By 1 July, over 3,000 men and 77 women had been arrested and taken to Richmond Barracks. About half were released without trial; but some 1,800 persons were interned in English prisons—among them Constance Markievicz, Winifred Carney, William Partridge, William O'Brien, Michael Collins, Eamon De Valera and others mentioned in this chronicle. The Irish public was shocked, for it knew these people and considered most of them to be inoffensive types holding ordinary jobs. The British did themselves great harm by these mass arrests, for the prisons turned out to be excellent training schools for converting people into future officers and members of the Irish Republican Army, office-holders of the Irish Free State and the Irish Republic, and administrators of agencies established by both governments.

The shift in public opinion came with astonishing speed. The first voice raised in protest was that of George Bernard Shaw. In a letter published in the *Daily News* of London two days before Connolly was executed, he said that he could not regard as a traitor 'any Irishman taken in a fight for Irish independence against the British Government, which was a fair fight in everything except the enormous odds my countrymen had to face'. He asserted, with a confidence that time has proved valid: 'It is absolutely impossible to slaughter a man in this position without making him a martyr and a hero. The shot Irishmen will now take their places beside Emmet and the Manchester martyrs in Ireland and nothing in Heaven or on earth can prevent it.'

The same prediction, as well as an interesting estimate of Connolly, was made in a letter written in May by George Russell (AE) to Sir Matthew Nathan, Under-Secretary of Ireland:

I am very sad over Ireland just now. I knew many of those now dead and had a genuine liking for them. They had no intellect. Connolly was the only one with a real grip in his mind. They were rather featherbrained idealists . . . and now they will be national heroes. If I had remembered Connolly was in the counsels of the Irish Volunteers I would have been frightened. He lay low, and I believe he cast the torch on the pile.

The liberal American periodical, *The Nation*, printed a report from Dublin that 'for one sympathizer with the Sinn Fein Easter Monday there are two today'. In the 18 May issue of the same magazine, William Dean Howells, the distinguished American novelist, wrote that 'in giving way to her vengeance England has roused the moral sense of mankind against her'. US indignation was fanned by the surprising number of rebels who had spent time or travelled in the US. Tom Clarke had lived there ten years, Connolly seven. Pearse, John MacBride and Francis Sheehy-Skeffington had conducted successful lecture tours: Joseph Plunkett and Roger Casement had made a fair number of acquaintances while making their plans for the rising. A recent biographer of Woodrow Wilson writes that, after the executions, 'Irish-American opinion turned massively and savagely against Great Britain'.

On 10 June, T. M. Healy wrote to his brother, 'I never knew such a transformation of opinion as that caused by the executions. Besides the looting by the soldiers and ruffianism against innocent people—the ill-treatment of prisoners, the insolence of the military in the streets, the foul language used to women, and the incompetence shown by officers, have aroused a contempt and dislike for which there is no parallel in our day.' Pearse had built better than he knew, Healy reported, and 'his executioners would now give a great deal to have him and his brother back in jail alive'.

The first cleric to raise his voice against the 'government terror' was Bishop O'Dwyer. Other voices soon followed suit. Even William Martin Murphy was affected. Though he had not yet recovered from the losses suffered by his department store, he confessed that when he heard Protestants gloating over the executions, every drop of Catholic blood in his veins surged up. Within two months of the rising, the insurgent leaders had been given places beside Wolfe Tone and Robert Emmet.

At least one Marxist spoke up in defence of the Easter Rising. He was an obscure Russian revolutionary named V. I. Lenin. In an article published in October 1916, he termed 'doctrinaire and pedantic' Karl Radek's opinion that the rising was merely a *putsch*. Lenin asserted that social revolution was inconceivable without simultaneous or preceding outbursts by a section of the petty bourgeoisie, with all its prejudices, 'against landlord, church, monarchical, national or other oppression . . .' It was completely unrealistic to expect that 'one army will line up in one place and say, "We are for socialism," while another will do so in another place and say, "We are for imperialism." Whoever expects a "pure" social revolution will *never* live to see it.'

One need not be an admirer of Lenin's goals to appreciate the realism and pragmatism he displays in this article.

The socialist revolution in Europe *cannot* be anything but an outburst of mass struggle by all and sundry oppressed and discontented elements. Sections of the petty bourgeois and of the backward workers will inevitably participate in it—without such participation, *mass* struggle is not possible, *no* revolution is possible—and just as inevitably they will bring into the movement their prejudices, their reactionary fantasies, their weaknesses and errors. But *objectively* they will attack *capital*, and the class-conscious vanguard of the revolution . . . will be able to unite and direct it, to capture power . . . and to introduce other dictatorial measures that in their totality constitute the overthrow of the bourgeoisie and the victory of socialism, which, however, will by no means immediately 'purge' itself of petty-bourgeois slag . . .

The misfortune of the Irish is that they have risen prematurely, when the European revolt of the proletariat has *not yet* matured . . .

On the other hand, the very fact that revolts break out in different times, in different places, and are of different kinds, guarantees wide scope and depth to the general movement; only in premature, partial, scattered and therefore unsuccessful, revolutionary movements do the masses gain experience, acquire knowledge, gather strength, get to know their real leaders, the socialist proletarians, and in this way prepare for a general onslaught . . .

A year later, in Russia, Lenin had the opportunity to put into practice some of his theories. But the continent-wide revolution he envisaged in Europe has not come to pass, nor does Ireland today resemble much the 'workers' republic' that Connolly sought to establish. Nevertheless, the rising did (in the words of Lennox Robinson) 'cut down to the heart of Irish nationality'. Nothing in Ireland thereafter was the same. W. B. Yeats said it in another way.

> I write it out in a verse—
> MacDonagh and MacBride
> And Connolly and Pearse
> Now and in time to be,
> Wherever green is worn,
> Are changed, changed utterly:
> A terrible beauty is born.

*   *   *

It is time to take a last look at the nature of James Connolly. The most striking elements are the consistency of his thought and work, and the tenacity with which he pursued his goal of a socialist republic free of British rule.

The claim is made that, when World War I broke out, Connolly scrapped his faith in socialism and the brotherhood of the working class in order to embrace pure and simple nationalism. The passage of time has softened the controversy resolving around this issue; radicals today believe that the combination of nationalist and socialist struggles strengthens both, and that Connolly was a pioneer in understanding this position.

A slight change in emphasis did take place, I think, but on the whole Desmond Ryan was correct in calling Connolly's socialism 'the most vital and consistent thing about him'. Connolly was not likely to make a drastic change in his thinking at the age of forty-six, when the war started.

There is further evidence of his consistency. Only a week before the rising, Connolly told his Citizen Army that, 'in the event of victory, hold on to your rifles, as those with whom we are fighting may stop before our goal is reached. We are out for economic as well as political liberty. Hold on to your rifles.'

During the rising Connolly dispatched the starry plough flag, the symbol of Irish labour, to be hoisted over the Imperial Hotel, owned by William Martin Murphy. The symbolism (writes Donal Nevin) is clear. Though Murphy had defeated labour in 1913, now labour was triumphing over him and his class.

However tenacious Connolly was in clinging to his ideology and long-range goals, he was in other respects an impatient man. He could not endure the same obstacles for more than a certain period of time. That period works out to seven years—a circumstance which should delight those who subscribe to the ideas of numerology and should astonish all others. From fourteen to almost twenty-one, Connolly was a soldier in Her Majesty's army, stationed in Ireland. From twenty-one to twenty-eight he was living in his native city of Edinburgh. From twenty-eight to thirty-five he was in Dublin, trying to establish an Irish Socialist Republican Party as impressive as its name. He worked and lived in the United States from thirty-five to forty-two. He lived in Ireland for six years before he was executed; one has reason to wonder that, if he had not been executed at forty-eight, would he have been ready to move elsewhere at forty-nine?

I see nothing magical in these figures, of course. But they are important as part of a pattern—the pattern of a man who could endure repression and suppression only for a limited period of time, and then he had to burst out. In a way, the Easter Rising represented for him, I think, this kind of escape for the frustration that had built up inside him. It was his way of lashing out at circumstances that thwarted him personally or the revolution he sought (he drew little distinction between the two). In most years, release took the form of migration. In 1916 it took the form of armed revolt.

This does not mean that the reasons he gave for his migrations were simply camouflage for thwarted psychological drives, that they had no basis in fact. His financial circumstances in Edinburgh in 1896 were indeed dismal, and the controversy with his comrades in 1903 was bitter enough to cause anyone to leave Dublin, but the fact remains that, under similar circumstances, most men would have stayed put. In more than one way, Connolly was always looking for a better world and ready to gamble to get it. He rarely put this emotion into words, preferring to find and state objective reasons for his sometimes rash actions. The radical Jesuit priest, Father Berrigan, believes that, in view of the way things are, it is necessary for everyone to 'prod the world, and enter into *some* kind of jeopardy'. Connolly would have understood.

In the same way that impatience marked Connolly's brand of tenacity, a number of contradictions flawed his consistency. Based on his own service in the British Army, Connolly had a deep and lasting hatred of the military. On the eve of the Boer War he called the army 'a veritable moral cesspool corrupting all within its bounds . . . a miasma of pestilence upon every spot so unfortunate as to be cursed by its presence'. But he assisted in forming the Irish Citizen Army, displayed great zeal in training it, and, as commanding general of the Dublin insurgents during the rising, acted like a veritable Napoleon, assigning men to their stations, ordering barricades to be built, and dispatching military bulletins with authority and unmistakable gusto.

Connolly believed that only 'proletarians' could be trusted to provide leadership for honest trade unions and revolutionary groups, but in practice got on remarkably well with such upper-class Anglo-Irish as Maud Gonne and Countess Markievicz. He sought to obtain the services of Helena Molony for his union because he thought her bourgeois background would make her specially useful.

Though a loving husband and father, he was away from home an astonishing amount of time. It is clear that the cause always came first, there were always good reasons why he was away, and Mrs Connolly rarely complained about his absences. But one feels she had reason to.

At one time Connolly thought that reviving the Irish language would do nothing to feed a starving man, but later argued that all manifestations of the ancient Gaelic culture deserved support.

Connolly performed practically no religious duties during his adult life, but returned to the Church before his death. Though he preached political action, he seemed to think that the organization of trade unions on industrial lines was the only sure guarantee of a successful revolution. On the day of the rising, he confessed that it was doomed to defeat, but he acted throughout as if it had a chance to succeed.

For a man who was always seeking popular support against overwhelming odds, he showed little of the geniality and charm that might have smoothed his path. He acquired his share of young ardent followers (such as Cathal O'Shannon) but he was frequently impatient with his comrades, mainly because they were not as committed to the cause as he was.

In the General Post Office during the Easter Rising, a young man with literary inclinations, Desmond Fitzgerald, had a good chance to observe Connolly's personality. He got the impression that Connolly 'viewed anyone who was not associated with the Citizen Army as only dubiously well-disposed'; and that 'it would take very little to make him angry ... I always felt when I went to talk with him that he was likely to round on me and rend me'. After Connolly was wounded and the building started to go up in flames, 'I felt that I was received in a more friendly way.'

Some contemporaries believe that Connolly's reserve and abrupt manner have been made too much of. It does seem true that the women he enrolled in his Belfast textile union had little difficulty in appreciating his wit and in seeing through his mask of gruffness to the concern lying underneath it. How genuine his concern was is indicated by an incident told by Eva Gore-Booth, poet and social worker. In June 1915, she was visiting her sister, Constance Markievicz. As Eva and her friend Esther Roper were discussing socialism with Connolly while preparing dinner (in Ireland, supper) for the three of them, a woman rushed into the house in great agitation. She said that a young member of the Irish Women Workers' Union had left her home and disappeared into the slums. It was an odd way of putting it, since most members lived in the slums, but apparently the implication was that she had become a delinquent. Connolly immediately left the table to start searching for her, and did not return until he had succeeded and brought her home. It was after midnight when he finally got back to continue the conversation and drink tea instead of having the dinner he had left. This was hardly the action of a person who considered the individual in terms of a Marxist worker stereotype.

All of Connolly's inconsistencies, even when true, matter little when compared to the massive, single-purpose resolve he brought to his cause of transforming Ireland into a workers' republic. At most they show that even professional revolutionaries have human frailties.

What matters is Connolly's writings, the labour struggles he led, and the kind of revolution he tried to effect. What matters more is what impelled him towards revolution—the desire for a more decent and more just life for the Irish people—and the devotion with which he pursued that goal. What matters most, in my opinion, is not what he made of Ireland but what he made of himself; how he managed to reach distinction as a writer, thinker, labour organizer and patriot, against a staggering host of handicaps and disabilities: grinding poverty, his position as member of a despised minority in Scotland, inadequate education, limited vocational opportunities, unimpressive height, a squint, bowlegs, a speech impediment (to the end of his life he pronounced socialism 'socy . . . ism'), and an accent which stamped him as a foreigner, an 'outside agitator', in every community outside of Edinburgh's Irish ghetto.

Someone has said that Connolly was born in the wrong country and at the wrong time. If he had been born in Russia and staged his revolution one-and-a-half years later, he might have been another Lenin. Speculating along more factual lines, Conor Cruise O'Brien thinks it possible that, if the Easter Rising had taken place in 1918 instead of 1916, it might have been, in Connolly's metaphor, the 'pin in the hands of a child' that would have 'pierced to the heart' the giant of European capitalism. In either case Connolly would have emerged as an important figure in European history—'a great man'. It is the point of this book that, even without such advantageous circumstances, Connolly was precisely that.

Bibliography

CONNOLLY's principal works, such as *Labour in Irish History*, and many of his other writings, are contained in a four-volume set published between 1948 and 1951 by Three Candles, Dublin. Titles are: *Labour in Ireland, Socialism and Nationalism, The Workers' Republic,* and *Labour and Easter Week 1916.* An anthology edited by Proinsias MacAonghusa and Liam O Reagain was published in paperback by Mercier Press, Cork, in 1967.

Numerous letters by and to Connolly, and many other manuscripts relating to him are contained in the National Library of Ireland. Some were left by William O'Brien at the time of his death a few years ago.

In 1961 there was published in London *The Life and Times of James Connolly.* C. Desmond Greaves, a founder of the Connolly Clubs of England, spent ten years researching and writing this biography, which has dwarfed and made obsolete all previous ones: Desmond Ryan, *James Connolly: His Life and Writings*, London, 1924; R. M. Fox, *James Connolly, the Forerunner*, Tralee, 1946; and one in the Irish language by Prioinsias Mac an Bheatha. *Portrait of a Rebel Father*, Dublin, 1935, is the memoirs of Connolly's daughter, Nora Connolly O'Brien. The memoirs of another daughter, Ina Connolly-Heron, were serialized in *Liberty*, organ of the Irish Transport and General Workers' Union, March–October 1966.

In the preface to his biography of Connolly, Mr Greaves thanks me warmly for letting him use an early, unpublished Connolly biography I had written. Since I have, in the present book, made far greater use of his work than he made of mine, I consider myself the gainer by far.

The 1967 (No. 7) issue of *Studia Hibernica*, an annual published at St Patrick's College, Dublin, contains a hundred-page article entitled '1916—Myth, Fact, and Mystery'. In the process of discussing almost every issue and every important figure connected with the Easter

Rising, the author, F. X. Martin, OSA, lists and analyses almost all relevant material published up to that time. The availability of this exhaustive study was one of the reasons which convinced me that only a brief bibliography was required, and that it should contain only the most serious, relevant, or recent works.

BOURKE, MARCUS, *The O'Rahilly*, Dublin, 1967.

COFFEY, THOMAS, M., *Agony at Easter*, New York, 1969, and London, 1970.

COLUM, MARY, *Life and the Dream*, New York, 1947.

EDWARDS, OWEN DUDLEY, and PYLE, FERGUS, eds., *1916, The Easter Rising*, London, 1968.

FITZGERALD, DESMOND, *Memoirs of Desmond Fitzgerald 1914–1916*, London, 1968.

FOX, R. M., *Jim Larkin*, London, 1957.

—— *Louie Bennett, Her Life and Times*, Dublin, 1958.

HANDLEY, JAMES E., *The Irish in Scotland*, Glasgow, 1964.

HOBSON, BULMER, *Ireland Yesterday and Tomorrow*, Tralee, 1968.

KING, CLIFFORD, *The Orange and the Green*, London, 1965.

LARKIN, EMMET, *James Larkin Irish Labour Leader, 1876–1947*, London, 1965.

MACBRIDE, MAUDE GONNE, *A Servant of the Queen*, Dublin, 1938.

MACENTEE, SEAN, *Episode at Easter*, Dublin, 1966.

MCCAY, HEDLEY, *Padraic Pearse*, Cork, 1966.

MARRECCO, ANNE, *The Rebel Countess, The Life and Times of Countess Markievicz*, London, 1967.

MARTIN, F. X., OSA, ed., *The Easter Rising, 1916 and University College, Dublin*, Dublin, 1966.

—— ed., *The Irish Volunteers 1913–1915*, Dublin, 1963.

—— ed., *Leaders and Men of the Easter Rising*, Cornell U. Press, 1967.

O'BRIEN, NORA CONNOLLY, *Portrait of a Rebel Father*, Dublin, 1936.

O'BRIEN, WILLIAM, *Forth the Banners Go*, Dublin, 1969.

O BROIN, LEON, *Dublin Castle and the 1916 Rising*, Dublin, 1966.

O'CASEY, SEAN, *Drums Under the Windows*, New York, 1950.

—— *The Story of the Irish Citizen Army*, Dublin, 1919.

O'FAOLAIN, SEAN, *Constance Markievicz* (revised, paperback), London, 1967.

RYAN, DESMOND, *The Man Called Pearse*, Dublin, 1919.

—— *The Rising*, Dublin, 1949.

STEPHENS, JAMES, *The Insurrection in Dublin*, New York, 1916.

THOMPSON, WILLIAM IRWIN, *The Imagination of an Insurrection: Dublin, Easter 1916*, London, 1967.

VAN VORIS, JACQUELINE, *Constance de Markievicz in the Cause of Ireland*, U. of Mass. Press, 1967.

The latest additions to this bibliography include: Edwards, Owen Dudley, *The Mind of an Activist—James Connolly*, Dublin, 1971; *Connolly in America*, by Manus O'Riordan, multilithed, 81 pages, issued by the Irish Communist Organization; 'James Connolly 1868–1916', a Thomas Davis lecture by Donal Nevin, mimeographed, 17 pages; 'The American Career of James Connolly, Irish Agitator', by Kara P. Brewer, of Stockton, California, MA thesis, 96 pages; and Samuel Levenson, articles in the Winter 1971 issue of *Eire-Ireland* and the Autumn 1972 issue of *Dissent*. Of special interest are articles relating to Connolly written by Manus O'Riordan in the May and December 1972, January 1973 issues of *The Irish Communist*, official organ of the British and Irish Communist Organization. No fewer than twenty-three such communist, socialist and left-wing groups exist in Ireland, according to a list appearing in the 23 June 1972 issue of *Hibernia*. These organizations represent various trends in national and international politics but all, without exception, lay claim to James Connolly as their model and inspiration.

Index

Connolly, James—(*cont*).

character, 14–15, 22–3, 50, 74, 103, 106, 119, 125–6, 150, 170–171, 291, 334–5; his attitude to the Church and religion, 12, 16, 78–9, 92–3, 112–13, 148–50, 180–2, 195–6, 218, 222, 252–3, 285–6, 317–18, 321–2; on women's rights, 14–15, 16, 111–12, 113, 213–14, 222, 224, 300; Greaves's biography of, 17, 23, 26, 41, 121, 124, 127, 128, 323; Ryan's biography of, 326, 331; his political thought, 12, 16, 47–50, 54–5, 56–7, 71–2, 111–13, 145–7, 148–50, 171–2, 181–2, 190, 191–2, 197–8, 209–10, 212–14, 253–4, 278–80, 285–6, 291, 322–3, 331–3; his birth and childhood, 21–2; early jobs, 22–3; joins Royal Scots Regiment, 23; first sight of Ireland, 24; meeting with Lillie Reynolds, his desertion from army, and marriage, 24–6; becomes involved in politics, 28–30; years of activity in Edinburgh and his disillusionment, 31–43; goes to Dublin, 43; builds Irish Socialist Republican Party, 44–7; organizes demonstrations against the monarchy, 51–4, 69; refusal to support Home Rulers, 55–7; campaigns during the famine, 57–9; founds and edits *Workers' Republic*, 59–61; in financial trouble, 62–3, 71; campaigns against Boer War, 63–7; differences with Fabians and ILO, 68, 72; attacks on Miller-

and, 70–1; tours Scotland and England, founds IRSP branches, stoned in Oxford, disappointment with London, 73–8; as itinerant agitator in Britain, 79–87; leaves for America, 88; his work in America, 89–97; back in Ireland, 98–103; discord within IRSP and its collapse, 98–108; in Scotland, 103–7; leaves again for America, 108; failure to obtain work, 110–11; differences with De Leon, 113–16, 121, 127, 129–32, 134–7, 154–5, 160; family joins him in US, 116–17; the search for work, 117–18, 119, 120; in New Jersey, 120–2; his work there with Italian Socialist Federation and IWW, 123–7; resigns from job, 128; quarrels with SLP, 133; forms Irish Socialist Federation in New York, 137–139; organizer for IWW in New York, 139–41; news from Ireland, 142–3; publishes *The Harp*, 144–5, leaves SLP and joins SP, 147; recruiting for IWW and attends convention, 150–3; establishes ISF in Chicago, publishes *Socialism Made Easy*, campaigns for ISF with some success, 153–4; receives news from Ireland, desires to return, 155–7, 161–3; lecturer for SP and national organizer, 158–74; has idea to move *Harp* to Ireland, 164–9; thoughts on uniting trade unions, 167–8; arranges tours

346